Welfare Regimes and the Experience of Unemployment in Europe

Edited by

DUNCAN GALLIE

and

SERGE PAUGAM

OXFORD
UNIVERSITY PRESS

OXFORD

UNIVERSITY PRESS

Great Clarendon Street, Oxford OX2 6DP

Oxford University Press is a department of the University of Oxford.
It furthers the University's objective of excellence in research, scholarship,
and education by publishing worldwide in

Oxford New York

Athens Auckland Bangkok Bogotá Buenos Aires Calcutta
Cape Town Chennai Dar es Salaam Delhi Florence Hong Kong Istanbul
Karachi Kuala Lumpur Madrid Melbourne Mexico City Mumbai
Nairobi Paris São Paulo Singapore Taipei Tokyo Toronto Warsaw
and associated companies in Berlin Ibadan

Oxford is a registered trade mark of Oxford University Press
in the UK and certain other countries

Published in the United States
by Oxford University Press Inc., New York

British Library Cataloguing in Publication Data

Data available

Library of Congress Cataloging in Publication Data
Welfare regimes and the experience of unemployment in Europe / Duncan Gallie and
Serge Paugam.
Includes bibliographical references and index.
1. Public welfare—Europe. 2. Unemployment—Europe. 3. Unemployed—Europe.
4. Welfare state. I. Gallie, Duncan. II. Paugam, Serge.
HV238.W43 2000 331.13'79—dc21 99-087084

ISBN 0-19-828039-4
ISBN 0-19-829797-1 (pbk.)

Typeset by Graphicraft Limited, Hong Kong
Printed in Great Britain
on acid-free paper by
Biddles Ltd, Guildford and King's Lynn

WELFARE REGIMES AND THE EXPERIENCE OF UNEMPLOYMENT IN EUROPE

ACKNOWLEDGEMENTS

The book presents the results of a large-scale collaborative research programme, bringing together researchers from eight EU countries. The project was funded by the European Commission (DGXII) under the Fourth Framework Programme (TSER). Many of the chapters make use of the European Community Household Panel (ECHP), the first major comparative data set for issues of social exclusion. This was made available to us by Eurostat, which is responsible for the co-ordination of the data collection and the construction of the comparative data set. We are also grateful to DGV for making available the Employment in Europe Survey, used in Chapter 6. We would like particularly to acknowledge the help given in the provision of data by Fadila Boughanemi, Christine Kotarakos, Eric Marlier, and Jean-Paul Tricart. We are also grateful to Geoffrey Jones, Sarah McGuigan and Mandy Roberts, at Nuffield College, for their assistance in the administration of the project and to the staff at Oxford University Press for their work in the preparation of the book.

Duncan Gallie   Serge Paugam
Nuffield College, Oxford   CREST/INSEE, Paris

CONTENTS

PART 3   UNEMPLOYMENT AND SOCIAL INTEGRATION

CONCLUSION

LIST OF FIGURES

LIST OF TABLES

NOTES ON THE CONTRIBUTORS

Editors:

Duncan Gallie is Professor of Sociology at the University of Oxford.

Serge Paugam is a Directeur at the Centre Nationale de la Recherche Scientifique and a member of the Laboratoire de sociologie quantitative, CREST, INSEE, France.

Contributors:

Susanne Alm is a Research Fellow at the Swedish Institute for Social Research, Stockholm.

Paolo Barbieri is a Research Officer at the University of Trento, Italy.

Fabrizio Bernardi is a Research Officer at the University of Trento, Italy.

Ivano Bison is a Research Officer at the University of Trento, Italy.

Paul de Graaf is a Research Officer at the University of Nijmegen, The Netherlands.

Philippe De Vreyer is Maître de Conférences, Centre d'Etudes des Politiques Economiques de l'Université d'Évry (EPEE), Université d'Evry, Val d'Essonne.

Gøsta Esping-Anderson is a Professor of Sociology at the University of Trento, Italy.

Torben Fridberg is a consultant at the Danish National Institute for Social Research.

Richard Hauser is Professor of Social Policy at the Goethe University, Frankfurt.

Mohammad Azhar Hussain was formerly a researcher at the Danish National Institute of Social Research; currently undertaking doctoral research at the Aarhus Business School.

Sheila Jacobs is a Research Officer at Nuffield College, Oxford.

Richard Layte is a Research Fellow at the Economic and Social Research Institute, Dublin, and was formerly a Research Officer at Nuffield College, Oxford.

Henrik Levin is a Project Manager at the Swedish National Board for Industrial and Technical Management (NUTEK) and was formerly a Research Officer at the Swedish Institute for Social Research, Stockholm.

Frances McGinnity is a Research Officer at Nuffield College, Oxford.

Brian Nolan is a Professor at the Economic and Social Research Institute, Dublin.

Lisbeth Pedersen is a consultant at the Danish National Institute of Social Research.

Niels Ploug is Director of Research at the Danish National Institute of Social Research.

Helen Russell is a Research Fellow at the Economic and Social Research Institute, Dublin, and was formerly a Prize Research Fellow at Nuffield College, Oxford.

Antonio Schizzerotto is a Professor of Sociology at the University of Milan, 'Bicocca' Italy.

Hanne Weise is a Research Officer at the Danish National Institute of Social Research.

Christopher T. Whelan is a Professor at the Economic and Social Research Institute, Dublin.

Michael White is a Senior Research Fellow at the Policy Studies Institute, London.

Maarten Wolbers was formerly a researcher at the University of Nijmegen; currently Project Manager at the Research Centre for Education and the Labour Market (ROA), Faculty of Economics and Business Administration, Maastricht University.

Jean-Paul Zoyem is a Research Officer at the National Institute for Social Statistics, France.

1

The Experience of Unemployment in Europe: The Debate

Duncan Gallie and Serge Paugam

When the social status of individuals depends primarily on their participation in the systems of economic production and exchange of their society, there is a high probability that unemployment will lead to a loss of status and a feeling of failure, especially if it extends for any length of time. It involves more a *process* of what might be termed 'social disqualification' than a static state. It brings about a sharp drop in living standards, a weakening of social life, and marginalization with respect to those in work—effects which can become cumulative and lead to a situation of intense poverty and, at the extreme, of social rupture.

It is notable that the first major sociological enquiries on the unemployed date from the 1930s (Lazarsfeld *et al.* 1933; Bakke 1940a), at a time of economic crisis and unprecedented levels of unemployment. It was an issue that drew the attention of researchers much less in the period of economic prosperity after the war. Research focused much more on the effects of technical, social and cultural change on the social structures of Western societies. It was only towards the end of the 1970s that there was a renewal of research on unemployment by sociologists,[1] economists and social-policy analysts. Our knowledge has expanded considerably over the 1980s and 1990s, but it remains highly fragmented since there was little co-ordination between the research carried out in different countries. Comparisons across countries in Europe are very rare, not least because they have had to confront the technical difficulty of the lack of standardization in the way data has been collected. In the absence of genuine comparison, the tendency has been to fall back on the mere juxtaposition of national monographs.

This book seeks to advance our understanding by drawing on a research programme that has made an intensive effort to achieve a high level of comparability of data. The research, which lasted over a three-year period, brought

---

[1] In France the work of Dominique Schnapper entitled *L'épreuve du chômage* (1981) marked the beginning of a new phase in studies of unemployment; in Britain, the first major research programme on the social consequences of unemployment was carried out in the mid-1980s (see Gallie *et al.* 1993).

Duncan Gallie and Serge Paugam

TABLE 1.1. *Comparison of characteristics of unemployed* (%)

	GER	SW	DK	NL	BE	FR	UK	IRE	IT	GR	S	PT
Average unemployment rates												
1991–4	6.8	7.1	9.1	6.7	8.2	11.0	9.7	15.4	10.2	8.3	20.4	5.1
1995–7	9.0	9.4	6.5	6.1	9.6	12.2	8.0	11.3	12.0	10.4	22.0	7.1
Proportion of long-term unemployed												
1991–4	37.2	8.5	29.8	47.4	58.3	37.1	38.2	60.0	61.6	49.9	48.7	37.9
1995–7	36.7	18.4	20.5	36.2	46.0	29.5	30.5	44.4	48.9	40.9	39.8	39.8
Average unemployment rates by sex 1991–4												
Men	5.7	8.2	8.4	5.5	6.1	9.2	11.3	15.1	7.5	5.4	16.4	4.2
Women	8.3	5.9	10.0	8.4	11.3	13.3	7.7	15.8	14.9	13.3	27.4	6.3
Composition of the unemployed 1994												
Sex												
Males	49.5	59.8	48.2	53.8	47.0	48.0	66.5	62.1	49.1	42.7	51.5	48.0
Females	50.5	40.2	51.8	46.2	53.0	52.0	33.5	37.4	50.9	57.6	48.5	52.0
Age group												
15–24	12.9	n.a.	22.2	27.7	25.2	25.0	28.3	31.2	39.5	39.0	33.1	34.2
25–49	60.6	n.a.	60.4	64.2	66.8	65.2	53.8	57.4	53.7	51.9	56.6	54.0
50+	26.5	n.a.	17.3	8.2	8.1	9.9	17.9	11.4	6.8	9.1	10.2	11.8

Notes: GER: Germany, SW: Sweden, DK: Denmark, NL: Netherlands, BE: Belgium,
FR: France, UK: United Kingdom, IRE: Ireland, IT: Italy, GR: Greece, S: Spain, PT: Portugal.
Source: Figures for unemployment rates and long-term unemployment are drawn from
European Commission, *Employment in Europe*, 1996, 1998. Figures on composition of the
unemployed are from Eurostat, *Labour Force Survey*, 1994. n.a. = not available

together research teams from eight countries: Denmark, France, Germany,
The Netherlands, Ireland, Italy, Sweden, and the UK. It aimed to provide an
overview of the experience of unemployment, partly by re-analysing national
data sources with a view to increasing their comparability and partly by using
the European Community Household Panel Study (ECHP),[2] which started
in 1994 and represents the first major source of information on the unemployed in the European Union.

   The comparison of the experience of unemployment in Europe is all
the more interesting in that it addresses a wider concern by researchers to
understand the forms of social regulation in European societies. To begin
with, it is clear that, even though there are some common features, the relative risks of unemployment of specific categories of the population differs
considerably between countries.

   As can be seen in Table 1.1, women have a much higher risk of unemployment than men in several of the countries of Southern Europe—Italy,
Greece, and Spain—as well as in Belgium and France. While women are
still disadvantaged, there is considerably less difference in the relative

---

[2] For details, see Appendix A, pp. 375–80.

unemployment risks of men and women in Denmark, Germany, Portugal and Ireland. In contrast, in Sweden and the UK, it is men that are most affected. The effect of such sex differences in unemployment rates on the composition of the unemployed depends in part on the level of participation of women in the labour market. At one extreme, in Greece, women represent 58 per cent of the unemployed; at the other, in the UK, only 34 per cent. There are also considerable differences in the age composition of the unemployed. Younger people, aged 15 to 24, constitute a much larger proportion of the unemployed in the Southern European countries than in other countries. In Italy, Greece, Spain, and Portugal they represent more than 30 per cent of all unemployed people, compared with 22 per cent in Denmark and only 13 per cent in Germany.

These differences point to the need to analyse the experience of unemployment not as something homogeneous, but as a phenomenon that takes place within particular economic, social and political structures and which, because of this, may have a different dynamic within each national culture.

One factor that could well be important is the nature and the forms of intervention of the welfare state. It is a plausible hypothesis that the living standards of the unemployed will depend to a considerable extent on the system of unemployment benefits. The probability of people experiencing long spells of unemployment is also likely to depend on both the extent of development of active employment policies and on the availability of specific policies to assist women's employment, for instance through the provision of childcare. Further, one could hypothesize that the degree of social integration of the unemployed within society will depend on the form and the stability of family structures, in particular as these affect their capacity to provide opportunities for sociability and material or affective support. Finally, it is important to consider the experience of unemployment in the context of the pattern of economic development and the rapidity of sectoral change in particular societies, since the chance of finding work is likely to be heavily affected by the nature of demand in the market. The differences between European societies in terms of these three dimensions—welfare provision, the family and the market—are very great, and it would be worth recalling the most salient points of divergence.

WELFARE REGIMES AND UNEMPLOYMENT

The conception of 'welfare regime' is taken in a broad sense. It refers to a system of public regulation that is concerned to assure the protection of individuals and to maintain social cohesion by intervening, through both legal measures and the distribution of resources, in the economic, domestic and community spheres. The usefulness of any regime model for understanding the empirical pattern of welfare provision may differ between welfare domains, either because of the distinctiveness of the problems addressed or because of the specific historical conditions at the time of institutional formation. It is quite possible, for instance, that the principles underlying the provision of welfare with respect to health may differ from those with respect to protection in the labour market. This wider issue of the degree of integration or segmentation of the principles underlying different aspects of welfare provision in a society is not one that can be pursued here. Rather it needs to be emphasized that we are concerned to use such types to explore one particular sphere of welfare provision. Our central concern is with those aspects of welfare regimes that provide protection from misfortunes in the labour market, primarily through the system of financial support for the unemployed and the institutional arrangements for intervention in the process of job allocation.[3]

The degree of coverage is likely to be a critical factor for the way the welfare state affects the experience of unemployment. It is, to a considerable degree, the very fact of receiving benefits to compensate for being without work that underlies conventional definitions of the unemployed. A person who is not receiving, or who has ceased to receive benefits is less likely to be socially recognized as a 'genuine' unemployed person. Coverage includes both those who receive insurance benefits and those who rely upon means-tested benefits. The balance between these can vary substantially between countries and, arguably, the nature of this balance may be important for the experience of unemployment. The higher the reliance on means-tested benefits, the greater may be the risk that unemployment will be stigmatic. In recent years, there has been a considerable expansion of means-tested assistance in most European countries, largely reflecting the deterioration of the labour market (Paugam 1999). But it should be noted that the link between these trends is stronger in countries where there is only weak coverage of the unemployed by insurance-based systems of social protection, revealing the importance of the underlying characteristics of the system.

The level of financial compensation is also likely to have an important effect on the experience of unemployment. In countries where a high level of replacement of earnings is provided over a relatively long period, the unemployed are more likely to be able to live in similar conditions to when they were in work. This also gives them greater opportunity to search thoroughly

<hr/>

[3] This emphasis on domain specificity is one of the factors that distinguishes our approach from the influential analysis developed by Esping-Andersen (1990). It should also be noted that the concept of welfare regime used here relates to provision by public authorities, in contrast to Esping-Andersen's revised conception of a welfare regime in terms of 'the ways in which welfare production is allocated between state, market and households' (Esping-Andersen 1999: 73).

TABLE 1.2. *Unemployment welfare regimes*

Regime	Coverage	Level & duration of cover	Active employment policy
1. Sub-Protective	Very incomplete	Very weak	Quasi non-existent
2. Liberal/Minimal	Incomplete	Weak	Weak
3. Employment-centered	Variable	Unequal	Extensive
4. Universalistic	Comprehensive	High	Very extensive

when they are looking for a job. It seems plausible that the degree of social stigmatization to which they are subjected will be lower, since there are fewer visible signs of their temporary loss of position. In countries where financial compensation is much more limited, the risk of poverty and of the cumulative growth of difficulties is likely to be much higher.

Finally, the extent of development of active employment policies is likely to have an effect on the experience of unemployment, given that these can reduce the risk of long-term marginalization from the labour market. When the unemployed have the possibility of improving their skills through training, they are likely to be in a better position to find a job. This argument cannot be accepted without qualification. When the number of available jobs in a region is limited, training courses can become little more than ways of keeping the unemployed occupied, giving them a minimum level of activity rather than providing any serious career perspectives. None the less, it has been shown that at least some types of employment policy which have been developing—albeit in different forms—across European societies in recent years can have real effects on job chances.

In taking these three criteria—coverage, level of compensation and expenditure on active employment policies—it is possible to distinguish at least four 'unemployment welfare regimes' in Europe: the sub-protective regime, the liberal/minimal regime, the employment-centred regime, and the universalistic regime.

A sub-protective regime is a system that offers the unemployed less than the minimum level of protection needed for subsistence. Few of the unemployed receive benefits, and when they do the amount is low. Active employment policies are virtually non-existent. In this type of regime, it could be expected that the unemployed will experience severe financial difficulty and live under the poverty threshold. The probability of long-term unemployment is also high, even though this is also likely to be conditioned by other factors such as the level and pattern of economic development.

The liberal/minimal regime provides a higher level of protection for the unemployed than the sub-protective. It does not, however, cover those at risk of unemployment as a whole and, above all, it provides a low level of financial compensation. Similarly, there is little development of active employment policies. This type of regime is also distinguished by its general philosophy. Whereas the sub-protective regime reveals a chronic absence of organized and planned intervention by the state, the liberal/minimal regime rather reflects an explicit political will not to intervene too heavily in the protection of the unemployed so as not to undermine the laws of the market. The underlying idea is to encourage the unemployed to take responsibility for themselves in order to avoid becoming dependent on social assistance. In order to minimize the possibility of a financial disincentive to work, there is a particularly strong reliance on benefits that are subject to means-testing, taking account of wider household income. It is a type of regime in which there is a strong risk that the unemployed will suffer from poverty. Given the emphasis on means-tested household income, it could be expected to provide particularly weak support for unemployed married women.

The employment-centred regime provides a much higher level of protection for the unemployed than the liberal/minimal. The level of financial compensation is higher and the development of active employment policies reflects the concern of the public authorities to avoid the effective withdrawal from the labour market of the most disadvantaged sectors of the active population. Nevertheless, the coverage of the unemployed remains far from complete as a result of the principles of eligibility for compensation. These are primarily defined in terms of previous employment experience. The system is concentrated on those who have built up the greatest rights. It tends then to create a division between 'insiders' and 'outsiders'. Vulnerability to poverty is likely to vary greatly depending on the status of the unemployed person, as well as on the length of time they have been unemployed. It is a type of regime that will disadvantage people who have only been able to obtain temporary jobs or those with little work experience. It could be expected to disadvantage particularly sharply, women and younger people since these are less likely to have either lengthy or continuous employment experience.

Finally, the universalistic regime is distinguished from the other three by the fact that it offers comprehensive coverage of the unemployed, a much higher level of financial compensation and a more ambitious active employment policy. Universalism also tends to be associated with the individualization of rights. Benefits are granted relatively independently of the resources of other household members. This should lead to both a low level of poverty among the unemployed and a lower risk of labour market marginalization. Given relatively easy eligibility rules and the individual basis of rights, this type of regime could be expected to discriminate the least between unemployed people in terms of either sex or age.

Welfare regimes have been seen as differentiated in terms of the extent to which they lead to 'decommodification', that is to say the progressive detachment of the individual's status from the logic of the market (Esping-Andersen 1990). The introduction of modern social rights in capitalist societies has helped to give people resources that are independent from the market, thereby making them other than merely an exchangeable commodity. But the extent to which this has occurred varies significantly between countries. With respect to the concept of 'decommodification', there is a clear gradient between the four types of unemployment welfare regime. The regime that is furthest from achieving this is the sub-protective regime; that which is closest is the universalistic regime.

A further common distinction is between 'beveridgian' and the 'bismarkian' systems, with the former characterized by the widest possible approach to social protection founded on the notion of social citizenship, and the latter by a more restrictive approach derived from participation in productive activity. It can be seen that the employment-centred regime reflects a bismarckian approach while the universalistic is closer to beveridgian principles. Both of the two other types of regime—the sub-protective and the liberal/minimal—are far from either principle.

Finally, as will be discussed in more detail later, the regimes differ in terms of the extent to which they lead to de-familialization, that is to say ensuring the independence of the individual from reliance on other family members. This is likely to have particularly important implications for the experience of women (Lewis 1992; Orloff 1993; O'Connor 1996; Daly 1996). The universalistic regime stands out from the others in terms of the extent to which it provides support irrespective of other household resources.

In considering this typology of unemployment welfare regimes, our view is that such models are best regarded as ideal-types rather than as descriptions of the institutional arrangements of particular countries. They are ways of describing the logic of particular *processes* of welfare regulation. It should not be expected that any country would represent a pure example of any such process. Rather, in reality, the welfare regimes of specific societies are likely to reflect, albeit to different degrees, a mixture of these different logics, and indeed their relative importance may change over time.

However, there are grounds for thinking that the countries upon which we are focusing approximate *more closely* to one type of welfare model than another. We have taken three empirical indicators reflecting the different constitutive dimensions of these regimes. These are: the proportion of the unemployed who receive benefits (see Table 1.3), the average expenditure on benefits per unemployed person as a percentage of per capita gross domestic product (see Table 1.4), and finally expenditure on active employment policies as a percentage of gross domestic product (see Table 1.5). These have been chosen as providing a reasonable level of comparability and, in the case of the last two, for giving a picture of the stability of the pattern across time. They must however be regarded as providing approximate indicators. The issue

TABLE 1.3. *Proportion of unemployed in receipt of benefit*

Country	Men	Women	Total
Belgium	81.3	81.6	81.5
Denmark	66.9	66.2	66.5
France	47.6	42.8	45.0
Germany	75.4	65.7	70.5
Greece	10.6	7.1	8.6
Ireland	81.4	42.8	66.8
Italy	7.7	6.0	6.8
Netherlands	64.3	35.0	49.6
Portugal	29.2	25.5	27.3
Spain	32.3	15.6	23.8
Sweden	86.6	85.1	86.0
UK	71.8	36.6	59.4

Note: The unemployed are defined in terms of the ILO criteria.
Source: European Labour Force Survey, 1995 (see Employment Gazette, 1995), except for Sweden. Figures for Sweden are drawn from register data for 1993 collected for the sample interviewed in the Level of Living Survey of 1991.

TABLE 1.4. *Expenditure on unemployment benefits per unemployed person* (% of per capita GDP)

Country	1980	1990	1993
Belgium	65.3	59.6	48.2
Denmark	88.0	61.3	61.8
France	38.6	33.2	36.1
Germany (West)	58.7	36.0	45.0
Germany*	—	—	46.8
Greece	64.9	32.6	31.1
Ireland	51.9	35.8	35.8
Italy	14.6	5.1	6.2
Netherlands	83.5	107.5	108.5
Portugal	13.2	9.4	23.7
Spain	79.6	52.5	73.7
Sweden	n.a.	n.a.	n.a.
UK	48.1	29.8	34.9

* includes the new Lander.
n.a.: data not available.
Note: Expenditure includes social assistance as well as insurance benefits.
Source: European Commission, 1995, *Social Protection in Europe*.

of the level of compensation, in particular, has led to quite diverse estimates for particular countries of the extent to which unemployment benefit replaces income in work, depending on the assumptions used. These are discussed further in Appendix 2. However, despite such variations, there emerges a reasonably consistent pattern of the broad differences between countries.

TABLE 1.5. *Expenditure on active employment policies* (% of GDP)

Country	1985	1990	1996
Belgium	1.3	1.2	1.4
Denmark	1.2	1.3	2.3
France	0.7	0.8	1.3
Germany	0.8	1.0	1.4
Greece	0.2	0.4	0.3
Ireland	1.5	1.4	1.7
Italy	n.a.	n.a.	n.a.
Netherlands	1.3	1.2	1.4
Portugal	0.4	0.6	1.1
Spain	0.3	0.8	0.7
Sweden	2.2	1.6	3.2
UK	0.7	0.6	0.4

n.a.: data not available.
Source: European Commission, 1998, *Social Protection in Europe*.

It is clear, to begin with, that there is a strong similarity between the countries of Southern Europe.[4] The proportion of the unemployed receiving benefits is lower than 10 per cent in Greece and Italy and lower than 30 per cent in Portugal and Spain.[5] These figures are almost sufficient in themselves to justify considering these countries as closest to a sub-protective regime. If one takes, in addition, the criteria of expenditure per unemployed person as a percentage of per capita GDP, it can be seen that Italy is below the 10 per cent threshold, Portugal is lower than 25 per cent and Greece around 30 per cent. Only Spain stands out from this pattern at 73.7 per cent. Moreover, expenditure on active employment policies is also very low in these countries. It amounts to less than 1 per cent of GDP in Greece and Spain and to only 1.1 per cent in Portugal. Such policies are considered virtually non-existent at the national level in Italy (Saraceno 1992), which possibly explains why this indicator is not available in the national statistics.

While the most notable feature of these systems is the gaps in their provision, it is possible none the less to detect a bismarckian influence. The Italian system of financial assistance for the unemployed is interesting in this respect: it is characterized by a very strong dualization. It is a system that reflects a particular way of handling employment issues in very specific sectors of the economy, particularly in large firms where employers and

[4] A number of writers have pointed to broad similarities in the structure of welfare arrangements in the Southern European countries (see Liebfried 1992; Castles 1993; Ferrera 1996; Saraceno 1994).
[5] The unemployed are defined in terms of the ILO criteria: people without employment, available to start work, and actively seeking employment.

employees have negotiated agreements that protect the workers and at the same time reinforce their loyalty to the organization. Through the mechanism of the '*Cassa Integrazione Guadagni*', employees of such firms receive 90 per cent of their daily salary through the period of inactivity. Moreover, people covered by this scheme are not officially classified as unemployed. There are also special schemes for workers in industries characterized by a high level of seasonal variation in activity. With the '*Trattamento speciale di dissoccupazione*', employees from construction and agriculture receive an allowance representing more than half of their daily salary if they become unemployed—66 per cent in the construction industry, 60 per cent in agriculture—and this continues for a period of three to six months, with possible further extensions. But, in Italy, as in the other Southern European countries, such protection has not been extended to the unemployed as a whole. The absence of more comprehensive coverage is likely to be particularly disadvantageous for young adults.

The countries which are closest to a liberal/minimal regime are the UK and Ireland. The proportion of the unemployed covered by benefits is relatively high in the UK at 59 per cent, but expenditure on benefits is quite low: less than 30 per cent in 1990 and less than 35 per cent in 1995. It is also important to note the more and more restricted role of insurance benefits. The principal benefit 'Job Seekers' Allowance' is subject to means-testing from the seventh month, and the obligation has been imposed to subscribe to a 'Job Seekers Agreement'. All these measures have the objective, following the liberal logic, of encouraging the unemployed to actively seek work and to accept, if necessary, a precarious job. Since insurance benefit is for such a short period, the majority of the unemployed in the early 1990s were receiving means-tested benefit (Evans *et al*. 1995). Ireland is also close to this type of regime, with relatively high coverage at 67 per cent, but low levels of benefit. It is, however, important to note that Ireland differed considerably from the pattern in the UK with respect to expenditure on active employment policies. These represented 1.7 per cent of GDP in Ireland compared with only 0.4 per cent in the UK.

Several countries approximate to the employment-centred model: France, Germany, The Netherlands, and Belgium. The proportion of the unemployed that receives benefits is high in Belgium (81.5 per cent) and in Germany (70.5 per cent) and lower in France (45 per cent) and The Netherlands (49.6 per cent). But the country order is no longer the same if one takes expenditure on benefits. In this respect The Netherlands is highest at 108.5 per cent of per capita income in 1993, followed by Belgium with 48.2 per cent and Germany with 46.8 per cent. France is at an even lower level with 36.1 per cent. The case of The Netherlands consists then of two rather different tendencies: a relatively low proportion of the unemployed are covered by insurance benefits, but these are quite generous for those who do get them.

This has the effect that large numbers of the unemployed have to look to social assistance for support. There are two such systems, one of which was created specifically for the unemployed, especially the long-term unemployed (Kemperman and Vissers 1999). The numbers on this have increased considerably in recent years, following closely the trend in the level of unemployment.

The same process has occurred in France. A low proportion of insured unemployed leads in a period of strongly rising unemployment to a sharp increase in the proportion receiving social assistance, especially the *revenu minimum d'insertion* introduced in 1988 (Paugam 1993). In Belgium and Germany where the coverage of unemployment insurance is more extensive, the increase in the numbers on social assistance has been less closely tied to changes in the labour market (Vranken, 1999; Breuer, 1999). Finally, it is notable that expenditure on active employment policies as a percentage of GDP is at a very similar level in these four countries and considerably higher than for countries closer to the first two types of regime. Such policies are an attempt by the public authorities to compensate for the gaps left in the system of insurance cover in a way that limits the pressure on social assistance schemes.

Finally, the two countries that are closest to the universalistic regime model are Denmark and Sweden. The proportion of the unemployed covered by benefits and the level of benefits are relatively high in these countries. It should be noted that between 1994 and 1996, Sweden introduced measures to reduce the level of compensation, but it was subsequently increased again. These two countries have also been characterized for many years by a particularly strong emphasis on active employment policies with expenditures of 2.3 per cent of GDP in Denmark in 1993 and 3.2 per cent in Sweden. For instance, the 'activation' agreement signed in 1992 in Denmark included the objective of integrating young people rapidly into the labour market, by increasing the number of public sector jobs and offering training to all. It also aimed to develop incentives and opportunities for the long-term unemployed, through social development programmes, the creation of free zones, and the development of public employment. The overall package of these measures, in combination with the encouragement of early retirement, is thought to have made a major contribution to reducing the level of long-term unemployment in the country.

The discussion to date has been mainly concerned with the broad implications of the social protection systems for the unemployed taken as a whole. However the type of unemployment welfare regime may also have important implications for the degree of equality or inequality in the treatment of men and women. Given that employment-centred systems depend to a considerable degree on the direct contributions of employees, there is a risk that women who have interrupted their careers for family reasons will be disadvantaged compared to men with a more continuous employment record. Women could also be expected to be disadvantaged in liberal/ minimal systems by the reliance on a system of means-testing which takes account of overall household income. In contrast, this type of effect could be expected to be least strong in universalistic systems, due to their easier eligibility rules and their individualized system of rights.

While it is difficult to find any simple metric for comparison, there are certainly important institutional differences between countries in eligibility rules (Rubery *et al.* 1998). The Danish system appears to be the particularly advantageous for women: only twelve months of contributions in the previous three years is sufficient to give eligibility for unemployment benefit, and this threshold has been reduced to thirty-four weeks for women who were in part-time work. It is notable that, although the unemployment system is a voluntary one, two-thirds of working women belong to it. In comparison, the British system is much less favourable for women. It gives greater importance to the amount than to the duration of contributions, which favours higher paid employees. As a result it takes a particularly long period for women to become eligible who are working in part-time jobs with low pay.

Taking the empirical evidence on benefit coverage (Table 1.3), it is notable that the sex differential is very small in both of the countries closest to the universalistic model: Denmark and Sweden. It is also relatively low in three of the four countries that were seen as close to the sub-protective system—Italy, Greece, and Portugal. This, however, constitutes relative sex equality in the virtual absence of provision. In contrast, women were much less likely to receive benefit when unemployed in both of the liberal/minimal countries—Ireland and Britain. Indeed these are the countries in which the sex differential is greatest. Women are also less likely to receive benefit in the majority of the employment-centred societies. It should be noted, however, that there is considerable diversity in pattern: the sex differential is very sharp indeed in The Netherlands, but it is relatively moderate in France and absent in the figures for Belgium. While in general the evidence supports the view that such systems work to the disadvantage of women, there are clearly mediating factors that lead to important differences in the extent to which this is the case. Given the emphasis of such systems on employment experience, it is likely that one such factor will be the pattern of women's labour market participation in specific societies.

Overall, these differences in benefit coverage for men and women confirm the earlier classification. Countries closest to the universalistic systems provide a high level of sex equality in coverage, while women are less well covered in the majority of countries closest to the employment-centred regime and in both of those closest to the liberal/minimal regime. While this is the only aspect of welfare for the unemployed for which comparable evidence for men and women is publicly available, it is clear that any full comparison of the degree of sex equality would require an assessment both of the level of benefits and of access to active employment policies.

There are good reasons then for thinking that the unemployment welfare regime is likely to have a major impact on the experience of unemployment. But it is also important to assess its relative importance in comparison with the role that may be played by the pattern of family organization.

THE ROLE OF THE FAMILY

It seems likely that the nature of the family will have an effect on the experience of unemployment. For instance, it seems probable that an unemployed person who lives alone, one who lives with their parents or one who has responsibility for several children will not live the same experience. It may also be the case that, in a situation in which the male partner has a job, unemployment will have a different significance for a female partner in countries where the general level of activity of women is high than in one where it is low.

In considering the possible impact of the family on unemployment experiences, the first factor that needs to be taken into account is the degree of stability of the family as an institution. The trends with respect to the rates of marriage, divorce and births outside marriage are generally used to provide a picture of the degree of 'de-institutionalization' of marriage and of the fragility of the traditional family model (Roussel 1989). Earlier research has suggested that family instability may aggravate the precarity of work careers, especially for unemployed people. But it is striking to note how strongly these demographic indicators vary from one country to another, suggesting that the unemployed will experience very different family situations depending on the country in which they live (see Table 1.6).

It is possible to distinguish at least three groups of countries with respect to the degree of de-institutionalization of the traditional family model. Sweden and Denmark share in common a high divorce rate and a high proportion of live births outside marriage. These are unquestionably the most advanced cases of de-institutionalization, even if the marriage rate is still high in Denmark. The UK resembles these countries with its high divorce rate, but the proportion of births outside marriage is somewhat lower. In contrast to the northern pattern, the Southern European countries, Greece, Portugal, Italy, and Spain, stand out with low rates both of divorce and of births outside marriage. Taking the 1980s cohort, the proportion of marriages ending in divorce was 12 per cent in Greece and only 7 per cent in Italy, compared with 46 per cent in Sweden. Note that Ireland comes close

TABLE 1.6. *Demographic indicators*

Country	Crude marriage rate (1/1000)	Crude divorce rate (1/1000)	Proportion of marriages ending in divorce for the 1980 cohort (1/100)	Proportion of live births outside marriage (1/100)
Belgium	5.1	3.5	34	15.0
Denmark	6.6	2.5	44	46.5
France	4.4	2.0	33	37.2
Germany	5.3	2.1	33	16.1
Greece	6.1	1.1	12	3.0
Ireland[a]	4.3	(0.5)	—	22.7
Italy	4.9	0.5	7	8.1
Netherlands	5.3	2.2	31	15.5
Portugal	6.6	1.2	14	18.7
Spain	5.0	0.8	—	10.8
Sweden	3.8	2.6	46	53.0
UK	5.5	2.9	42	33.6

[a] Given that divorce has been only recently legalized in Ireland, the figures presented are those of judicial separation rates (see Fahey and Lyons 1995). The legal separation rate for Italy for the 1980 cohort has been estimated at 8.7%. Employment Precarity, Unemployment, and Social Exclusion (EPUSE) programme data.
Source: Eurostat, data for 1995.

to the southern pattern in this respect. Even if the trends in most European countries have been similar over the 1980s and 1990s, the family model still remains more traditional in the Southern countries. Several countries occupy an intermediary position between the Scandinavian countries on the one hand and the Southern European countries on the other: this is the case for France, Germany, The Netherlands and Belgium.

There are also major differences between countries in the roles attributed to the family. This is evident with respect to the responsibilities of the family for young children. These are likely to be heavily affected by the nature of welfare policies, which determine the availability of childcare provision. The role of the welfare state in the construction of family models and their implications for inequalities between men and women has been emphasized by a number of writers in recent years (Lewis 1992; Orloff 1993; O'Connor 1996). Like unemployment benefit and employment policies, family policies differ considerably from one country to another.

There is a need, then, to complement the emphasis on decommodification, or detachment from the market, as a principle for comparing welfare regimes, with an emphasis on de-familialization, or detachment from the family. A social policy that leads to de-familialization implies a commitment to collectivising the weight of family responsibilities. This is likely to be an

TABLE 1.7. *Proportion of young children in publicly funded childcare* (%)

Country	Aged 0 to 2	Aged 3 to school-age
Belgium	20	95
Denmark	48	85
France	20	95
Germany	2	78
Italy	5	88
Netherlands	2	53
Sweden	32	79
UK	2	38

Source: Gornick *et al.*, 1997.

important condition for the ability of women to give equal importance to their career and family lives. At the other extreme, it is possible to point to societies where the family remains both the pivot of sociability and the principal legitimate mechanism for taking care of the social needs of all of its members.

It is striking to note, for example, the wide country variations in the socialization of children under school age in publicly funded childcare (see Table 1.7). This is a good indicator of de-familialization. The proportion of children under two years old with places in a creche is 48 per cent in Denmark and 32 per cent in Sweden compared with only 2 per cent in Germany, the UK and The Netherlands and 5 per cent in Italy. If one takes the proportion of children between 3 years old and school-age in publicly funded childcare, it is also weak in the UK (38 per cent) and in the Netherlands (53 per cent). It seems clear that women in the Scandinavian countries have much better opportunities to ensure the socialization of their children outside the family and thus to be less disadvantaged relative to men in their professional careers.

The nature of the family also differs very considerably with respect to the responsibilities for older children and the length of time over which they continue to reside with their parents. When one compares the proportion of adult children of 20 to 29 years of age living with their parents, it is evident that the process of de-familialization is much more advanced in the Northern than in the Southern European countries or in Ireland (see Table 1.8). Over two-thirds of such young adults continue to live with their parents in Italy, Spain, and Portugal, and more than half in Greece and Ireland. The corresponding figure is only 16 per cent in Denmark and 29 per cent in The Netherlands. If one takes the proportions among the unemployed, the divergences are even greater: 14 per cent in Denmark compared with 87 per cent in Italy.

TABLE 1.8. *Proportion of adult children aged 20 to 29 living with their parents*

Country	All 20–29 year olds	Unemployed 20–29 years olds
Belgium	54.4	58.6
Denmark	16.4	13.6
France	39.5	48.5
Germany	35.9	28.6
Greece	57.4	78.1
Ireland	61.8	71.6
Italy	77.1	87.0
Netherlands	29.2	33.3
Portugal	69.8	74.2
Spain	72.3	76.7
UK	32.4	41.7

Source: European Community Household Panel (ECHP), 1994, wave 1.

It is possible, then, to detect three models of *family residence*: an extended dependence model, a model of relative autonomy between generations, and finally a model of advanced inter-generational autonomy.

The extended dependence model characterizes a situation where different generations are brought together in the same household under the wing of the core generation. Adult children—and possibly older parents—are taken care of within the same home. Sociologists and demographers have often provided descriptions of this model emphasizing that it is based simultaneously on reciprocal exchange between the members of the household and on strict norms defining the obligations of each person within the group. It is a model that is reinforced by a very strong institutionalization of marriage (Jurado Guerrero and Naldini 1997). While it restricts the autonomy of the individual, it has the advantage of offering everyone a minimum of protection. The long-term unemployed for instance would benefit from direct family support.

The relative autonomy model defines an intermediary situation between the extended dependence and the advanced autonomy models. In this model, adult children living with their parents are under an obligation to look for an alternative solution. They must be actively preparing their entry to the labour market. The normative system underlying this model is primarily one of autonomy, and individual responsibilities in the household are much more weakly defined. It is above all the difficulty that young people encounter in trying to enter the labour market that creates the necessity for parental solidarity. While this system is less rigid, it is also more fragile. Adult children and older parents live the experience as a temporary situation. The ties between parents and children can easily break up as a result of misunderstandings in the household, especially when a relationship

TABLE 1.9. *Unemployment welfare regime and model of family residence, by country*

Unemployment Welfare Regime	Model of Family Residence		
	Extended Dependence	Relative Inter-Generational Autonomy	Advanced Intergenerational Autonomy
Sub-protective	Italy, Spain, Portugal, Greece		
Liberal/Minimal	Ireland		UK
Employment-centred		France, Belgium	Netherlands, Germany
Universalistic			Denmark, Sweden

of dependence without possible exchange develops, which is commonly the situation for the young long-term unemployed.

Finally, the model of advanced autonomy represents the normative system that contrasts most strongly with the extended dependence model. The self-realization of the young adult is regarded as inconceivable without acquiring autonomy from the parents. This does not of course mean that there is breakdown of affective ties. The children may remain to some degree financially dependent, but the norm is to live separately. This model allows people to cohabit with a partner earlier than is possible in the case of the two previous models.

What is the nature of the link between the unemployment welfare regime and the type of family residence model? We can begin by looking at the location of countries when the two dimensions are taken into account simultaneously (see Table 1.9). It is evident straight away that for the countries of Southern Europe there is a very strong correspondence between the sub-protective regime and the extended dependence model. It is also clear that there is a perfectly symmetrical relationship between the universalistic regime and the advanced autonomy family model in the Scandinavian countries.

It might be tempting to conclude that there is a continuum between these two poles and to attribute the decisive role in the creation of family residence models to the type of unemployment welfare regime that prevails in each country. But any such conclusion would be over hasty. This is evident if one takes the example of the UK. Given the minimal character of unemployment benefits and the liberal policies aimed at keeping them low, it could be expected that young people would stay for a long time at home with their parents, much as is the case in Ireland. Similarly, given its system of unemployment protection, it could be expected that the situation in The Netherlands and in Germany would be very similar to that in France and Belgium. But, in fact, The Netherlands and Germany, like the UK, are closer to Denmark and Sweden in their family residence models. It has to be concluded then that the dynamic of family residence is not entirely determined by the social protection regime, and that it is preferable to distinguish in our analysis the aspects of the experience of unemployment which are linked to the welfare regime from those which are linked to the family.

For these reasons, we prefer to speak in terms of welfare or unemployment welfare regimes when considering the sphere of intervention of the public authorities and of family models when examining the sphere of domestic life. When seeking to characterise the joint influence of several institutional factors linked to the experience of unemployment, we will use the notion of systems of social regulation.

THE ROLE OF THE MARKET

The concept of unemployment is inseparable from that of work, which provides the core interpretative framework in industrial societies. It is linked both to the idea of full employment and to the modern conception of paid work (Salais *et al.* 1986; Topalov 1994). Since unemployment is so closely linked to the conception of work that exists in an industrial society, its meaning may well vary depending on the degree of industrialization and of economic development. In a region or a country with a relatively low level of economic development, the inhabitants may not even define themselves in terms of the employment relationship, in the sense that it has acquired in large-scale enterprises. They may consider their work as self-employed or carry it out, on an occasional or permanent basis, in the informal sector. Since work is primarily a matter of survival rather than a social status, the consciousness of being an unemployed person may be less strong, especially since formal financial compensation on grounds of unemployment is negligible or even non-existent.[6] Qualitative research in the less developed

---

[6] Pierre Bourdieu, in his research in Algeria in the early 1960s, found that it was only the peasants of the Kabylie who had internalized the conception of work common in industrial societies, largely due to the close links they had maintained with Western culture through their tradition of immigration to the large cities and to France (Bourdieu *et al.* 1963). Even when they had been out at work in the fields for long hours in the previous days, they reported themselves as unemployed since they looked upon this agricultural work merely as a temporary way of getting by. It was only paid employment that they regarded as having true value. The situation was completely different among the more traditional peasants of Southern Algeria. These considered work simply in terms of its social function and paid little attention to the notions of unemployment or sub-employment, even in periods when there was not a great deal of economic activity and they were only at work part of the time.

TABLE 1.10. *Economic restructuring in Europe, 1974–1993* (% of total employment)

	Agriculture			Industry		
	1974	1993	Change	1974	1993	Change
Belgium	3.8	2.5	−1.3	31.2	19.7	−11.5
Denmark	9.6	5.2	−4.4	21.4	22.3	0.9
France	10.6	5.1	−5.5	28.3	19.1	−9.2
Germany	7.0	3.5	−3.5	35.8	28.5	−7.3
Greece	36.0	21.3	−14.7	18.5	15.6	−2.9
Ireland	22.8	12.7	−10.1	21.7	19.4	−2.3
Italy	17.5	8.0	−9.5	28.0	22.5	−5.5
Netherlands	5.7	3.9	−1.8	25.7	17.2	−8.5
Portugal	34.9	11.4	−23.5	24.9	23.8	−1.1
Spain	23.2	10.1	−13.1	26.3	23.0	−3.3
Sweden	6.7	3.4	−3.3	28.3	18.3	−10.0
UK	2.8	2.0	−0.8	34.6	24.1	−10.5

Source: OECD (1997) *Historical Statistics* 1960–1995.

regions of Southern Europe suggests that the conventional notion of unemployment is not as salient in the way people think about their society, in part because the 'unemployed' are mainly women or young people—see for instance Krief (1998). The adult men have the responsibility of ensuring the protection and survival of their families, and the economic system is organized to assist them to do this, even when conditions are harsh.

It also seems likely that the experience of unemployment will be affected by the extensiveness and timing of sectoral restructuring of the economy. For instance, in all countries, the transition from an essentially rural to an industrial economy has been associated with major changes in the skills and work attitudes of the workforce. In much of Europe, this transformation was completed in the three decades following World War II, when there was an overall shortage of labour and there were possibilities for re-integration into other economic sectors. But much greater problems inevitably arose for countries for which severe reductions in the agricultural workforce coincided with wider economic crisis and an inability to generate jobs that could compensate for those that had been lost. Unemployment became heavily concentrated on certain sectors of the population and involved severe marginalization from the labour market.

Since the mid-1970s, the degree and nature of sectoral change has varied very considerably between European countries (see Table 1.10). Taking employment change in the agricultural sector, it is notable that the Southern European countries have been by far the most affected in this period. The share of the agricultural sector went down from 35 to 11.4 per cent in Portugal, and from 36 to 21.3 per cent in Greece. In comparison to a country such as France the restructuring of agriculture in Southern countries was taking place in a much more difficult overall economic climate. The *Mezzogiorno* region in Italy represents a particularly extreme case where structural decline in the agricultural sector occurred with little compensation in terms of the development of other types of stable economic activity.

With respect to changes in manufacturing industry, it is clear that the heaviest employment losses occurred in the more developed industrial societies. The share of such industries in overall employment went down by about ten percentage points in Belgium, the UK, Sweden, France, and The Netherlands. The reduction was less sharp in Germany, but it was still considerable. Employment change in this sector was much lower in the Southern countries: Portugal, Spain, Greece, and Italy. Finally, Denmark stands out as the only country in which there was a slight increase in the share of this sector.

The European countries have then experienced different types and different intensities of shock to their employment systems in the period since the mid-1970s. There are three broad groups of countries. The Southern countries experienced a particularly severe reduction of their agricultural sectors, leaving endemic unemployment in certain regions. The societies that had developed large-scale industry earlier were subject to massive restructuring of the manufacturing sector. Unemployment in these cases was less likely to affect an entire sector of the workforce than to operate selectively, striking at those with lower skills and less ability to adapt to technological change. Finally, countries such as Denmark saw much less radical types of economic rupture which would have made it easier to handle the problems thrown up by unemployment. The transitions between different types of work were likely to require less drastic changes in skill and training, which should have helped to reduce the duration of unemployment spells.

STRUCTURE OF THE BOOK

Our starting point then is that the three types of factor that we have been considering—the nature of social protection for the unemployed, the type of family system, and the pattern of economic change—are each likely to have major implications for the experience of unemployment. While they are clearly not entirely autonomous, they do not determine each other in a way which can make it possible to simply logically deduce one from the other. Rather, the specific configuration of the relations between them is likely to lead to significant differences in the experience of unemployment between countries. In the course of this book, their impact will be examined with respect to three main dimensions of the experience of unemployment: financial deprivation, labour market marginalization, and social integration.

The first part of the book focuses on the relationship between unemployment and poverty. Chapter 2 looks at differences between countries in the risk of poverty for the unemployed and how these changed between the 1980s and 1990s. Chapter 3 examines the vulnerability to poverty and financial hardship of different types of unemployed people. Chapter 4 focuses on the situation of young unemployed adults, in particular considering whether family resources are effective in substituting for public welfare in countries where state provision is largely absent. Chapter 5 seeks to assess how far country differences in the risk of poverty for the unemployed can be attributed to the system of social transfers provided by the welfare state.

The second part of the volume turns to the processes that may heighten or reduce the risk of labour market marginalization. Chapter 6 considers whether there is any evidence that the generosity of welfare benefits affects the attitudes to work of the unemployed, leading them either to attach a lower importance to having a job or to be particularly inflexible about the type of work they will accept. Chapter 7 assesses the impact of labour market conditions at the time of first entry to the labour market on later risks of unemployment, seeking to establish whether entry at a time of high unemployment leads to a long-term penalty in terms of job security. Chapter 8 focuses on whether there are variations between countries in the 'scarring effect', whereby people who have been unemployed have a higher risk of unemployment in the future. Chapter 9 considers the effectiveness of childcare policies in limiting the risk of labour market marginalization for the particularly vulnerable group of lone mothers. Chapter 10 considers how the role of social networks in determining the job chances of the unemployed may vary with different national labour market institutions. Chapter 11 involves a detailed comparison of Britain and Italy, to explore the influence of institutional differences in determining the type of people who are most at risk of long spells of unemployment.

The third and final section is concerned with the issue of social integration. Chapter 12 looks at the impact of unemployment on people's social relationships in the household and the community. It considers how far unemployment is associated with social isolation and whether this varies between countries. Chapter 13 examines the tendency for unemployment and non-employment to become concentrated within households. Chapter 14 looks at the subjective side of social integration: the extent to which unemployment affects people's satisfaction with their lives. Chapter 15 seeks to assess how far the nature of the welfare regime affects differences between men's and women's experiences of unemployment. Finally, Chapter 16 looks at whether public attitudes to the employed are sympathetic or punitive, a factor which is likely to be important for the risk that unemployed people become socially marginalized.

The conclusion of the book both summarizes the results with respect to the different dimensions of deprivation, and argues that there are distinct models of social regulation of unemployment, which present quite different risks of social exclusion for the unemployed.

PART 1

Unemployment and Poverty

2

Unemployment and Poverty: Change over Time

*Richard Hauser and Brian Nolan with Konstanze Mörsdorf
and Wolfgang Strengmann-Kuhn*[1]

INTRODUCTION

The late 1980s and early 1990s were periods characterized by growing international competition accompanied by high unemployment in the countries of the European Union. Keynesian policies were substituted by more conservative policies based on neo-classical economic theory or supply-side economics. Deregulation, retrenchment and budget restrictions were key words in the debate about the welfare state all over Europe. The national strategies adopted, however, differed widely. This raises the issue of the implications of such differences both for the overall distribution of income and wealth, and for the living conditions of those at the lower end of the distribution, in particular the unemployed. This chapter examines the change over time in the poverty of the unemployed in countries that differed significantly both in their welfare regimes and in the policies that governments adopted towards the unemployed.

In the introduction to this book the theory of welfare regimes is used to create a classification of unemployment welfare regimes: the universalistic, the employment-centred, the liberal/minimal, and the sub-protective. This distinction of types of regime is an analytical instrument to highlight some important characteristics of the respective welfare states. If this classification has explanatory value it should allow one to predict political reactions to a marked increase in unemployment, and also broad tendencies in terms of outcomes for the living standards of the unemployed compared to the active population. Reactions and outcomes should be similar in countries dominated by the same welfare regime, and different in countries with different regimes.

[1] Data analyses also done by Beate Hock (GER), Paolo Barbieri (I), Mohammad Azhar Hussain (DK), Sheila Jacobs (UK), Charlotte Samuelsson (S), Jean-Paul Zoyem (F). For more detailed information about changes in unemployment and social policy from the mid-1980s to the mid-1990s see Hauser and Nolan (1998).

In an employment-centred welfare regime, the state provides extensive social insurance benefits instead of referring the unemployed mainly to the market. The aim of the social security system is the preservation of living standards, and, therefore, the entitlement to and the amount of benefits depend on previous contributions to the mandatory system. Those who were formerly employed are well protected, but those who had no chance to enter the labour market are excluded from the social insurance system. The universalistic unemployment welfare regime is dominated by the idea of universal social rights and offers equal basic benefits to all risk groups. To finance them and to avoid overly high costs for social protection—including high transfers to support families—a large proportion of the population has to participate in the labour force. An important component of social policy measures, therefore, is geared to enable as many as possible to work. In times of unemployment the state will probably increase its revenue by higher taxes and contributions, and extend active labour market measures.

The sub-protective unemployment welfare regime tends to offer neither passive nor active labour market policy measures. Few of the unemployed receive benefits and the level of protection is very low. The liberal/minimal unemployment welfare regime provides mainly means-tested assistance and only modest non-means-tested universal transfers. Because of its strong work-ethic norms, entitlement to benefits is strictly related to work effort.

The countries which we are examining can be seen as approximations of particular analytical types. Denmark and Sweden come closest to the universalistic type; France, Germany and The Netherlands to the employment-centred type; Britain and Ireland to the liberal/minimal type, and Italy to the sub-protective type.

To describe the outcomes of the different national strategies, in this chapter we focus on the following questions in a comparative perspective:

1. Were there changes in the distribution of income among the population of working age?
2. Is there more or less inequality among the unemployed than among the population of working age?
3. Are there higher poverty rates among the unemployed than among the whole population or the population of working age?
4. Did poverty rates among the unemployed increase from the mid-1980s to the mid-1990s as a consequence of deregulation and reductions in replacement rates?
5. Are there differences between the poverty rates of the short-term and the long-term unemployed or between the male and the female unemployed?

UNEMPLOYMENT AND SOCIAL POLICY—
CHANGES FROM THE MID-1980S
TO THE MID-1990S

Social Expenditure Relating to Unemployment

How did social expenditure for the unemployed change over the period, and were there clear differences in trends between countries depending on the model of welfare regime to which they approximated? When the percentages of relative social spending for active and passive labour market policies are aggregated, one gets a clear ranking. In 1985 the most generous countries were Denmark and The Netherlands, followed by Germany, Ireland and the UK. France and Italy spent least per unemployed person in relation to their Gross Domestic Product (GDP). In 1994 the ranking was still the same, but the UK had fallen to the same level as France. This ranking corresponds with the expectation that universalistic unemployment welfare regimes, such as Denmark, rank labour market policies high on the political agenda, and sub-protective unemployment welfare regimes, such as Italy, show little interest in this policy field. However it comes as a surprise that liberal welfare regimes, such as the UK and Ireland, spend relatively more per unemployed person in relation to their GDP per capita than France's employment-centred welfare state.

In both years all countries spent much higher proportions on passive than on active labour market measures. From 1985 to 1994 only three countries— Denmark, The Netherlands, and reunified Germany—increased their relative spending on passive labour market policies while the other countries remained at about the same level or reduced their relative spending. On the other hand, most countries—Italy is the only exception—increased their ratio of social expenditure on active labour market policy per unemployed person to GDP per capita.

Of the countries under review, The Netherlands and Denmark showed the highest relative spending on passive labour market measures in the mid-1980s and the mid-1990s while their unemployment rates were among the lowest (see Table 2.1). As expected, the universalistic welfare state, Denmark, also spent the highest proportion on active labour market measures. In contrast, Italy had the lowest relative expenditures on passive and, in the 1990s, also on active measures. The increase in the unemployment rate seems to have been compensated for by a decrease in the relative spending per unemployed person. These comparatively low expenditures for the social provision of the unemployed correspond with Italy's classification as a sub-protective welfare regime. But it has to be noted that Italy has a special benefit system for industrial workers in short-time work and temporary lay-offs, and the transfers from this system are not classified as unemployment benefits.

TABLE 2.1. *Harmonized unemployment rates 1985–1996* (yearly averages, in %)

	1985	1986	1987	1988	1989	1990	1991	1992	1993	1994	1995	1996
DK	7.1	5.4	5.4	6.1	7.4	7.7	8.4	9.2	10.1	8.2	7.1	6.0
GER[a]	7.2	6.5	6.3	6.2	5.6	4.8	5.6	6.6	7.9	8.4	8.2	9.0
W-GER[b]	7.2	6.5	6.3	6.2	5.6	4.8	4.2	4.5	6.0	6.7	n.a.	n.a.
F	10.1	10.2	10.4	9.8	9.3	8.9	9.5	10.4	11.7	12.3	11.6	12.3
IRE	16.9	16.8	16.6	16.1	14.7	13.4	14.8	15.4	15.6	14.3	12.4	12.3
I	8.5	9.2	9.9	10.0	10.0	9.1	8.8	9.0	10.3	11.4	11.9	12.0
NL	8.3	8.3	8.0	7.5	6.9	6.2	5.8	5.6	6.6	7.1	7.0	6.6
S	3.0	2.8	2.3	1.9	1.6	1.8	3.3	5.8	9.5	9.8	9.2	10.0
UK	11.5	11.5	10.6	8.7	7.3	7.0	8.8	10.1	10.4	9.6	8.8	8.2

[a] Figures until 1990 refer to West Germany, figures from 1991 onwards include East and West Germany.
[b] Data refer only to West Germany.
Notes: n.a. = not available. DK: Denmark, GER: Germany, F: France, IRE: Ireland, I: Italy, NL: The Netherlands, S: Sweden, UK: United Kingdom.
Source: Europäische Kommission 1997: 82–3.

In the mid-1980s, both countries with liberal/minimal welfare regimes, Ireland and the UK, had the highest unemployment rates, at 16.9 per cent and 11.5 per cent, and spent more on passive measures than the employment-centred welfare regime France. Ireland's spending was even higher than the Germany's. In the mid-1990s, relative expenditure on passive measures decreased in both countries. But relative expenditures on active measures rose, especially in Ireland, although the unemployment rates slightly decreased.

Among the employment-centred welfare regimes one cannot find a clear pattern. Germany's relative social expenditure for the unemployed was in an intermediate position in 1985, but it rose significantly by the mid-1990s, partly caused by more generous rules for the unemployed in East Germany. Because of the extraordinary event of reunification it cannot be compared directly with other countries. France's relative social expenditure was clearly below Germany's in 1985, and it also increased somewhat until 1994. The Netherlands' relative spending on passive labour market measures exceeded that of the other two employment-centred welfare regimes, but, surprisingly, in The Netherlands the proportion spent on active labour market measures was relatively low. This impression, however, may result from a different classification of total spending for labour market policies.

Social Policy Reforms Concerning the Unemployed

These changing patterns of expenditure have to be understood in the light of changes in the social security systems over this period. Daly (1997: 133) has summarized the general trend in the reform strategies of governments. Access to benefits was restricted by attaching additional conditions and tightening regulations. There was increased targeting of transfers by greater use of means-testing, the linking of the size of benefits to income, and by making benefits taxable. Privatization was extended, not only in terms of contracting out services to the private sector but also by according greater responsibility to individuals to provide for their own protection against risks, or to family members to provide financially for each other. Finally, there was a heightened emphasis on active measures to get people into employment so that they could support themselves.

But the extent of these changes varied considerably from country to country, due to differences in emphasis in social policy. For instance, in the mid-1990s, there remained very wide differences in the extent to which the unemployed were covered by unemployment benefit or assistance. In the universalistic welfare regime, Denmark, coverage reached nearly 70 per cent, but was not as high as in Germany and only a little higher than in Ireland. Coverage in the UK is about 10 percentage points lower, and in France and in The Netherlands only one-half of the unemployed received any benefits. The situation in Italy is striking: barely one out of ten unemployed persons received unemployment benefits or unemployment assistance. This is due firstly to a high rate of youth unemployment, because those without a prior job do not qualify for the insurance scheme, and secondly, to a highly selective system of social protection. Once again recall that beneficiaries of the special benefit system for industrial workers in short-time work and temporary lay-offs are not classified as receiving unemployment benefits.[2]

There were also very substantial differences by country in the extent to which living standards were protected for those who were in receipt of benefit. We define the income replacement rate as the disposable income of an unemployed person—including unemployment benefits and unemployment assistance, social assistance and housing benefits—as a proportion of the disposable income of an employed person. Calculation of the disposable income of an employed person is based on the average gross wage of an industrial worker, as estimated by the OECD, from which simulated amounts of national taxes and social insurance contributions are deducted.[3]

[2] Officially, the participants of this compensation program, '*Cassa Integrazione*', are not considered unemployed and do not appear in Italian unemployment statistics, even if they have been fully laid-off for months or even years. However, due to the Eurostat definition of unemployment, which includes all people who are without job and looking for a job, they appear in the harmonized unemployment statistics on which the results in Fig. 2.2 are based.

[3] We refer to a model which was developed by the European Central Planning Department in Den Haag on behalf of the Directorate General V of the European Commission. The model takes into account: age, previous income as a percentage of average income, the number of dependent persons, the length of former employment and so the length of contribution to unemployment insurance, and the duration of unemployment. The replacement rates refer to typical persons who are 24 years or 35 years old, who are single or have

In all countries the short-term unemployed suffer a substantial decrease in disposable income. The replacement rates for the long-term unemployed —after two years of unemployment—are even lower in most of the countries (European Commission 1996: 90–100), Denmark being the exception. Those in long-term unemployment who cannot rely on financial help from their family have a particularly high risk of poverty in Ireland, the UK, and Italy, with replacement rates below 50 per cent.[4] Young single people who have a low wage income of only 50 per cent of the average production worker wage, and a short contribution record, suffer a considerable decline in income when unemployed in the sub-protective welfare regime, Italy, as well as in the liberal/minimal regimes of Ireland and the UK, but also in the employment-centred welfare regime, Germany. In contrast, those who have a dependent family have higher replacement rates in all countries. In France, Ireland and The Netherlands, the replacement rates are even slightly above 100 per cent.

HYPOTHESES

Given the patterns of relative social expenditure for labour market measures, of coverage of the unemployed, and of replacement rates, one can formulate hypotheses about the way the size of the poverty problem among the unemployed is likely to have changed over time in the various countries:[5]

1. In Denmark, social expenditure on passive labour market measures and on active measures was relatively high compared to the other countries. Taking the rather high income replacement rates, the high coverage, and many institutional regulations in favour of the unemployed in a universalistic regime into consideration, we expect a low proportion of poor among the unemployed in the 1980s as well as in the 1990s.

2. Sweden, also a universalistic welfare regime, was the only country that in 1985 spent more on active than passive measures (OECD 1994:

a dependent spouse and two dependent children, who have been employed for 10 years or for two years, who have contributed to unemployment insurance and who have had an average income and an income of 50 per cent of the average, respectively. For details see European Commission (1996a: 85).

[4] This statement is true if the usual poverty line of 50 per cent of mean equivalent net income is applied. For details see Income Poverty—A comparison from the mid-1980s to the mid-1990s, later in this chapter.

[5] Additional information about the main changes in the labour market policies of the EPUSE countries can be found in Hauser and Nolan (1998).

101). At that time the Swedish unemployment rate was quite low at 3 per cent. Corresponding with the sudden increase in its unemployment rate at the beginning of the 1990s, Sweden increased relative social spending on passive measures. The poverty rate among the unemployed is thus expected to have remained unchanged.

3. The Dutch unemployment insurance system was for a long time thought to be a shining example of an effective employment-centred welfare state. But when, in the mid-1980s, unemployment reached an extremely high level the Dutch government reduced the replacement rate from 80 to 70 per cent, and also froze the minimum wage: the general assessment basis for a lot of benefits. In the early 1990s further cuts followed. Despite this retrenchment, social expenditure for the unemployed was still relatively high, and coverage was at a medium level. We expect, therefore, that the poverty rates of the unemployed were moderate, but increased during the previous decade.

4. In Germany, also an employment-centred welfare regime, relative social expenditure was far below The Netherlands in the mid-1980s, but rose somewhat during the following decade. Replacement rates were at a medium level, but coverage was high, especially in the new Eastern part of the country. In the early 1990s the replacement rates of unemployment benefits as well as of unemployment assistance were cut. Therefore, we expect that the poverty rates of the unemployed were moderate, but have risen.

5. The French system sticks to the traditional unemployment insurance of the employment-centred welfare regime, consequently excluding those not qualifying for the benefits. The proportion of those receiving unemployment benefits or assistance was less than 50 per cent in 1994, and relative expenditure for passive labour market policies was comparatively low. Thus, we suppose that there is a relatively high rate of poverty among the unemployed, and that the rate has increased during the decade under consideration.

6. Ireland was the country with the highest unemployment rate in the mid-1980s and the mid-1990s. In the 1990s, however, relative social expenditure on passive measures decreased, and changes were introduced to the Unemployment Assistance Scheme to make it 'more attractive' for the unemployed to take up casual work. On the other hand, a national Employment Support Service was established in 1993, and the lowest rates of social protection were increased relatively rapidly. Overall, it is possible that the presumably high poverty rate among the unemployed did not increase.

7. The British/liberal minimal welfare regime is thought to leave more unemployed in poverty than most employment-centred or universalistic welfare regimes, since relative social spending for passive labour

market measures is low, decreasing further from 1985 to 1994. Unemployment benefits as well as income support were cut to motivate the unemployed to take on badly-paid jobs. Finally, in 1996, the duration of the flat-rate insurance benefit was limited to six months. The proportion of poor unemployed, therefore, is likely to have increased from the mid-1980s to the mid-1990s.

8. The Italian sub-protective unemployment welfare regime favours those in 'normal' full-time employment. Coverage of the unemployed with respect to benefits is very low. In the 1980s, relative social expenditure for the unemployed was also low for active and passive measures, and during the 1990s they actually decreased, but from 1991 the income replacement rate for the unemployed was increased several times. Therefore, one can expect a rather high but decreasing poverty rate.

INCOME DISTRIBUTION AND INEQUALITY

The Measure of Income

The concept of income used here is a person's equivalent net household income. The net income of a household, its disposable income, is calculated from the sum of gross incomes of all household members by deducting personal taxes and social security contributions, and by adding all kinds of monetary transfers, and, as the only non-cash income, the rental value of owner occupied housing.[6] To compare the well-being of members of households of different size, it is necessary to assign a share of the household net income to each member. If *per capita* income were used, the smaller needs of children compared to adults, and the economies of scale resulting from common household consumption would not be taken into account. Therefore, a weighting formula, called an equivalence scale, is used that assigns a weight of 1 to the head of the household, and weights below 1 to further members of the household. Equivalent net income of each member of a household is then calculated by dividing household net income by the sum of the weights of the household members. Since there is no universally accepted

---

[6] We used *monthly* net income. Income information refers to the last month before the interview. Persons (households) with missing values or an income variable of zero were excluded. Although monthly income should refer to the same month as the information about unemployment of a person to get the most reliable indicator of the respective income situation, this could not be realized in all of the countries. With the French and the Dutch data sets it was not possible to calculate the net household income for the year the employment status refers to. Therefore, the income information of the previous year was used. This procedure presumably resulted in biased estimates giving too low values of the inequality measure for the unemployed and of the respective poverty ratios.

equivalence scale, we will apply two different scales: commonly known as the old, and the modified OECD scale.[7]

To assess change from the 1980s to the 1990s, the only feasible approach is to try to obtain the best possible matching of national data sources, since the collection of fully comparative data for the countries of the European Union only began in the 1990s. While the use of national data sources provides the most reliable evidence of change over time *within* countries, it necessarily provides only an approximate picture of the differences *between* countries. Although every effort has been made to standardize methods of calculation, differences of procedure remain. Most of our data sources are household surveys. In the case of Denmark, however, the source is a 3 per cent sample from tax records. The Swedish income data is obtained by matching the Level of Living Surveys with data from administrative records. The data for The Netherlands for 1987 from the Luxembourg Income Study Project includes only persons aged 15 years and older and, to maximize comparability over time, the same age limits were applied to the 1991 data. Leaving out children under 15 may result in biased estimates of the poverty ratios, probably giving lower ratios. It should also be noted that the available data sets do not refer to exactly the same years. The case of Sweden is problematic since the rise in unemployment came after 1991.

Income Inequality Among the Population of Working Age and the Unemployed

The inequality measure we use is the Gini coefficient. For details of this see for example, Atkinson (1983: 53–6) and Atkinson, Rainwater, and Smeeding (1995b). This widely applied inequality measure ranges from 0: completely equal distribution of equivalent incomes, to 1: extreme inequality, one person receives the whole income, the others nothing. Table 2.2 shows Gini coefficients for the population of working age, that is, at an age between 18 and 65 years, including all the workforce and the inactive, and the same measure only for the unemployed.

In the mid-1980s in Denmark, The Netherlands and Ireland, inequality among the unemployed was lower than among the population of working age, but in the other countries it was higher. Denmark and The Netherlands had the lowest levels of inequality among the unemployed, the UK and Italy had the highest levels, and the other countries were in between but closer to the top than to the bottom group. From the mid-1980s to the mid-1990s inequality among the unemployed increased further in the group with

---

[7] Person weights implied by the old OECD scale: head of household: 1.0, all additional members 14 years and over: 0.7, children under 14 years: 0.5. Modified OECD scale: head of household: 1.0, all additional persons 14 years and over: 0.5, children under 14 years: 0.3.

Richard Hauser and Brian Nolan

TABLE 2.2. *Gini coefficients*[a]

	Mid-1980s			Mid-1990s		
	Year	Population at working age	Unemployed	Year	Population at working age	Unemployed
DK	88	0.219	0.186	93	0.225	0.189
GER(W)	85	0.266	0.291	95	0.278	0.291
F	85	0.300	0.301	92	0.290	0.274
IRE	87	0.331	0.279	94	0.313	0.230
I	89	0.302	0.313	93	0.336	0.365
NL	87	0.253	0.215	91	0.261	0.272
S	81	0.225	0.297	91	0.270	0.303
UK	84/86	0.282	0.311	94/95	0.306	0.337

[a] Based on equivalent net income of the population at working age (18–65) and the unemployed in the mid-1980s and the mid-1990s. The modified OECD-scale is applied.
Source: EPUSE calculations; see the Appendix to this chapter for the data sets used.

highest inequality, Italy and UK, but also in The Netherlands, while it decreased in France, and most notably in Ireland. Among the population of working age, a tendency to increasing inequality can be found in most countries, but France and Ireland are exceptions.

INCOME POVERTY—A COMPARISON FROM THE MID-1980S TO THE MID-1990S

Poverty thresholds

Each definition of income poverty is based on the idea of a minimum of subsistence. One can distinguish an absolute minimum of subsistence based on a basket of goods that allows a person to survive, and a socio-cultural minimum that is sufficient to participate in the activities of a society at least at a modest level, related to the average living standards. Our analysis is based on a relative socio-cultural minimum that has to be reached by each member of a society if income poverty is to be avoided. To guarantee a socio-cultural minimum of subsistence is one of most important aims of social policy in all the member states of the European Union, although the instruments and the outcomes may be different. There is no universally accepted value-judgement, however, about the level of this socio-cultural minimum. The income level that is considered as acceptable may differ in absolute and relative terms from country to country.

To arrive at a broader insight into the situation of the low income groups in each country we will use, therefore, several poverty lines based on three different percentages of a central measure of the average living standard of a society, on two central measures of average living standard, and on two different equivalence scales. We will use 40, 50, and 60 per cent of the central measures as poverty lines; 50 per cent is the most commonly used percentage in poverty research and is also favoured by the European Commission for its poverty reports. Besides posing less of a problem with value judgements, the use of three thresholds has the advantage that one can evaluate policy effects much better. If the unemployment benefits in one country are cut, this might not affect the poverty rate of the unemployed when one only uses the most common 50 per cent line, whereas one might see a negative effect when applying the 60 per cent line.

The arithmetic mean as well as the median will be used as measures of central tendency. By using the mean, the 'pure' idea of relative income poverty is expressed. Whenever total income rises, no matter whose income increases, the poverty threshold also goes up. Using the median implies another idea. Since the median does not change if only the incomes of the better-off half of the society increase, in this case the poverty line does not change either. With the typically negatively skewed income distribution the median is lower than the mean. The central measures will be calculated for each country separately. The reason for this decision is that both citizens and politicians still use this national perspective. Social policy as well, still takes place at the national level. A view that an average of the European Union should be the point of reference has yet to be established in the minds of its populace.[8]

The weights for the household members will be taken from the two different equivalence scales, the old and the modified new OECD scale, already described. Since the assumptions concerning the economies of scale and the differences in need between children and adults are quite different with these two scales, the percentages and the composition of the population in poverty are different. By using the old OECD equivalence scale one finds more persons from multi-person households among the poor, but with the modified scale more of the poor come from single households.

Poverty Among the Whole Population from the Mid-1980s to the Mid-1990s

To get a general picture of the changes in income poverty from the mid-1980s to the mid-1990s we first compare income poverty among the whole population of the countries under review. Table 2.3 gives poverty figures based on poverty lines of 50 per cent of national mean and median equivalent

---

[8] Poverty figures on the basis of European mean income can be found in Huster (1996: 62).

Richard Hauser and Brian Nolan

TABLE 2.3. *Poverty rates of all individuals in EPUSE countries[a], mid-1980s and mid-1990s*

	Mid-1980s			Mid-1990s				
	Year	Epuse Median 50% %	Mean 50% %	Year	Epuse Median 50% %	Mean 50% %	Eurostat Year	Mean 50% %
DK	1988	7.6	7.9	1993	7.2	7.7	1993	6
D	1985	5.8	10.5	1995	7.4	12.7	1993	11
F	1985	10.3	14.1	1992	8.4	12.8	1993	14
IRE	1987	7.8	17.3	1994	4.9	18.7	1993	21
I	1989	9.9	15.6	1993	14.2	19.7	1993	20
NL[b]	1987	4.8	7.9	1991	4.9	8.1	1993	13
S	1981	11.6	11.7	1991	10.7	12.4		n.a.
UK	84–86	7.9	14.9	94–95	12.4	19.1	1993	22

[a] Based on the modified OECD equivalence scale.
[b] For the Netherlands, EPUSE calculations are for the population aged 15 years and older, Eurostat figures are for the total population.
Notes: n.a. = not available.
Sources: EPUSE calculations; see the Appendix to this chapter for the data sets used. Eurostat (1997) Based on data from the European Community Household Panel Study.

net incomes as calculated by the EPUSE project. For comparison, results calculated by Eurostat on the basis of the first wave of the Euro Panel referring to 1993 are also shown.

By first comparing the EPUSE results for the mid-1980s and the mid-1990s one can see rising poverty rates in most of the countries. Only in Denmark and France did the percentage of the poor, calculated with both poverty lines, decrease. In Ireland and Sweden, applying the median-based poverty line, the poverty rates are lower by the mid-1990s, while using the mean-based poverty line they are higher. The Eurostat figures for the mid-1990s differ only slightly from the EPUSE results. The discrepancy may partly be due to the different method of calculating mean or median equivalent net income: while Eurostat uses equivalent net income per household, the EPUSE project more correctly uses equivalent net income per person.[9] It may also be due to the differing years of reference. The rather large difference for The Netherlands may additionally result from the fact that the Dutch data set used by the EPUSE project only contains the population aged 15 years and older, while the figures based on the Europanel include the total population.

[9] Since each individual in a society has equal value as a human being, the calculation of the mean per person is appropriate. The calculation of the mean per household gives individuals less weight the greater is the number of household members.

Changes in Poverty Within the Population of Working Age

We now look at the development of income poverty within the population of working age, the 18 to 65 year-olds in each country containing both the employed and the unemployed. Table 2.4 shows how much difference the choice of poverty line makes to the level of income poverty. It is the choice between 40, 50, or 60 per cent of the measure of central tendency, rather than between the mean or the median, the old or the modified OECD equivalence scale, which makes the major difference.

In the mid-1980s, with the 50 per cent poverty line, France and Italy had higher poverty rates than the average for the eight countries, while 'West' Germany, The Netherlands, and the UK had below average rates. Denmark and Sweden show below average poverty ratios if the poverty line is based on the mean, but above average ratios if the line is based on the median, while the opposite is true for Ireland. The results of the 40 and 60 per cent poverty lines do not change this ranking crucially.

From the mid-1980s to the mid-1990s, in most countries the poverty rates increased at the 50 per cent line independent of the measure or the scale applied, but in France, Ireland and The Netherlands, poverty fell. Has this changed the ranking of the countries? At the 50 per cent lines the UK now joins Italy in the group with the highest rates. 'West' Germany and The Netherlands remained in the group with below average rates, and France and Denmark also have rates below or at least close to the average. For Ireland and Sweden their position again depends on the choice of mean or median, but Ireland is only a few percentage points above the average when the mean is used. When the 40 per cent poverty line is chosen the improvements in France and Ireland result more obviously in a better ranking position.

The most notable changes happened in the UK which clearly moved into the group with above average poverty rates, while France and also to some extent Ireland at least improved their rank at the two lower poverty lines. This is similar to the pattern of changes in inequality discussed earlier. Moreover, there exists a strong correlation between the rank order of countries with respect to income inequality among their population at working age and their poverty ratios. In a European perspective the Dutch employment-centred welfare state seems to be the most successful in preventing poverty among its population at working age, followed by the Danish and Swedish universalistic welfare states. From the mid-1980s to the mid-1990s, however, one cannot detect a clear pattern of change among the other countries related to their type of unemployment welfare regime.

Poverty Among the Unemployed in the Mid-1980s and Mid-1990s

We now turn to the analysis of poverty among the unemployed, first using all the different poverty lines. Table 2.5 shows that the ranking of countries changes considerably when only this specific group is looked at. Even though

Richard Hauser and Brian Nolan

TABLE 2.4. Poverty ratios of persons at working age[a], mid-1980s and mid-1990s

	40%				50%				60%			
Mid-1980s	Mean New	Mean Old	Median New	Median Old	Mean New	Mean Old	Median New	Median Old	Mean New	Mean Old	Median New	Median Old
Mean*[b]	**5.3**	**5.6**	**3.9**	**3.9**	**11.0**	**11.4**	**7.2**	**7.4**	**17.6**	**18.8**	**12.7**	**12.8**
DK	5.6	5.1	5.4	4.7	8.9	8.5	8.5	7.8	13.0	12.5	12.3	11.5
GER[c]	4.2	4.4	2.5	2.3	9.2	10.1	5.3	4.9	17.2	18.4	9.9	9.9
F	7.9	8.4	6.5	6.5	12.9	14.0	9.7	10.0	20.1	21.7	15.0	15.5
IRE	5.3	6.0	2.9	2.9	15.3	15.4	6.6	7.2	23.8	23.5	15.5	15.0
I	7.0	7.9	4.3	4.7	13.9	14.3	9.0	9.8	21.8	23.0	15.2	15.9
NL	3.3	4.1	2.2	2.6	8.1	9.8	5.0	5.7	14.7	18.3	9.4	10.6
S	6.0	5.7	5.8	5.5	8.9	9.1	8.4	8.7	12.3	13.8	12.0	13.0
UK	3.4	3.9	1.7	1.8	10.4	10.5	5.6	5.5	18.0	18.3	12.3	11.5
Mid-1990s												
Mean*[b]	**6.5**	**6.8**	**4.3**	**4.6**	**12.7**	**13.0**	**8.3**	**8.4**	**19.7**	**19.5**	**14.2**	**13.5**
DK	5.8	5.2	5.4	4.8	9.2	8.7	8.7	7.9	13.7	13.0	12.6	11.7
GER[c]	5.9	6.1	2.5	3.4	12.0	12.3	6.8	6.9	19.5	20.8	12.7	11.9
F	6.2	6.8	4.3	4.5	12.0	12.9	8.2	8.6	20.1	21.0	14.2	14.9
IRE	2.8	4.2	1.2	1.2	14.8	13.8	3.6	4.2	24.1	24.3	14.5	12.3
I	11.6	12.4	7.9	8.8	18.7	19.2	13.8	14.4	26.1	26.8	19.8	20.8
NL	3.9	4.0	3.0	2.6	8.0	9.2	5.1	5.0	15.5	17.9	9.5	9.5
S	7.7	7.6	6.7	6.8	11.6	11.7	9.9	9.8	16.2	17.3	13.8	14.5
UK	7.9	8.5	4.3	4.6	15.3	16.3	10.0	10.1	22.8	24.1	16.4	16.9

[a] 18–65 years old.
[b] mean* = Unweighted mean of the EPUSE countries in %.
[c] Figures only refer to West-Germany.
Note: Data presented according to poverty lines set at 40, 50 and 60 per cent, using different equivalence scales.
Source: EPUSE calculations; see the Appendix to this chapter for the data sets used.

TABLE 2.5. *Poverty ratios of unemployed persons, mid-1980s and mid-1990s*

	40%				50%				60%			
	Mean New	Mean Old	Median New	Median Old	Mean New	Mean Old	Median New	Median Old	Mean New	Mean Old	Median New	Median Old
Mid-1980s												
Mean*a	**12.9**	**13.9**	**8.9**	**8.3**	**26.5**	**26.9**	**17.5**	**17.9**	**37.6**	**37.6**	**29.6**	**29.0**
DK	4.2	3.9	3.9	3.5	7.6	7.2	7.2	6.6	12.3	11.8	11.6	10.7
GERb	22.0	19.5	11.9	10.9	35.5	35.5	26.1	21.4	52.5	50.6	36.5	34.8
F	11.8	14.9	10.5	10.6	23.0	24.6	17.2	18.0	33.9	35.1	26.6	26.8
IRE	6.1	12.5	1.4	1.4	37.3	39.4	11.7	16.4	52.6	52.7	37.3	39.4
I	23.7	26.6	16.1	17.8	37.1	37.8	28.0	30.0	48.3	49.7	38.9	39.8
NL	5.2	5.7	2.6	4.2	11.3	13.0	7.1	7.1	20.6	22.6	13.8	13.8
S	20.5	13.5	19.3	12.4	27.3	25.0	25.0	25.0	34.1	33.7	34.1	33.7
UK	9.9	13.0	5.3	5.6	32.9	32.0	17.9	18.5	46.8	45.5	37.8	33.3
Mid-1990s												
Mean*a	**17.5**	**18.7**	**12.1**	**12.2**	**32.0**	**31.2**	**19.3**	**21.0**	**44.9**	**43.5**	**34.7**	**32.6**
DK	4.2	3.8	3.8	3.4	7.6	7.1	7.0	6.3	12.9	12.2	11.7	10.7
GERb	23.2	22.1	14.6	13.9	41.7	36.2	25.6	24.5	53.2	56.8	41.9	35.5
F	13.1	14.3	9.8	9.5	23.3	23.9	16.0	16.9	34.6	36.7	27.1	27.8
IRE	4.0	7.6	1.3	1.5	33.4	29.5	6.1	7.6	52.8	50.6	33.0	27.3
I	34.0	35.5	23.5	27.0	45.7	46.0	37.2	38.1	55.0	56.0	47.1	48.0
NL	12.9	15.5	8.3	8.4	25.2	23.8	15.3	17.5	46.3	32.9	29.8	23.8
S	19.4	19.4	18.5	16.9	30.4	29.6	22.0	23.2	43.2	41.9	36.3	36.0
UK	29.0	31.5	16.3	16.6	49.4	50.6	35.8	34.1	61.5	60.7	51.2	51.5

a mean* = unweighted mean of the EPUSE countries in %.

b Figures refer only to West-Germany.

Note: Data presented according to poverty lines set at 40, 50 and 60 per cent, using different equivalence scales.

Source: EPUSE calculations; see the Appendix to this chapter for the data sets used.

the use of the different thresholds still makes a difference, the results are more consistent than for the population of working age.

In the mid-1980s the group with highest poverty rates among the unemployed at the 50 per cent line consisted of Italy and West Germany. Ireland and Sweden have relatively high and average rates, respectively, depending on the measure used. The UK and France had a middle rank, and The Netherlands and Denmark showed the lowest poverty rates. With a few exceptions this ranking was reproduced at the 40 and 60 per cent lines.

Comparing the mid-1980s with the mid-1990s one finds a robust result that is independent of the poverty lines used. On average, poverty among the unemployed has increased between 4 to 7 percentage points, comparing the lines labelled mean* in Table 2.5. Denmark is the only country that managed to keep the poverty rate at about the same low level. The general increase in the poverty ratios of the unemployed in the mid-1990s was accompanied by several changes in the ranking of countries. These ranks are now fairly independent of the equivalence scale chosen, but they vary depending on whether the mean-based or the median-based poverty lines at the 40, 50, or 60 per cent level are used.

Denmark remains at the lowest rank, meaning that it has the lowest poverty ratios on all counts and, therefore, the best rank from a social policy perspective.[10] This corroborates the hypothesis about the outcome of the Danish labour market policies formulated earlier. Sweden's ranking varies somewhat with the poverty line used, but except for the lowest poverty line Sweden maintained an intermediate position, broadly consistent with our initial hypothesis. Looking at Denmark and Sweden as a group with welfare states of the same type, one can conclude that they did fairly well in keeping poverty among the unemployed at a low or medium level, despite the generally unfavourable economic development from the mid-1980s to the mid-1990s.

The Netherlands had the second lowest rank in the mid-1980s but poverty among the unemployed increased considerably during the subsequent decade, as was hypothesized from an examination of the Dutch labour market policies. From the mid-1980s to the mid-1990s 'West' Germany improved its relative position a little, but did not reduce the very high poverty rates among the unemployed. Indeed they increased slightly, although less than in some other countries. Our expectation that poverty rates for the unemployed would turn out to be only moderate was not corroborated, but the hypothesis about a slight increase was. France occupied a middle rank in the mid-1980s, and as expected of an employment-centred welfare regime, its position was even better at the higher poverty lines than at the low one. From the mid-1980s to the mid-1990s France generally improved its relative position, keeping poverty rates at a medium level, so our hypothesis about

---

[10] To avoid misunderstanding it has to be emphasized that from a social policy viewpoint the rank of a country is the better, the lower it is.

high and still rising poverty rates was not confirmed. Levels of social protection for the unemployed differ widely across the three countries with an employment-centred welfare regime, with The Netherlands having poverty rates more similar to the countries with a universalistic welfare regime, and Germany protecting a much smaller percentage of the unemployed against the risk of poverty.

In the mid-1980s Ireland had a low rank at the 40 per cent poverty line but a very high rank at the 60 per cent line. That means it protected its unemployed only at a very low level of living. During the following decade Ireland managed to improve its situation so that it reached lower ranks with respect to all its poverty rates. Our hypothesis that the presumably high poverty rates did not further increase was not fully corroborated: although the poverty rates are quite high, they went down on all counts. The UK started with medium ranks in the mid-1980s, but in the mid-1990s it had reached the group with the highest poverty rates. This was clearly the severest deterioration in relative position among all the countries under review and fully confirmed our initial hypothesis. The two states with liberal/minimal welfare regimes, therefore, have reacted to the economic development from the mid-1980s to the mid-1990s in different ways, and with very different outcomes.

Italy in both periods occupied first or second rank with respect to poverty among its unemployed. As expected, poverty rates turned out to be extremely high, but the hypothesis of falling poverty ratios because of increases in the replacement rates of unemployment benefits, was not corroborated.

To compare the extent of poverty among the unemployed to that of the whole population, and the population at working age—see Figs. 2.1 and 2.2—we restrict our analysis to the most common mean-based 50 per cent poverty line calculated with the new OECD equivalence scale.

At first glance it is obvious that the differences between the poverty rates of the whole population, and the population of working age, are small in all countries. The poverty rates of the unemployed, however, with the exception of Denmark, are much higher than the rates of the population of working age. In most countries unemployed people and their families bear a much higher risk of becoming poor than other groups. In the mid-1980s the discrepancy between the poverty rates of the unemployed and the population of working age were extremely large in Germany, Ireland, Italy, Sweden and in the UK. Only Ireland was able to reduce this discrepancy during the following decade while it increased in the other countries of this group, and The Netherlands joined it.

Poverty Among the Short-term and the Long-term Unemployed

Finally, we examine differences in poverty risk between short-term and the long-term unemployed, and between men and women, among the countries

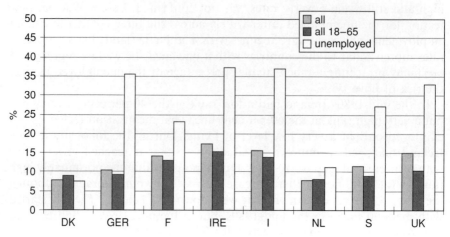

FIG. 2.1. Poverty rates, mid-1980s

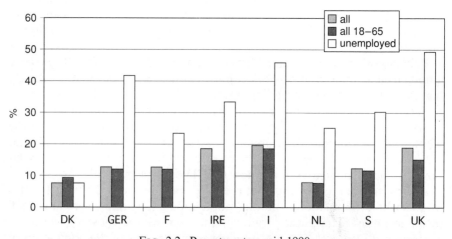

FIG. 2.2. Poverty rates, mid-1990s

Notes: 'Germany' refers to 'West' Germany. For The Netherlands, the column for 'all' only includes those 15 years and older. For both Figs. 2.1 and 2.2 the 50% mean and new OECD equivalent scale have been used.

Source: EPUSE/own calculations; see the Appendix to this chapter for the data sets used.

under review. Short-term unemployment is defined as a period of unemployment of less-than, or equal-to twelve months, while long-term unemployment consists of periods longer than twelve months. We restrict our analysis to poverty rates calculated by using the mean-based and the median-based 50 per cent poverty lines and the new OECD equivalence scale. Table 2.6 provides the results.

TABLE 2.6. *Poverty rates of the short-term and long-term unemployed*[a], *mid-1980s and mid-1990s (%)*

	1980s						1990s					
		50% Mean			50% Median			50% Mean			50% Median	
	All	Male	Female	All	Male	Female	All	Male	Female	All	Male	Female
DK				1988						1993		
all unemployed	7.6	7.4	7.9	7.2	7.0	7.5	7.6	7.9	7.4	7.0	7.2	6.7
<=12 months	7.9	7.6	8.2	7.5	7.2	7.8	8.2	8.3	8.0	7.5	7.7	7.3
>12 months	4.7	5.2	4.2	4.5	5.0	4.1	4.1	4.9	3.3	3.5	4.1	2.9
GER(W)				1985						1995		
all unemployed	35.5	33.7	37.3	26.1	25.0	27.3	41.7	50.1	33.3	25.6	32.0	19.2
<=12 months	24.1	22.3	25.9	17.2	16.4	17.9	41.8	48.7	36.0	23.2	(25.3)	(21.4)
>12 months	51.5	48.5	55.0	38.6	36.0	41.6	41.4	52.5	(26.1)	30.5	43.0	(13.2)
F				1985						1992		
all unemployed	23.0	25.9	20.5	17.2	20.6	14.2	23.3	29.6	18.6	16.0	19.8	13.1
<=12 months	19.1	19.6	18.6	13.2	13.7	12.7	16.7	22.5	11.9	10.6	13.7	8.2
>12 months	26.4	32.8	21.7	20.6	28.1	15.2	29.6	36.6	24.6	21.1	25.9	17.6
IRE				1987						1994		
all unemployed	37.3	41.4	14.5	11.7	13.8	—	33.4	38.4	19.6	6.1	6.9	4.0
<=12 months	31.0	33.8	20.2	11.6	34.6	—	23.9	22.2	26.4	6.2	5.6	7.2
>12 months	40.5	44.8	9.7	11.8	13.5	—	39.1	45.6	10.9	6.1	7.5	—
I				1989						1993		
all unemployed	37.1	37.8	36.3	28.0	30.5	25.0	45.7	48.7	42.3	37.2	41.6	32.0
<=12 months	n.a.	n.a.	n.a.	n.a.	n.a.	n.a.	59.1	67.6	49.2	50.4	57.4	44.4
>12 months	n.a.	n.a.	n.a.	n.a.	n.a.	n.a.	44.4	46.9	41.5	35.9	40.1	31.0

continued p. 44

TABLE 2.6. (cont'd)

	1980s						1990s					
	50% Mean			50% Median			50% Mean			50% Median		
	All	Male	Female	All	Male	Female	All	Male	Female	All	Male	Female
NL												
	1987						1991					
all unemployed	11.3	13.5	10.0	7.1	(7.9)	(6.6)	25.2	(28.2)	(18.2)	15.3	[16.8]	[11.6]
<=12 months	n.a.	n.a.	n.a.	n.a.	n.a.	n.a.	n.a.	n.a.	n.a.	n.a.	n.a.	n.a.
>12 months	n.a.	n.a.	n.a.	n.a.	n.a.	n.a.	n.a.	n.a.	n.a.	n.a.	n.a.	n.a.
S												
	1981						1991					
all unemployed	(27.3)	(30.2)	(24.4)	(25.0)	(27.9)	(22.2)	30.4	(35.1)	(23.5)	22.0	(23.3)	(20.0)
<=12 months	(28.2)	(30.6)	(26.2)	(25.6)	(27.8)	(23.8)	30.0	(33.3)	(25.5)	(21.9)	(22.0)	(21.7)
>12 months	[20.0]	[28.6]	—	[20.0]	[28.6]	—	[33.3]	[42.9]	—	[22.2]	[28.6]	—
UK												
	1984–86						1994/95					
all unemployed	32.9	39.2	20.3	17.9	21.5	10.7	49.4	52.0	44.9	35.8	37.4	33.0
<=12 months	22.7	26.6	16.3	13.3	16.1	8.9	30.7	30.8	30.4	20.4	19.8	21.6
>12 months	45.6	52.7	27.0	23.6	27.3	13.9	63.9	67.7	56.8	47.6	50.4	42.4

[a] 18–65 years old.

n.a. = not available.

( ) unweighted number of cases < 30; [ ] unweighted number of cases < 10.

Notes: Using the new OECD equivalent scale.

Source: EPUSE calculations; see the Appendix to this chapter for the data sets used.

In the mid-1980s the poverty rates of the long-term unemployed were higher than the rates of the short-term unemployed in most of the countries, though not in Denmark and Sweden. Disaggregated figures are not available for The Netherlands. With the exception of Germany this pattern remained valid in the mid-1990s. In the German case the poverty rate of the long-term unemployed fell, and that of the short-term unemployed rose, so that both groups now have the same very high poverty risk. In the UK the poverty risk of the long-term unemployed is extremely high, and it has risen considerably from the mid-1980s to the mid-1990s. Partially, the differences between the poverty rates of the short-term and the long-term unemployed can be explained by institutional factors, especially a reduction of the replacement rate when the duration of unemployment exceeds a certain time limit. A composition effect is also presumably at work since unskilled workers whose income was low even during employment are over-represented among the long-term unemployed.

Comparing the differences in poverty rates among male and female unemployed, with only very few exceptions—Denmark, and Germany in the 1980s—unemployed women have a lower poverty rate than men. While a large proportion of unemployed men still live in households where they are, if not the only, then at least the main breadwinner, women are often second earners and can still rely on other work-related incomes and not only on low unemployment benefits or unemployment assistance. Between the mid-1980s and the mid-1990s this relationship has not changed very much.

CONCLUSIONS

In most of the countries analysed in this chapter, inequality among the unemployed is greater than among the population of working age. Moreover, poverty rates are much higher among the unemployed than the population of working age. In most of the countries poverty increased from the mid-1980s to the mid-1990s, and the gap between the poverty rates of the unemployed and the population of working age became even greater. Poverty rates among the long-term unemployed are generally higher than among the short term unemployed, and poverty rates of unemployed women are mostly lower than those of unemployed men.

Neither the extent of poverty among the unemployed nor the changes of the poverty rates over time can be explained purely in terms of the social policies of the different countries, though these did clearly play a major role. Countries belonging to the same type of unemployment welfare regime were not homogeneous. There were considerable differences between the United Kingdom and Ireland although both were liberal/minimal welfare regimes;

between employment-centred welfare regimes The Netherlands on the one hand and France and Germany on the other; and between universalistic welfare regimes Denmark and Sweden. Assessed in terms of poverty among the unemployed, Denmark and The Netherlands fared best over the period examined while the position of the UK deteriorated considerably.

APPENDIX

TABLE 2A. *Data sets*

	1980s data set		1990s data set	
DK	1988	Register Data from the Danish Statistical Bureau[a]	1993	Register Data from the Danish Statistical Bureau[a]
GER	1985	German Socio-Economic Panel	1995	German Socio-Economic Panel
F	1985	Situations Défavorisées 1986/87	1992	Situations Défavorisées 1993/94
IRE	1987	ESRI Survey of Income Distri-bution, Poverty and Use of State Services	1994	Living in Ireland Survey (incorporates the European Community Household Survey)
I	1989	Bank of Italy Income Survey	1993	Bank of Italy Income Survey
NL	1987	Luxembourg Income Study	1991	Luxembourg Income Study
S	1981	Level of Living Survey[a]	1991	Level of Living Survey[a]
UK	1984/6	Family Expenditure Survey (pooled)	1994/5	Family Expenditure Survey (pooled)

[a] administrative income data.

Note: A more detailed description of the data sets can be found in the working papers of the national teams that did the calculations.

3

Poverty and Financial Hardship among the Unemployed

Duncan Gallie, Sheila Jacobs, and Serge Paugam

The previous chapter depicted the broad differences between countries in the implications of unemployment for poverty. But to what extent do countries also differ in terms of the distribution of financial deprivation among the unemployed: the types of unemployed people that are most at risk, and the degree of differentiation in the experience of unemployed people? If welfare institutions are of critical importance, it could be expected that countries closest to a universalistic regime would provide relatively equal treatment for different types of unemployed people while those closest to an employment-centred regime should be characterized by sharper differences. Eligibility for financial assistance in the latter type of regime is heavily dependent on a person's past employment record. Those with a long continuous record of employment are provided with relatively generous benefits, but those who are either at the start of their work careers or who have had periods out of the labour market are much less well covered. This type of regime then could be expected to be associated with particularly sharp disadvantage for both younger people and for women.

This chapter begins by looking at the relationship between income poverty and two measures of financial hardship. It then examines how the financial vulnerability of unemployed people varies with respect to their individual and household characteristics. Finally, it considers the specific case of Italy, a country in which particularly strong regional divisions lead to very different financial experiences of unemployment.

INCOME POVERTY AND FINANCIAL HARDSHIP

The poverty measures examined in the previous chapter are measures of *relative* income poverty. They may well then reflect rather different levels of financial difficulty between countries. How, in practice, do measures of relative income poverty relate to the experience of financial hardship? The European Community Household Panel gives us the opportunity to assess the financial risks associated with unemployment not only with respect to 'poverty status', but also with regard to reported financial difficulty, and deprivation in terms of household living conditions.

The comparisons in the last chapter were based on income poverty measures produced by the alignment of national data sets. These data sets are well tested within each country and they alone have the continuity over a relatively long period needed to show the evolution of poverty among the unemployed over time. For the 1990s, however, income data is also available from a survey which used a similar format of questions in twelve of the countries of the European Union (the European Community Household Panel). Sweden was not covered, and, given the small sample numbers for the unemployed, Luxembourg has been excluded from the present analyses. The survey contains very detailed income information on annual income, but this is difficult to relate to specific employment statuses, which may well change over the year. However, it also includes a relatively simple question, focusing on the time of interview, asking people to state their overall household income after taxes in the previous month. This has been used to construct a measure of the 50 per cent mean poverty line following the same principles as in the last chapter.

Two measures can be taken of financial hardship. The first is a self-reported measure of immediate *financial difficulty*. People were asked how difficult they found it 'to make ends meet'. The second is a measure of *material or 'life-style' deprivation* that tries to capture the longer-term deterioration in people's economic circumstances (see Nolan and Whelan 1996; Fleurbaey *et al.* 1997; Lollivier and Verger 1997). It is based on whether or not people possess a range of normal household items.

Table 3.1 shows the correlations between the income poverty measure, that is below 50 per cent of mean household income, and the two measures of financial hardship. It confirms that income poverty is systematically related to financial hardship in all of the countries. Part A of the table gives the association for the whole population of working age, while Part B is restricted to unemployed people. The pattern for the unemployed is very similar to that for the wider population. In each case and for every country the associations are of a high level of statistical significance. However, it also should be noted that the associations are not particularly strong, although they are more marked with respect to material deprivation than for immediate financial pressure. It is clear then that income poverty and financial hardship cannot be regarded as synonymous. There is considerable variation between countries in the strength of the associations. Taking the unemployed, income poverty is least closely related to the experience of financial hardship in Denmark and Ireland. It is most closely related to immediate financial difficulty in Germany, The Netherlands and the UK, and in two of the Southern European countries—Italy and Spain. It is most strongly linked to material deprivation in Germany, France, the UK, Italy, and Spain.

TABLE 3.1. *Correlations of poverty status with indicators of financial hardship*

A. Overall Sample 18–65

Parameter	Total	GER	DK	NL	BE	FR	UK	IRE	IT	GR	SP	PT
Inc. Pov. & Fin. Diff.	0.278	0.265	0.190	0.268	0.212	0.233	0.356	0.188	0.353	0.255	0.266	0.243
Inc. Pov. & Mat. Dep.	0.351	0.327	0.245	0.286	0.229	0.309	0.409	0.256	0.387	0.353	0.363	0.373
Fin. Diff. & Mat. Dep.	0.557	0.380	0.437	0.586	0.475	0.497	0.578	0.460	0.553	0.561	0.535	0.464

B. Unemployed aged 18–65

Parameter	Total	GER	DK	NL	BE	FR	UK	IRE	IT	GR	SP	PT
Inc. Pov. & Fin. Diff.	0.296	0.316	0.209	0.385	0.248	0.276	0.373	0.138	0.388	0.258	0.292	0.258
Inc. Pov. & Mat. Dep.	0.352	0.451	0.296	0.336	0.357	0.413	0.388	0.251	0.395	0.325	0.382	0.339
Fin. Diff. & Mat. Dep.	0.538	0.413	0.458	0.583	0.458	0.514	0.564	0.487	0.532	0.500	0.532	0.437

Notes: Financial difficulty (very/quite); Mat. Dep. = Material deprivation; All associations were significant at the P < 0.001 level.
Source: European Community Household Panel, 1994. For details see Appendix A.

TABLE 3.2. *Financial hardship, by 50% poverty threshold*

	% Finding it very/quite difficult to make ends meet		Material deprivation score	
	Non-poor	Poor	Non-poor	Poor
Belgium	9.7	35.0	2.0	4.1
Denmark	11.6	38.3	1.7	4.1
France	16.2	46.7	2.7	5.1
Germany	6.1	40.9	2.1	5.4
Greece	48.8	85.9	5.9	9.7
Ireland	23.0	49.7	2.6	5.1
Italy	14.3	57.5	2.7	6.0
Netherlands	6.9	31.8	1.0	2.6
Portugal	30.3	58.1	6.1	9.8
Spain	32.5	67.0	4.3	7.4
UK	10.7	47.6	2.1	4.9
Total	20.1	56.5	3.2	6.6

Note: ECHP respondents in the workforce, aged 18–65.
Source: European Community Household Panel, 1994.

Given this varying relationship between income poverty and financial hardship, the extent to which people under the 50 per cent poverty threshold experienced financial difficulty varied very considerably between countries (see Table 3.2). Taking the extremes, only 32 per cent of the 'poor' in The Netherlands reported that they found it difficult to make ends meet, while this was the case for 86 per cent of the 'poor' in Greece. With respect to the material deprivation score, the average in Portugal, the most deprived country, was nearly four times that of The Netherlands, the least deprived. Taking the overall pattern, it was particularly in the less developed Southern countries—Greece, Spain and Portugal—that 'poor' people found it difficult to make ends meet and had relatively high levels of lifestyle deprivation. It should be noted that Italy is different in pattern to the other Southern countries, lying in an intermediate position between these countries and those of Northern Europe.

In short, while the income poverty status measure is clearly related to the experience of financial difficulty within each country, the same poverty threshold can conceal large differences in hardship between countries.

THE RISK OF POVERTY AND FINANCIAL HARDSHIP AMONG THE UNEMPLOYED

The differences between countries in the proportions of the unemployed in income poverty that emerge from the European Community Household Panel are broadly similar to those from the national data sets. The very low

TABLE 3.3. *Financial hardship among the unemployed*

	<50% mean income (%)	In financial difficulty (%)	Material deprivation score
Belgium	22.7	32.6	4.0
Denmark	8.1	26.6	3.3
France	28.1	41.0	4.8
Germany	26.8	26.7	4.2
Greece	25.7	72.6	7.9
Ireland	31.3	55.4	5.6
Italy	37.2	44.8	5.0
Netherlands	25.1	30.6	2.9
Portugal	29.6	53.1	8.1
Spain	33.2	56.1	6.3
UK	48.5	45.0	5.1

Source: European Household Community Panel, 1994.

risk of poverty in Denmark again stands out in a striking way (Table 3.3), while the UK is again far and away the country in which the unemployed have the greatest risk of being in poverty. Indeed the estimates for these two countries from the two data sources are very close. Italy is still the country with the second highest poverty level, although it should be noted that there are considerable differences between the various Southern countries. France, Germany, and The Netherlands have intermediate poverty levels. The figures for Germany are much lower than those previously presented, but the coverage of the samples is quite different. The present sample covers Germany as a whole, whereas the data analysed in Chapter 2 was restricted to West Germany to provide comparability over time.

Turning to the measures of financial hardship, the importance of the level of economic development stands out clearly. As can be seen in Table 3.3, it was in Greece, Spain, and Portugal that the unemployed were particularly likely to find it difficult to make ends meet, and where they also had the worst material living conditions. Ireland also showed relatively high levels of financial hardship. It should be noted that Italy is rather different from the general southern pattern: it comes in an intermediate position, close to the UK. It was the unemployed in Denmark, Germany, and The Netherlands who were the least likely to experience financial pressure, while the unemployed in Denmark and The Netherlands were also the least deprived in terms of their material living standards.

But while the unemployed suffered the greatest hardship in the poorer Southern European countries, this may not be specifically because they were unemployed. It is possible that those in work in these countries also experienced greater financial difficulty and had worse material living conditions than their equivalents in other countries. To provide a test of the 'unemployment effect', we carried out a regression analysis to compare countries

TABLE 3.4. *Effect of unemployment on income poverty, financial difficulty and material deprivation*

	Income Poverty	Financial Difficulty	Material Deprivation
Belgium	0.41	0.36	0.51*
Denmark	Ref.***	Ref.***	Ref.***
France	0.14	0.24	0.48*
Germany	0.87***	0.36	0.34
Greece	−0.26	−0.56**	0.12
Ireland	0.04	0.13	0.97***
Italy	0.34	0.10	0.41*
Netherlands	−0.09	0.87**	0.00
Portugal	−0.68**	−0.49*	−0.14
Spain	0.03	−0.32	−0.29*
UK	1.05***	0.61**	1.30***
Model Type	Logistic	Logistic	OLS
N	70632	70686	70827

Note: The models include the unemployed and those in work (18–65). Coefficients are from the interaction terms unemployment* country. Main country effects were included in the models. Ref. = Reference Country. Significance: * = $P < 0.05$, ** = $P < 0.01$, *** = $P < 0.001$.
Source: European Community Household Panel, 1994.

in terms of the relative disadvantage of the unemployed compared to those in work on the different measures. The results are given in Table 3.4, with countries compared to the situation in Denmark.

The countries where the risk of income poverty for the unemployed was exceptionally high, compared to that for people in work, were the UK and Germany. In contrast, two of the poorer Southern countries, Portugal and Greece, have a negative coefficient indicating that the relative disadvantage of the unemployed was less great, and in Portugal the result is statistically significant. The differences among other countries were not strong enough to reach significance, suggesting that in general the prevalence of poverty among the unemployed was closely related to the broader risk of poverty in each society.

Taking the measures of financial hardship, the relative experience of the unemployed with respect to immediate financial difficulty was particularly difficult in the UK and The Netherlands, and again it was less difficult in two of the Southern countries, Greece and Portugal. The coefficient for Spain is also negative, although not statistically significant. Finally, deprivation in terms of material living conditions was particularly great for the unemployed in the UK and Ireland, followed by Belgium, France, and Italy. In contrast, Spain stands out with a lower relative disadvantage of the unemployed.

Thus, while the experience of financial hardship in absolute terms was particularly great for the unemployed in the poorer Southern European countries, this largely reflected the more general prevalence of financial difficulty in these societies. There was no evidence of a particularly sharp gap between the unemployed and those in work in these societies. Rather both groups experienced harsh financial conditions and, in some of the poorer countries, unemployment made less difference than it did in the wealthier societies. The country which stands out most clearly as having a particularly marked effect of unemployment on each of the measures is the UK. Thus not only did unemployment have the strongest effect of all for income poverty in the UK, but this appeared to translate directly into a much greater sense of financial difficulty and worse material living conditions.

Overall, it has been seen that the income poverty measure is meaningful in terms of experiences of financial difficulty within countries. However, those classified as 'poor' in one country may confront very different levels of financial hardship to the 'poor' in another country. A major determinant of financial hardship was the general level of economic development of the national economy. The unemployed were much more likely to experience financial hardship in the Southern European economies, but at the same time the position of the unemployed was less distinctive in these countries compared to people in work. The results here point to the need to retain measures both of income poverty and financial hardship. They also underline the importance of the distinction between absolute and relative measures of financial deprivation.

THE IMPLICATIONS OF INDIVIDUAL CHARACTERISTICS AND HOUSEHOLD STRUCTURE

To what extent did the experience of financial deprivation differ between types of unemployed people, as a result either of their personal characteristics, such as sex and age, or the characteristics of their households? Did the type of welfare regime affect the relative risks of particular groups? We will consider this respectively for the measures of income poverty, financial difficulty, and material deprivation.

Income Poverty

From a welfare perspective, one might expect a particularly strong contrast between universalistic systems, such as Denmark and Sweden, on the one hand, and employment-centred regimes on the other. Universalistic systems, with their broad coverage and low barriers to entry, could be expected to minimize differences in experience between different types of unemployed people. In contrast, employment-centred welfare regimes, as in France,

Belgium, The Netherlands, and Germany, might be expected to favour males with established employment records and to discriminate against women and the young.

Table 3.5 presents the proportions in poverty by sex, age, and a number of household characteristics. The data for Sweden are taken separately, from the Level of Living Survey, and may not be fully comparable. The evidence for a distinctive pattern in the employment-centred regimes is decidedly limited. In all countries, with the exception of Denmark, and regardless of welfare regime, men were more likely than women to be below the poverty line. While younger people were more disadvantaged in Germany and Denmark, in all other countries the youngest were no worse off than were some of the prime-age groups.

While there was little support for a welfare-regime effect, there were a number of individual and household characteristics that had quite consistent relationships with the poverty risk. The proportions in poverty varied considerably depending on characteristics which reflected their past income-earning capacity—which presumably affected the income from savings on which people could continue to draw while unemployed. In all but The Netherlands and Spain, people who had been unemployed for twelve months or more were more likely to be in poverty than the shorter-term unemployed. Education and social class of previous job can be taken as proxies of the level of earnings in the previous job. In all countries poverty rates were highest among those who came from lower-class jobs, and the pattern was similar for those with very low educational qualifications.

Type of household was also very important for the risk of poverty in a wide range of countries. With the exception of Portugal and Italy, people who were in single adult households had a much higher risk of poverty. Moreover, in all countries, there was a particularly high poverty risk if people lived with other adults who were also not employed. It is clear that the presence of another earner in the household was a major protection against poverty. Among people in partnerships, the presence of a child increased the risk of poverty in most countries, although the percentage differences were particularly small in Denmark and Sweden. Lone parents, most of whom were lone mothers, also frequently had higher poverty rates, and this was particularly the case in France and Spain. This suggests that the implications of welfare systems for the resources of unemployed individuals may be mediated in an important way by the effects of household structure.

In order to look at the net effect of each of these factors once other characteristics were taken into account, we used a logistic regression procedure. Given the high correlation between social class and education, it was decided to select education as the main indicator of prior earnings potential. A first set of models looked at the combined sample, including both men and women. An initial analysis was carried out examining just the

TABLE 3.5. *Comparison of the unemployed in poverty* (%)

	GER	DK	SW	NL	BE	FR	UK	IRE	IT	GR	SP	PT
Sex												
Male	30.1	6.8	35.1	27.7	28.5	31.5	53.1	34.1	42.6	29.9	35.5	37.4
Female	24.5	9.6	23.5	22.3	17.3	25.2	38.2	26.3	33.0	22.9	31.3	24.9
Age group												
18–24	33.9	15.7	—	25.6	22.2	29.6	49.0	28.5	39.3	25.8	32.9	29.1
25–34	27.9	7.2	9.1	25.7	20.8	25.1	47.8	25.1	33.1	21.4	27.2	27.4
35–49	26.2	8.5	18.2	23.0	23.0	31.4	54.1	39.2	39.8	29.9	38.8	33.6
50–65	21.7	1.5	35.9	29.4	32.3	25.9	39.4	34.1	39.5	28.7	39.9	27.8
Education												
Higher	24.1	3.7	71.4	7.1	19.7	13.6	29.5	10.7	16.1	13.5	15.8	22.2
Intermediate	24.9	7.8	36.0	25.1	23.7	26.4	44.9	27.3	29.1	24.6	27.7	21.1
Minimum	31.3	10.6	25.8	31.7	25.5	36.9	57.3	36.8	46.3	34.9	40.1	31.8
Social class												
Managerial/Professional	9.3	—	16.7	5.2	7.1	8.0	23.6	15.9	11.8	17.1	8.6	22.2
Intermediate	18.8	6.0	25.0	19.8	14.6	20.3	33.6	17.3	23.9	18.7	17.8	11.8
Working	35.0	9.5	31.2	27.6	25.6	34.4	57.5	30.3	42.2	28.6	37.5	32.3
Length of unemployment												
<12 mths	25.7	7.3	30.0	28.0	21.0	25.2	42.2	26.1	33.5	24.9	33.5	28.6
12 mths+	28.5	9.4	33.3	22.4	23.6	33.0	56.2	34.8	39.7	27.4	32.8	31.4
Dep. child <30 yrs												
No	28.1	7.9	23.6	26.8	24.0	27.7	51.0	35.8	34.4	26.0	34.5	31.2
Yes	16.7	10.0	72.2	16.4	19.2	29.4	38.4	23.4	39.3	25.4	31.3	26.3
Partner/Parental status												
Single no child	38.2	12.5	47.1	20.3	24.2	30.7	47.4	25.2	38.1	27.5	31.7	33.6
Partner no child	11.4	1.0	13.8	18.2	15.6	17.3	34.4	6.6	26.1	17.4	25.2	19.6
Partner + child	27.8	4.4	18.8	35.7	24.1	27.4	60.0	42.9	39.7	25.7	37.7	29.1
Lone parent	40.0	35.7	33.3	47.1	26.1	57.1	45.0	35.7	40.7	41.7	54.9	46.2
Household employment												
1 adult	49.5	14.9	45.9	27.9	35.3	41.8	61.5	41.8	33.3	34.0	52.1	25.0
>1 adult, 0 emp.	36.7	11.9	16.3	44.9	40.5	42.8	68.5	43.5	55.0	43.1	54.5	52.6
2 adults, 1 emp.	11.5	1.8	10.0	9.8	4.4	10.5	22.4	6.7	11.2	12.6	14.4	22.9
>2 adults, at least 1 emp.	16.0	1.9	—	14.1	11.2	25.1	31.3	13.9	36.8	20.1	22.7	25.8
N=	403	347	80	367	375	972	613	855	1457	943	2171	487

Sources: European Community Household Panel, 1994; Swedish Level of Living Survey, 1991.

effects of sex, age, and duration of unemployment. Then other individual and household characteristics were added to the model. The initial results showed that, in the countries for which there was a gender difference in the poverty risk—all except Denmark, The Netherlands, and Ireland—it was men rather than women that were at greater risk. However, when education and household characteristics were taken into account, the difference by sex persisted only for France and Portugal. With the exception of Greece, households with children were at far greater risk of poverty. But the strongest factor was household employment status. One adult households were at greatest risk but, in general, the unemployed living in households where there was no employed adult were also particularly likely to be poor.

Tables 3.6 and 3.7 present the results for men and women separately. It can be seen that household variables had a very powerful effect for most countries. For those living with others, the presence of another employed adult was important in protecting the unemployed from poverty in all countries except Denmark and Sweden. This is consistent with the view that more universalistic regimes make it easier to escape poverty without dependence on the resources of other adults in the household. Both unemployed men and unemployed women who lived on their own were particularly sharply deprived in France, the UK, and Spain. In addition, unemployed men living alone were particularly vulnerable to poverty in Germany and Ireland, and this was also the case for unemployed women in Belgium and Italy. Young people living at home with their parents were no less likely to experience income poverty; indeed women in this position in Italy were particularly disadvantaged. This suggests that they were members of households that were themselves poor.

The data for all the countries except Denmark and Ireland include information on the region in which people lived. Further logistic regression analyses were run adding region to the previous models. In Northern and Central Europe, Spain and Portugal, few regional effects were significant. In Italy, however, regional differences were marked in both the risks of unemployment and more particularly that of poverty of the unemployed. South Italian men and women have a much higher poverty risk than those in the North, as will be discussed more fully later (p. 63ff). In Greece, too, there are significant regional variations in vulnerability to poverty. For many unemployed Italians and Greeks, location appears to be a vital factor determining their financial situation.

The Risk of Financial Hardship

To explore the extent to which the risk of financial hardship varied between subgroups of the unemployed the previous analyses were repeated for the

TABLE 3.6. *Logistic regression of the probability of unemployed men being in poverty*

Parameter	Odds Multipliers											
	GER	DK	SW	NL	BE	FR	UK	IRE	IT	GR	SP	PT
Age 18–24	n.s.	n.s.	n.s.	n.s.	n.s.	n.s.	2.72*	n.s.	n.s.	n.s.	n.s.	n.s.
Age 25–34	n.s.	n.s.	n.s.	n.s.	n.s.	n.s.	n.s.	n.s.	n.s.	n.s.	0.55*	n.s.
Age 35–49	n.s.	n.s.	n.s.	n.s.	n.s.	n.s.	n.s.	n.s.	n.s.	n.s.	n.s.	n.s.
Inter. quals.	n.s.	n.s.	n.s.	n.s.	n.s.	2.81*	n.s.	n.s.	3.50*	n.s.	2.12*	n.s.
Min. quals.	n.s.	n.s.	n.s.	n.s.	n.s.	2.99*	n.s.	n.s.	6.53***	3.76**	3.54***	n.s.
Single, no child	n.s.	n.s.	n.s.	n.s.	n.s.	n.s.	n.s.	n.s.	n.s.	n.s.	n.s.	5.77*
Partner, + child	n.s.	n.s.	n.s.	n.s.	n.s.	2.16*	2.09*	5.82**	n.s.	n.s.	2.65***	3.72*
Unemp. 12+ mths	n.s.	n.s.	n.s.	0.20**	n.s.	1.99**	1.58~	n.s.	1.40*	n.s.	n.s.	n.s.
Dep. child <30	n.s.	n.s.	n.s.	n.s.	n.s.	3.34~	n.s.	n.s.	n.s.	n.s.	n.s.	0.20*
One adult h'hold	18.45*	n.s.	n.s.	n.s.	7.53~	10.5***	5.63***	35.6***	n.s.	n.s.	6.07***	n.s.
>1 adult, 0 emp.	4.45**	n.s.	n.s.	9.75**	7.02**	4.57***	3.69***	4.91***	2.71***	2.87***	4.14***	3.65**
Constant	0.66	0.00	0.00	2.27	0.43	0.83	1.58	0.40	0.10	0.33	0.64	0.01
N=	155	171	40	110	150	406	407	415	702	362	993	174

Notes and *Source*: see Table 3.7.

TABLE 3.7. *Logistic regression of the probability of unemployed women being in poverty*

Parameter	Odds Multipliers											
	GER	DK	SW	NL	BE	FR	UK	IRE	IT	GR	SP	PT
Age 18–24	n.s.	n.s.	n.s.	n.s.	n.s.	n.s.	6.79*	n.s.	0.42~	n.s.	n.s.	n.s.
Age 25–34	n.s.	n.s.	n.s.	n.s.	n.s.	n.s.	n.s.	n.s.	n.s.	n.s.	n.s.	n.s.
Age 35–49	n.s.	n.s.	n.s.	n.s.	n.s.	n.s.	4.59*	n.s.	n.s.	n.s.	n.s.	3.27~
Inter. quals.	n.s.	n.s.	n.s.	n.s.	n.s.	2.37*	n.s.	n.s.	2.15~	2.71**	1.70*	n.s.
Min. quals.	n.s.	n.s.	n.s.	8.17*	n.s.	5.52***	n.s.	n.s.	6.12***	6.52***	3.18***	n.s.
Single, no child	8.45**	n.s.	n.s.	n.s.	n.s.	n.s.	4.73*	n.s.	n.s.	n.s.	n.s.	2.99~
Partner, + child	4.29*	n.s.	n.s.	43.0**	n.s.	n.s.	3.27~	n.s.	n.s.	n.s.	2.15**	n.s.
Lone parent	n.s.	n.s.	n.s.	20.90*	n.s.	2.70~	n.s.	n.s.	n.s.	n.s.	3.69**	n.s.
Unemp. 12+ mths	0.09~	n.s.	n.s.	n.s.	n.s.	n.s.	0.18*	n.s.	2.84**	2.38~	n.s.	n.s.
Dep. child <30	n.s.	n.s.	n.s.	n.s.	n.s.	n.s.	n.s.	n.s.	n.s.	n.s.	n.s.	n.s.
One adult h'hold	n.s.	n.s.	n.s.	7.12~	10.47**	4.41**	8.41**	n.s.	5.63**	n.s.	3.74**	n.s.
>1 adult, 0 emp.	5.01**	n.s.	n.s.	7.63**	5.47**	4.03***	8.57***	11.5***	3.81***	3.88***	5.65***	n.s.
Constant	0.16	0.01	0.00	0.07	0.13	0.49	0.30	0.05	0.66	0.43	0.64	0.18
N=	231	166	35	181	186	550	204	232	896	577	1103	257

Notes: Reference: Age 50–65, Higher quals., Partner, no child, Not dependent child, >1 adult h'hold 1 emp.

~ = $P < 0.07$, * = $P < 0.05$, ** = $P < 0.01$, *** = $P < 0.001$.

Source: European Community Household Panel, 1994.

measures of financial difficulty and material deprivation. Sweden was excluded this time, as no comparable measures were available.

Taking first financial difficulty, we again found no evidence that particular regimes were associated with a greater vulnerability of either women or younger people. The simplest model showed a sex effect in France, the UK, Italy, Greece, and Portugal. But in each case, it was men that were particularly likely to be under financial pressure. The only country in which people aged 18–24 had a distinctively high level of financial difficulty was Italy, while those aged 25–34 stood out in Italy, Spain, and France.

When the other variables are introduced (Table 3.8), age and sex effects dwindle and, once more, the household variables are important. The sex effect disappears in all countries other than Portugal. In contrast, household effects are evident in all countries. Except in the case of Germany, the absence of an employed adult in the household is associated with a greatly increased probability of experiencing severe financial difficulty. In Germany the pressures seem to be particularly great on unemployed families where there is a dependent child. The impact of household factors is evident across all types of welfare regime including the universalist regime as represented by Denmark.

A similar analysis was carried out with the measure of material deprivation, or the absence of essential household equipment, using an ordered logit procedure. Again a simple analysis was carried out to begin with, including just age, sex, and duration of unemployment. This was then extended to take account of education and a number of different household characteristics. The results of the initial analysis are shown in Model 1, and those of the extended analysis in Model 2, of Table 3.9. Whichever set of results is examined, there is no evidence that women and younger people were particularly vulnerable in employment-centred regimes. In contrast to the pattern for financial difficulty, a sex effect was evident in several countries, even when other individual and household characteristics had been taken into account. This was the case for Germany, France, the UK and Ireland. But in none of these countries were women specifically disadvantaged; rather it was men who experienced greater deprivation as a result of unemployment.

The pattern of age effects is particularly interesting. The initial analyses, which included just age, sex, and duration of unemployment, showed that younger people suffered particularly strongly from material deprivation in Germany, Denmark and the UK. This was true both for youngest group aged 18 to 24 and for the 25 to 34 year olds. Moreover, even when household type was controlled for, the age effects persisted in these countries. It is difficult, however, to attribute this to any specific welfare regime effect, since the countries where the young suffered particularly sharply include universalistic, employment-centred, and liberal/minimal types of regime.

TABLE 3.8. Unemployed: logistic regression of difficulty making ends meet

| | Odds Multipliers | | | | | | | | | | |
Parameter	GER	DK	NL	BE	FR	UK	IRE	IT	GR	SP	PT
Age 18–24	n.s.	n.s.	n.s.	n.s.	n.s.	n.s.	n.s.	0.51*	n.s.	n.s.	3.76*
Age 25–34	n.s.	n.s.	n.s.	n.s.	n.s.	n.s.	0.47~	n.s.	n.s.	n.s.	n.s.
Age 35–49	n.s.	n.s.	n.s.	n.s.	n.s.	n.s.	n.s.	n.s.	n.s.	n.s.	n.s.
Male	n.s.	n.s.	n.s.	n.s.	n.s.	n.s.	n.s.	n.s.	n.s.	n.s.	1.72*
Inter. quals.	n.s.	n.s.	n.s.	n.s.	1.80~	n.s.	n.s.	4.85**	n.s.	n.s.	n.s.
Min. quals.	3.78~	n.s.	n.s.	n.s.	2.76**	n.s.	n.s.	9.30***	2.68***	2.20***	n.s.
Single, no child	n.s.	n.s.	n.s.	n.s.	n.s.	n.s.	n.s.	n.s.	n.s.	n.s.	n.s.
Partner, + child	5.25**	n.s.	n.s.	n.s.	n.s.	n.s.	n.s.	n.s.	n.s.	1.40*	n.s.
Lone parent	n.s.	n.s.	n.s.	15.48**	n.s.	n.s.	5.86**	n.s.	n.s.	2.90***	n.s.
Unemp. 12+ mths	n.s.	n.s.	n.s.	n.s.	1.62**	n.s.	1.64*	n.s.	1.33~	n.s.	0.56**
Dep. child <30	n.s.	11.96*	n.s.	n.s.	n.s.	n.s.	n.s.	1.84*	n.s.	n.s.	n.s.
One adult h'hold	n.s.	6.35**	7.12*	n.s.	5.88***	2.72*	n.s.	8.54***	n.s.	4.39***	7.76***
>1 adult, 0 emp.	n.s.	5.37***	6.58**	2.44*	3.13***	4.69***	2.44***	2.91***	1.41*	2.20***	1.85*
Constant	0.05	0.30	0.12	0.19	0.34	0.28	0.24	0.38	0.77	0.83	0.08
N=	388	344	294	369	1008	615	675	1632	940	2096	439

Notes: Reference: Age 50–65, Female, Higher quals., Partner, no child, Not dependent child, >1 adult h'hold, 1 emp. 'Difficulty make ends meet' = Most extreme coding.
~ = P < 0.07, * = P < 0.05, ** = P < 0.01, *** = P < 0.001.
Source: European Community Household Panel, 1994.

But it is notable that people in the same age groups in the sub-protective regimes of Italy, Greece, and Spain were in a sharply contrasting situation. They were more likely than older people to be protected in terms of their material living standards. This was most probably attributable to the fact that they benefited from their ability to continue living with their parents. It should be remembered that, in contrast to the countries of Northern and west central Europe, these were countries in which a majority of the young unemployed continued to live with their parents. In Italy, 87 per cent of those aged 20 to 29 were living with their parents, while this was the case for 78 per cent in Greece and 77 per cent in Spain. The central importance of household position becomes clear when household structure is taken into account in the analyses. The relative protection of young people becomes weaker in Italy, disappears in Greece and is reversed in Spain, leading to the pattern of results seen in Model 2 of Table 3.9.

Another point of interest is that educational qualifications, as the proxy of past earning power, have a very strong influence on material deprivation in all countries other than Denmark. This contrasts with the rather selective influence of low qualifications on more immediate financial pressure which was only significant for France, Italy, Greece, and Spain. The low level of household resources is likely to reflect the fact that the currently unemployed were previously in low-paid jobs and were not in a position to build up levels of savings, which could help cushion them against the sharp fall of income that accompanied unemployment. Finally, the great importance of household position for the financial hardship unemployed people confront is once more confirmed. The presence or absence of an employed adult had a marked effect in all countries other than Greece and Portugal.

It is evident that, in comparing the poverty situation of the unemployed in these countries, a simple explanation in terms of the characteristics of the welfare regime typology is not feasible. In particular, there is no evidence that either women or younger people are more heavily penalized in specific types of regime. However, certain of the results are consistent with expectations from a welfare perspective. First, there is some evidence that universalistic welfare regimes reduced the dependence of unemployed people on the earnings of other members of the household. In most countries the risk of income poverty was heavily affected by the type of household to which a person belongs, and in particular by whether or not there was another earner present. However, such household effects were less strong, failing to reach statistical significance in Denmark and Sweden, the two countries that came closest to the universalistic welfare regime. Second, it is notable that the dependence on the family associated with the sub-protective regimes tended to provide some protection for the young with respect to household material living conditions, although there was no comparable effect for income poverty or for the experience of financial difficulty. Indeed, in Italy, younger

TABLE 3.9. *Unemployed: ordered logit of material deprivation index, by country*

	Coefficients										
Parameter	GER	DK	NL	BE	FR	UK	IRE	IT	GR	SP	PT
Model 1											
Age 18–24	1.04**	0.75*	n.s.	n.s.	n.s.	0.60*	n.s.	−0.84***	−0.46*	−0.24~	n.s.
Age 25–34	0.67**	1.27***	n.s.	n.s.	n.s.	0.75***	n.s.	−0.72***	−0.75**	−0.44**	n.s.
Age 35–49	0.54*	0.83**	n.s.	n.s.	n.s.	0.64**	0.67**	−0.44*	n.s.	n.s.	n.s.
Male	0.36~	0.35~	n.s.	n.s.	0.44***	0.64***	n.s.	0.19*	0.23~	0.20*	0.39*
Unemp. 12+ mths	n.s.	n.s.	n.s.	n.s.	0.39**	0.55***	0.86***	n.s.	n.s.	n.s.	−0.68***
Model 2											
Age 18–24	1.23**	1.01*	1.50**	n.s.	1.33***	1.26***	0.95*	−0.63*	n.s.	0.46*	n.s.
Age 25–34	0.56*	1.04**	0.93*	n.s.	0.84***	0.96***	n.s.	−0.53*	n.s.	n.s.	n.s.
Age 35–49	n.s.	0.71*	n.s.	n.s.	0.55*	0.63**	n.s.	−0.61**	n.s.	n.s.	n.s.
Male	0.47*	n.s.	n.s.	n.s.	0.45***	0.33*	0.36*	n.s.	n.s.	n.s.	n.s.
Inter. quals.	n.s.	n.s.	n.s.	n.s.	0.52**	0.58**	0.84**	n.s.	0.50**	0.44**	1.71**
Min. quals.	0.84**	n.s.	1.09***	0.96***	1.06***	0.92***	1.20***	1.21***	1.35***	1.21***	3.31***
Single, no child	0.44*	n.s.	n.s.	n.s.	n.s.	n.s.	n.s.	n.s.	n.s.	0.35*	0.91**
Partner, + child	0.61**	n.s.	n.s.	n.s.	n.s.	n.s.	0.62*	0.41*	n.s.	0.87*	n.s.
Lone parent	n.s.	n.s.	1.69**	n.s.	n.s.	n.s.	2.13***	n.s.	n.s.	n.s.	1.11*
Unemp. 12+ mths	n.s.	n.s.	n.s.	n.s.	0.36**	0.29~	0.68***	n.s.	n.s.	n.s.	−0.61**
Dep. child, <30	−0.95~	n.s.	−2.35**	n.s.	n.s.	n.s.	n.s.	n.s.	n.s.	n.s.	n.s.
Single adult	1.12*	2.44***	n.s.	1.71**	1.93***	1.80***	0.76~	0.99***	n.s.	1.05***	n.s.
>1 adult, 0 emp.	0.69**	1.22***	1.04***	1.38***	0.85***	1.55***	0.89***	0.80***	n.s.	0.86***	n.s.
N=	387	342	291	337	961	612	651	1601	939	2097	432

Notes: Reference: Age 50–65, Female, Higher quals., Partner, no child, Not dependent child, >1 adult h'hold 1 emp. ~ = P < 0.07, * = P < 0.05, ** = P < 0.01, *** = P < 0.001. 'Difficulty making ends meet' = Most extreme coding.
Source: European Community Household Panel, 1994.

unemployed people were more likely than others to experience immediate financial pressure, even though they were better off with respect to material conditions in the household.

POVERTY AND THE REGIONAL CONCENTRATION OF UNEMPLOYMENT: THE CASE OF ITALY

The previous sections have raised a number of issues about the relationship between unemployment and poverty in Italy. It was seen first that Italy did not follow the pattern of the other Southern European countries—Greece, Spain, and Portugal—with their very high levels of financial hardship but relatively low gap between the unemployed and those in work. Second, it was noted that Italy stood out from most other countries in the strong impact on risks of financial deprivation of the region in which a person lived. This suggests that it may be crucial for understanding the experience of the Italian unemployed to look more carefully at the differences between regions. The distinctive feature about Italy is its exceptionally high regional concentration of unemployment in Southern Italy, and this may have important implications for the way poverty is viewed and coped with.

The Mezzogiorno is economically much poorer than the rest of Italy (Trigilia 1992: *Commissione di indagine sulla poverta e sull' emarginazione* 1996). In comparison with Northern Italy, the unemployed in this region have fewer chances of escaping unemployment and are likely to be subject to greater destitution. According to data published by the Istituto Nazionale di Statistica (ISTAT) in 1996, the rate of unemployment was 6.6 per cent in the North, 10.3 per cent in the Central region, and 21.7 per cent in the South;[1] 21.1 per cent being the overall rate for Italy. At 3.3:1, the South/North ratio is considerable. Equally, the nature of unemployment differs from North to South. In the South, almost 50 per cent of the unemployed are seeking first time employment, in contrast with less than one-third in the North; which suggests that the young are at a greater disadvantage in the South as a result of the chronic shortage of jobs in this region.

It can be seen from Table 3.10 that the rates of income poverty vary in relation both to a person's employment situation and to the region they are

---

[1] ISTAT defines the North in terms of the following regions: the North West, Lombardia, North East and Emilia-Romagna. The Centre includes: Centro (Toscana, Umbria, Marche), Lazio. Finally, the South covers: Abruzzo-Molise, Campania, South (Puglia, Basilcata, Calabria, Sicilia, Sardegna). For our own analyses, we have followed this classification, except that, on the advice of several experts, we have placed Abruzzo-Molise in the Centre, since it is an economically more developed region than the others of the South.

TABLE 3.10. *Frequency of people living below poverty line*[a] *by labour market situation and region*

	Stable job	Insecure job	Precarious job	Unemployment		Total
				<1 yr	>1 yr	
North	3.0	3.9	10.0	7.3	11.6	5.2
Center	4.8	6.1	14.4	17.9	31.6	9.3
South	19.0	37.0	50.7	51.7	65.2	37.0
Ratio S/N	6.3	9.5	5.1	7.1	5.6	7.1

[a] Based on a 50% mean, new OECD.
Source: ECHP, 1994, wave 1, Coverage: population 18–65 years of age

living in. The contrast is remarkable when the two extremes are compared: among those who have a stable job, the rate of poverty is at 3 per cent in the North as opposed to 19 per cent in the South; among those unemployed for over 1 year it is at 11.6 per cent in the North and 65.2 per cent in the South. The risk of poverty for both those unemployed for over 1 year and under 1 year remains rather modest in the North: the rate for these two categories bears a resemblance to the figures which we recorded from Denmark—a country which has a completely different cultural tradition and social security system for the unemployed to that of Italy. In part, this can be explained as a result of the unemployment compensation system which protects primarily those working in the branches of industry pre-dominantly to be found in the North (see Chapter 1). In Southern Italy, on the other hand, with little probability of escaping unemployment, and a quasi-non-existent indemnity system, the long-term unemployed are at a much greater disadvantage.

As Nicola Negri has observed, working does not necessarily decrease the risk of poverty in the Mezzogiorno, since the unemployed tend to end up accepting, for want of other options, the precarious and poorly-paid jobs available (Negri 1998). It can be seen that in the South, effectively one in two people with a precarious job lives beneath the poverty line, which roughly corresponds with the proportion for people who have been unemployed less than a year in the same region. If one calculates the ratio of long-term unemployed to those with an insecure job, it works out to 3.0 in the North, 5.2 in the Central region and 1.7 in the South. Poverty thus appears to be more diffused in the South and is a situation affecting wide sectors of the population; whereas in the North, it is more marginal.

This finding, however, is based on an approach that focuses on an exclus-ively monetary method of assessing poverty. Would the contrasts between the North and South of Italy be as strong if a different definition of poverty

TABLE 3.11. *Logistic regressions of the risk of poverty of unemployed in Italy, using different measures*

	Income Poverty (1)		Financial Difficulty (2)		Material Deprivation (3)		Financial Dissatisfaction (4)	
	B	Sig.	B	Sig.	B	Sig.	B	Sig.
North	*Ref.*		*Ref.*		*Ref.*		*Ref.*	
Centre	0.56	*	0.72	**	0.87	**	0.37	*
South	2.42	***	1.50	***	1.50	***	−0.08	n.s.

(*): P < 0.1, *: P < 0.05, **: P < 0.01, ***: P < 0.001.
(1) Probability of living under the poverty threshold (50% mean).
(2) Probability of finding it very difficult to make ends meet.
(3) Material deprivation poverty index.
(4) Probability of financial dissatisfaction.
Notes: Models include controls for sex, age, family situation, household composition, level of education and duration of unemployment. Ref. = Reference region.
Source: European Community Household Panel, 1994, Coverage: population 18–65 years of age.

were to be used? We look in turn at the two measures of financial hardship used earlier: financial difficulty and deprivation in material living conditions. In addition, we will examine a measure of the extent to which people were satisfied or dissatisfied with their financial situation.[2] Table 3.11 compares these measures for the unemployed, using in each case the same logistic regression model with a range of controls for individual and household characteristics. It shows that the risk for the unemployed in Southern Italy is not only greater than for those in the North with respect to income poverty, with a coefficient of 2.42; but also with respect to the indicators of great financial difficulty and material deprivation: albeit with a weaker coefficient of 1.50. The coefficients are lower though also significant for the central region.

However, there is no evidence of a significant effect of living in the South for the most subjective measure—financial dissatisfaction. This suggests that the unemployed in this region were no more dissatisfied with their financial situation than those in the North, despite being considerably poorer objectively. To test this more rigorously, we pooled the sample for the country as a whole and introduced interaction terms representing the regional location of the unemployed. Table 3.12 shows the effects of these interaction terms once sex, age, the composition of the household, the level of education, household income, and employment status have been taken into account.

[2] The question format was: 'How satisfied are you with your present situation in the following areas? Using the scale 1 to 6 again please indicate your degree of satisfaction . . . (with 'your financial situation').

TABLE 3.12. *Effect of regional location on financial satisfaction in Italy after controls* (ordered logit)

	B	Sig.
Centre	*Ref.*	
Northern Region	0.17	**
Southern Region	−0.27	***
Unemployment	−2.21	***
[Unemployment/North]	0.11	n.s.
[Unemployment/South]	0.46	*

*: P < 0.05, **: P < 0.01, ***: P < 0.001.
Note: The model included controls for gender, age, household structure and household income. Ref. = Reference region.
Source: European Community Household Panel, 1994,
Coverage: population 18–65 years of age.

Even when these factors have been controlled for, it can be seen that there are still clear regional effects. The unemployed in the central region, shown by the coefficient 'unemployment', had a markedly lower level of satisfaction than that of people in work. Unemployed people who lived in the North were not significantly different. But unemployment had a less severe effect on the financial satisfaction of people who lived in the South than it had for the unemployed in other regions, with a positive coefficient of 0.46.

At first glance, this result may seem a little strange. It might seem logical for financial dissatisfaction to coincide with both the degree of poverty and with the economic problems of development. If this is not the case, one must consider the possibility that the level of aspiration of those at greatest disadvantage varies depending on the opportunities for satisfying needs available in the region in which they live. The norms relating to well-being may depend in part on the degree of economic development, with frustrations stronger when deprivation occurs in the middle of abundance.

It may be that lack of work and of material wealth are not as great a source of dissatisfaction when the region in which a person lives is more widely deprived of employment and economic opportunities of development. In a prosperous and dynamic region, the unemployed become more aware of the distance which separates them from other categories of the population, and hence experience greater bitterness and frustration. It is likely to be the discrepancy between the objective situation and the level of aspiration, which is conditioned by the general level of well-being, which generates resentment about deprivation among the unemployed. Alexis de Tocqueville, who was sensitive to the importance of regional contrasts, mentioned the existence of an analogous phenomenon in his study of America. He contrasted the forgotten poor with free men placed in the best possible cultural and material conditions. He noticed that the former were generally serene, and apparently happy in mood, while the latter seemed solemn and almost sad even when they were supposed to be enjoying themselves. He concluded that 'The chief reason for this contrast is that the former do not think of the ills they endure, while the latter are forever brooding over advantages they do not possess' (de Tocqueville 1994: 136).

It may also be that the relationship between unemployment and poverty differs when unemployment is heavily concentrated regionally because the informal economy plays a more important role. Estimates based on ISTAT data (Reyneri 1996) suggest that informal work constitutes 28 per cent of jobs in the Mezzogiorno compared with less than 8 per cent in the rest of Italy. Such informal activity may play an important role in supplementing the resources of poor households. Research carried out in Southern Italy shows that the unemployed often look to it as a way of coping with the low level or even absence of unemployment benefits (Pugliese 1993). When the informal economy develops to this extent, it becomes a regular system of exchange, involving so many individuals and businesses that it can no longer be regarded as marginal. As an integral part of the economy, it is likely to provide a recognized social status for those thereby giving both material and symbolic protection from social disqualification.

The lower level of dissatisfaction shown by the unemployed living in Southern Italy may then reflect the effect of a high regional concentration of unemployment. This may alter the way that unemployment is viewed, given that insecurity is so highly generalized, and lead to greater reliance on the informal economy as a means of coping with poverty and providing protection against cumulative disadvantage.

CONCLUSION

This chapter has been concerned with the way that the distribution of income poverty and financial hardship among the unemployed may vary between countries. It was seen that while income poverty was systematically related to other indicators of financial disadvantage, namely the experience of financial difficulty and material deprivation with respect to living conditions, these different measures reflected distinct aspects of people's financial experience. The main commonality was that the UK emerged as the country where unemployment had a particularly sharp effect on all three of the measures.

The expectation from a welfare regime approach was that universalistic systems would lead to relatively little difference in the disadvantage suffered by various types of unemployed people, while employment-centred systems would create a sharp division between some unemployed who were relatively well protected and others who were much more vulnerable. It was particularly women and younger people who were considered to be at risk in such systems. The hypothesis concerning universalistic regimes received support with respect to income poverty. Denmark and Sweden, the two countries that came closest to such regimes, were countries in which the relatively low risk of poverty was broadly similar across unemployed people with different individual and household characteristics.

The view that employment-centred regimes would be associated with particularly high levels of poverty among women and the young received little support. There were certainly significant sex differences in a number of countries and on each of the indicators of financial disadvantage. But in every case these pointed to a greater vulnerability of men. There was also little in the way of a systematic pattern linking type of welfare regime to the vulnerability of younger people.

For the societies that were not close to the universalistic model, the most consistent finding was the importance of the nature of the household for the extent to which a person was protected from, or exposed to, income poverty and financial hardship. In particular, people who lived on their own or who were in households where none of the other adults were in work had very much higher risks of poverty. It is clear that the household mediates, in a crucial way, the relationship between welfare benefits and the financial experience of the unemployed.

Finally, the experience of financial hardship was heavily affected by the level of economic development of the society. By far the sharpest levels of financial difficulty and material deprivation were to be found in the poorer Southern countries—Spain, Greece, and Portugal. While Italy did not at first sight conform to this pattern, a more detailed analysis revealed that this was because of the very sharp degree of polarization between the level of economic development of the different regions in Italy. In Southern Italy, the unemployed had exceptionally high levels of income poverty, financial difficulty and material deprivation. But such financial hardship did not imply that there was a greater gap between the experience of the unemployed and of those in work in these societies. Rather the severe hardship experienced by unemployed people reflected the generally higher levels of financial difficulty and material deprivation in these societies. While family support was greater, and to some degree offset the lack of any guaranteed system of state support, the families offering this protection were themselves relatively poor and were doubtless further impoverished by their responsibilities for looking after the unemployed. At the same time, this shared situation of disadvantage in a context of high regional concentration of unemployment may help to account for the fact that the very high levels of hardship of the unemployed in Southern Italy did not generate the type of resentment that might have been expected.

4

Unemployment, Welfare Regime, and Income Packaging*

Ivano Bison and Gøsta Esping-Andersen

INTRODUCTION: INCOME PACKAGING AND WELFARE REGIMES

People can derive income from a combination of market activity—earnings and various investment incomes—the welfare state, through the bundle of income transfers, or from inter-personal, mainly familial, networks. The sum total constitutes a person's or household's income package. Micro-level studies of how individuals and households acquire income reveal patterns of institutional dependencies: of how people manage to mobilize resources in the struggle to maximize well-being. At the macro-level, income packages help describe the distributional system of a society.[1]

A nation's structure of income packaging tells us a great deal about the prevailing welfare *regime*, within which the welfare *state* occupies a more or less central role. The comparative welfare state literature typically distinguishes three dominant welfare regimes, although some authors have recently argued that Mediterranean Europe constitutes a possible fourth.[2] The Nordic model is characteristic for its deliberate attempt to guarantee adequate economic resources independently of market or familial reliance. It is at once individualistic and universalistic. The pivotal role of public income maintenance should be evident for all citizens' income packages but, of course, especially for those whose connection to employment is tenuous.

The more liberalistic, Anglo-Saxon model is tendentially equally individualistic but insists that the state should occupy a residual, last-resort, position relative to markets; social benefits are typically subject to an income test,

* We would like to thank Nuffield College and Department of Economics, Goethe University Frankfurt and, in particular, Duncan Gallie, Richard Layte, Richard Hauser and Konstanze Mörfdorf, for their generous help and hospitality. We also thank Brian Nolan, Richard Hauser, Wolfgang Strengmann, Sheila Jacobs, and Luis Toharia for their help and comments on this paper.
[1] See Rainwater *et al.* (1986) for a pioneering comparative study of income packaging in the welfare state. For a recent application, see Andress and Strengmann (1994).

[2] The three-way typology is argued by Titmuss (1958), Furniss and Tilton (1977), and Esping-Andersen (1999). Ferrera (1996) proposes a fourth, Mediterranean regime.

and targeted to abject 'market failures'. Hence, it is quite likely that the unemployed will benefit from public support, but that support is less likely to be generous or universal.

The Continental European model is centred on social insurance, implying that rights to benefits depend on being *already* inserted in the labour market. This, in turn, means that family members' welfare needs come to depend on the principal, usually male, breadwinner's entitlements. The case for a special Southern European regime stems, in part, from its especially strong emphasis on familial support ('familialism'), a direct legacy of the age-old Catholic subsidiarity principle.

Such regime differences should translate into distinct income packaging profiles, especially in the case of unemployed youth, the primary focus of this study.

Regime differences notwithstanding, in the 'Golden Era' of full employment it was largely assumed that unemployment, at worst, would be of the frictional or cyclical kind, that is, brief and marginal. Social benefits to the unemployed were accordingly tailored as temporary bridges. Modest labour supply coupled with an abundance of relatively low-skilled manufacturing and construction jobs meant that even basically unqualified and inexperienced workers could find well-paid employment.

All this has changed. A large proportion of today's unemployment appears 'structural' and of long duration, and easy-entry jobs are disappearing. In many European countries, youth, the less-skilled, and women find themselves heavily over-represented among the excluded. In such a scenario, first-time and inexperienced job-seekers constitute a particularly knotty problem in that they will usually not be eligible for traditional unemployment support.

The income consequences of the new unemployment will depend on the combination of two factors. One, who is at risk? Is it primarily young, first-job seekers; persons whose partner is fully employed; primary breadwinners; or families? Two, how strong are welfare state guarantees for the unemployed? Is coverage narrow or broad, and are benefits adequate?

Table 4.1 provides data on the generosity of coverage relative to the average wage among youth and the extent of coverage among all workers. Public support for the unemployed falls into three distinct groups: in one group, exemplified by Belgium and Denmark, benefits are generous and coverage extensive; a second, middling group including France, Germany, Spain, and the UK, offers more modest levels of benefit and coverage; and a third group including Italy, Greece, and Portugal is characteristic for its residual public support.[3] These features, as we shall see, have

---

[3] To the extraordinarily residual Italian programme must be added the system of '*Cassa Integrazione*', a lay-off or reduced-hours compensation programme for workers employed in industry. Officially, participants in the *Cassa Integrazione* are not considered unemployed (and do not appear in unemployment statistics) even if they have been fully laid-off for months

TABLE 4.1. *Gross unemployment insurance replacement rates, early 1990s*

	Unemployment benefit as a percent of average wage among youth[a]	Coverage rates all workers[b]
Belgium	58	81
Denmark	56	85
France	19	44
Germany	55	64
Greece	n.a.	9
Italy	0	19
Netherlands	75	38
Portugal	24	17
Spain	27	29
UK	47	62

[a] Youth = 20 year-old. The data refer to 1994–95 (OECD 1998b).
[b] Coverage data refer to 1991 (European Commission 1993).
Notes: The table relates to workers with average earnings and insurance coverage rates.
We present data as near as possible to 1993, which is the basis for our empirical analyses.

decisive implications for the income position and welfare packaging of the unemployed.

As emphasized, the welfare *state* is but one of three legs in welfare delivery. Market or family-derived welfare may be substitutes, or a complementary source of well-being. Even where the welfare state is generous, the market may furnish substantial revenue even for the unemployed. Firstly, not everybody is necessarily unemployed on a full-time basis. Some incomes from work are therefore to be expected—especially if we measure income streams on an annual or even monthly basis.[4]

Secondly, the unemployed may receive incomes from informal work or black market activities. Some categories of the unemployed are more likely to do this: some may pick up odd jobs, such as baby-sitting, or seasonal employment, for example in the tourist industries; others have skills that are amenable to informal employment, like plumbers or electricians. It is also known that in some countries, especially Southern Europe, black market jobs are quite widespread. Recent estimates for Italy suggest that 16 per cent of all jobs are of this kind (Reyneri 1996). Thirdly, the unemployed may receive non-work related market incomes, such as investment or rental incomes. Most unemployed, of course, are not likely to command large resources of this kind.

or even years. One way to characterize the Italian system is that it combines high-level *Cassa Integrazione* benefits for the (predominantly male-breadwinner) 'insider-workforce' and a truly residual and ungenerous programme for the 'outsiders'.

[4] In this study our income estimates are based on annualized monthly incomes.

If the unemployed engage in remunerated market activity, it is none the less unlikely that it will furnish income adequacy. Hence, most can be expected to depend primarily on welfare state transfers or on the resources of family members. It remains, however, an open question whether, and to what extent, one substitutes for the other: if welfare state benefits are modest, does the market or the family fill the gap?

As we saw in Table 4.1, welfare state protection of the unemployed is very uneven. In some countries, such as Denmark, eligibility is very liberal and even persons without prior employment experience receive aid.[5] In others, such as Italy, it is restrictive, assuming lengthy employment records or covering effectively only certain clienteles. Such differences affect how persons of different status, in particular young, first-time job seekers, returning women, or those with frequent and repeated unemployment spells, secure protection. Duration of benefit entitlements can be decisive. In some countries, such as Germany, insurance benefits are exhausted within a year or so, after which the unemployed are moved to less generous assistance benefits; in others, like Belgium, benefits can be held for several years. This is, in principle, also possible in Denmark where, however, most unemployed will be moved to a training or job creation programme with benefits. We should, in other words, expect that income attainment strategies and consequent economic well-being will differ among the unemployed across Europe. The weaker the welfare state, the more likely is it that the unemployed will be income-poor, and the more likely is it that they will compensate with some form of market income, aid from family members, or both. A key question is whether such compensatory strategies permit the unemployed to approach adequate welfare standards.[6]

METHODOLOGY

The data that follow derive from the first (1994) wave of the European Community Household Panel (ECHP), using the retrospective data that refer to the calendar year 1993. The variables are comparable and standardized except in a few cases. Since, unfortunately, we only have access to one wave, it is not possible to examine how the duration of unemployment affects incomes and income packaging.

Our comparison includes: Belgium, Denmark, France, Germany, Greece, Ireland, Italy, Portugal, Spain, and the United Kingdom (UK). The Nether-

[5] The Danish unemployment insurance scheme is based on the Ghent model. Persons who are members of a trade union fund can be eligible even without past employment experience.

[6] Note that several EU member countries have introduced special assistance schemes for unemployed youth, such as the French RMI, typically assuring little more than an absolute minimum. For an overview, see OECD (1998a).

lands and, for some analyses, also Ireland and Portugal, are excluded for reasons of data comparability.[7] Our nation-sample provides a good representation of the divergent welfare regimes: Denmark, the Nordic model; the UK, the 'liberal'; Belgium, France, and Germany represent a less familialistic version of the Continental European social insurance approach; Italy, Greece, Spain, and Portugal are the epitomy of familialism.

Our approach is to focus first on unemployed individuals, and then examine them in their household context. In this study we measure unemployment retrospectively for 1993. Our definition of unemployment is that a person declares having been unemployed for at least five months in 1993. We have chosen to limit our study to young adults (aged 20–29) for several reasons.[8] Firstly, teenagers are excluded since it is not always easy to distinguish participation in education from unemployment or out-of-labourforce status. This age group exhibits too much flux. But our decision is also motivated by the particularly difficult position in which those in their twenties find themselves in today's Europe. Not only are they often heavily over-represented among the unemployed—in Southern Europe they constitute the lion's share—but they are at special risk of long-term unemployment. This, in turn, has potentially severe consequences, such as prolonged income precarity and exclusion, and delayed family formation.

Because the configuration of unemployment differs across Europe, the civil status and living arrangements of the unemployed become quite important. Much of European—especially Southern European—unemployment is concentrated among young first-job seekers. Since social benefits for youth with little labour market experience are essentially non-existent in these countries, their dependence on kin is likely to be unusually high. Families can potentially substitute for welfare states and markets either in terms of cash, that is money transfers, or 'in-kind' provisions, where the unemployed live with kin.

The income-concept used in this study is *declared* annual income for the calendar year 1993.[9] Market incomes include all revenue from remunerated

---

[7] The Irish and Portuguese panels are not comparable because they measure only steady-stream incomes. They are therefore likely to underestimate income transfers, especially those that come from family. We have left out The Netherlands because the Dutch file provides no information on incomes for 1993. We have been forced to exclude Germany, Ireland, and Portugal from the logistic analyses of poverty probabilities because access to the data files arrived too late.

[8] We are in effect studying young adults. A priori, there are reasons to believe that the situation of the 20–29 year olds should differ substantially between the younger (say less than 25) and older (25–29). The data suggest that this is *usually* not the case. In the following, we shall note such differences if they are substantial; otherwise, for the sake of economy of exposition, we shall treat the group without finer age-distinctions.

[9] We have excluded from the sample persons and households where one or more members declared having an income, but did not furnish information on the amount.

work as well as investment income. Welfare state income includes unemployment benefits and all other cash transfers: child allowances, social assistance benefits, housing allowances, and so forth. 'Family'-derived incomes including also from friends, are cash transfers, either of the lump-sum or steady-stream type. The implicit value of living with parents or relatives cannot be quantified. When we examine household-level incomes, the sum of revenues received by all household members is added. We use the new OECD equivalence scale to adjust for household size: for a discussion, see Atkinson, Rainwater and Smeeding (1995), and Chapter 2 in this volume.

WHO ARE THE YOUNG UNEMPLOYED?

In some countries, such as Greece, Italy, Ireland, and Spain the youth bias is unusually strong; in others, most unemployment affects mature adults; and in still others, France and Denmark for example, the distribution is rather 'democratic'.[10] Women are disproportionally unemployed except in the UK. Table 4.2 below shows how much of total unemployment is concentrated among the young. 'Youth' includes only the age-group 20–29.

Youth unemployment varies a little by age—the 20–24 year olds are tendentially more unemployed in Southern Europe, while the 25–29 year

TABLE 4.2. *Youth[a] share of total unemployment* (%)

	Young Males	Young Females
Belgium	11.0	21.3
Denmark	13.3	21.9
France	14.6	17.0
Germany	10.4	12.0
Greece	17.7	34.5
Ireland	26.6	15.9
Italy	31.1	28.9
Portugal	13.9	15.9
Spain	21.9	20.0
UK	24.1	6.0

[a] Youth = 20–29 yr-olds.
Note: This table includes all unemployed, whether or not they have declared any income.
Source: ECHP 1994.

[10] One should be careful in the case of Germany since the heavy rates of older worker unemployment are an attribute of the German practice of early retirement.

olds are slightly more unemployed in Northern Europe; by sex, as women are typically over-represented; or by education—unemployment rates are systematically higher among the less-educated, and much lower among persons with tertiary education.

Living arrangements are of direct relevance for social well-being. In Denmark, 86 per cent of the young unemployed live independently, either as singles or in a couple, 40 per cent of whom also have children. At the other extreme, young unemployed Southern Europeans are heavily dependent on their family of origin and few, therefore, have children (see Table 4.4).

Indeed, very few in the Mediterranean countries live independently—less than 10 per cent in Italy, and less than 20 per cent elsewhere—so the norm is continued co-residence with parents. Ireland, with 72 per cent living with parents, is the only country that approximates the Mediterranean profile.[11] Parental dependence is somewhat greater in Britain, France, and Belgium than in the Northern countries, but still well short of the Southern pattern. This North-South contrast is, as we shall see, closely connected to access to economic resources.

ECONOMIC RESOURCES AMONG UNEMPLOYED INDIVIDUALS

We can examine the relative *individual* well-being of unemployed youth by comparing them to the population mean. This we do in Table 4.3, which presents estimates of total income and the value of welfare state benefits as a percentage of total population mean income for unemployed youth, aged 20–29.

Surprisingly, most young unemployed *individuals* in Europe find themselves living on incomes that are below 50 per cent of mean individual income, or what could be regarded as poverty-level incomes. Denmark is the only case in which they arrive at close to average incomes. The economic status of unemployed youth is—again except Denmark—substantially inferior. In many countries it is unrealistic to assume that they can set up independent households, at least without pooling the resources of others, through roommates, co-habitation or marriage. The welfare state's income guarantee for youth is, then, fairly strong in Denmark, Germany, Ireland, and Belgium, and dramatically low in Southern Europe.[12] Indeed, the income levels of unemployed

---

[11] This is not the place to speculate on the Irish 'anomaly'. It may reflect a Catholic culture of subsidiarity similar to that of Southern Europe.

[12] Excepting participants in the Italian *Cassa Integrazione*, which almost no young unemployed is likely to benefit from.

TABLE 4.3. *Relative income levels of young unemployed: individuals*

	Income of the unemployed, % of average income	Value of welfare state benefits, % of average income	N. of unemployed
Belgium	45.5	35.1	153
Denmark	62.5	50.2	167
France	29.2	20.1	208
Germany	41.3	31.7	71
Greece	13.6	2.3	245
Ireland	44.7	38.5	270
Italy	6.9	1.3	637
Portugal	18.0	9.0	476
Spain	26.3	16.3	630
UK	33.0	25.0	136

Note: This table includes all unemployed, including those who declare zero income.
Source: ECHP 1994.

youth in Southern Europe amount to little more than 'pocket money'. The monthly average of ca. 80,000 Lire among unemployed young Italians would just about cover the cost of a daily coffee and cigarettes, assuming they are not heavy smokers.

The averages we present in Table 4.3 are not very meaningful if the underlying distribution is skewed. One way to take this into account is to examine what percentage claim that they receive *zero* revenue. Additionally, 80,000 Lire a month may not imply poverty if the unemployed live free with their parents—see Table 4.4.

The just mentioned Italian average of 80,000 Lire reflects the reality that 81 per cent of young unemployed receive no income whatsoever from either welfare state or market. In fact, if we restrict our inquiry to the welfare state, asking what proportion of the *young* unemployed live solely on welfare state benefits, EC Europe presents itself bi-modally: in one group the rate lies between 40 and 70 per cent of all: Belgium (56 per cent), Germany (47 per cent), Denmark (37 per cent), Ireland (67 per cent), and the UK (59 per cent). In another group the rate is below 20 per cent: Italy (2 per cent), Greece (4 per cent), Portugal (10 per cent), and Spain (16 per cent). France falls in the middle with 28 per cent. There is of course a strong coincidence between not receiving welfare state support and living with parents.

The data do not suggest any simple, one-to-one income-substitution effects. Meager welfare state support is not automatically picked up by more revenues from either the market or family. Granted, reliance solely on income from the market, presumably through informal, occasional, or black market employment, tends to be somewhat higher in Southern

TABLE 4.4. *Unemployed with zero market or welfare state revenue, and young unemployed who receive aid from family* (%)

	% Unemployed with zero income		% of young unemployed	
	All (20–65)	Youth (20–29)	with income from family[a]	who live with parents[b]
Belgium	2.1	3.3	13.7	58.6
Denmark	0.4	0.0	12.6	13.6
France	13.7	20.8	4.8	48.5
Germany	5.4	8.5	15.5	28.6
Greece	48.9	59.6	7.8	78.1
Ireland	2.1	3.0	0.4	71.6
Italy	69.8	81.3	4.2	87.0
Portugal	40.7	54.2	0.0	74.2
Spain	31.8	42.6	2.6	76.7
UK	3.6	2.2	5.2	41.7

[a] This refers only to income transfers *between* households.
[b] Based on unemployed at time of interview in 1994.
Note: This table includes all unemployed, including those who declare zero income.
Source: ECHP 1994.

Europe, at about 15–25 per cent, than in Northern Europe, where it lies between 1 and 6 per cent. But the level of market income remains typically low: among Italians, only 5 per cent of average individual income, while their Danish equivalents, notwithstanding generous social protection, actually earn twice as much in the market.

Young unemployed with inadequate, or no revenue rely, therefore, primarily on an 'in-kind' type of substitution strategy: residing with their parents. This is clearly the common welfare solution in Southern Europe generally, and in Italy *par excellence*. Youth living with their parents have generally very low market incomes. In brief, the market, black, informal or whatever, is not an effective welfare state substitute.[13] This stands to reason because, for youth, even the black economy is likely to 'fail'. Access to 'irregular' earnings or capital income normally assumes that people already have developed networks, considerable savings, or desirable skills. The single clearest fact is that families may help fill the welfare gap, via free room-and-board, but not the income-gap. Oddly enough, more unemployed receive cash from family members in the two most luxurious unemployment scheme countries, Belgium and Denmark, than in Italy, Portugal, or Spain.

---

[13] Of course, for youth living on 'free' room and board with parents, 10 per cent of average individual income may constitute adequate daily spending money.

These findings apparently contradict two widespread assumptions in much of the contemporary debate on welfare reform. The first is that welfare providing institutions are substitutable. Hence, contrary to what the privatization strategy assumes, it is quite clear that the market is no automatic substitute for the welfare state.

Hence, we discover a new dimension to the traditional income packaging approach to measuring welfare. The prototypical welfare packaging strategy of young unemployed in Southern Europe combines continued residence with parents, coupled with occasional 'pocket' money income from either market or kin, or both. Whether family can effectively secure adequate welfare depends, of course, on whether unemployment bundles within families. On this count it is evident that the Mediterranean model of familialistic welfare packaging 'works' because almost all young unemployed live in a household with a full-time earner—typically the traditional male breadwinner. On average, a young unemployed person in Italy, Spain, Greece, or Portugal resides in a household with roughly 1.2 income earners from market activity. In France, where continued residency with parents is more common than in Northern Europe, the rate is 1.0. Elsewhere, the average number of earners is systematically below 1.0—as low as 0.3 in Denmark, and around 0.5 in most other countries. Clearly, this indicates that young unemployed are capable of setting up their own, independent households.

There exists a clearly demarcated 'Mediterranean' model of unemployment on both the structural side—who is unemployed—and the welfare side—how do they live. Its opposite is found in Denmark, where even young unemployed live independently, mainly on welfare state benefits. An unemployed Danish, Belgian, German, Irish, and British youth receives 80 per cent of their total income from the state: see Table 4.5. In Denmark, and possibly also in Belgium, welfare state benefits may also be enough to live on.

The unemployed Europeans, therefore, experience very different institutional revenue dependencies. If we consider gender, these differences should be even more accentuated. Since women's integration in the labour market is generally weaker, they will have less capacity to draw upon welfare benefits or work incomes. As a result, we would expect greater family dependencies. Yet any such gender-effect just does not show up. In no single country is there any gender difference in the proportion that receives incomes solely from the market, and in only two countries, France and the UK, are women more likely than men to receive income support from family. The absence of any gender-effect is, however, less startling when we consider the age-group under study: young men and women today will differ much less in terms of their labour force integration.

TABLE 4.5. *Income packages among unemployed youth* (20–29)

	% Income From:			Total income of unemployed as % of average adjusted income of all households (age 20–65)	N. of unemployed
	Welfare State	Market	Family		
Belgium	78.4	18.3	3.2	42.3	167
Denmark	79.9	19.0	1.1	58.1	167
France	59.3	37.5	3.2	26.1	164
Germany	80.4	16.2	3.5	35.2	65
Greece	13.6	71.4	15.0	11.4	99
Ireland	87.1	12.5	0.4	41.2	259
Italy	11.6	69.2	19.3	6.0	124
Portugal	36.8	63.2	0.0	15.5	49
Spain	49.1	48.6	2.2	21.7	358
UK	82.7	16.2	1.1	29.9	133

Notes: This Table presents the % of total received income deriving from welfare state, market and family*, and total revenue of individual unemployed as a % of average adjusted income of all households (age 20–65).**
*) Excludes persons with zero income.
**) Including those who declare zero income.
Source: ECHP 1994.

INCOME PACKAGING AMONG INDIVIDUALS

What share of income derives from the three distinct sources, and how does the final package assure welfare? As we already have seen, the unemployed experience a very different structure of revenue dependencies. Let us now examine how incomes are bundled.

Again, Europe divides in two. The welfare state is omnipresent in the income package of Northern Europeans, and truly marginal among Italians and Greeks. But omnipresence may not automatically guarantee income adequacy. In the case of Denmark it certainly does, possibly also in Belgium and Ireland. But the combined income package of French, British, and even German unemployed youth is quite low even if the welfare state also dominates here. In other words, unless the welfare state dominates the income package, the risk of very low income is very high. But dominance alone is not always a sufficient condition.

Lack of income sources in general, and welfare state support in particular, can be countered by choice of living arrangement. One way to gauge this is to examine how unemployed individuals with incomes below 50 per

TABLE 4.6. *Living arrangements of unemployed youth with total income below 50 per cent of mean youth income*[14]

	Alone	Couple	With parents
Belgium	2.9	42.8	48.6
Denmark	16.7	41.7	33.3
France	8.5	28.2	56.4
Germany	9.7	35.6	35.5
Greece	2.0	14.8	57.6
Ireland	0.0	10.7	73.2
Italy	0.9	7.0	84.8
Portugal	0.0	19.3	56.8
Spain	0.0	9.6	73.3
UK	20.0	25.2	47.4

Note: This Table includes all unemployed, including those who declare zero income. 'Alone' includes lone parents. 'Couple' includes couples with children. The rows do not add to 100 because 'other' living arrangements have been omitted.
Source: ECHP 1994.

cent of mean individual income live. As Table 4.6 demonstrates, low incomes are much more likely to discourage independent living, especially as a single, and push the unemployed to live with their parents.

THE INCOME POSITION OF HOUSEHOLDS WITH UNEMPLOYED MEMBERS

The experience of unemployment is therefore not always individual. Real well-being is a matter of household resource pooling, and household type is accordingly critical. Some households, for example, are far less capable of 'playing the market' or of counting on generous intra-family money transfers. Single-person, single-parent, and single-earner families are much more at risk of poverty than are dual-earner units. The employment status of a partner is especially decisive. If unemployment bundles in households, the risk of poverty is especially grave.

Certainly, even households with multiple unemployment can attain socially adequate income levels if the array of welfare state benefits, including rent allowances, family benefits, or social assistance, permit so. If this is not the case, and if market revenue is also low, family remains the venue of last resort.

The problem with families, however, is that they are unequally endowed with money and social capital. It is a well-established sociological fact that

[14] The 'other' category of living arrangements, not shown in the table, includes unclear responses as well as situations such as renting a room in the house of others.

privilege and underprivilege are passed on inter-generationally (Erikson and Goldthorpe 1992; Shavit and Blossfeld 1993). If unemployment is more likely to afflict persons with less privileged social origins, family 'failure' may easily accompany welfare state and market 'failures'. It is precisely for this reason that strong welfare state guarantees are important, and this is why familialistic *or* liberalistic welfare regimes can be problematic.[15]

In some countries, the combined household income package succeeds in securing incomes above poverty, in others not. Put differently, youth unemployment may catalyse poverty because of their household characteristics, their capacity to combine revenues, or because of the welfare regime in which they happen to find themselves. Table 4.7 addresses these issues with the aid of a logistic regression in which the dependent variable is household poverty (scored 1), defined as less than 50 per cent of median income (adjusted for household size).

As we have known since the early studies of Seebohm Rowntree (1901), large families are especially likely to fall into poverty. Since we apply an equivalence scale to adjust for household size, it is almost by definition the case that additional non-earning family members will contribute positively to poverty. Note in any case that the number of children has no significant effect on poverty, as very few families have more than two children; also, there are no significant effects of household type other than 'singles', which is our reference group. The single category includes unemployed lone parents. In Denmark and Belgium, these achieve 80 per cent of mean income; in France and the UK, around 50 per cent; and in Greece and Italy, around 40 per cent.

It does, however, matter how many household members are employed or inactive. Each additional income recipient has a powerful effect on reducing poverty: the odds-ratio suggests that the risk is reduced by roughly four times. Surprisingly, if unemployment bundles, chances of poverty are not greater.

Turning to our income packaging variables, it is by now rather evident that the most effective guarantee against *income* poverty is the welfare state together with market incomes that derive from other family members. In other words, the best hedge against poverty for the unemployed is to have employed relatives, or to be blessed with a strong welfare state. More generally, the income packaging variables suggest that when, at the household level, families manage to *combine* the income sources of various members, the risk of poverty declines significantly.

The country dummies in Table 4.7 can be interpreted as 'welfare regime' effects. Since Denmark is the omitted reference country, the country odds indicate the relative risks of poverty compared to Denmark, our most

---

[15] Although, as we have shown above, it is quite likely that an unemployed person in Southern Europe lives in a household with at least one full-time earner.

TABLE 4.7. *Logistic regression of the probability of poverty among unemployed youth*

Parameter	B	S.E.	Odds	Sig.
Constant	−0.768	0.57	0.46	n.s.
1. The Impact of:				
Household characteristics[a]				
- number members	0.59	0.08	1.81	***
- being couple	0.06	0.38	1.06	n.s.
- being couple with children	0.11	0.33	1.11	n.s.
- living with parents	−0.51	0.34	0.60	n.s.
- other typology	−0.72	0.37	0.49	n.s.
2. Labour market status of household				
- number employed	−1.26	0.18	0.28	***
- number unemployed	0.21	0.12	1.23	n.s.
- number inactive	−0.31	0.11	0.74	**
- number income sources	0.19	0.09	1.21	*
3.a. Individual income packaging[b]				
- log market income	−0.18	0.04	0.83	***
- log social benefits	−0.35	0.04	0.71	***
- log family transfers	−0.26	0.07	0.77	***
3.b. Household income packaging[b][c]				
- log market income	−0.46	0.04	0.63	***
- log social benefits	−0.36	0.04	0.70	***
- log family transfers	−0.21	0.06	0.81	***
4. Citizenship[d]				
- Belgium	0.88	0.48	2.43	n.s.
- France	1.60	0.47	4.95	***
- Greece	1.36	0.49	3.89	**
- Italy	1.78	0.48	5.92	***
- Spain	1.56	0.46	4.75	***
- UK	2.46	0.45	11.66	***
N=2266				

[a] reference category for household types is 'single'.
[b] income revenues (in ECU equivalents) are logged.
[c] contribution to total family income of *other* household members. The sum of 3.a. and 3.b. equals total household income.
[d] Denmark is reference country. Germany, Ireland, and Portugal have been omitted for technical reasons.
Notes: Significance: * = 0.05% level; ** = 0.01% level or less; *** = 0.001% level or less. Percentage observations correctly classified = 83.9. Chi-square = 808.8 d.f. = 21 and pseudo-R squared 0.30. We have ascertained that there exist no problems of multi-colinearity.

generous and comprehensive welfare regime. It seems clear that all other countries 'produce' a comparatively quite high risk of poverty. The UK is an extreme case since the odds of poverty are almost 12 times greater than for Denmark.

Here we seem to have a puzzle because, as we know, welfare state provision for young unemployed in the UK may not exactly be generous but it

TABLE 4.8. *Total household income of families*
with one unemployed youth, as % of income of
all households (aged 20–65)

Denmark	73.2
Belgium	68.2
France	75.0
Germany	68.8
Greece	78.0
Ireland	77.2
Italy	77.8
Portugal	87.7
Spain	77.1
UK	56.2

Note: This table includes all unemployed, including
those who declare zero income.
Source: ECHP 1994.

is certainly superior to that in Greece or Italy. Why, then, is the poverty risk
of being British greater than that of being Greek, Italian, or Spanish? The
most convincing answer lies in nationally-specific substitution strategies. The
unemployed in the UK are likely to live independently, but on poverty-level
social benefits; the Italians receive nothing from the public purse but they
do live with parents.

But this does not explain the entire puzzle because if, as in the UK, the
unemployed live in independent households, they are also much more likely
to be married or cohabiting—meaning the availability of multiple potential
income earners.[16] The question is therefore whether partners of the unemployed can boost household income through market earnings? The evidence
suggests that this is not easily the case. In Britain, the average number of
persons receiving market income in *households* with children and one
unemployed is very low: 0.14 persons on average, by far the lowest among
our countries. Denmark and Belgium are, respectively second and third but
they provide much more generous social benefits. Hence, the net income
position of families in the UK with one unemployed is much inferior to
elsewhere. See Table 4.8.

Table 4.8 is in its own right somewhat of a paradox. As the reader may
recall, we started out emphasizing the vast national differences in welfare
regime and unemployment structure. Our analyses along the way stressed
the equally evident variations in income packaging profiles and *individual-*
level poverty risk. Now that we examine incomes in the household context,
what we find is convergence. Except for the UK, the young unemployed are,
in one way or another, inserted in households that are not doing especially

---

[16] In fact, almost half (46 per cent) live independently.

poorly, achieving from 70–86 per cent of mean household income. And now, suddenly, Belgium and Denmark are no longer shining examples of well-being.

The answer is of course simply that in Southern Europe—once again—the unemployed may have very little money but they live in a family that does. The Danes live independently and they fare rather well, all said. The British also live independently, but here modest welfare state benefits and low *household* levels of labour supply conspire to produce internationally low net income levels. Since the unemployed person in the UK is most likely male, low household levels of labour supply are possibly due to the well-known combined disincentive effects of weak childcare coverage and the implicit taxation of social benefits through spouses' earnings. In fact, this can be shown in an indirect way by introducing an interaction term (UK*number employed persons in household) in the logistic model presented in Table 4.7. This interaction variable reduces the risk of poverty significantly: coefficient = −1.27, odds ratio = 0.28. Yet, the simple UK dummy variable now becomes dramatically more powerful: in this case, the odds of being poor 'if British' are 67 times greater than 'if Danish'. In other words, unemployed households in the UK would be about three times less likely to be poor if partners worked.[17]

Notwithstanding previous UK governments' avowed dedication to the market, unemployed households in the UK appear extraordinarily distant from the labour market. This distance is surely related to the well-known 'welfare traps' built into social assistance in the UK, an inherent negative work incentive for spouses and single parent families (Atkinson and Mogensen 1993). For most other countries, the unemployment of one spouse, partner, or child does not appear apocalyptic as far as access to market incomes is concerned.

CONCLUSIONS

Our study suggests implications both for social policy and for the contemporary debate on European mass unemployment. Beginning with the former, our income packaging approach indicates that a nation's profile of social support matters greatly as far as income adequacy and poverty risks are concerned. A Nordic style, welfare-state dominated approach is clearly superior from the point of view of income adequacy. To an extent, a Mediterranean model dominated instead by familial support also succeeds in securing adequate welfare, although not income, through continued

---

[17] Repeating the same estimation for Italy yields no such effect.

residence with parents. The associated consequences are, however, dramatically different: the ability to live independently and form families in the Nordic model; delayed independence in the Southern. The UK exemplifies a third pole, one characterized by weak family and welfare state support. This automatically implies a relatively stronger dependency on markets if the aim is welfare adequacy. Yet, here markets seem to 'fail'. Households with unemployed persons are, in the UK, not able to substitute for meager welfare state and family support, arguably because of the assistance-based transfer system that is typical of residual welfare states: they actually discourage added labour supply. In brief, due to institutional factors, we cannot easily assume functional substitution between state, market and family—at least in the case of guaranteeing welfare among young unemployed.

Turning to labour market consequences, it is often held that labour market deregulation is the single most effective remedy against the European unemployment problem. Concepts such as insider-outsider labour markets, hysterisis of unemployment, or Eurosclerosis in one way or another seek to depict European unemployment as predominantly structural. Often, Europe's persistent unemployment levels and the extraordinary disadvantage that youth and women find themselves in is diagnosed as a 'supply-side' problem: the unemployed have a too high reservation wage which inhibits market clearing through wages.

Our approach to income packaging presents a broader conception of the reservation wage than is usual. On one side it includes the conventional welfare state guarantees. On the other side it includes also the implicit or explicit value of familial support. If exiting from unemployment implies geographical mobility, then the cost of movement will be weighed against the value of living free with parents. There is an opportunity cost involved that, in many cases, can be very steep.

Our data do not suggest that the welfare state is the chief culprit of excessive reservation wages. The lion's share of unemployed *young* Europeans does not receive welfare state benefits that even tangentially approach average market incomes. Where they do, as in Denmark and less so in Belgium, unemployment in general, and youth unemployment in particular, is not higher, nor of longer duration, than where they do not, as in Italy.

Yet, for institutional reasons the impact of the reservation wage may very well be idiosyncratic, that is to say, nationally unique. If an unemployed person must live on, say, 20 per cent of average income, it makes a huge difference if he or she must maintain another adult and perhaps children, or whether he or she resides with kin. In Southern Europe there may be exclusion, but since the family breadwinner is almost never unemployed, the excluded can attain adequate welfare standards by rallying around the breadwinner: derived welfare. Unemployment rarely becomes economic hardship.

The reservation wage of the Southern European unemployed is therefore a wholly different phenomenon from that of Northern Europe. Put bluntly, in the former case the calculus is based on the differential between living conditions in the parental home and the alternative of living independently. The micro-level cost of unemployment in Southern Europe is not individualized, but familialized. The macro-level cost is, in turn, delayed family formation and extremely low fertility. Denmark offers the most telling contrast in the sense that the unemployed, whether young or adult, will be able to expect an income level that assures adequacy.

Several lessons emerge from this kind of comparison. The first, and perhaps foremost, is that the simple US-European comparison that underpins so much of the current debate on jobs-versus-social protection is, simply put, erroneous.[18] It is erroneous because the profile of unemployment, and the economic conditions of the unemployed, are so different across Europe. It may very well be that unemployed youth shun the market in Southern Europe but if they do so it just cannot be the fault of the welfare state—unless by welfare state we mean a system that familializes the burden of taking care of the unemployed. This brings us to the second 'lesson': deregulation, as in the United States or the UK, may have a positive effect on aggregate unemployment rates but this does not necessarily affect the nation-specific unemployment profile. Deregulating the Italian or Greek labour market might very well produce job growth at low-level entry wages, but supply might not automatically follow if, as our study has shown, the youth reservation wage includes the value of parental co-residence. In some countries, Denmark perhaps, 'structural unemployment' may be higher than necessary because of welfare state benefits.[19] But these very same benefits encourage earlier independence, family formation and, hence, fertility. Clearly, it is not the unemployment benefit system that creates 'structural unemployment' in Italy or Greece. Indeed, if these countries were to follow the Danish example, they just might restore their record-low fertility levels.

---

[18] This is also the conclusion that emerges from Blank (1994), Nickell (1997), and Esping-Andersen (1999).

[19] Indeed, two successive reforms, in 1994 and 1996, have brought about radical change since the maximum allowable period of obtaining 'passive' benefits has been limited to 6 months whereafter the unemployed are compelled to accept either education or job offers with benefits.

5

The Changing Effects of Social Protection on Poverty

Brian Nolan, Richard Hauser, Jean-Paul Zoyem*

INTRODUCTION

One of the principal concerns of this volume is the extent to which institutional differences across countries with respect to the labour market and social protection are a significant factor mediating the relationship between labour market precarity and social exclusion. This chapter focuses on the effectiveness of cash transfers, the central element of social protection systems, in alleviating the effects of unemployment on income poverty. The structures of social protection systems vary greatly across European Union member states, and in many cases have altered significantly in recent years in response to high unemployment, as discussed in Chapter 2. We now take as a starting-point the analysis in that chapter of how poverty rates among the unemployed vary across countries, and analyse in depth the role of social protection cash transfers. Using data from the mid-1980s and the mid-1990s for six member countries, we compare the effectiveness of different systems in lifting or keeping the unemployed out of poverty, and how this has been affected by the way systems have responded to the challenges produced by developments in the labour market in the 1990s. The specific role of social insurance-based unemployment-linked transfers versus other cash transfers is also considered, to assess the extent to which social insurance has been able to cope with changes in the labour market over the period. The data come from a variety of national large-scale household surveys.

The chapter is structured as follows. The second section discusses the data and methods to be employed in measuring the impact of cash transfers on poverty risks for the unemployed. The third looks at the overall risks of poverty for the unemployed before and after cash transfers, and how these changed between the mid-1980s and mid-1990s. The fourth looks at the role of social insurance-based unemployment payments versus other cash transfers. The

* With the collaboration of Beate Hock, Mohammad Azhar Hussain, Sheila Jacobs, Charlotte Samuelsson and Wolfgang Strengmann-Kuhn.

fifth examines the extent to which the impact of transfers varies by gender and by duration of unemployment. The sixth highlights the key patterns identified and what these tell us about the relationship between the type of welfare regime a country operates and effectiveness in alleviating poverty among the unemployed.

DATA AND METHODS

As well as studies of the overall effectiveness of social protection systems in alleviating poverty in specific countries (for example Weinberg 1987; Paugam and Zoyem 1996), cross-country comparisons of anti-poverty effectiveness have been made by, for example, Beckerman (1979a,b), Mitchell (1991), and Deleeck, Van den Bosch and De Lathouwer (1992). Many other studies have looked at the impact of transfers and of direct taxes on income distribution as a whole, including Atkinson, Smeeding and Rainwater (1995b). Here our specific focus is on the unemployed, and on the impact of cash transfers on the risk of poverty for that group. Following the approach adopted in the research programme as a whole, unemployment is measured where possible following ILO definitions, incorporating job search and availability for work criteria.

In analysing poverty risks we concentrate on income-based poverty measures, using relative income poverty lines. We build on the in-depth analysis of income poverty rates in Chapter 2, measuring poverty in exactly the same way. The income recipient unit is the household, with an adjustment for household size and composition using adult equivalence scales. Two alternative scales are employed to see whether the results are sensitive to the way this adjustment is carried out, namely the 'New' and 'Old' OECD scales. Household poverty status is measured vis-à-vis a set of relative income poverty lines, calculated as 40, 50 and 60 per cent of mean equivalent disposable household income.[1] The simplifying assumption is made that all members of a given household share the same living standards, and thus the same income poverty status. Each unemployed individual is thus identified as in a household below/not below a particular income poverty line.

This chapter examines the impact of social security transfers on the risk of income poverty amongst the unemployed. To do this, we not only look at whether a household is presently in poverty, using disposable income, but also the position of each household in the absence of cash transfers.

---

[1] Chapter 2 also looked at poverty rates for the unemployed with relative income lines constructed as proportions of the median rather than the mean: while poverty rates themselves are quite different, there is no reason to expect the pattern of results of our analysis of the impact of transfers to be significantly affected by this choice.

This involves calculating the income aggregate 'income less social security transfers' for each household, by deducting transfers from disposable income. Any tax paid on transfers should in principle be added back in, but this was not possible with the data available and the amounts involved would generally not be large. Poverty status vis-à-vis the income poverty lines is then reassessed on the basis of this pre-transfer income. The income poverty lines themselves are held unchanged in this exercise, rather than being recalculated as proportions of mean pre-transfer rather than disposable income. The comparison of actual poverty rates for the unemployed with these counterfactual 'no transfers' poverty rates, with the different relative income lines, provides outer bounds on the effectiveness of transfers in reducing income poverty.

The estimates are outer bounds because we do not believe that incomes from the market would in fact be unchanged in the absence of transfers. This problem with the 'no transfers' counterfactual is widely recognized, and indeed the same point was made with respect to standard static analyses of the impact of taxes and transfers as far back as the 1950s. However, we will be focusing not on the absolute difference between poverty rates before and after transfers, but on the way these vary across countries and change over time. The overall effectiveness of cash transfers will be measured for each participating country at two points in time, a year around 1985 and one around 1995.

In addition to looking at the impact of all state cash transfers on poverty risks for the unemployed, the analysis will also compare the role of social insurance-based unemployment compensation and other cash transfers. In the same way, income 'before Unemployment Insurance' and 'before other transfers' will be calculated, poverty rates employing these income aggregates will be derived, and estimates produced on this basis of the impact of each of these components of cash transfers in reducing poverty rates for the unemployed. These estimates cannot be seen as distinct additive effects of each component on poverty risks, as we shall see, but are none the less instructive. The results will also distinguish men and women, and the short-term and long-term unemployed.

The analysis concentrates on the comparison of the simplest summary poverty measure before and after transfers, namely the 'headcount' of the proportion of persons in poverty, as do, for example, Deleeck *et al.* (1992). Beckerman (1979a) in contrast looked at the size of the aggregate poverty gap—the difference between the income of all those below the poverty line and the line itself—and the extent to which this is reduced by transfers. This takes into account the impact of transfers on the depth of poverty as well as the numbers in poverty. Here we utilize the headcount measure but capture the depth of poverty by using a range of relative income poverty lines from 40 to 60 per cent of mean income rather than a single line.

Nolan, Hauser, and Zoyem

TABLE 5.1. *Data sources*

Country	Survey	Year of survey	Income measure	Unemployment measure
Denmark	3% sample from administrative registers	1988, 1993	Annual	registered unemployed
France	Situations défavorisées	1986/7, 1993/4	Annual (previous year)	ILO
Ireland	Survey of income distribution etc., Living in Ireland Survey	1987, 1994	Weekly/ Monthly	ILO
Germany	Socio-Economic Panel	1985, 1993	Annual	registered unemployed
Sweden	Level of Living Survey	1981, 1991	Annual	looking for work, unemployed or laid off in the week before interview.
United Kingdom	Family Expenditure Survey	1984–86 (pooled), 1994–95 (pooled)	Current	ILO

The countries for which results are presented are Denmark, France, Germany, Ireland, Sweden, and the UK. The results have been produced by project participants from the country in question using large-scale household surveys described in detail in Chapter 2; the key features of these surveys are summarized in Table 5.1. It is important to note at this stage some differences across countries in the nature of the data available, which must be taken into account in interpreting the results. Most of the data sources are household surveys, but in the case of Denmark the source is a 3 per cent sample from administrative records so the income data comes from tax records. While the Swedish results are from the Level of Living Surveys, the income data is in that case obtained by matching to administrative records. Income data from tax records may differ from income data provided as survey responses, the source for the other countries covered.

Second, the income measure differs across countries in the period it covers: for Denmark, France, Germany, and Sweden it is annual income, whereas for Ireland and the UK it is for the most part income last week or month. While this distinction can be significant in measuring income poverty—a household could be in poverty this week or month but have annual income over the poverty line—it is particularly important in examining the relationship between unemployment and poverty. For the countries using 'current' weekly or monthly income, unemployment is measured on the basis of status when surveyed, and so labour market status and income refer to the same time period. For some of those using annual income, unemployment is also defined in terms of status when interviewed, but for others, notably Germany, an individual is counted as unemployed if he or she experienced unemployment at any point during the year in question. For France there is the added complication that income refers to the previous year but unemployment to the current year, which is obviously unsatisfactory when the aim is to relate income and unemployment experience but is the only data available. In the case of Germany, it should be noted that in Chapter 2 monthly income was employed whereas annual income is used here, because in the German Socio-Economic Panel (SOEP) detailed information about transfers are given only for the whole year.

THE IMPACT OF TRANSFERS ON POVERTY RATES FOR THE UNEMPLOYED

We now look at the overall impact of cash transfers on poverty rates for the unemployed in the countries covered, in the mid-1980s and mid-1990s. Pre- and post-transfers poverty rates have been produced using three relative income poverty lines and two sets of equivalence scales, so for ease of presentation we begin with the intermediate, 50 per cent relative income poverty line which also tends to be the one most widely referred to internationally. Table 5.2 shows poverty rates for the unemployed in each country before and after cash transfers, for both income equivalized using the 'New' and the 'Old' OECD equivalence scales.

The post-transfer poverty rates for the unemployed in these countries, and the level of unemployment itself, have been analysed in depth in Chapter 2 and this discussion will not be repeated here. It is sufficient to note two central features of these poverty rates after transfers. The first is the very wide variation across countries in poverty rates for the unemployed. The percentage below the 50 per cent poverty line ranges from as low as 8 per cent in Denmark to as high as 50 per cent in the UK in the mid-1990s, with the rates for the other countries between 23 and 38 per cent. The second is the diverging trends in these poverty rates across countries between the mid-1980s and the mid-1990s. A sharp increase in the proportion of the unemployed falling below half average income was seen over this period in the UK and to a lesser extent in Germany, with a more marginal increase in Sweden, stability in Denmark and France, and a decline in Ireland.

The primary focus of this chapter, however, is the impact of cash transfers on poverty rates for the unemployed. Table 5.2 shows that, unsurprisingly, poverty rates would have been much higher in the absence of transfers in all countries. In the mid-1980s, household income before transfers was below the 50 per cent poverty line for almost three quarters of the unemployed in

TABLE 5.2. *Poverty rate for unemployed, before and after transfers, 1980s and 1990s*

	1980s		1990s	
	before transfers	after transfers	before transfers	after transfers
Denmark				
New	58.5	7.6	66.6	7.6
Old	58.3	7.2	66.4	7.1
France				
New	41.6	23.1	49.0	23.3
Old	43.0	24.7	49.5	23.9
Germany				
New	48.1	25.5	55.6	37.8
Old	48.0	27.6	55.4	37.9
Ireland				
New	73.1	38.7	79.6	33.4
Old	72.9	41.7	79.4	29.5
Sweden				
New	37.1	27.3	62.3	30.4
Old	32.6	25.0	61.5	29.6
UK				
New	53.2	32.9	61.0	49.4
Old	53.7	32.0	61.5	50.6

Note: Poverty line 50% of mean equivalent income (new/old OECD equivalence scale).
Sources: See Table 5.1.

Ireland, for about half the unemployed in the UK and Germany, and for between 33 and 44 per cent in the other three countries. The Table also shows that pre-transfer poverty rates had risen in all countries by the mid-1990s. This increase was particularly pronounced in Sweden, where the pre-transfer poverty rate rose from the relatively low figure of about one-third to over 60 per cent. A much smaller but still substantial increase in pre-transfer poverty rates was also seen in each of the other countries.

With pre-transfer poverty rates going up universally but some countries seeing stable or declining post-transfer poverty rates, cash transfers are clearly having a greater impact in some cases by the mid-1990s than they were in the mid-1980s. Even where both pre- and post-transfer poverty rates are rising, transfers are of course also being more effective if the increase is less post-transfers. Table 5.3 shows one measure of the impact of transfers: the percentage of the pre-transfer poor unemployed who are not in poverty post-transfers—in other words, the percentage of the pre-transfer poor un-employed lifted above the poverty line by the cash transfers received by their household. Still using the 50 per cent poverty line, this shows that in the mid-1980s transfers were most effective in alleviating poverty for the

TABLE 5.3. *Impact of transfers on poverty rates for the unemployed*

	% of pre-transfer poor unemployed lifted above poverty line		% of all unemployed lifted above poverty line	
	1980s	1990s	1980s	1990s
Denmark				
New	87.0	88.6	50.9	59.0
Old	87.6	89.3	51.1	59.3
France				
New	44.5	52.4	18.5	25.7
Old	42.6	51.7	18.3	25.6
Germany				
New	47.0	32.0	22.6	17.8
Old	42.5	31.6	20.4	17.5
Ireland				
New	47.1	58.0	34.4	46.2
Old	42.8	62.8	31.2	49.9
Sweden				
New	26.4	51.2	9.8	31.9
Old	23.3	51.9	7.6	31.9
UK				
New	38.2	19.0	20.3	11.6
Old	40.4	17.7	21.7	10.9

Note: Poverty line = 50% of mean equivalent income.
Sources: See Table 5.1.

unemployed in Denmark, where more than 80 per cent of those who were poor before transfers had been lifted out of poverty by transfers. In France, Germany, Ireland, and the UK, about 40–45 per cent of the pre-transfer poor were lifted above the poverty line by transfers, while in Sweden the figure was only about one-quarter.

By the mid-1990s, the impact of transfers on this measure had increased in France, Ireland, and particularly Sweden, where a much larger proportion of the pre-transfer poor unemployed were being lifted above the poverty line. In Denmark the very high 'escape rate' seen in the mid-1980s was maintained. In Germany and even more so in the UK, however, the percentage of the pre-transfer poor lifted above the poverty line by transfers fell sharply.

Distinct underlying patterns over the 1980s–1990s period can thus be identified as follows: In Denmark, France, Ireland, and Sweden, the pre-transfer poverty rate rose but cash transfers either became more effective or, in the Danish case, remained very effective in lifting the pre-transfer poor above the poverty line, so the post-transfer poverty rate for the unemployed fell or at worst increased only marginally. In Germany and the UK, the pre-transfer poverty rate rose while cash transfers became much less effective, so the post-transfer poverty rate rose a good deal more.

Both the scale of unemployment and the extent of pre-transfer poverty among the unemployed obviously differ across countries, and thus so does the size of the problem being tackled by the cash transfer system. Table 5.3 also shows the absolute reduction in the poverty rate for the unemployed which transfers succeed in bringing about in each country. Cash transfers lift half or more of the unemployed out of poverty in Denmark and in Ireland, considerably more than in the other countries. This reflects the very high level of effectiveness of transfers in the Danish case, but in Ireland reflects a lower, though still relatively high, level of effectiveness together with a very high pre-transfer poverty rate for the unemployed. In Germany and even more so in the UK, the percentage of the unemployed lifted out of poverty by transfers in the mid-1990s is relatively low. In each case this is not because the pre-transfer poverty rate was low, but rather reflects the ineffectiveness of transfers in lifting the substantial numbers in pre-transfer poverty above the poverty line.

These overall results for the 50 per cent relative income poverty line in Tables 5.2 and 5.3 have been given for both the 'New' and the 'Old' OECD equivalence scale, and the pattern we have described holds irrespective of which of these scales is employed. The scale used does in some instances make a difference to the level of poverty rates for the unemployed—Ireland in both years and Sweden in the 1980s, for example—and to the impact of transfers—particularly for Germany in the 1980s and Ireland at both points in time. The choice between these two equivalence scales can influence the size of the measured differences between countries or the change between the mid-1980s and 1990s, but does not affect the general pattern described across countries or over time. Since there is little justification for focusing simply on the 50 per cent line, it is particularly important to see whether the same holds true when the level of the income poverty line is altered. Table 5.4 shows the pre- and post-transfer poverty rates for the unemployed with the 60 per cent relative income poverty line, and the proportion of the pre-transfer poor lifted above that line by transfers. Poverty rates are now of course substantially higher, with post-transfer rates in the mid-1990s reaching about 50 per cent in Germany and Ireland and over 60 per cent in the UK. The lowest rates are still for Denmark, where about 13 per cent of the unemployed were below the 60 per cent line in the mid-1980s, with France and Sweden once again in an intermediate position at about 35–40 per cent. As with the 50 per cent line, post-transfer poverty rates once again rose substantially between the mid-1980s and the mid-1990s in the UK and Germany, rose but to a lesser degree in Sweden, and remained

TABLE 5.4. *Poverty rates for unemployed before and after transfers and
impact of transfers, 1980s and 1990s* (60% poverty line)

	1980s			1990s		
	% poor before transfers	% poor after transfers	% of pre-transfer poor lifted out of poverty	% poor before transfers	% poor after transfers	% of pre-transfer poor lifted out of poverty
Denmark						
New	64.7	13.0	79.9	72.3	12.9	82.2
Old	64.6	11.8	81.7	72.3	12.2	83.1
France						
New	52.7	33.9	35.7	57.5	34.6	39.8
Old	53.3	35.1	34.1	58.7	36.6	37.6
Germany						
New	56.9	39.9	29.9	63.0	52.7	16.3
Old	56.8	39.9	29.8	62.1	49.3	20.6
Ireland						
New	77.6	53.8	30.7	83.0	52.8	36.4
Old	77.2	54.0	30.1	84.3	50.6	40.0
Sweden						
New	46.1	34.1	26.0	69.1	36.3	47.5
Old	42.7	33.7	21.1	65.9	41.9	36.4
UK						
New	58.7	46.8	20.3	65.9	61.5	6.7
Old	58.7	45.5	22.5	67.2	60.7	9.7

Notes: Poverty line 60% of mean equivalent income (new/old OECD equivalence scale).
Sources: See Table 5.1.

stable in Denmark and France. In Ireland the poverty rate for the unemployed now declines marginally whereas with the 50 per cent line it had fallen much more.

Table 5.4 also shows that, as with the 50 per cent income line, pre-transfer poverty rates once again went up between the mid-1980s and the mid-1990s in every country. The effectiveness of transfers in lifting the pre-transfer poor above the line is again greatest in Denmark, and rose between the mid-1980s and mid-1990s in France, Ireland, and particularly Sweden. In Germany and the UK effectiveness in these terms fell sharply, so that by the mid-1990s only 7–9 per cent of the pre-transfer poor unemployed were lifted above the line by transfers in the UK. The 60 per cent income line thus shows a very similar pattern, in terms of cross-country comparisons and changes over time, to that revealed by the 50 per cent line. The choice of 'New' versus 'Old' OECD equivalence scale again leaves this broad pattern unaffected; though in the case of Sweden, transfers appear a good deal more effective with the 'New' scale in both the mid-1980s and mid-1990s.

Nolan, Hauser, and Zoyem

TABLE 5.5. *Poverty rates for unemployed before and after transfers and impact of transfers, 1980s and 1990s* (40% poverty line)

	1980s			1990s		
	% poor before transfers	% poor after transfers	% of pre-transfer poor lifted out of poverty	% poor before transfers	% poor after transfers	% of pre-transfer poor lifted out of poverty
Denmark						
New	52.2	4.2	92.0	60.3	4.2	93.0
Old	52.3	3.9	92.5	60.1	3.8	93.7
France						
New	32.0	11.8	63.1	40.2	13.1	67.4
Old	31.9	14.9	53.3	40.2	14.3	64.4
Germany						
New	41.3	13.8	66.6	45.1	24.9	44.8
Old	41.2	11.9	71.1	44.5	24.2	45.6
Ireland						
New	69.5	6.7	90.4	74.8	4.0	94.7
Old	70.4	13.0	81.5	75.1	7.6	89.9
Sweden						
New	28.1	20.5	27.0	50.4	19.4	61.5
Old	24.7	13.5	45.3	50.4	19.4	61.5
UK						
New	48.5	9.9	79.6	55.0	29.0	47.3
Old	48.2	13.0	73.0	56.1	31.5	43.9

Notes: Poverty line 40% of mean equivalent income (new/old OECD equivalence scale).
Sources: See Table 5.1.

In order to further assess the sensitivity of the results to the level of the poverty line, Table 5.5 shows the corresponding figures with the poverty line set at 40 per cent of mean equivalent income. Post-transfer poverty rates are now quite low, although in the mid-1990s they still reach about 20 per cent for Sweden, 25 per cent for Germany, and 30 per cent for the UK. The ranking of countries in terms of post-transfer poverty rates in the mid-1990s thus differs somewhat from the 50 and 60 per cent lines. The UK still has the highest rate, but Germany and then Sweden are next highest, with France considerably lower, and Denmark and Ireland now with by far the lowest rates. These post-transfer poverty rates are now significantly higher than the mid-1980s only for Germany and the UK: Denmark, France, Ireland, and Sweden saw little change over the period.

With the 40 per cent line pre-transfer poverty rates once again went up between the mid-1980s and the mid-1990s in every country. The effectiveness of transfers in lifting the pre-transfer poor above the line is now greatest in Denmark and Ireland, where about 90 per cent of the pre-transfer poor are lifted above the poverty line. Effectiveness of transfers in this sense once again remained high between the mid-1980s and mid-1990s in Denmark, rose in France, Ireland, and particularly Sweden, and fell sharply in Germany and the UK where by the mid-1990s less than 50 per cent of the pre-transfer poor were lifted above this relatively low threshold by transfers.

THE ROLE OF UNEMPLOYMENT INSURANCE VERSUS OTHER CASH TRANSFERS

So far we have looked at the impact of social security cash transfers as a whole on poverty among the unemployed. It is of particular interest from a policy perspective to assess the role played by unemployment insurance (UI)—cash transfers to the unemployed arising from social insurance coverage of that contingency—as opposed to other parts of the social security system, in alleviating the impact of unemployment. In this section we therefore disaggregate cash transfers into these two distinct components and carry out an analysis of their impact on poverty rates for the unemployed. Since the household is being used as the income recipient unit, transfers other than UI include means-tested or universal payments being made either to the unemployed individual or to other household members; and social insurance payments other than UI being made to the unemployed individual or, more often, to other household members. Where more than one individual in the household is unemployed, UI itself may be received by other household members. Rather than focusing on transfers to the unemployed individual, we are looking at the impact of UI versus other transfers in lifting the equivalent income of the household in which the unemployed person lives above the poverty line.

To assess the effectiveness of UI versus other cash transfers, we derive two new income concepts: 'income before UI' and 'income before other transfers'. These are analogous to the 'income before all transfers' employed in the third section, and calculated in the same way by deducting the relevant component of transfers from disposable household income. Poverty rates based on each of these income aggregates are then derived, again using the same relative income poverty lines based on mean disposable income. From these poverty rates we estimate the impact which each of these components of cash transfers has on its own in reducing poverty rates for the unemployed, assuming that the other element remains unchanged at its actual level. These estimates are not distinct additive effects of each component on poverty risks, which would in any case depend entirely on an arbitrary assumption about which element 'comes first'. They do however provide a picture of the variation in the relative importance of each element across countries and over time.

Nolan, Hauser, and Zoyem

TABLE 5.6. *Impact of different types of transfers on poverty among the unemployed* (50% relative income line)

	1980s			1990s		
	impact of UI alone	impact of other transfers alone	impact of all transfers	impact of UI alone	impact of other transfers alone	impact of all transfers
Denmark						
New	62.2	15.7	87.0	64.6	13.5	88.6
Old	61.9	16.1	87.6	65.5	13.6	89.3
France						
New	23.3	18.3	44.5	24.7	20.4	52.4
Old	24.7	19.8	42.6	26.5	21.2	51.7
Germany						
New	11.8	31.6	47.0	19.6	22.5	32.0
Old	11.0	32.3	42.5	19.5	25.4	31.6
Ireland						
New	11.5	25.6	47.1	5.4	46.1	58.0
Old	11.9	23.2	42.8	5.7	50.1	62.8
Sweden						
New	0	26.4	26.4	36.9	13.2	51.2
Old	0	23.3	23.3	37.9	11.4	51.9
UK						
New	8.8	30.1	38.2	1.8	17.4	19.0
Old	8.9	31.3	40.4	2.6	15.5	17.7

Sources: See Table 5.1.

Using the 50 per cent relative income line, in the mid-1980s poverty rates in the absence of UI would have been much higher than poverty rates in the absence of other transfers only in Denmark. The converse was true in Germany, Ireland, Sweden, and the UK: in that sense, transfers other than UI were more important than UI for the households of the unemployed. For France, poverty rates before UI were slightly higher than those before other transfers.

Derived from these poverty rates, Table 5.6 shows the percentage of the pre-transfer poor lifted out of poverty by the different transfer types. In the mid-1980s, the percentage lifted out of poverty by UI alone is seen to be much less than the percentage lifted out by other transfers in the case of Germany, Ireland, Sweden, and UK: indeed in the case of Sweden UI taken alone had little or no impact. In Denmark, on the other hand, UI has a much greater impact than other transfers.

By the mid-1990s, as illustrated in Fig. 5.1, the most striking change is that the impact of UI taken alone had fallen very sharply in Ireland and

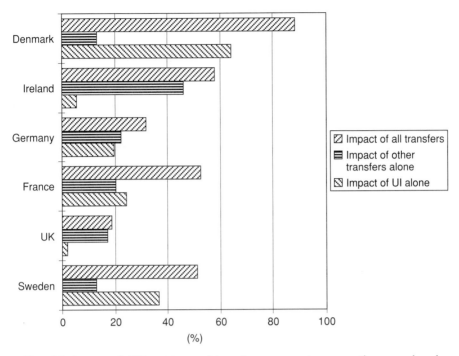

FIG. 5.1. Impact of different types of transfers on poverty among the unemployed,
mid-1990s

Note: 50% Relative income line, new OECD scale.

Sources: See Table 5.1.

the UK. Indeed in both these countries, most certainly in the UK, UI now
has very little impact indeed in lifting the unemployed above the 50 per cent
poverty line. These two countries differ markedly however as far as trends
in the impact of other transfers are concerned. In the Irish case, other
transfers have a much greater impact in the mid-1990s than they did in
the mid-1980s, so much so that the overall effectiveness of transfers rose
considerably over the period, as seen in the previous section. In the UK,
other transfers declined in effectiveness just as much as UI, producing the
result already described whereby the overall effectiveness of transfers fell very
sharply.

In the other countries, the impact of UI taken alone rose in Germany,
and especially in Sweden between the mid-1980s and mid-1990s, and
remained stable in France and, at a very high level, in Denmark. Other
transfers played a smaller role in lifting the unemployed out of poverty in
Germany and Sweden, and to some extent in Denmark, in the mid-1990s
compared to the mid-1980s but remained stable in France. The overall

pattern over the period is therefore of little change in the impact of UI versus other transfers, taken alone, in the case of France and Denmark. For Sweden the increase in overall effectiveness of transfers reflected an increasing impact of UI, whereas for Germany the marked decline in overall effectiveness reflected a fall in the impact on poverty of transfers other than UI.

Once again it is important to assess whether these results hold over alternative poverty lines. With the 60 per cent relative income line, the pattern is very similar indeed to that seen with the 50 per cent line. UI had a greater impact than other transfers in Denmark and to a lesser extent in France; its importance relative to other transfers rose between the mid-1980s and the mid-1990s in Sweden and to a lesser extent in Germany, and the impact of UI declined over the period from an already low base in Ireland and the UK. Once again this was more than offset in the Irish case by an increased impact for other transfers, but compounded in the UK by a fall in the already-low impact of those transfers. With the 40 per cent relative income line, the main deviation from this pattern is that the impact of UI compared with other transfers is lower in Germany in the mid-1990s and in the UK in both periods than it was with the higher income lines.

IMPACT OF TRANSFERS BY DURATION AND GENDER

Having looked at the effects of cash transfers on poverty rates for the unemployed as a group in each country, we now distinguish among the unemployed on the basis of key characteristics which may influence those effects: the duration of unemployment experienced, and gender. In doing so we present results for poverty rates using only the 50 per cent income line and the 'New' OECD equivalence scale.

As far as unemployment duration is concerned, for most countries we focus on the duration of the current spell of unemployment, and distinguish where possible durations of up to 6 months, 6–12 months, and 12 months and over. In the case of France, at this stage we are only able to distinguish spells of up to 12 months from those of 12 months and over. In the case of Germany total unemployment experienced in the previous year rather than duration of current spell is used, distinguishing where this total was up to 6 months or 6–12 months. Table 5.7 shows pre- and post-transfer poverty rates, and the percentage of pre-transfer poor lifted above the 50 per cent line by total transfers, by duration.

This shows first that post-transfer poverty rates are almost invariably higher for longer than shorter durations, Denmark being the exception. Pre-transfer poverty rates are also almost always higher for longer durations,

TABLE 5.7. *Poverty rates for unemployed before and after transfers and impact of transfers, 1980s and 1990s, by duration*

	1980s			1990s		
	% poor before transfers	% poor after transfers	% of pre-transfer poor lifted out of poverty	% poor before transfers	% poor after transfers	% of pre-transfer poor lifted out of poverty
Denmark						
<6 months	44.5	8.4	81.1	51.7	9.4	81.8
6–12 months	87.8	6.2	92.9	86.7	5.2	94.0
>12 months	97.4	4.7	95.2	97.1	4.1	95.8
France						
<12 months	32.6	19.1	41.4	34.2	16.6	51.5
>12 months	49.7	26.4	46.9	63.0	29.6	53.0
Germany						
<6 months	28.4	13.9	51.1	42.8	28.0	34.6
6–12 months	69.3	37.9	45.3	69.2	48.3	30.2
Ireland						
<6 months	65.8	28.1	57.3	66.9	28.2	57.8
6–12 months	68.2	33.3	51.2	76.0	10.9	85.7
>12 months	76.0	41.8	45.0	85.9	39.1	54.5
Sweden						
<12 months	37.0	28.2	23.8	62.6	30.0	52.1
>12 months	37.5	20.0	46.7	60.0	33.3	44.5
UK						
<6 months	34.5	19.5	43.5	38.5	28.8	25.2
6–12 months	53.1	31.2	41.2	44.9	36.2	19.4
>12 months	70.3	45.6	35.1	77.0	63.9	17.0

Note: Poverty line 50% of mean equivalent income (new OECD equivalence scale).
Sources: See Table 5.1.

the exception in this instance being Sweden. The effect of transfers, measured by the percentage of pre-transfer poor unemployed lifted above the poverty line by transfers, does not however have a consistent relationship with duration. Transfers are more effective in lifting those with short than long durations out of poverty in the case of Germany and the UK, but the opposite is true for France and Denmark, and effectiveness is greatest for those with intermediate-length durations in Ireland in the mid-1990s.

We can again distinguish the impact of UI and other transfers on the unemployed by duration. In the case of Ireland and the UK, UI has more impact on the shorter rather than longer durations, reflecting the fact that insurance-based transfers are time-limited and most of those with longer durations will have exhausted entitlement. For Denmark, and for France in the mid-1980s, however, UI has a greater impact in lifting the unemployed

Nolan, Hauser, and Zoyem

TABLE 5.8. *Poverty rates for unemployed, by gender, before and after transfers and impact of transfers, 1980s and 1990s*

	1980s			1990s		
	% poor before transfers	% poor after transfers	% of pre-transfer poor lifted out of poverty	% poor before transfers	% poor after transfers	% of pre-transfer poor lifted out of poverty
Denmark						
Male	58.0	7.4	87.2	67.7	7.8	88.5
Female	58.9	7.9	86.6	65.5	7.4	88.7
France						
Male	45.8	25.9	43.4	57.9	29.5	49.1
Female	38.3	20.5	46.5	42.3	18.6	56.0
Germany						
Male	51.4	23.7	53.9	62.2	42.9	31.0
Female	43.7	27.9	36.2	44.5	29.6	33.5
Ireland						
Male	76.5	42.7	44.2	81.6	38.4	52.9
Female	53.6	15.7	70.7	74.3	19.6	73.6
Sweden						
Male	31.8	30.2	5.0	74.0	35.1	52.6
Female	40.9	24.4	40.3	44.9	23.5	47.7
UK						
Male	61.1	39.2	35.8	66.3	52.0	21.6
Female	37.6	20.3	46.0	51.5	44.9	12.8

Note: Poverty line 50% of mean equivalent income (new OECD equivalence scale).
Sources: See Table 5.1.

out of poverty for long rather than short durations. For Germany and for France in the mid-1990s, UI has about the same impact on long as on short durations.

Turning to gender, Table 5.8 shows pre- and post-transfer poverty rates and the impact of total cash transfers for male and female unemployed, again with the 50 per cent relative income poverty line. Generally, unemployed men have higher post-transfer poverty rates than women; exceptions are Denmark, where poverty rates are about the same for male and female unemployed, and Germany in the mid-1980s, where unemployed women had slightly higher poverty rates. This mostly reflects lower pre-transfer poverty rates for the female unemployed—everywhere except Sweden in the mid-1980s—though cash transfers are also more effective for women in the case of Ireland. Cash transfers are more effective for men than women for the UK in the mid-1990s, but this is not enough to offset the gap in their pre-transfer poverty rates.

We can again also look at the impact of UI versus other transfers by gender. In the case of Denmark and France there is little difference between male and female unemployed in these terms. For Germany, both UI and other transfers have less impact for women than men, while for Ireland the opposite is true. For the UK other transfers had a greater impact for women than men in the mid-1980s, but by the mid-1990s this had been reversed.

POVERTY AND THE ROLE OF SOCIAL PROTECTION

What is the relationship between the results we have presented on the impact of cash transfers on poverty among the unemployed, and the nature of the welfare regimes in the different countries included in the study? The relationship between welfare regime and the extent of poverty and unemployment is itself of course highly controversial. Much of this debate, particularly among economists, has concentrated on the links between the level of unemployment and the generosity of welfare provision for the unemployed. In this chapter however we have, in a sense, taken the level of unemployment in different countries or at different points in time as given, and sought to measure the effectiveness of cash transfers in lifting the unemployed out of poverty. How does this vary with welfare regime?

With reference to the welfare regimes discussed in Gallie and Paugam's introductory chapter, the six countries included in the study fall fairly neatly into three groups. Sweden and Denmark represent countries that aim to provide a high level of protection of living standards to all unemployed people—the universalistic model. Germany and France have systems based on the protection of living standards of those with longer-term experience of employment and minimum protection for those who have not—the employment-centred model. The UK and Ireland have systems of universal minimum protection with an increasing emphasis on means-testing—the liberal/minimal model. Some relevant differences in family structures were also noted in that discussion, in some instances distinguishing countries with similar welfare regimes—Ireland and the UK for example, or France and Germany have rather different family structures.

How well have these different systems responded to the challenges of the changing labour market between the mid-1980s and the mid-1990s? The results presented here have shown that in the mid-1980s cash transfers were more effective in lifting the pre-transfer poor unemployed out of poverty in Denmark than any of the other countries. Denmark maintained that high level of effectiveness through to the mid-1990s, at which point post-transfer poverty rates—with the 50 per cent relative income line—among the unemployed were still below 10 per cent. The situation in Sweden, where unemployment rose very sharply from a very low level over the period, was quite different. Cash transfers had been relatively ineffective in the early 1980s in dealing with poverty among the small number then unemployed. By the early 1990s transfers had become more effective in those terms, but the post-transfer poverty rate among the unemployed was still much higher than in Denmark at 30 per cent below half average income. The fact that the data available for Sweden allowed us to cover only up to 1991 is particularly unfortunate, since unemployment had only begun its very rapid increase there at that point.

France and Germany, with broadly similar welfare regimes, also had diverging experiences over the period. In France the effectiveness of cash transfers increased, so post-transfer poverty rates for the unemployed remained stable, despite an increase in pre-transfer poverty. For Germany, effectiveness fell so that post-transfer poverty rose quite sharply.

In the final group of Ireland and the UK, the divergence in experience was if anything even more pronounced. The two countries began the period with Ireland having a somewhat more effective cash transfer system for the unemployed but, because of much higher levels of pre-transfer poverty, still having higher post-transfer poverty among the unemployed. Between the mid-1980s and mid-1990s pre-transfer poverty rose in both countries—as it did in the other four—but the transfer systems responded very differently. The Irish cash transfer system became more effective in lifting the pre-transfer poor unemployed out of poverty, while the UK saw a marked decline in the effectiveness of its transfer system. As a result, poverty rose sharply for the unemployed in the UK, whereas it fell in Ireland. The results illustrate how similar institutional structures in terms of broad welfare regime can yet produce radically diverging responses to a changing labour market.

These changes over time in the measured effectiveness of social protection systems in alleviating poverty among the unemployed could reflect changes in the structures of these systems, but could also be a product of changes in the demographic make-up of the unemployed themselves. If the composition of the unemployed shifted over time towards groups for which social protection is relatively ineffective, then this could produce a fall in overall effectiveness, and conversely for a shift towards groups for which social protection is relatively effective in the country in question. For example, if the system is less effective in lifting the long-term than the short-term unemployed out of poverty, and the proportion of unemployed who are long-term increases, then this would, all other factors being equal, produce a decline in overall effectiveness.

Changes in the composition of the unemployed in each of the countries included in this study over the period in question have been examined to assess the possible importance of this effect in terms of both duration and the male/female balance. Changing composition, but holding effectiveness fixed for each duration by gender group, one can calculate how overall effectiveness would then have moved over the period. This shows that while there were some significant shifts in composition, this on its own would not have made a major contribution to explaining the observed changes in overall effectiveness. In some countries, indeed, composition shifts would have pushed effectiveness in the opposite direction to that observed—in Ireland, for example, the proportion of the unemployed who were long-term rose substantially, which would in itself have produced lower effectiveness, whereas in fact as we have seen overall effectiveness rose sharply.

This brings us back to the social protection structures themselves, and the way they changed over the period. Some important structural changes did take place in certain countries. In the case of France, the most significant was the introduction of the *Revenu Minimum d'Insertion* (RMI) in 1988, providing a safety-net payment for, among others, some of those without entitlement to unemployment-related income support. Income support for housing costs was also extended over the period and would have become more important for the unemployed. In Sweden, a variety of changes in the unemployment compensation system occurred over the period, but perhaps the most important factor in the current context is that membership in the unemployment insurance funds increased substantially over the 1980s and 1990s so that a growing proportion of the unemployed has been covered by regular unemployment insurance (Bjorklund and Holmlund 1989). As a consequence, the percentage of the unemployed in the samples used here who received unemployment benefits rose from 19 per cent in 1981 to 64 per cent in 1991. In Germany, in 1994 the duration of unemployment assistance was limited in certain circumstances to one year. The UK introduced a series of measures affecting the structure of unemployment compensation: for example in 1988 entitlement to unemployment benefit was tied more closely to recent employment, and in 1989 testing that recipients were actively seeking work was made more rigorous. In 1996, just after the end of our period, unemployment benefit duration was cut from 12 to 6 months and transition to Job Seeker's Allowance set in train. In Denmark, by contrast, the period of entitlement to unemployment benefit was extended in 1994. In Ireland it became easier for women to obtain means-tested unemployment assistance from 1986, leading to increasing numbers in receipt of assistance over the 1987–1994 period examined here.

It would be a mistake however to focus entirely on changes in social protection structures in seeking to understand the evolution of anti-poverty effectiveness for the unemployed over the period. In the case of Ireland and the UK, the results in fact illustrate how similar institutional structures, developing over time in quite a similar fashion, can yet produce radically different outcomes. Each evolved over the 1990s towards greater reliance on means-testing and a reduced role for social insurance-based unemployment compensation, but the crucial factor has quite simply been in trends in the level of cash transfer paid relative to other incomes. In the Irish case, transfers to the unemployed, particularly means-tested support, rose a good deal more rapidly than average household income over the period. In the UK the level of safety-net support lagged significantly behind mean incomes: see the detailed comparison in Callan and Sutherland (1997). It is this, rather than the increased role of means-testing *per se* which had the most direct impact on poverty rates for the unemployed and produced such divergent trends in the two countries.

The results presented here have highlighted the scale of differences in the effectiveness of various European social protection systems in alleviating poverty among the unemployed in the mid-1980s, and in how well they coped with the challenges posed by the labour market in this respect in the subsequent decade. They have shown that similar institutional structures in terms of broad welfare regime can yet produce radically diverging responses to a changing labour market. Differences in the manner in which governments operate within the structure of their welfare regimes, as well as in the nature of those regimes, clearly play a crucial part in understanding the changing effects of social protection. In a framework where income poverty lines linked to average incomes are the point of reference in measuring poverty among those depending on social protection cash transfers, the extent to which those support levels keep up with increases in incomes in the broader society is of central importance.

PART 2

Unemployment and Labour Market Marginalization

6

Unemployment, Gender, and Attitudes to Work

Duncan Gallie and Susanne Alm

For some, vulnerability to unemployment and, even more, vulnerability to long-term unemployment are seen as strongly linked to deficiencies in employment commitment among unemployed people. There are different views about the causes of this, but perhaps the most influential is the argument that it is the result of a calculative response to the incentives or disincentives for work provided by welfare systems. This has inspired, in several countries, an attempt by governments to cut back on welfare payments to the unemployed. Yet despite the prevalence and influence of such views, the evidence that has been adduced to date to support the underlying assumption that there is a problem of the 'work motivation' of the unemployed is remarkably slim, and there is correspondingly little well-grounded evidence about its determinants. This chapter sets out to use data from a new European survey to provide a more satisfactory description of the work attitudes of the unemployed, and to make an initial assessment of how far these are affected by the characteristics of benefit systems.

The theoretical drive behind most of the research in this area has come very much from the work of economists. The assumption is that work is inherently a disutility, so that the willingness to work will crucially depend on the structure of financial incentives (Lane 1991). Where the welfare system provides high replacement rates, it is suggested, this will lead both to a lower commitment to having a job and to greater inflexibility over job choice. In some countries, studies have been carried out using longitudinal microdata. Although attitudes to work are central to the explanation offered, they are rarely studied directly. The most relevant evidence is thought to lie in the strength of the relationship between the replacement ratio and the duration of unemployment. Even with respect to this rather indirect test, the results have been far from clear-cut (Atkinson and Mogensen 1993).

Arguably, however, the most interesting test of the impact of different levels of welfare provision should come from cross-cultural analysis. As has been seen in the Introduction, there are very striking differences in the extent to which national welfare systems protect the standard of living of people who are unable to find work. At one extreme, the welfare systems of the 'Northern' European countries have provided relatively good levels of support for a high proportion of unemployed people. At the other end of the spectrum, there are countries such as Italy and Greece, where public financial assistance for the unemployed is minimal. Clearly, if the level of financial assistance is a major determinant of work attitudes, we would expect to see very substantial variations between countries.

The implications of welfare systems may also vary depending on gender differences in work attitudes that are rooted in broader socialization processes, relating for instance to family values. There have been very wide variations between countries in women's levels of labour market participation and this may reflect, or have contributed to, substantial national differences in women's psychological commitment to employment. It is plausible that there is a spectrum of women's attitudes to employment, which potentially ranges from a point where employment is regarded as women's primary role in life, to one where it is secondary in importance to the domestic role. This suggests an alternative hypothesis, namely that women's work motivation is more sensitive to the effects of the level of benefit in societies which culturally value more traditional gender role patterns.

Clearly any serious examination of these issues requires comparable micro-level data for all EU countries, providing information about individuals' work attitudes, their benefit status, and their attitudes towards gender roles. It also requires a sample that includes sufficient numbers of unemployed people to carry out country-level analysis. In the past, this has simply not been available. However, in 1996, the EU carried out a survey—the *Employment in Europe Survey*—that does open the possibility for a closer examination of these issues.[1] It provides an unweighted sample of 7926 people in employment, both employed and self-employed, and 5134 unemployed people across the full range of member states in the EU. The samples were randomly selected, and were designed to provide a nationally representative picture of the relevant population in each country.

This chapter will address the issue of employment commitment and then turn to that of flexibility over job choice. In each case, we will first consider the general characteristics of the work attitudes of the unemployed and then examine in more detail the way these relate to welfare assistance on the one hand, and to cultural assumptions about gender roles on the other. However, there are three initial problems that need to be addressed: the nature of the work attitudes on which the analysis should focus, the way in which unemployment should be defined, and the principles for classifying welfare regimes with respect to the unemployed.

Arguments about work motivation sometimes confuse two different dimensions of people's attitudes to work. The first is the extent to which

---

[1] The survey was carried out as part of Eurobarometer 44.3. For technical details, see Gallie (1999: 164–5).

they are committed to employment as such. This is what is usually meant when it is suggested that the unemployed are for some reason not socialized into a strong work ethic, and therefore are to some degree self-selected into unemployment. Such employment commitment is usually conceived as independent of the purely financial reasons for working: it is a desire to work for its own sake. The second dimension of work attitudes relates to how flexible people are about the types of job that they would be willing to take. For instance, do they have a very strong commitment to a particular type of occupation, such that they would be very hesitant before taking a different type of job? It is difficult to draw any simple implications about employment commitment from the flexibility of attitudes towards job choice. Clearly, at one extreme, a high degree of rigidity about types of work might indicate low employment commitment, if there was little chance of obtaining the preferred type of work. But, equally, in cases where job opportunities were less bleak, a concern to retain a given skill-level might reflect strong intrinsic employment commitment, even though it might well result in a longer period of job search.

The second issue is the definition of unemployment. The most commonly used definition for comparative purposes is that based on the ILO criteria. People are regarded as unemployed if they are without work, actively looking for work, and available for work. While the general advantages of the ILO approach are unquestionable, it raises a difficulty with respect to the issue of work motivation. In order to be considered to be unemployed people must have been looking for work in the recent past—say the last month. This tends to exclude unemployed people who may have become discouraged from job search, a particularly important category for arguments about work motivation among the unemployed. Our procedure then, has been to take as unemployed, for the analysis of employment commitment, all those who *either* defined themselves as unemployed *or* met the ILO criteria. When we move on to the issue of flexibility about job choice, we focus exclusively upon those who are looking for work, that is the ILO unemployed, as the questions are necessarily framed in this context.

Finally, there is the question of the criteria that should be used to classify welfare provision for assessing arguments about their motivational effects for the unemployed. In broad terms it is the generosity of the welfare system, rather than its regime type as discussed in the introductory chapter, that is regarded as potentially corrosive of work motivation. Our approach has been to try to isolate for comparison a limited number of countries that stand out as relatively generous or ungenerous. We take two measures as of primary importance for the classification. We assume that for a disincentive effect to be present, there must be a reasonable chance of getting some type of assistance in the first place and that it should offer a relatively high level of replacement of salary. The first measure then is whether or not a significant proportion of the unemployed are eligible for assistance. As can be seen in Table 1.3, there are four countries that stand out on this basis as having a low level of welfare provision, with less than one-third of the unemployed in receipt of benefits: Italy, Greece, Spain, and Portugal. There is a considerable gap between these four and the next lowest ranked country—France with 45 per cent coverage—so they do appear to form a distinct constellation.

The second criteria, which we apply to those countries with an acceptable level of coverage, is a summary measure of the generosity of the replacement rate devised by the OECD (OECD 1994). It is based on the replacement rates for single people during the first year of unemployment, averaging the rate for two earnings levels—average and two-thirds of average earnings.[2] On the basis of this measure, it is possible to distinguish, among countries with reasonable levels of coverage, a group of countries with relatively high replacement rates of 70 per cent or higher, namely Denmark, The Netherlands, and Sweden, from a group with relatively low replacement rates of less than 40 per cent: Germany, Ireland, and the UK. As the figures for Germany appear to be particularly uncertain, being estimated from the net figures, we leave this country aside in the final selection of the contrasting types of welfare regime.

Our final classification, taking account both of coverage and the replacement rate, gives us three relatively 'high welfare' societies: Denmark, The Netherlands, and Sweden; and six 'low welfare' societies: Italy, Greece, Portugal, Spain, Ireland, and the UK. In terms of the typology presented in Chapter 1, the former include the countries closer to the universalistic model, but also one country nearer to the employment-centred type. The latter include the countries closest to both the sub-protective and liberal minimalist types.

EMPLOYMENT COMMITMENT

The Level of Employment Commitment

Is it the case that the unemployed were less committed to employment than those in work, and therefore may be to some degree self-selected into unemployment? We take as our principal measure an indicator of non-financial employment commitment—that is to say the desire to have some type of

---

[2] The OECD also produces a measure that gives an unweighted average replacement ratio across different household types and durations of unemployment. However, the unemployed are drawn disproportionately among single people and the unweighted measure makes little sense for a country such as Sweden where the regulations provide a cut-off of one year together with the provision of employment or training opportunities.

TABLE 6.1. *Comparison of employment commitment of the employed and unemployed*

	% committed		
	Unemployed	In Work	Unemp. minus In Work
Austria	66.7	54.0	12.7
Belgium	60.4	44.4	16.0
Denmark	82.8	76.3	6.5
Finland	57.5	55.2	2.3
France	59.4	36.9	22.5
Germany E	69.0	61.2	7.8
Germany W	48.7	43.2	5.5
Great Britain	78.3	53.0	25.3
Greece	74.8	49.4	25.4
Ireland	71.4	62.1	9.3
Italy	75.6	42.7	32.9
Netherlands	80.4	67.3	13.1
Portugal	70.7	58.8	11.9
Spain	51.7	35.8	15.9
Sweden	78.7	75.9	2.8
EU15	63.7	48.0	16.7
N	5144	7783	

Source: Employment in Europe Survey (Eurobarometer 44.3).

paid job irrespective of financial need. The survey includes a well-tried indicator of this, a question that has been used both in the American 'Quality of Working Life' surveys and in a number of British studies. There is a variant for the employed and for the unemployed. For the employed, it asks: 'If you were to get enough money to live as comfortably as you would like for the rest of your life, would you continue to work, not necessarily in your present job, or would you stop working?' For the unemployed the format was: 'If you were to get enough money to live as comfortably as you would like for the rest of your life, would you want to work somewhere or would you want to remain without a job?'

Table 6.1 presents the proportions of unemployed people and of people in work, who would have wished to continue in a paid job even if there were no financial need. A first point to note is the high level of commitment of unemployed people in the EU as a whole. Nearly two-thirds of the unemployed said that they would want to work somewhere even if there were no financial necessity.

Further, it is interesting that not only were the unemployed highly committed in absolute terms but they were more committed than people who were currently in work. As can be seen in Table 6.1, only 48 per cent of those who were in a job would have wished to continue to work irrespective of

financial necessity, compared to 64 per cent of the unemployed. What is particularly striking is the systematic nature of this pattern at country level. In
all of the individual country samples the unemployed are more committed
than the employed.

This degree of consistency of pattern is relatively rare in comparative
research. It is difficult to escape the conclusion that unemployment in some
way heightens people's awareness of the advantages of employment. Given
the sheer diversity of different types of welfare system across these societies,
it seems rather unlikely that it simply reflects the institutional pressures
associated with unemployment benefit regulations. The effect is strong even
in societies where public welfare provision for the unemployed is fairly negligible—for instance, Italy. More plausibly it may be that unemployment
highlights some of the less visible benefits of employment that those in work
tend to take for granted. Marie Jahoda (1982) for instance has suggested
that employment provides an important source of psychological stability
through providing a time structure, participation in a collective purpose and
identity, and a regular required source of activity. It may be that it is only
when there is a rupture in the continuity of employment that people are in
a position to fully assess effects of this type.

It might be the case, however, that those with low motivation were disproportionately concentrated among the long-term unemployed. This
might reflect either processes of self-selection or gradual demoralization as
unemployment lengthens. To assess this, commitment was examined by
length of experience of unemployment. The decision to include self-defined
unemployed people, even if they did not meet the ILO criteria of seeking
work, made it necessary to use a measure of the overall time spent unemployed during the previous five years, as this was the only indicator available for this category. However, the analysis was replicated with very similar
results for the sub-sample of the 'ILO unemployed', using a measure of the
duration of the *current* spell of unemployment.

Taking the EU as a whole, if those that have been unemployed for less
than a year are compared with those unemployed for a year or more (Table
6.2) the proportion committed to employment is 3 percentage points lower
among the long-term unemployed. Taking the duration of the current spell
of unemployment for the ILO unemployed, the difference is even smaller,
the comparable figures being 65 per cent and 66 per cent. Further, a more
detailed breakdown for current duration shows that there is very little difference at all between those unemployed for less than a year and those
unemployed for between one and two years, at 66 and 67 per cent respectively.
The lower level of commitment is primarily among people who have been
unemployed for over two years (60 per cent). The countries in which the lower
commitment of the long-term unemployed is most marked are Belgium,
Denmark, Finland, Greece, The Netherlands, and Portugal. The salient fact,

TABLE 6.2. *Employment commitment by duration of unemployment*

	% Committed		% Committed (ILO unemployed only)	
	Unemployed <12 months in last 5 yrs	Unemployed 12+ months in last 5 yrs	Unemployed <12 months current spell	Unemployed 12+ months current spell
Austria	61.9	71.4	68.6	71.4
Belgium	67.9	61.2	75.0	66.7
Denmark	89.5	81.6	88.2	82.4
Finland	77.1	48.2	75.8	40.0
France	63.6	59.0	60.3	62.1
Germany E	69.1	69.8	71.9	67.1
Germany W	49.7	48.5	49.2	52.3
Great Britain	67.4	80.5	69.6	89.9
Greece	86.7	73.5	77.4	73.9
Ireland	77.8	75.0	65.0	81.3
Italy	73.3	74.5	77.2	75.0
Netherlands	88.5	78.0	84.6	75.5
Portugal	78.9	68.9	75.8	70.8
Spain	53.2	49.5	53.9	49.7
Sweden	80.5	75.5	81.1	82.9
EU15	65.0	62.1	66.2	64.6
N=	1463	3032	2556	1660

Source: Employment in Europe Survey (Eurobarometer 44.3).

however, remains that, with the exception of Finland, even these countries share the general pattern that the long-term unemployed have a higher level of commitment than those in work.

The Tables examined so far do not allow for the fact that there may be differences in the background characteristics of the unemployed and those in work which may be independently related to work motivation, for instance differences in age, sex, and class background. To examine this we have carried out a logistic regression analysis for the pooled European data controlling for these factors. The first two rows of Table 6.3 show the coefficients for ILO and non-ILO unemployed net of such influences. The results confirm that the ILO unemployed are significantly more likely to be committed to employment than those in work. The coefficient for the non-ILO unemployed is also positive, but it is only just statistically significant at 0.05. The third and fourth rows of Table 6.3 repeat the analysis distinguishing the short-term from the long-term unemployed. Again both categories of the unemployed are more likely to be committed than people in work, although the effect is a little stronger among those who have been unemployed for less than a year. It seems clear that any general characterization

TABLE 6.3. *Coefficients for effect of unemployment status on employment commitment*

	B	Sig.
ILO Unemployed	0.58	***
Non-ILO Unemployed	0.13	*
Short-term Unemployed	0.53	***
Long-term Unemployed	0.45	***

Note: The coefficients are drawn from a logistic regression based on the pooled sample of those in work and unemployed (N = 14247) controlling for age, sex, country and class. Ref = those in work, * = $P < 0.05$, ** = $P < 0.01$, *** = $P < 0.001$.
Source: Employment in Europe Survey (Eurobarometer 44.3).

of the European unemployed as a weakly motivated group, with little interest in employment, fits poorly with the evidence available.

Welfare Systems and Employment Commitment

Even if there are no general grounds for considering the unemployed deficient in employment commitment, do the variations between countries suggest that the relative generosity of the welfare system may have an important impact on work motivation? Taking the simple figures of the proportions committed to employment (Table 6.1), there is certainly no indication that relatively generous welfare systems give rise to low motivation among the unemployed. Employment commitment was highest among the unemployed in Denmark (83 per cent) and The Netherlands (80 per cent), while Sweden came in third position (79 per cent). Overall, welfare states that were designed to provide a relatively high level of protection of living standards were associated with high levels of employment commitment.

Exactly the same picture emerges if the analysis is refined to take account of the fact that there may be compositional differences between the unemployed in the different countries in terms of age, sex, and class. It is necessary to take one country as the reference point for comparison. In Table 6.4 the coefficients for any particular country indicate whether the unemployed in that country have a relatively high or low probability of commitment compared to those in Belgium. Belgium represented a case of relatively low commitment, and a majority of the countries emerge as significantly higher. It is only in West Germany that the unemployed have a lower probability of being committed, while the unemployed in France, Spain and Austria are very similar to the Belgians. But turning to the countries with positive coefficients, it is clear that the largest coefficients, suggesting particularly high levels of commitment among the unemployed, are for The Netherlands and

TABLE 6.4. *Coefficients for employment commitment of the unemployed relative to Belgium*

	All Unemployed		Unemployed on Benefit	
	B	Sig.	B	Sig.
Austria	0.12	n.s.	0.11	n.s.
Belgium	ref.		ref.	
Denmark	0.49	***	0.66	***
Finland	0.49	***	0.68	***
France	−0.20	n.s.	−0.09	n.s.
Germany E	0.42	**	0.59	**
Germany W	−0.64	***	−0.67	***
Great Britain	0.55	***	1.18	***
Greece	0.48	***	0.76	n.s.
Ireland	0.41	**	0.84	n.s.
Italy	0.31	*	−0.28	n.s.
Netherlands	0.89	***	1.00	***
Portugal	0.44	**	0.68	*
Spain	−0.24	n.s.	0.13	n.s.
Sweden	0.82	***	1.00	***

Note: Controlling for sex, age and class. Sample Size = 6347 for whole sample, 3213 for those on benefit. * = P < 0.05, ** = P < 0.01, *** = P < 0.001, n.s. = not significant.
Source: Employment in Europe Survey (Eurobarometer 44.3).

Sweden, while Denmark is fifth in order. Again, there is nothing in this pattern to suggest that relatively generous welfare provision for the unemployed leads to lower levels of employment commitment.

The comparison can be focused more closely by restricting the analysis to unemployed people who were in receipt of some type of financial benefit, since these are the people whose attitudes are most likely to be affected. While the coefficients are generally higher, the overall conclusions are similar. Britain certainly stands out as the country where employment commitment was highest, which is consistent with the view that low replacement ratios increase motivation. But the coefficients for The Netherlands and Sweden, countries with high replacement rates, are also relatively high. There is, then, no clear relationship between relative welfare generosity and work motivation.

The Influence of Perceived Replacement Ratios

Such comparisons between countries can give only an approximate view of replacement ratios at the individual level. Country welfare systems tend to be classified in terms of their implications for supposedly 'typical' types of unemployed people, for instance someone earning the average industrial wage and having a number of years of continuous employment in their previous

TABLE 6.5. *Effect of receipt of benefits and of perceived replacement rate on employment commitment*

	B	Sig.
Receiving Benefits (ref. not receiving)	−0.05	n.s.
Comparison with income in work (only those on benefit)		
Benefit income same or better	ref.	
Benefit income a little lower	−0.01	n.s.
Benefit income much lower	0.09	n.s.

Notes: Controlling for age, sex, country, and class.
Source: Employment in Europe Survey (Eurobarometer 44.3).

job. But in practice the implications of given benefit systems for the maintenance of resources may vary substantially depending on previous employment history.

The current survey does not offer the detailed information about incomes in and out of work that would be needed to calculate replacement ratios. It does however give us a broad measure of people's perception of how far their benefits compensate for lost income. Arguably, it is the perception of the differences between income from benefits and income from a job which is the critical factor affecting work motivation. Those who received benefit were asked: 'Compared with the pay you would get if you had the type of job you are looking for, would you say that your income from this financial assistance is: much higher, a little higher, about the same, a little lower or much lower?' Those on benefit have been divided into three groups. The first were those who said that their benefit income was either higher or the same as they could earn in a job. The second group consisted of those who reported that their benefit income was a little lower, and the third was comprised of those who said that it was much lower.

If the economic deprivation theory of work motivation is correct, it could be expected that those who felt that their income was much lower on benefit than in work would be significantly more committed to employment than those who felt that unemployment made little financial difference. This was tested with regression analysis, controlling for age, sex, country and class. Two regressions were fitted: the first tested whether receiving benefit had an effect on commitment. The second, restricted to those who did receive benefit, contrasted those who thought they had low replacement ratios with those who thought that benefits provided a similar income to what they would receive if they had a job. It can be seen from Table 6.5, that there was no general effect of receiving benefit: those on benefit were as committed to employment as those who were not. Moreover, among the unemployed who

TABLE 6.6. *Comparison of employment commitment of the unemployed, by gender*

	% committed, unemployed	
	Men	Women
Austria	60.0	78.3
Belgium	65.4	56.6
Denmark	84.0	84.4
Finland	56.7	59.3
France	58.5	60.2
Germany E	68.0	69.6
Germany W	52.5	42.5
Great Britain	72.3	86.9
Greece	72.9	76.2
Ireland	74.2	66.7
Italy	67.1	84.0
Netherlands	77.5	83.1
Portugal	76.0	67.3
Spain	46.4	57.0
Sweden	75.9	80.5
EU15	59.7	68.0
N	2661	2483

Source: Employment in Europe Survey (Eurobarometer 44.3).

did receive benefit, the level of income replacement by the benefit system had no importance for employment commitment.

Gender, Traditionalism, and Employment Commitment

It has been suggested that unemployed women may show lower levels of commitment to employment than unemployed men because they have the possibility of sustaining an alternative self-identity based on their domestic or caring responsibilities. However, it can be seen in (Table 6.6) that, at the level of the EU as a whole, unemployed women were more likely than unemployed men to say that they would want a job even if they did not need the money: 68 per cent compared with 60 per cent. Moreover, this was the case for all countries other than Belgium, 'West' Germany, Ireland, and Portugal. The overall differences by sex, however, did not reach statistical significance once country, age, and class were controlled. So the safest conclusion is that there was no effective difference in the employment commitment of men and women.

Similarly, when separate regression analyses were run for men and women to examine the association between benefits and employment commitment, there was no evidence for a greater effect among women than among

TABLE 6.7. *Effect of receipt of benefit and perceived replacement ratios on employment commitment for unemployed men and women*

	Men		Women	
	B	Sig.	B	Sig.
Receiving benefits (ref. not receiving)	−0.19	n.s.	0.02	n.s.
Comparison with income in work (only those on benefit)				
Benefit income same or better	ref.		ref.	
Benefit income a little lower	0.19	n.s.	−0.18	n.s.
Benefit income much lower	0.27	n.s.	−0.11	n.s.

Note: Controlling for age, country, and class.
Source: Employment in Europe Survey (Eurobarometer 44.3).

men (Table 6.7). In both cases, those who received some type of benefit were indistinguishable for those who did not. Moreover, there was no significant difference in employment commitment, for either men or women, between those who thought that their benefit income was much lower than the pay they would get from a job and those who thought there was little difference. Indeed, it should be noted that, in contrast to men, the women's coefficient is negative which is the opposite of what would be predicted if the view were correct that women were more sensitive to replacement ratio effects.

But while there was no support for the general argument that women are more sensitive to the incentive effects of benefit systems, might it be the case that women's attitudes vary substantially depending on the extent to which they adhere to traditional views about gender roles? To examine this, we constructed a scale of 'gender traditionalism' based on four items in the survey.[3] The items, with which people were asked to express agreement or disagreement, were:

'A mother must give priority to her young child rather than to her work'
'It is a must for a woman to have her own income'
'It is as important for a woman as for a man to have a job'
'When jobs are scarce, men should have more right to a job than women'.

Whereas 72 per cent of women who were low in terms of gender traditionalism—defined in terms of the lowest two scores—were committed to employment, the proportion fell to 63 per cent among those at the midpoint on the scale, dropping to only 59 per cent among those who were highly traditional—the highest two scores. Regression analysis showed that traditionalism continued to have a highly significant negative association with

---

[3] A factor analysis confirmed that the items related to a single underlying factor (eigenvalue 1.52, accounting for 38% of the variance).

commitment even when country, age, and class were controlled. There are, then, grounds for thinking that women's employment commitment is at least partially rooted in their broader beliefs and values about gender roles.

However, our central concern is with the implications of traditionalism for responses to the incentives or disincentives to work provided by benefit systems. Our hypothesis is that such effects may be mediated by the wider normative system within a society, since this conditions the social acceptability of given types of behaviour. In societies with more traditional gender cultures, married women may prefer, or feel a greater moral pressure, to emphasize their domestic roles. By reducing the financial constraints, unemployment benefit may make it easier for them to give a lower salience to employment.

To explore this, the measure of traditionalism of gender culture was used to distinguish a group of relatively 'traditional' from a group of relatively 'non-traditional' countries. The average score of the *whole* female sample aged 16 or older was examined for each country. The European female mean on the scale was 5.66. Five countries stood out as having relatively high traditionalism scores of over 5.80: Austria, 'West' Germany, Britain, Ireland, and Italy. Three countries had particularly low traditionalism scores of less than 5.25: Denmark, Finland, and Sweden.

The principal focus is on the attitudes of women in partnerships since these women were in a position to give greater centrality to their identity as housewife or mother in response to unemployment. Was it the case that in societies with more traditional gender cultures, benefits were associated with lower employment commitment among such women? We carried out separate regression analyses for women in the two groups of countries—those with traditional and non-traditional gender cultures—in order to contrast the employment commitment of single and married women who received benefit from those who did not. As can be seen in Table 6.8, in the traditional societies, women in partnerships who received benefit were significantly less likely to be committed to employment. In sharp contrast, in the non-traditional societies, the reverse is the case, and such women are significantly more likely to be committed. The benefit effect, then, is indeed very different between the two types of society.

In conclusion, our evidence does not provide any support for the view that unemployed women are less committed to employment than unemployed men or that their commitment to employment is in general more affected by unemployment benefit. However, there does appear to be an association between benefits and lower commitment in the specific case of married, or cohabiting, women in societies with more traditional gender cultures. This suggests that economistic arguments that assume universal effects of given types of incentive structure are unsatisfactory; rather the implications of such 'incentives' will depend crucially on the specific cultural context.

TABLE 6.8. *Welfare benefits, partnership status and employment commitment for women in countries with traditional and non-traditional gender cultures*

	Traditional countries		Non-traditional countries	
Household status of unemployed women	B	Sig.	B	Sig.
Partners not on benefit	ref.		ref.	
Single not on benefit	−0.04	n.s.	0.29	n.s.
Single on benefit	0.15	n.s.	0.16	n.s.
Partners on benefit	−0.67	***	0.74	**
N	924		605	

Note: ** = P < 0.01, *** = P < 0.001. Controlling for age.
Source: Employment in Europe Survey (Eurobarometer 44.3).

FLEXIBILITY IN JOB SEARCH

The second aspect of work attitudes that we are concerned with is people's flexibility about the type of job that they would be willing to accept. As was mentioned earlier, this may be a sign of lower or higher commitment depending on the real nature of labour market opportunities. But, independently from its connection with employment commitment, it could be argued that a high degree of inflexibility about job choice is likely to be a factor that leads to longer unemployment.

The analysis is concerned in particular with three types of flexibility in job choice: about the level of pay that a person is willing to accept, about the type of skill the work involves, and finally about geographical location. A series of questions were designed to tap these different dimensions. People were initially asked: 'Would you only take a job that offers at least the same rate of pay as your last job, or would you be prepared to accept a lower rate of pay'? Subsequent questions asked whether they would be prepared or not to accept a job which, by comparison with their previous work, involved 'a lower level of skill or qualification', 'a different type of skill', and 'training in a different type of skill'. Finally, people were asked whether they would accept a job that involved 'moving house to a different area?'

Taking first pay-flexibility, there has been a widespread concern that one of the consequences of a relatively generous welfare system is that people become more resistant to a reduction of pay levels. Overall, it is clear that this was an area of relatively low flexibility (Table 6.9). Only 45 per cent of the unemployed in the EU reported that they would be willing to consider a job offering lower pay than their previous employment.

TABLE 6.9. *Pay, skill and residential flexibility*

	% unemployed who would accept:					
	Lower pay	Lower level of skill	Different skill	Training for different skill	Skill flexibility index	Moving area
Austria	24.4	48.9	66.0	62.9	1.78	16.3
Belgium	22.9	60.2	86.2	76.8	2.24	33.3
Denmark	32.0	40.8	75.2	69.8	1.86	17.6
Finland	57.9	85.4	91.7	71.7	2.49	25.2
France	38.9	56.2	80.0	86.3	2.22	36.7
Germany E	48.8	73.7	86.5	78.5	2.40	15.7
Germany W	54.2	53.7	73.9	65.7	1.94	13.2
Great Britain	42.1	69.5	88.3	88.5	2.49	19.0
Greece	22.2	48.7	78.5	77.2	2.06	20.9
Ireland	34.8	70.6	75.8	77.4	2.22	22.2
Italy	49.3	50.6	87.9	84.3	2.30	40.2
Netherlands	68.9	62.5	85.2	80.1	2.30	31.4
Portugal	37.1	47.2	71.7	76.0	1.94	24.4
Spain	43.0	71.4	85.8	89.4	2.46	43.8
Sweden	53.5	77.7	84.0	81.8	2.43	25.7
EU15	45.1	63.7	83.5	82.1	2.29	30.6
N	3240	3447	3830	3906	3381	4019

Source: Employment in Europe Survey (Eurobarometer 44.3).

The unemployed were more willing to be flexible about skill than about pay (Table 6.9). As much as 84 per cent were willing to move to a job that required a different type of skill. Similarly 82 per cent were prepared to undertake training to take a job with a different type of skill. There was somewhat greater reluctance to take on less-skilled work, with 64 per cent of the unemployed saying that they would accept a job requiring a lower level of skill. But, overall, occupational identities did not seem to be a major barrier to re-employment.

The unemployed were least flexible with respect to residential mobility. Very few were willing to contemplate moving house to a different area to get a job. In not a single country was a majority of the unemployed prepared to move to a different area. The reasons why there is such reluctance to move may be quite diverse. It may be that long-term prospects are not thought to be better elsewhere, it may be that the growth of the two-earner family acts as a substantial constraint on the ease of moves, or it may reflect the importance of local familial and community attachments. It is clearly an issue that needs much more detailed research.

TABLE 6.10. *Coefficients for pay, skill and residential flexibility of the unemployed receiving benefit relative to Belgium*

Unemployed in:	Pay		Skill		Residence	
	B	Sig.	B	Sig.	B	Sig.
Austria	−0.10	n.s.	−0.50	***	−0.51	n.s.
Belgium	ref.		ref.		ref.	
Denmark	0.82	**	−0.05	n.s.	−0.31	n.s.
Finland	1.32	***	0.16	n.s.	0.28	n.s.
France	0.60	n.s.	0.19	n.s.	0.84	**
Germany E	1.00	***	0.24	*	−0.05	n.s.
Germany W	1.18	***	−0.13	n.s.	−0.34	n.s.
Great Britain	0.61	(*)	0.27	*	0.14	n.s.
Greece	0.01	n.s.	−0.23	n.s.	−0.04	n.s.
Ireland	0.39	n.s.	0.23	*	−0.05	n.s.
Italy	1.71	**	0.56	*	−1.03	(*)
Netherlands	1.64	***	0.27	**	0.49	n.s.
Portugal	0.60	n.s.	−0.28	(*)	0.15	n.s.
Spain	1.20	***	0.28	*	0.48	n.s.
Sweden	1.20	***	0.28	**	−0.06	n.s.

Note: Controlling for sex, age and class. Sample Sizes: 2718 for pay flexibility, 2740 for skill flexibility, and 2802 for residential flexibility. Logistic regression was used for pay and residential flexibility, OLS regression for the skill flexibility scale. (*) = $P < 0.1$, * = $P < 0.05$, ** = $P < 0.01$, *** = $P < 0.001$, n.s. = not significant.
Source: Employment in Europe Survey (Eurobarometer 44.3).

Welfare Systems and Flexibility

How did the relative generosity of welfare systems affect people's willingness to 'trade down' in order to get a job? Table 6.10 shows the country coefficients for each of the three types of flexibility. The comparison has been restricted to those in receipt of benefit or state assistance, since these are the people that will be directly affected by differences in incentives linked to national welfare regimes. The different countries are compared as previously with Belgium. The most significant variations between countries are with respect to pay flexibility. But there is no evidence that more generous welfare would reduce flexibility. In contrast, all of the three 'high welfare' countries—Denmark, The Netherlands, and Sweden—show relatively high levels of pay flexibility. In contrast, among the 'low welfare' countries, only Italy and Spain had relatively high levels of pay flexibility. The coefficient for the UK is positive but is only significant at the 10 per cent level.

To compare countries with respect to skill flexibility, an index was constructed by summing the items relating to willingness to take a job with a different skill, to train in a different skill and to take a job with lower skill.

TABLE 6.11. *Effects of receipt of benefits and of perceived benefit income on pay, skill, and residential flexibility*

	Pay		Skill		Residence	
	B	Sig.	B	Sig.	B	Sig.
Receiving benefits (ref. not receiving)	−0.07	n.s.	0.05	n.s.	0.08	n.s.
Comparison with income in work (only those on benefit)						
Benefit income same or better	ref.		ref.		ref.	
Benefit income a little lower	0.05	n.s.	0.04	n.s.	−0.16	n.s.
Benefit income much lower	0.31	**	0.12	**	0.02	n.s.

Note: Controlling for age, sex, country and class. ** = $P < 0.01$, n.s. = not significant.
Source: Employment in Europe Survey (Eurobarometer 44.3).

In three of the less generous welfare systems—Italy, Ireland, and Britain—the unemployed did show a relatively high willingness to change their type of occupation. However, there is again no evidence for a welfare effect, given that unemployed people on benefit in Sweden and The Netherlands were also relatively high on skill flexibility. This was not the case for Denmark, so the unemployed in high welfare societies can differ considerably in attitudes to skill. Finally, with respect to residential mobility, the notable point is just how similar the societies are. It is only the unemployed in France that stand out as being more willing to move area, and the Italians may be less prepared than the unemployed in most countries to be geographically mobile. Overall, whichever measure of flexibility is taken, there is no consistent difference between the high and low welfare societies in the job search flexibility of the unemployed.

As with employment commitment, the analysis of benefit effects can be extended by looking at the effect of the individual's perception of the difference in income of being unemployed and having a job. Two sets of regression analyses were carried out. The first simply examined the effect of whether or not a person was in receipt of some type of benefit for each of the three types of flexibility. The second contrasts those who felt that their income from benefit was lower than it would be if they were in a job, with those who thought it was similar to what they would be earning in work. The regressions controlled for age, sex, country and class. The coefficients refer to the overall effect in the pooled sample of European unemployed.

It can be seen in the first row of the Table 6.11 that there was no significant difference on any of the dimensions of flexibility between those who received benefit and those who did not. However, what did make a difference was people's perception of the relationship between their benefit income and what they would be earning if they were in work. Those who perceived the replacement ratio to be much lower were significantly more willing to be flexible about skill, and especially about pay, than those who felt that there was not much difference between their income in and out of work. The perception of financial loss, however, made no difference with respect to the willingness to move area in order to find a job.

In contrast to the findings for employment commitment, there would appear to be an association at the individual level between the extent to which people's living standards are maintained when they are unemployed and their willingness to take a job with lower pay or to change their occupation. However, it is clear from the country pattern that other institutional and cultural characteristics are also very strong determinants of such flexibility. It is notable that, despite such replacement ratio effects, two of the three 'high welfare' societies have managed to maintain relatively high levels of flexibility.

Gender and Job Search Flexibility

Were there differences between unemployed men and women in their flexibility in job search, possibly reflecting women's stronger identification with their domestic roles? Do the disincentives to work linked to the benefit system have stronger implications for the job search behaviour of women than of men?

Table 6.12 compares the flexibility of men and women on the three measures of pay, skill and geographical mobility. The skill measure is the overall scale score produced by summing the three separate items relating to skill. Taking first pay, the proportions of men and women in the overall European sample who would accept lower pay are very similar indeed: 46 per cent of men would take a pay cut, compared with 44 per cent of women. Turning to skill flexibility, the scores of men and women are virtually identical for the European unemployed as a whole: 2.29 and 2.30 respectively. It is only with respect to geographical mobility that there is a clear sex difference. Women were considerably less likely to be willing to move area in order to get a job than men. Whereas 37 per cent of men would change area, this was the case for only 23 per cent of women. Moreover, in contrast to pay and skill flexibility, the gender pattern is remarkably consistent across the different countries. Women were less prepared to consider residential mobility in every country except Ireland.

There are no grounds then for thinking that women's domestic roles lead in general to lower flexibility in terms of either pay or skill. But it does seem to be the case that women are systematically less likely to be willing to consider moving from the area in which they currently live. Further analysis showed that this effect is primarily due to the reluctance of married women

TABLE 6.12. *Pay, skill, and residential flexibility, by gender*

	Pay (% flexible)		Skill flexibility (scale score)		Residence (% flexible)	
	Men	Women	Men	Women	Men	Women
Austria	22.7	31.6	1.63	1.95	21.7	5.3
Belgium	20.8	25.0	2.11	2.36	39.3	25.8
Denmark	37.5	29.6	2.16	1.58	20.8	15.4
Finland	71.4	43.5	2.41	2.59	32.1	16.7
France	35.3	42.5	2.18	2.26	49.2	25.2
Germany E	48.7	48.8	2.28	2.47	18.9	13.2
Germany W	57.9	46.9	1.94	1.94	16.2	9.0
Great Britain	42.7	39.0	2.48	2.54	23.9	7.5
Greece	26.9	20.7	2.04	2.08	25.0	18.9
Ireland	21.4	50.0	2.12	2.45	20.0	25.0
Italy	46.3	53.6	2.34	2.24	51.4	29.5
Netherlands	70.3	66.7	2.20	2.43	35.6	26.9
Portugal	42.1	31.3	1.88	2.00	31.0	19.5
Spain	45.5	40.1	2.55	2.36	52.5	34.8
Sweden	56.1	51.7	2.49	2.36	26.8	24.1
EU15	46.1	44.1	2.29	2.30	37.4	23.3
N	1793	1448	1821	1560	2074	1946

Source: Employment in Europe Survey (Eurobarometer 44.3).

to move. Only 12 per cent were willing to take a job that required geographical mobility.

It was seen earlier that, while receipt of financial benefits did not in itself affect flexibility, the perception of the level of benefit income relative to earnings was significant for both pay and skill flexibility. Might it be that this effect was more pronounced among women as the result of the greater importance attached to their domestic roles? To the extent that men still perceive themselves primarily in terms of their work identities, there may be stronger pressures to search for work of a non-financial type, thereby reducing the significance of financial incentives.

In Table 6.13 the effects both of receipt of benefits and of the perceived level of benefits are given separately for unemployed men and women. It is clear that there is no sex difference linked simply to the receipt of benefit. Further, there is no support overall for the view that the perceived replacement ratio has a stronger effect for women than for men. There was however an interesting difference between the sexes in the *type* of flexibility that is related to the replacement ratio. Unemployed men who believed that their benefit income was particularly low, relative to the earnings they would get if they had a job, were more likely to be flexible about pay. In contrast, there

TABLE 6.13. *Effects of receipt of benefits and of perceived benefit income on pay, skill, and residential flexibility, by gender*

	Pay		Skill		Residence	
	B	Sig.	B	Sig.	B	Sig.
Men						
Receiving benefits (ref. not receiving)	0.12	n.s.	0.07	n.s.	0.01	n.s.
Comparison of benefit income with income in work						
same or better	ref.		ref.		ref.	
a little lower	−0.06	n.s.	0.10	n.s.	−0.36	n.s.
much lower	0.39	**	0.10	n.s.	0.01	n.s.
Women						
Receiving benefits (ref. not receiving)	−0.21	n.s.	0.05	n.s.	0.12	n.s.
Comparison of benefit income with income in work						
same or better	ref.		ref.		ref.	
a little lower	0.18	n.s.	−0.01	n.s.	0.08	n.s.
much lower	0.23	n.s.	0.16	*	−0.23	n.s.

Notes: Controlling for age, country, and class. * = P < 0.05, ** = P < 0.01, n.s. = not significant.

was no comparable effect on pay flexibility among women. However, with respect to skill, the reverse is the case. It was women who perceived that their benefit income was much lower than their potential income from a job who were more willing to change type of occupation, whereas there was no difference for men.

Any explanation of this difference must at present be purely speculative. It may be that the jobs that men apply for offer a greater range of salaries, so that a concession on pay is more feasible, whereas women's jobs are heavily crowded into a very low-paid sector. Correspondingly, the key to a woman's capacity to get work quickly may lie in being flexible about the type of work that she is willing to do, given that the pay may not vary a great deal between jobs. It may also be the case that men tend to be socialized into stronger occupational identities that make it more difficult for them to contemplate a change in type of work.

It was seen earlier, with respect to employment commitment, that there was some evidence that the type of gender culture in a society was an important factor mediating the effect of benefits. Welfare benefits were associated with lower employment commitment among women in societies with a traditional gender culture, but with higher commitment in the countries with non-traditional gender cultures. Was it also the case that the broader gender culture affected the relationship between welfare assistance and job search

TABLE 6.14. *Welfare benefits, partnership status and job search flexibility for women in countries with traditional and non-traditional gender cultures*

Household Status of Unemployed Women	Traditional Countries		Non-Traditional Countries	
	B	Sig.	B	Sig.
Pay Flexibility				
Partners not on benefit	ref.		ref.	
Single not on benefit	−0.46	n.s.	−0.15	n.s.
Single on benefit	0.19	n.s.	−0.13	n.s.
Partners on benefit	−0.44	*	−0.03	n.s.
N	599		432	
Skill Flexibility				
Partners not on benefit	ref.		ref.	
Single not on benefit	−0.12	n.s.	−0.08	n.s.
Single on benefit	0.21	n.s.	−0.03	n.s.
Partners on benefit	−0.04	n.s.	−0.23	n.s.
N	600		431	
Geographical Mobility				
Partners not on benefit	ref.		ref.	
Single not on benefit	−0.13	n.s.	0.71	n.s.
Single on benefit	0.38	n.s.	−0.39	n.s.
Partners on benefit	−1.50	***	−0.78	n.s.
N	685		437	

Notes: Controlling for age. * = P < 0.05, *** = P < 0.001, n.s. = not significant.
Source: Employment in Europe Survey (Eurobarometer 44.3).

behaviour? The hypothesis once more is that it is women who are partners who will be most affected, since it is they who have the opportunities and constraints of an alternative domestic role.

In Table 6.14, the coefficients are given separately for the two groups of countries that were previously classified as 'traditional' and 'non-traditional' in their norms about women's employment. The results add further support to the pattern that emerged with respect to employment commitment. In the group of countries with traditional gender cultures, female partners in receipt of benefit were significantly less likely to be flexible about pay and, in particular, they were less likely to be flexible about geographical mobility than female partners who do not receive benefit. In contrast, in the societies with non-traditional gender cultures, the coefficients are much lower and they are not statistically significant. Once more, it is not the general effect of receiving benefits that appears to be important, but rather the interaction of the benefit system and specific gender cultures.

TABLE 6.15. *Job search flexibility and perceived difficulty of finding a job*
(% considering it very difficult)

	Pay		Skill Flexibility		Geographical Mobility	
	Flex	Inflex	Flex	Inflex	Flex	Inflex
All	41.9	31.6***	37.0	34.7 n.s.	33.1	38.3**
Men	41.9	28.0***	34.1	33.8 n.s.	31.3	35.0 n.s.
Women	41.9	35.9**	40.4	36.0***	36.2	41.2***

Notes: ** = P < 0.01, *** = P < 0.001, n.s. = not significant.
Source: Employment in Europe Survey (Eurobarometer 44.3).

Job Search Flexibility and Job Opportunities

While there is no evidence for a benefit effect with respect to employment commitment, there are grounds for thinking that high replacement ratios are associated with greater reluctance to accept a drop in pay and with a lower willingness to take a job with a rather different type of skill. These factors may contribute to longer durations of unemployment. However, they may also be associated with more beneficial labour market outcomes (see OECD 1996: 38). One function of providing a reasonable level of income maintenance to unemployed people is to ensure that they have the time to look for a job that matches well their skills. If they do not, they are likely to be more dissatisfied with their job, to work less well in the job, and to leave it more quickly for another, with the attendant turnover costs for the employer.

Far too little is known at the moment about the implications of such job search attitudes for longer-term labour market outcomes. The appropriate design for such a study is longitudinal. The current survey—which is cross-sectional—cannot provide strong evidence on this issue. But it is perhaps informative to consider the relationship between job search flexibility and people's perception of how difficult it is likely to be to obtain a job. It can be assumed that lack of flexibility is likely to be most dangerous where it substantially reduces the flow of job opportunities. However, if people retain high expectations in a situation where opportunities are relatively good, then it may have the positive consequence of improving matching.

Table 6.15 gives the proportions among those who were flexible or inflexible with respect to pay, skill, and geographical mobility considering that it would be very difficult to find a job. Taking first pay flexibility, it is clear that those who were inflexible were actually somewhat more confident about their ability to find work than those who were flexible. The difference is particularly sharp for men. With respect to skill flexibility, there is no overall difference in the perceived difficulty of finding work between the flexible and the inflexible, but it is notable that skill inflexibility among women was associated with a more optimistic view about labour market opportunities. In the case of pay and, for women, of skill flexibility, then, the pattern is consistent with the argument that people maintain expectations when they feel that job opportunities are relatively good, rather than with the view that inflexibility brings about a deterioration in job prospects.

The contrasting case is that of geographical mobility. Here there is precisely the pattern that would be expected if inflexibility made it less likely that people would find work. It is clear from the overall figures and particularly from the figures for women that there was a significant association between unwillingness to move and a belief that it would be very difficult to find a job. However, it was seen earlier that this type of inflexibility had no association with benefits. Attitudes to geographical mobility were clearly determined by rather different factors.

Finally with respect to the country patterns, it is revealing to look at the relationship between the average levels of flexibility and the prevalence of long-term unemployment. There were five countries that had below average flexibility on each of the three types of flexibility. These were Austria, Denmark, Greece, Ireland, and Portugal (see Table 6.9). These had diverse proportions of the unemployed in long-term unemployment in 1996 (Eurostat 1996). Three of these countries had levels of long-term unemployment that were above the average for the EU: these were Greece, with 56.7 per cent, Ireland, with 59.5 per cent, and Portugal, with 53.1 per cent. In contrast, two had levels of long-term unemployment that were well below the EU average: Austria, with 25.6 per cent, and Denmark, with 26.5 per cent. The association between low levels of flexibility and high long-term unemployment occurs only in the countries with weak welfare systems for the unemployed. The only 'high welfare' society with below average flexibility was Denmark. But, in this case it was associated with particularly low levels of long-term unemployment. It seems possible that in Denmark generous benefit levels provided the conditions for a type of job search that permitted more careful matching between people's skills and the available jobs, in a relatively buoyant labour market.

While overall higher replacement ratios may be associated with lower flexibility with respect to pay and skill, it is far from clear that this leads in the longer term to greater labour market marginalization. In particular, people who retain high expectations about pay have a somewhat more optimistic view of their labour market opportunities. If this reflects a realistic assessment, then the effect of higher replacement rates on expectations could be to permit better matching between the individual and the job, rather than leading to a higher risk of long-term unemployment.

CONCLUSIONS

The central concern of the chapter has been to examine whether welfare arrangements that provide relatively high levels of material support to the unemployed undermine work motivation. Taking measures of both employment commitment and job search flexibility, we have focused both on the comparison between societies with rather different welfare regimes and on the effects of perceived replacement ratios at the individual level. We have also considered a variant of the conventional argument which suggests that the incentives and disincentives provided by benefit systems may be particularly important in the case of married women, given the greater salience of their domestic roles.

The general argument that the generosity of welfare provision influences people's underlying commitment to having a job received little support from our evidence. The unemployed in all of the European countries attached greater importance to having a job than people who were actually in paid work. This pattern is consistent with the argument that employment may have vital latent functions for psychological well-being which tend to be taken for granted until people have the experience of being without them. A closer examination of the association between people's perception of replacement ratios and employment commitment also indicated that the level of benefits was of little relevance for commitment. Finally, comparisons between countries with very different welfare regimes showed that those countries which had the most generous welfare were among those where the unemployed had the highest level of employment commitment.

There was also no evidence that unemployed women were less committed to having a job than unemployed men. Similarly, overall, the level of benefits had as little effect on women as on men. However, we find marked differences between the responses of women in societies with more traditional views about women's employment and those where they were non-traditional. Where gender norms were traditional, a high level of benefit compensation was associated with lower employment commitment, while in the group of non-traditional societies the reverse was the case. This suggested that there was no simple 'benefit effect'; rather financial incentives have different implications for women depending on the broader gender culture.

The results with respect to job search flexibility were rather different. We examined three types of flexibility—pay flexibility, skill flexibility, and the willingness to be geographically mobile. While it made little difference whether people were in receipt of benefit or not, there was a tendency for those with low perceived replacement ratios to be more flexible with respect to both pay and skill than those who thought that their incomes in and of work were similar. However, it should be noted that this did not mean that 'high welfare' societies were characterized by lower levels of flexibility. Two of the three 'high welfare' societies—Sweden and The Netherlands—were characterized by both high pay flexibility and high skill flexibility. While benefit levels may in general have the effect of reducing these types of flexibility, other institutional and cultural factors clearly can more than compensate for this.

There was no evidence that this effect was generally stronger for women than for men. Rather there was a difference in the type of flexibility that was affected. Among men, low levels of income support were associated with increased pay flexibility, but among women with greater flexibility about the type of work. However, there was again a difference between women's responses in the more traditional group of societies compared with the non-traditional. In the former case there was a clear association between higher benefit levels and lower flexibility, whereas this was not the case in the non-traditional societies.

The evidence about employment commitment conflicts rather sharply with the view that benefit systems may contribute to high levels of unemployment by undercutting the work ethic. However, the finding that benefit levels are linked to pay and skill flexibility in job search would be consistent with the view that the level of benefits might contribute to longer unemployment, even for people who attach considerable importance to work. The extent to which this should be seen as a social problem depends very much on the final outcome. Where it leads to entrapment in long-term unemployment it is clearly undesirable; where it simply prolongs a period of job search sufficiently to ensure a good match between skills and the job, it must be judged a positive result of the benefit system. Our data was not of a type to permit strong conclusions about which of these situations best characterizes the experience of unemployed people. However, we did not find that those that were relatively inflexible felt that they had poorer job chances as might be expected if job search inflexibility was a major determinant of the risk of long-term unemployment. Rather they were somewhat more optimistic about their job chances. Retaining high aspirations where there are reasonable job opportunities may lead to more careful job search and hence more stable employment over the longer term.

Overall, our evidence leads to some scepticism about the importance that is frequently attached to the influence of benefit systems in affecting work motivation. The theoretical argument is heavily premised on the view that work is for most people a disutility, and that people only take a job because of the financial benefits that it brings. Our results tend to confirm the alternative view that work in general is seen as an important source of personal satisfaction and social integration. The great majority of unemployed people in the European member states would appear to prefer to have a job rather than remain unemployed irrespective of the level of benefit they receive.

7

The Permanent Effects of Labour Market Entry in Times of High Unemployment

Philippe De Vreyer, Richard Layte, Maarten Wolbers,
and Mohammad Azhar Hussain*

INTRODUCTION

Are young workers that first participated in the labour market in times of high aggregate unemployment permanently disadvantaged, compared to other workers that entered in more favourable periods, or do they catch up later? In this chapter we address this issue by looking at the career paths of several generations of workers, focusing on their relative risk of unemployment in relation to the level of aggregate unemployment when they first participated in the labour market. Our hypothesis will be that a first participation at a time of high aggregate unemployment can be detrimental to the future working careers of young workers, if they experience difficulties in getting into a stable job and, as a result, become outsiders in a segmented labour market. Our study uses data from Denmark, England, France, Italy, and The Netherlands. These countries have experienced high levels of unemployment since the mid-1970s, but at different degrees, and have adopted different labour market regulations. In what follows, after a brief presentation of insider/outsider theory, which predicts a dichotomy of the labour market that could explain a potential permanent handicap of the kind we are looking for, we present the features of labour markets that we think are likely to reinforce such a dichotomy. We then examine the effect of unemployment at the time of labour market entry on the current probability of being unemployed, using a pseudo-panel built from a time-series of cross sectional labour force surveys.

* In the process of this work we have benefited from the comments and suggestions of members of the EPUSE research group and particularly from Paul De Graaf, Richard Hauser, John Hendrickx, and Wout Ultee. We also wish to thank David Margolis for useful comments and suggestions and Paolo Barbieri for helpful comments and for providing us with the Italian data. We remain responsible for any error or imperfection.

UNEMPLOYMENT PERSISTENCE: INSTITUTIONAL AND SOCIOLOGICAL EXPLANATIONS

Hysteresis and the Insiders/Outsiders Theory of Wage-Setting

The so-called 'hysteresis' hypothesis (Blanchard and Summers 1986) challenges the view that there is a natural rate of unemployment, the level of which depends upon structural characteristics of the economy and towards which the economy tends in the long term. Instead, it raises the possibility that a temporary increase in the level of current unemployment could result in an increase in the natural rate of unemployment. Several theoretical explanations have been put forward to explain why a rise in unemployment, that one might think as being temporary, could turn permanent. One of them relies on the distinction between 'insider' and 'outsider' workers (Lindbeck and Snower 1988). In insider/outsider theory, wages are set by a process of bargaining between employed workers, or insiders, and employers. Unemployed workers, or outsiders, play no role in this process. Insiders are concerned with maintaining their jobs and with their wage level, and the employment of outsiders is not their prime priority. As long as the economy is not submitted to any external shock, insiders negotiate so as to obtain the highest possible wage level compatible with maintaining their employment. Nothing changes and outsiders remain unemployed. Suppose now that the economy is submitted to an exogenous shock that makes some insiders lose their jobs. Once the economy recovers, the remaining insiders negotiate their wage so as to maintain this new lower level of employment. In this case unemployment shows no tendency to return to its previous level. Such a process of wage bargaining could also induce segmentation of the labour market (Cahuc and Zylberberg 1996). Insiders, belonging to the primary segment of the labour market, can, for instance, benefit from specific human capital or from their position as insiders if redundancy payments or hiring costs are important. Outsiders are either constrained to accept low-paid and/or unstable jobs, or are unemployed.

Insider/outsider theory has interesting implications, in that it stresses the potential role of the wage bargaining process in explaining unemployment, and the importance of the institutional setting in which this negotiation takes place. In the remaining paragraphs of this section we shall first examine, for the five countries that are included in this survey, the institutional features that we think are likely to reinforce or reduce the insiders/outsiders dichotomy. Then we shall look at the individual characteristics that are likely to affect the probability of being an outsider.

Institutional Setting and Unemployment Persistence

A number of factors have been seen as reinforcing the insider/outsider dichotomy, by interfering with the institutional setting of wage bargaining. It has been frequently suggested that the length and replacement ratio of unemployment benefits, by improving the fall-back position of insider workers in their wage negotiation with firms, are likely to increase the dichotomy between insiders and outsiders. From the point of view of the generosity of unemployment insurance benefits the British system is probably the least favourable to the unemployed, since it provides only low coverage and for a limited duration: one year before 1996, six months since then. In contrast the Danish, French, and Dutch systems are much more generous, with a higher coverage and a much longer duration for benefits: up to five years in France and The Netherlands, eventually followed by a social assistance scheme. Italy is a particular case, since the '*Cassa Integrazione*' together with the '*Lista di Mobilità*' systems, even though very limited in their coverage of unemployed workers, make dismissal very difficult and guarantee their potential beneficiaries very generous unemployment benefits in the case of dismissal. There is no doubt that such a system is likely to reinforce the position of insiders. See also Chapter 11 in this volume.

The existence of high hiring and firing costs, induced by restrictive labour legislation and/or the costs supported by firms in their search for suitable workers are also potential candidates for explaining unemployment persistence and a potential dualism of the labour market. In a study conducted at the OECD in 1993, David Grubb and William Wells have ranked European countries according to the degree of employment protection and strictness of labour legislation. In Table 7.1 we reproduce some of the results they obtained for the five countries that we consider in this chapter. The countries which have the least restrictive legislation receive the lowest rank. Table 7.1 also includes results of surveys conducted for the EC and the Employers International Organisation in 1985 and 1989 reproduced in the same study. According to these data the UK is by far the least restrictive in terms of labour legislation, and this is confirmed by the perception of employers. In contrast, Italy and, to a lesser extent, France, are the most restrictive. Denmark and The Netherlands are in an intermediate position between these extremes. Denmark is closer to the UK, with few restrictions on hiring and dismissal procedures, but more restrictive legislation on normal weekly hours; and The Netherlands closer to France, with the same degree of legal restriction for dismissal, but fewer controls on the employment of workers on fixed-term contracts. The evidence for The Netherlands is somewhat contradictory. Employers perceive labour legislation to be very strict, yet only 51 per cent think that unemployment would be reduced by more flexible procedures on hiring and dismissal, compared with 81 per cent

TABLE 7.1. *Measures of the strictness of employment legislation*

	Denmark	France	UK	Italy	Netherlands
Legal requirements and procedures for dismissal	2	5.5	1	9	5.5
Ability to employ workers on fixed term contracts	2	8	2	10	4.5
Restrictions on normal weekly hours	11	7	1	6	8.5
Restrictions on overtime, week-end or night work	2	7.5	1	3.5	7.5
Perception of labour legislation strictness by employers (scale from 0 to 3)[a]					
- Dismissal	1	3	0	3	3
- Fixed term contracts	1	2	1	3	3
Proportion of employers thinking that unemployment would be reduced if:[a]					
- Hiring and dismissal were made easier	—	81	26	83	51
- Required notice for dismissal were reduced and legal procedures were simplified	—	48	28	88	47
- Required compensation for dismissal were reduced	—	22	23	78	12
- Hiring on fixed-term contracts were made easier	—	53	27	63	32
Proportion of employers mentioning restrictions in legal procedures for hiring and dismissal as reasons for not employing more personnel[b]	—	53	27	62	58

[a] Survey conducted in 1985.
[b] Survey conducted in 1989.
Note: The first part of the Table presents the relative strictness of employment legislation. The countries with the *least* restrictive legislation receive the *lowest* ranking.
Source: Grubb and Wells 1993.

in France. Similarly, only about one-third think that less restrictive legislation on fixed term contracts would lower unemployment, compared with 53 per cent in France.

How to be an Outsider

By definition outsiders are due to remain outsiders, unless they can benefit from exceptionally favourable circumstances or insiders lose their status. Of course, the process of wage bargaining is likely to be only one dimension of this exclusion process. The negative effect that unemployment exerts on the accumulation of human capital is likely to play a role as well. Indeed, since those that are unemployed lose the opportunity to maintain and update their skills by working, then the longer their unemployment spell the lower is their probability of finding a job, everything else being equal. However if this can explain why the long-term unemployed do not succeed in finding new jobs, it does not account for why newly unemployed workers become long-term unemployed. The same line of argument invokes biased technological shocks that reduce the demand for unqualified labour to explain the rise of unemployment. Recent studies show that the structure of employment has shifted to the disadvantage of low qualified workers (Drèze and Malinvaud 1994; Lescure and L'Horty 1994; Sneessens and Shadman-Mehta 1995) and this effect is the prime justification for the retraining programmes that have been developed throughout Europe in the 1980s.

Sociological research has underlined that labour market precarity may often be linked to a process of resource deprivation and desocialization, that can translate into a weakening of family and social ties, and reduces the probability of finding a stable job. But the intensity of this process depends upon several factors that vary widely between countries. First, it may be mediated by the specific cultural patterns of household structure and sociability—see De Vreyer *et al.* (1996); Gallie (1999); and Chapter 12 in this volume. Second, labour market policies that keep individuals in the labour market and efficient retraining programmes can help counteract the process. Third, the nature and extent of unemployment insurance and assistance benefits can help unemployed workers to sustain a decent standard of living, and make their search for a job more efficient—see Chapter 6 in this volume.

It has also been argued, however, that labour market policies and the various sorts of benefits unemployed workers may receive can have adverse effects on their future employability. For instance generous unemployment benefits have been viewed as a disincentive to finding a job. However, the large number of micro-econometric surveys that have been done of this subject have not pointed to a strong effect of this sort (De Vreyer *et al.* 1996) as confirmed in Chapter 6 in this volume. However, active labour market policies have been criticized for failing to promote full-time and stable jobs. Surveys in France (Bonnal, Fougère, and Sérandon 1994; Fougère, and Kamionka 1992; Florens, and Fougère 1993) and Sweden (Korpi 1995), for instance, have pointed to the risk that such policies can result in a significant proportion of workers permanently alternating between unemployment and unstable jobs.

RESEARCH HYPOTHESES

It is clear that most young workers that participate for the first time in the labour market are, *de facto*, outsiders. The likelihood that they remain durably on the secondary part of the labour market will depend upon such characteristics as education, social capital, and sex. It should also depend upon the level of unemployment at the time they participate for the first time in the labour market, since a higher level increases the average duration of their first job search, and reduces the chances that this job will be a stable one. The question here is whether this initial handicap could turn into a permanent one. In what precedes we have identified several mechanisms by which this could occur: loss of human capital, the potential perverse effects of active labour market policies, the stigma that unemployed workers carry with them when unemployment has been too long, and the process of desocialization. Our hypothesis is that such an exclusion process is more likely to take place in some countries than in others, either because of the particular form of the welfare state and of social organization, or because the institutional setting of the labour market is unfavourable to outsiders.

The classification of countries according to these two criteria is not clear cut. On the one hand, the process of wage bargaining and the strictness of labour market legislation point to France and Italy as prime candidates for unemployment persistence. The UK and Denmark fare very well from this point of view. On the other hand, the welfare system is not very efficient in protecting unemployed workers in the UK. This might decrease the likelihood of unemployment persistence, if labour supply is sensitive to unemployment and social assistance benefits. But, as mentioned before, micro-economic surveys have not pointed to any strong effect of this sort.[1] The protection provided by the welfare state is even worse in Italy than in the UK, but Italy is characterized by a 'familistic' model of welfare state, in which family support to the unemployed provides adequate welfare in terms of living conditions, though not in terms of income—see Chapter 4 in this volume. In the other three countries, the welfare state appears to protect the unemployed rather efficiently from poverty, thus counteracting the process of social exclusion.

Among these factors, one can expect the institutional organization of the labour market to dominate in the determination of unemployment, since the prime reason for which unemployed workers do not find jobs is that they are not hired by firms. The process of social exclusion and the problems created by poverty come later, with increasing unemployment duration. As a result we expect France and Italy to be the two countries in which the effect of early unemployment on the further risk of being unemployed should be the strongest. In contrast Denmark and the UK are the countries in which we expect these effects to be the lowest. The Netherlands should be in an intermediate position.

---

[1] It is true that the unemployment rate is low in the UK in the late 1990s, but at the same time the number of working poor is very large. Thus it is possible that in this country the process of social exclusion does not translate into persistent unemployment, but rather into increasing poverty.

LOOKING FOR THE INSIDERS/OUTSIDERS DICHOTOMY

In this section, we examine whether the initial handicap of workers that participate for the first time to the labour market in a period when the unemployment rate is high, is likely to be permanent or not. We will do so by looking at the career path of several generations of workers to see if the level of unemployment at the time of first participation in the labour market has an effect on the future probability of being unemployed.

Methodology

The identification of cohort effects cannot be realized with cross-sectional data, since it is not possible to distinguish age from cohort effects. Panel data provide the ideal information to perform such an analysis, however such data sets are rare, and often lack a sufficient time-span. An alternative is to use a time-series of cross-sectional data sets and create a pseudo-panel by way of aggregation over individuals having a given time-invariant characteristic. This is the solution that has been adopted in this chapter.

In what follows we call 'labour market cohort', a group of individuals having the following characteristics:

(1) first participation in the labour market in the same year;
(2) of the same sex;
(3) of the same education level.

We assume that once an individual has left school and entered the labour market, they do not go back to school, so that their education level remains the same throughout their working career. With this assumption, the combination of date of entry, sex, and education level is time-invariant and can be used to define cohorts. There are as many cohorts as there are combinations of those three criteria. For each country a pseudo-panel is thus created in the following way: for each year of observation, we grouped all individuals belonging to a given labour market cohort, and created a data set having the representative individual of each cohort as the unit of observation. In order to keep a large enough number of observations in each cell defined in this way, we restricted the number of education levels to four: Primary or no education, Junior Secondary, Senior Secondary, and Tertiary.

Data

The data we use are from several cross-sectional surveys and have been collected in Denmark, the UK, France, Italy, and The Netherlands. The following table gives the main characteristics of each data set used.

TABLE 7.2. *The country data sets*

Country	Survey years	Approximate no. of individuals in each year (included in sample)
Denmark	1984, 1986, 1988, 1992, 1994	100,000
France	From 1978 to 1996	50,000
UK	1979, 1981, 1984 and from 1985 to 1991	60,000
Italy	From 1985 to 1997	95,000
Netherlands	1973, 1977, 1985 and 1991	40,000

Notes: UK data is drawn from the ONS Labour Force Surveys; French data from INSEE, Enquêtes sur l'emploi; Italian data from ISTAT, Rilevazione trimestrale delle forze di lavoro. Danish data from Statistics Denmark, Integrated Data Base for Labour Market Research; Dutch data from Statistics Netherlands, Labour Force Surveys 1973, 1977, 1985 and 1991.

For each country our analysis only concerns active men and women aged between 16 and 55. The labour market cohorts that are considered in the sample are all those that first participated in the labour market since 1960.

Model Specification and Estimation Methods

Let $u_{c,t}$ be the labour market cohort c unemployment rate in year t. We can specify:

$$u_{c,t} = E(u_{c,t}) + u_{c,t} - E(u_{c,t})$$

We assume that $u_{c,t} - E(u_{c,t}) = \varepsilon_{c,t}$ is randomly distributed and that $E(u_{c,t}) = u_t + z'_{c,t} \cdot \gamma$ where u_t is the aggregate unemployment rate in year t, $z'_{c,t}$ is a set of cohort specific variables and γ is a vector of parameters to estimate. Thus the econometric model is written:

$$u_{c,t} = u_t + z'_{c,t} \cdot \gamma + \varepsilon_{c,t}$$

However in this model we cannot exclude the occurrence of unobservable random shocks, that could be correlated both with the cohort and the aggregate unemployment rates and that would bias the estimate of γ. One simple way of avoiding this problem is to transform the model in order to make the difference between the cohort and aggregate unemployment rates the dependant variable:

$$\Delta u_{c,t} = u_{c,t} - u_t = z'_{c,t} \cdot \gamma + \varepsilon_{c,t}$$

The set of cohort specific variables that can explain the relative probability of being unemployed when belonging to a particular cohort is assumed to include sex, education level, and labour market experience and, potentially, the aggregate unemployment rate during the year of labour market entry.[2]

[2] The time series of unemployment rates have been taken from OECD economic perspectives.

Experience on the labour market is computed by the difference between current age, and age when leaving school. This last variable is only observed for France. For other countries the year of labour market entry is estimated using the normal age for leaving school, given the education level. As a result, the date of labour market entry is imprecisely observed and measurement error is likely to occur in the year of labour market entry unemployment rate variable. For this reason we substituted this variable with a moving average of order 3. Experimentation showed that this significantly improved results in most cases. To these variables, in order to control for pure cohort effects that have nothing to do with unemployment rates, we also add as explanatory variable 5-years band cohort dummies. Such pure cohort effects could result from the labour force composition at the date of entry or from the structure of the labour demand. For instance, if a given cohort enters the labour market at a time that a particular sector of the economy is expanding, then the proportion of workers in this cohort employed in this sector is likely to be higher. Depending upon whether this sector has been expanding or contracting afterwards, the proportion of unemployed in that cohort will change.

We have experimented with several variations of this model,[3] one of which included among the explanatory variables the point increase in the unemployment rate during the year of labour market entry, instead of the aggregate measure of unemployment. One would expect this variable to have a significant positive impact on the current cohort proportion of unemployed, if young workers' unemployment is very sensitive to changes in the aggregate level of unemployment. This experiment proved fruitful, so we present the results for this, as well as those obtained for the aggregate unemployment rate at the time of first participation.

In this model, one could expect the residuals to be serially correlated when the data include consecutive years of observation, even though the number of controls that we add in the list of explanatory variables is likely to reduce the extent of serial correlation. Given the nature of our data sets, this problem is likely to occur for the French and Italian data only. As a rough way to control for this, we removed first order serial correlation by first estimating the residuals correlation coefficient and then by transforming the data in creating quasi-first differences between successive observations. Finally, in order to account for the possible heteroscedasticity of residuals between different cohorts, White standard errors are computed for the OLS estimates.

---

[3] In particular we also estimated a model in which the dependant variable is the Box-Cox transformation of the ratio between $u_{c,t}$ and u_t, using Stata Boxcox command. This did not improve the results.

Results

The results are presented in Tables 7A–F in the Appendix to this chapter. Estimations have been performed on the total sample, and on the male and the female samples separately. For each sample a series of four models has been estimated. Models 1 and 2 do not include the controls for pure cohort effects, in contrast to models 3 and 4. In models 1 and 3 the aggregate measure of unemployment at the time of entry is used as an explanatory variable, whereas in models 2 and 4 it is the point increase in unemployment during the year of first participation that is used. In Table 7F partial results of the estimations conducted by education level are presented.[4]

One of the prime difficulties in estimating such models is the potentially high level of multicolinearity that can occur between the explanatory variables. Indeed experience, cohort dummies, and the unemployment rate variables are likely to be more or less correlated together. For this reason we decided to estimate different specifications of the same model. There are good reasons to believe that, *a priori*, the least parsimonious model—either model 3 or 4—should be the preferred one, since it makes the least restrictive assumptions. But it is also the model in which multicolinearity is likely to be the most severe. However, if, in this model, we find a significant effect of the aggregate unemployment rate at the time of first participation or an effect of the point increase in aggregate unemployment, we can be fairly confident of the reality of such an effect. If not, then we have to determine whether the cohort dummies are significant. In the affirmative, this would mean that the measure of unemployment at the time of first participation captures other cohort effects that we must control for. If not, then one can turn to the estimation results of models 1 and 2.

Effects of Sex, Education and Experience

In all countries but The Netherlands and the UK, the percentage of the unemployed is lower in the male cohorts than in the female ones. As for education, we find, in all five countries, that it significantly reduces the odds of being unemployed. Such an effect of education is expected if the structure of employment has shifted to the disadvantage of low-qualified workers. A shift of this kind could occur in the case of a biased technological shock, as already mentioned, or if companies screen workers for level of education. The experience and experience squared variables are included in the models in order to control for the risk of unemployment associated with labour market experience. As expected the risk of unemployment decreases with

---

[4] The regressions from which these estimates have been obtained included cohort dummies as explanatory variables, and were conducted on samples including both male and female workers.

the time spent in the labour market, which confirms the high incidence of unemployment in the youth population in all five countries.

Effects of Unemployment Rate at the Time of First Participation

We start by examining estimates reported in Tables 7A–E. As expected the results for France and Italy display a strongly significant, positive, and robust effect of the level of unemployment during the year of first participation. Indeed this effect is quite sizeable, since a 1 per cent increase in the rate of unemployment at the time of first participation can translate in up to a 1.6 per cent increase in the cohort current unemployment rate (France, female sample). However, the point increase in unemployment during the year of first participation is not found to be significant, apart from in the French results, for which it is small. This might result from the relatively large measurement error in this variable, since the year of labour market entry is not always correctly observed, and the level of unemployment fluctuates much less than the increase in unemployment.

In sharp contrast to France and Italy are the UK and The Netherlands. In these two countries, we do not find any significant effect of aggregate unemployment—whether one takes level or difference—at the time of first participation. For both countries, for model 1, we find a well determined effect of the year of first participation unemployment rate on the cohort proportion of unemployed, but this does not hold once pure cohort effects are controlled for—as in model 3. The point increase in aggregate unemployment during the year of labour market entry also has no significant effect for the UK, while the effect is very small and not robust to the inclusion of cohort dummies for The Netherlands. For the UK this corresponds to what was expected from the earlier discussion. As for The Netherlands, the results are more surprising, considering the strong institutional similarities with France: the main difference being the fewer restrictions on employing workers on fixed-term contracts in The Netherlands.

The Danish results are mixed. On the one hand, in the male sample we find a positive and very significant coefficient of the point increase in aggregate unemployment, that holds when cohort dummies are included. On the other hand, the results obtained with the female sample display a significant negative effect of the level of unemployment at the time of first participation.

One could expect the effect of the aggregate unemployment rate at the time of first entry on the labour market to differ between education levels. Indeed, if firms use education as a screening device then the low-qualified workers have lower probabilities of being employed, and the gap between low- and highly-qualified workers is likely to increase in times of high unemployment. For this reason we have run separate regressions for each of the four education levels. The results are presented in Table 7F.

For France the results confirm what we find when all education levels are pooled together. As expected, the coefficient of the unemployment rate during the year of first participation is positive and significant for the primary and the secondary levels of education, but not significant for the tertiary level. Moreover, the coefficient for the primary level is more than two times larger than the coefficients for the secondary levels. It is true that the results obtained with the point increase in unemployment rate as an explanatory variable are not so clear-cut since, in particular, the coefficient for the tertiary level appears to be positive. But it is only marginally significant.

In Italy the results are a little different from those obtained with the pooled sample, since only the unemployment rate at the time of first participation appears significant, and the highest value is obtained for the tertiary level. For other levels the coefficients are quite large and decreasing with the level of education, but they are insignificant so that we cannot reject the possibility that they are equal to zero.

The Dutch results are interesting. The aggregate unemployment rate at the time of first participation is found to have a positive effect on the current cohort proportion of unemployed for the primary level, and a negative one for the tertiary level. Such a pattern is consistent with what can be expected if workers are screened by education levels, and if the labour market is divided between insiders and outsiders. Indeed in such a case when unemployment is high, young workers with high credentials have a higher comparative advantage than is usually the case, and this initial advantage can result in a lower than average probability of being unemployed later in the working career. These differences in the results obtained with each education level can explain why we do not find any significant effect with the pooled sample.

The British results confirm what has been obtained when the sample is not split since, as expected, no coefficient is found to be significant. Finally, as with the pooled sample, the Danish results are puzzling since for the tertiary level of education we find a negative effect of the aggregate unemployment rate when measured in level, but a positive one once this variable is entered in difference.

CONCLUSION

In this chapter we have examined whether first participation on the labour market at a time of high aggregate unemployment increases the probability of being unemployed later. We have found that this is indeed the case in France and Italy, and to a lesser extent in The Netherlands, an effect that we attribute to a segmented labour market. In these countries, handicaps seem to be built very early in the working career and do not depend only on individual characteristics that might result from individual choices, but also upon exogenous characteristics, such as birth date and the particular state of the labour market when first participation occurs. Our analysis suggests that this could partly result from the institutional features of the labour market, in the sense that the countries in which it is most flexible do fare better in terms of their unemployment rate. However, the fact that the UK succeeds better than any of the other four countries in reducing the effects for later unemployment of people's early experiences of the labour market does not mean that the average level of welfare is higher in this country, given the large number of working poor. Denmark combines labour market legislation that does not appear much more restrictive than in the UK, together with the features of the social-democratic welfare state that provides extended social protection, thus reducing the extent of poverty. Among the five countries included in this survey, Denmark is probably the one in which the process of 'decommodification' (Esping-Andersen 1990), that is to say the detachment of the individual's status from the logic of the market, is most advanced. This probably contributes to explaining the pattern of unemployment in this country, characterized by an unemployment rate that results from a high rate of job destruction and not from a low probability of leaving unemployment. Consequently, in Denmark the proportion of long term unemployed is much lower than in any of the other four EC countries included in this survey. This underlines the limits of the present study, which is based on an evaluation of the risk of unemployment, and indicates the direction in which the analysis should be extended. The description of a segmented labour market as opposing employed and unemployed workers is certainly too restrictive. It would be of considerable interest to see whether the ranking of countries would remain the same if the analysis were carried out not just on the probability of being unemployed, but on the likelihood of holding either a low-paid precarious job *or* of being unemployed.

APPENDIX

TABLE 7A. *Determinants of LMC unemployment rates, Denmark, 1984–1994*

Model	Total sample				Male sample				Female sample			
	1	2	3	4	1	2	3	4	1	2	3	4
Variable												
Male	-0.024***	-0.024***	-0.024***	-0.024***	—	—	—	—	—	—	—	—
Education:												
- Primary or less	ref.	ref.	ref.	ref.	ref.	ref.	ref.	ref.	ref.	ref.	ref.	ref.
- Junior secondary	-0.047***	-0.050***	-0.048***	-0.049***	-0.086***	-0.090***	-0.086***	-0.084***	-0.009	-0.009	-0.011	-0.013
- Senior secondary	-0.134***	-0.136***	-0.135***	-0.135***	-0.162***	-0.166***	-0.162***	-0.160***	-0.107***	-0.107***	-0.108***	-0.111***
- Tertiary	-0.224***	-0.226***	-0.225***	-0.225***	-0.250***	-0.254***	-0.251***	-0.249***	-0.198***	-0.198***	-0.200***	-0.202***
Experience (β*10)	-0.055***	-0.039***	-0.077***	-0.076***	-0.057***	-0.020	-0.066***	-0.074***	-0.053**	-0.057**	-0.089***	-0.077***
Experience² (β*100)	-0.008*	-0.010**	0.000	0.000	-0.007	-0.013**	-0.004	-0.002	-0.009	-0.007	0.004	0.001
Year of 1ˢᵗ participation Unemployment Rate	-0.281*	—	-0.418	—	-0.588***	—	0.632	—	0.026	—	-1.468**	—
Year of 1ˢᵗ participation Point increase in U.R.	—	0.016**	—	0.012*	—	0.019**	—	0.029***	—	0.014*	—	-0.004
Labour Market Cohort:												
- 1960–64	—	—	0.007	0.052**	—	—	0.109*	0.079**	—	—	-0.096	0.024
- 1965–69	—	—	0.001	0.045*	—	—	0.101*	0.065**	—	—	-0.098	0.024
- 1970–74	—	—	0.032	0.072***	—	—	0.128**	0.091***	—	—	-0.065	0.053
- 1975–79	—	—	0.046	0.063***	—	—	0.066*	0.036	—	—	0.026	0.089***
- 1980–84	—	—	0.031	0.037*	—	—	0.023	0.017	—	—	0.039	0.058**
- 1985–89	—	—	0.006	0.026	—	—	0.012	0.028	—	—	0.000	0.025
- 1990–94	ref.	ref.	ref.	ref.	ref.	ref.	ref.	ref.	ref.	ref.	ref.	ref.
Intercept	0.353***	0.318***	0.348***	0.295***	0.368***	0.300***	0.239***	0.286***	0.314***	0.311***	0.433***	0.280***
R² (adjusted)	0.4620	0.4640	0.4689	0.4699	0.4938	0.4928	0.4985	0.5052	0.4519	0.4541	0.4690	0.4655
Number of cohorts	1412	1412	1412	1412	706	706	706	706	706	706	706	706

(*) Significant at the 10% level, (**) Significant at the 5% level, (***) Significant at the 1% level.

Appendix

TABLE 7B. *Determinants of LMC unemployment rates, France, 1978–1996*

Variable	Total sample				Male sample				Female sample			
Model	1	2	3	4	1	2	3	4	1	2	3	4
Variable												
Male	-0.053***	-0.053***	-0.053***	-0.053***	—	—	—	—	—	—	—	—
Education:												
- Primary or less	ref.	ref.	ref.	ref.	ref.	ref.	ref.	ref.	ref.	ref.	ref.	ref.
- Junior secondary	-0.088***	-0.088***	-0.088***	-0.088***	-0.078***	-0.078***	-0.078***	-0.078***	-0.098***	-0.098***	-0.098***	-0.098***
- Senior secondary	-0.126***	-0.126***	-0.126***	-0.126***	-0.103***	-0.103***	-0.103***	-0.103***	-0.150***	-0.150***	-0.150***	-0.150***
- Tertiary	-0.162***	-0.162***	-0.162***	-0.162***	-0.124***	-0.124***	-0.124***	-0.124***	-0.199***	-0.200***	-0.199***	-0.199***
Experience ($\beta*10$)	-0.194***	-0.208***	-0.197***	-0.200***	-0.173***	-0.179***	-0.179***	-0.181***	-0.211***	-0.234***	-0.211***	-0.215***
Experience² ($\beta*100$)	0.043***	0.046***	0.044***	0.044***	0.039***	0.041***	0.041***	0.041***	0.047***	0.050***	0.047***	0.047***
Year of 1st participation Unemployment Rate	0.313***	—	1.186***	—	0.129	—	0.725***	—	0.508***	—	1.566***	—
Year of 1st participation Point increase in U.R.	—	0.016***	—	0.010**	—	0.015***	—	0.013**	—	0.015***	—	0.006
Labour Market Cohort:												
- 1960–64	—	—	0.087***	-0.015	—	—	0.079**	0.020	—	—	0.083**	-0.054***
- 1965–69	—	—	0.087***	-0.011	—	—	0.077**	0.019	—	—	0.085**	-0.045***
- 1970–74	—	—	0.074***	-0.014	—	—	0.077**	0.014	—	—	0.072**	-0.046***
- 1975–79	—	—	0.055***	-0.013	—	—	0.066**	0.009	—	—	0.049*	-0.039***
- 1980–84	—	—	0.047***	0.014*	—	—	0.052***	0.034***	—	—	0.030*	-0.011
- 1985–89	—	—	-0.005	-0.005	—	—	0.057*	0.021**	—	—	-0.030**	-0.032***
- 1990–96	ref.	ref.	ref.	ref.	ref.	ref.	ref.	ref.	ref.	ref.	ref.	ref.
Intercept	0.274***	0.298***	0.175***	0.299***	0.194***	0.201***	0.112***	0.186***	0.296***	0.339***	0.192***	0.359***
R² (adjusted)	0.4631	0.4581	0.4694	0.4668	0.4228	0.4237	0.4331	0.4324	0.5527	0.5395	0.5597	0.5553
Number of cohorts	3812	3812	3812	3812	1906	1906	1906	1906	1906	1906	1906	1906

(*) Significant at the 10% level. (**) Significant at the 5% level. (***) Significant at the 1% level.

TABLE 7C. *Determinants of LMC unemployment rates, UK, 1979–1991*

	Total sample				Male sample				Female sample			
Model	1	2	3	4	1	2	3	4	1	2	3	4
Variable												
Male	-0.000	-0.000	-0.000	-0.000	—	—	—	—	—	—	—	—
Education:												
- Primary or less	ref.	ref.	ref.	ref.	ref.	ref.	ref.	ref.	ref.	ref.	ref.	ref.
- Junior secondary	-0.092***	-0.092***	-0.092***	-0.092***	-0.112***	-0.112***	-0.112***	-0.112***	-0.073***	-0.072***	-0.073***	-0.073***
- Senior secondary	-0.121***	-0.121***	-0.121***	-0.121***	-0.137***	-0.137***	-0.138***	-0.138***	-0.105***	-0.105***	-0.105***	-0.105***
- Tertiary	-0.118***	-0.117***	-0.118***	-0.118***	-0.138***	-0.137***	-0.138***	-0.138***	-0.098***	-0.097***	-0.098***	-0.098***
Experience	-0.073***	-0.090***	-0.077***	-0.075***	-0.112***	-0.130***	-0.118***	-0.113***	-0.033**	-0.049**	-0.036***	-0.037***
Experience[2]	0.015***	0.018***	0.021***	0.020***	0.027***	0.031***	0.034***	0.033***	0.003	0.006**	0.008**	0.007**
Year of 1st participation Unemployment Rate	0.201***	—	0.092	—	0.210***	—	0.050	—	0.192**	—	0.135	—
Year of 1st participation point increase in U.R.	—	0.070	—	-0.408	—	0.072	—	-0.817*	—	0.069	—	0.001
Labour Market Cohort:												
- 1960–64			-0.046***	-0.053***			-0.052***	-0.054***			-0.040**	-0.053***
- 1965–69			-0.020	-0.027***			-0.024	-0.026**			-0.017	-0.029**
- 1970–74			-0.017	-0.022***			-0.019	-0.019*			-0.015	-0.025**
- 1975–79			-0.006	-0.007			-0.004	0.002			-0.009	-0.016
- 1980–84			-0.007	0.000			-0.003	0.011			-0.011	-0.011
- 1985–91	ref.	ref.	ref.	ref.	ref.	ref.	ref.	ref.	ref.	ref.	ref.	ref.
Intercept	0.135***	0.162***	0.152***	0.160***	0.172***	0.200***	0.193***	0.192***	0.098***	0.124***	0.112***	0.129***
R² (adjusted)	0.5246	0.5217	0.5322	0.3253	0.6132	0.6104	0.6207	0.6219	0.4468	0.4435	0.4531	0.4527
Number of cohorts	2124	2124	2124	2124	1062	1062	1062	1062	1062	1062	1062	1062

(*) Significant at the 10% level, (**) Significant at the 5% level, (***) Significant at the 1% level.

Appendix

149

TABLE 7D. *Determinants of LMC unemployment rates, Italy, 1985–1997*

Variable	Total sample				Male sample				Female sample			
Model	1	2	3	4	1	2	3	4	1	2	3	4
Variable												
Male	-0.052***	-0.052***	-0.052***	-0.052***	—	—	—	—	—	—	—	—
Education:												
- Primary or less	ref.	ref.	ref.	ref.	ref.	ref.	ref.	ref.	ref.	ref.	ref.	ref.
- Junior secondary	-0.086***	-0.087***	-0.085***	-0.085***	-0.071***	-0.072***	-0.069***	-0.069***	-0.099***	-0.100***	-0.098***	-0.098***
- Senior secondary	-0.127***	-0.129***	-0.125***	-0.125***	-0.098***	-0.100***	-0.094***	-0.094***	-0.152***	-0.154***	-0.151***	-0.151***
- Tertiary	-0.166***	-0.167***	-0.165***	-0.165***	-0.123***	-0.124***	-0.121***	-0.121***	-0.204***	-0.205***	-0.203***	-0.203***
Experience (β*10)	-0.122***	-0.208***	-0.100***	-0.112***	-0.130***	-0.209***	-0.115***	-0.125***	-0.126***	-0.211***	-0.101***	-0.113***
Experience² (β*100)	0.019***	0.034***	0.013***	0.015***	0.024***	0.037***	0.017***	0.019***	0.017***	0.033***	0.012***	0.015***
Year of 1st participation Unemployment Rate	2.035***	—	1.050***	—	1.861***	—	0.895**	—	2.087***	—	1.076***	—
Year of 1st participation Point increase in U.R.	—	0.001	—	-0.002	—	-0.003	—	-0.004	—	0.004	—	0.004
Labour Market Cohort:												
- 1960–64	—	—	-0.103***	-0.152***	—	—	-0.078***	-0.121***	—	—	-0.124***	-0.172***
- 1965–69	—	—	-0.109***	-0.150***	—	—	-0.086***	-0.121***	—	—	-0.125***	-0.167***
- 1970–74	—	—	-0.110***	-0.152***	—	—	-0.094***	-0.131***	—	—	-0.120***	-0.162***
- 1975–79	—	—	-0.108***	-0.145***	—	—	-0.104***	-0.135***	—	—	-0.107***	-0.145***
- 1980–84	—	—	-0.107***	-0.132***	—	—	-0.104***	-0.127***	—	—	-0.102***	-0.128***
- 1985–89	—	—	-0.082***	-0.088***	—	—	-0.076***	-0.081***	—	—	-0.081***	-0.088***
- 1990–97	ref.	ref.	ref.	ref.	ref.	ref.	ref.	ref.	ref.	ref.	ref.	ref.
Intercept	0.175***	0.363***	0.303***	0.395***	0.104***	0.280***	0.234***	0.313***	0.207***	0.393***	0.332***	0.424***
R² (adjusted)	0.4960	0.4550	0.5408	0.5374	0.4548	0.4066	0.5428	0.5390	0.6074	0.5836	0.6512	0.6484
Number of cohorts	2884	2884	2884	2884	1442	1442	1442	1442	1442	1442	1442	1442

(*) Significant at the 10% level, (**) Significant at the 5% level, (***) Significant at the 1% level.

TABLE 7E. *Determinants of LMC unemployment rates, The Netherlands, 1973–1991*

Model	Total 1	Total 2	Total 3	Total 4	Male 1	Male 2	Male 3	Male 4	Female 1	Female 2	Female 3	Female 4
Variable												
Male	0.015***	0.015***	0.015***	0.015***	—	—	—	—	—	—	—	—
Education:												
- Primary or less	ref.	ref.	ref.	ref.	ref.	ref.	ref.	ref.	ref.	ref.	ref.	ref.
- Junior secondary	-0.068***	-0.068***	-0.068***	-0.068***	-0.077***	-0.077***	-0.077***	-0.077***	-0.058***	-0.058***	-0.058***	-0.058***
- Senior secondary	-0.089***	-0.089***	-0.088***	-0.089***	-0.102***	-0.102***	-0.102***	-0.102***	-0.077***	-0.077***	-0.077***	-0.077***
- Tertiary	-0.088***	-0.088***	-0.088***	-0.088***	-0.102***	-0.102***	-0.102***	-0.102***	-0.075***	-0.075***	-0.075***	-0.075***
Experience	-0.071***	-0.089***	-0.073***	-0.074***	-0.070***	-0.087***	-0.073***	-0.074***	-0.072***	-0.092***	-0.074***	-0.074***
Experience²	0.015***	0.019***	0.016***	0.016***	0.015***	0.019***	0.016***	0.017***	0.015***	0.020***	0.016***	0.016***
Year of 1st participation Unemployment Rate	0.453***	—	0.032	—	0.421***	—	0.153	—	0.485***	—	-0.088	—
Year of 1st participation Point increase in U.R.	—	0.008***	—	-0.003	—	0.007*	—	-0.007	—	0.010**	—	0.001
Labour Market Cohort:												
- 1960–64	—	—	-0.022	-0.022**	—	—	-0.010	-0.015	—	—	-0.034	-0.029**
- 1965–69	—	—	-0.021	-0.020**	—	—	-0.010	-0.013	—	—	-0.032	-0.027**
- 1970–74	—	—	-0.020	-0.019*	—	—	-0.007	-0.008	—	—	-0.033*	-0.030**
- 1975–79	—	—	-0.010	-0.008	—	—	0.000	0.002	—	—	-0.020	-0.018
- 1980–84	—	—	0.020**	0.027**	—	—	0.019*	0.036*	—	—	0.021*	0.018
- 1985–91	ref.	ref.	ref.	ref.	ref.	ref.	ref.	ref.	ref.	ref.	ref.	ref.
Intercept	0.098***	0.124***	0.125***	0.125***	0.121***	0.146***	0.135***	0.141***	0.089***	0.117***	0.130***	0.124***
R² (adjusted)	0.5425	0.5219	0.5473	0.5471	0.4975	0.5611	0.5783	0.5791	0.4975	0.4739	0.5042	0.5041
Number of cohorts	720	720	720	720	360	360	360	360	360	360	360	360

(*) Significant at the 10% level, (**) Significant at the 5% level, (***) Significant at the 1% level.

Appendix

TABLE 7F. *Results by education level*

		Year of 1st participation Unemployment Rate	Year of 1st participation point increase in U.R.
Denmark	*Primary*	0.079	0.018
	Junior Secondary	0.641	−0.003
	Senior Secondary	0.312	0.008
	Tertiary	−0.857**	0.014***
France	*Primary*	1.705***	0.007
	Junior Secondary	0.717***	0.010
	Senior Secondary	0.590**	0.011**
	Tertiary	0.324	0.006*
UK	*Primary*	0.197	0.158
	Junior Secondary	0.013	−0.113
	Senior Secondary	−0.035	−0.492
	Tertiary	0.109	−0.694
Italy	*Primary*	0.706	−0.012
	Junior Secondary	0.533*	−0.001
	Senior Secondary	0.486	0.001
	Tertiary	0.942***	−0.002
Netherlands	*Primary*	0.929*	0.001
	Junior Secondary	−0.092	−0.007
	Senior Secondary	−0.246	−0.001
	Tertiary	−0.462*	−0.005

(*) Significant at the 10% level, (**) Significant at the 5% level, (***) Significant at the 1% level.

8

Unemployment and Cumulative Disadvantage in the Labour Market

Richard Layte, Henrik Levin, John Hendrickx, and Ivano Bison

INTRODUCTION

The general rise in unemployment and labour market instability experienced by most OECD countries since the late 1970s masked large differences within and between countries as to the groups effected. A number of explanations have been put forward to explain such differences in vulnerability to unemployment. Within countries, industrial restructuring and sectoral change have meant that skilled and unskilled manual occupations have become both less numerous and more unstable. It also has been argued (Averitt 1968; Galbraith 1969; O'Conner 1973) that OECD economies have been dividing into 'core' and 'periphery' sectors, the 'core' sector having greater employment stability because of the predominance of larger, unionized organizations. More recently, it has been suggested that employment instability is the outcome of increasingly dualistic labour market practices *within organizations* (Atkinson 1984; Atkinson and Meager 1986). Lastly, explanations have also been put forward which emphasize the link between an individual's present risk of unemployment, and employment instability in their past work life.

However, none of these positions takes account of the possibility of the mediating effect of national labour market and welfare institutions. To do this, comparative analysis is needed. In this chapter, data from Britain, Sweden, The Netherlands, and Italy is used to analyse the effect of national regimes and their interaction with the employment structure. These countries offer us contrasting environments within which to assess the role of employment and welfare regimes in shaping employment instability. In the first section of the paper we examine different hypotheses about vulnerability to unemployment and attempt to situate these within the context of Britain, Sweden, The Netherlands, and Italy. The second section analyses the risk of unemployment in each country, exploring the interactive relationship between the employment structure, and national employment and welfare regimes in shaping vulnerability to unemployment. The third section concentrates on the processes of cumulative disadvantage and attempts to evaluate alternative explanations for the effect of past employment instability.

EXPLAINING VULNERABILITY TO UNEMPLOYMENT

Labour Market Structure and Vulnerability to Unemployment

A number of theorists have posited the existence of a dual economy with 'core' and 'peripheral' sectors differentiated along two main dimensions: an internal one concerning the complexity of organizational forms, and an external one of market dominance. The 'internal' dimension of segmentation relates to the way systems of work rules, hierarchical job ladders, and limited points of entry into large corporations produce a 'core' employment sector buffered from the exterior labour market and thus a dual labour market structure within the economy as a whole (Edwards 1975; Edwards 1979; Reich *et al.* 1973). However, these internal labour markets only develop within larger organizations, due to their advantages with respect to the second dimension of segmentation, that of market dominance. As such, core firms populate key segments of the economy which they control and stabilize, sometimes on a global scale, using strategic planning and co-ordination, whilst smaller firms occupy more vulnerable markets on the margin.

Reviewing the literature of segmentation, Baron and Bielby (1984: 471) argue that 'if there is any single "imperative" shaping the organization of work, it is [organizational] size'. The reason for the importance of organizational size is that 'large unionized, multi-product, differentiated, and technically sophisticated establishments are presumed to possess greater internal resources and capacity, thus diminishing their vulnerability'. Whereas, 'organizations at the other end of the spectrum are expected to be more susceptible to the dictates of their environments' (Baron and Bielby 1984: 458). Differentiation by size can be taken as a rough proxy of firm market dominance. Unions are also far more likely to be found in larger establishments (Rubery and Wilkinson 1994) and their presence can have important effects on the stability of the employment relationship above and beyond economic conditions and employment protection legislation (Lindbeck and Snower 1988).

From a rather different perspective, Goldthorpe (forthcoming) has outlined a theory of class differentiation *within* organizations that accounts for differential risks of unemployment. Using the transaction cost theories of Williamson (1985, 1994), he argues that the 'contractual hazards' associated with monitoring the quality and quantity of employees output, and the severity of the penalty the employer suffers if the employee leaves, lead to very different types of employment relationship for different categories of employee. If a job has few problems associated with the monitoring of the quality or quantity of the work done, and demands skills that are widely available in the general population, it is efficient for an employer to offer that employee a contract based upon 'labour contract' principles, in which employment takes the form of short, discrete exchanges of money for time. In contrast, where monitoring is difficult and perhaps may produce negative effects, and where the cost of the employee leaving is high, it is efficient for the employer to offer a 'service type' contract where salaried payment, profit, or performance-related benefits and a long-term career structure are exchanged for a more multi-faceted and diffuse effort in the employers best interests. The theory suggests that the semi-skilled and unskilled workers will be most at risk of unemployment since they are the most likely to be employed on 'labour contract' principles.

Recent research has also emphasized the link between employment instability within an individual's past work history and their present vulnerability to unemployment, although explanations for this link differ substantially. On the one hand, the segmentation of labour markets and entrapment within a more vulnerable segment has been offered as one explanation for the link (Payne and Payne 1992; Gallie *et al.* 1998; Gershuny and Marsh 1994). Thus, workers in the secondary labour market find it increasingly difficult to move into the primary labour market over time, as any initial disadvantage they had is compounded by the experience of work in precarious or short-lived jobs which offer little in the way of career development or training. On the other hand, it has also been argued that the link between one's present risk of unemployment and past instability is a consequence of innate personality deficiencies or attitudes and values learnt in primary socialization which are unfriendly to the work ethic and which decrease an individuals ability to hold down a job for extended periods (Murray 1992; Willetts 1992).

The National Context and Unemployment

Even if vulnerability to unemployment is strongly affected by the nature of the employment structure and past work history, it may also be the case that forms of national labour market regulation influence the distribution of unemployment. Although organizations may seek to offer certain forms of contract that minimize the contractual risks they face, their ability to do this will be shaped by employment legislation and the power of employee organizations in the environment in which they are operating.

The countries upon which we focus in this chapter—Britain, Sweden, Italy, and The Netherlands—provide a range of institutional contrasts. Britain is an example of the 'liberal' welfare regime with minimal regulation of employment, relatively weak trade union presence, and little investment in active labour market policies. Overall, welfare and employment policy in the UK has been directed at increasing labour market flexibility through decreasing direct labour costs, and undermining employment rights whilst using passive measures to deal with the consequences of unemployment. In contrast to the UK, active labour market measures amongst the unemployed have been emphasized in The Netherlands—an 'employment-centred' welfare regime. At the same time, protection against unfair dismissal and control of fixed-term and non-standard employment have been central planks of Dutch employment policy.

Italy can be seen as a country representative of the 'sub-protective' type of welfare state, but which is nonetheless characterized by a highly regulated labour market. It is also marked by strong corporatist elements in the role of non-state organizations, such as unions, in the regulation of the labour market. In the context of this chapter, it is the regulation of the labour market which is of prime importance since this has significant effects on the structure of organizations and jobs. Regulations on individual dismissals in Italy are particularly restrictive as decisions have to be justified to local authorities on the grounds of misconduct, or an objective reason to do with the enterprise (Samek Lodovici 1997). Until 1990, much employment regulation was restricted to firms of sixteen employees or more, although since then controls have become somewhat stronger even for very small firms.

Sweden is an example of the 'social democratic' or 'universalistic' welfare state where social rights are individually based, universal, and levels of 'decommodification' are high. Although the Swedish labour market regime has always emphasized labour mobility—albeit within high aggregate levels of employment—actual job security has remained high partly because of the influence of Swedish trade unions, and legislation on non-standard employment contracts. Since the early 1980s, however, Sweden has attempted to introduce greater flexibility into the labour market through the use of six-month fixed-term 'screening' contracts. These contracts allow an employer to screen the productivity of an employee for a period of six months, after which they can choose either to terminate the contract or make the position permanent. These types of contract have become very common with almost half of new contracts since 1982 being of this type (Kazamaki 1991).

Overall then, these institutional contrasts lead to a number of expectations about country differences in unemployment risks. First, compared to the UK, the nature of employment regulation in Italy and The Netherlands means that once in a job, employees are in a fairly secure position, except that Dutch workers on short-duration contracts will be more insecure until they have passed the twelve-month legal threshold and been made permanent. In Sweden, *de facto* regulation through corporatist agreements means that employees are in a more secure position than in the UK, but are relatively unstable in the first six months of employment. These different forms of regulation should lead to distinctive temporal patterns of exit from employment in each country in the models to come.

Second, employment protection legislation is only applied to medium to large organizations in Sweden and Italy—those with less than twenty-five and sixteen employees respectively; thus we may only see differences between small and large organizations here compared to effects across the size range in the UK and The Netherlands where there is no differentiation by organizational size.

Third, we may see different effects for past unemployment on the probability of reoccurrence between Sweden and The Netherlands on the one hand, and Italy and Britain on the other. As just outlined, Sweden spends a great deal more of its welfare budget on active, as opposed to passive, labour market measures compared to the UK or Italy. This means that unemployed people in Sweden will receive training, or in the last resort, a job from the state. The Netherlands has a less well developed structure of active labour market policies, but nonetheless, compared to the UK and Italy, these could still ameliorate some of the secondary effects of unemployment such as discrimination from employers, the degradation of skills or a decline of work norms among the unemployed themselves that make entrapment in unemployment more likely.

DATA AND VARIABLES

The empirical analyses in this paper use retrospective work-history data from the Employment in Britain Survey[1] (Gallie 1992), Swedish Level of Living Survey[2] (1991), the Italian Household Longitudinal Survey[3] (1997), and the Households in The Netherlands Survey[4] (1995)—from here on referred to as EIB, LofL, IHLS, and HIN. The EIB work history file includes 5622 individuals, the LofL 3303, IHLS 7914, and the HIN 3354. All four

---

[1] Data used with the permission of Duncan Gallie, Nuffield College, Oxford.

[2] Data used with the permission of the Institutet för Social Forskning, Stockholms Universitet.

[3] Università degli Studi di Trento & Instituto Trentino di Cultura, Indagine longitudinale sulle famiglie italiane, 1997 (anno ultima ondata). File dati su supporto magnetico. Responsabile scientifico: A. Schizzerotto.

[4] Data used with the permission of the Department of Sociology, Utrecht University, The Netherlands.

surveys used standardized interviews which included questions about the life courses of respondents thus allowing us to look at longitudinal information about individuals over a number of different areas. There is very little information on the reliability of retrospective data (cf. Moss and Goldstein 1979), but there is some evidence (Elias 1996) that short spells of employment and unemployment may be forgotten the further back in time the event. This may mean that estimates of the length of employment events may be upwardly biased by the loss of short spells of unemployment, but there is no evidence that such attrition is unevenly distributed. Any such bias may however lead to an underestimation of the effect of past unemployment on the probability of future unemployment and it would increase the propensity to exit employment spells the closer one came to the date of interview.

In all the data sets, events of one month or more are recorded in the 'processual' record along with other, event-specific information about the nature of the organization: industry, number of employees, EGP (Erikson/ Goldthorpe) class category, whether a new or same employer. A range of other time constant information, such as sex, or ethnicity is also available from each main survey. Unemployment is defined in terms of respondents' self-report of their labour market position.

A range of variables were included in the analysis to examine the hypotheses considered earlier. A variable that represents the Erikson/Goldthorpe (Erikson and Goldthorpe 1993) class schema is included as a six-level variable, with the lower routine non-manuals (Class IIIb) combined with the unskilled groups. To examine the hypothesis about the size of the organization, a three-level variable is entered. This was coded as <25, 25–499, 500+ employees in Britain, The Netherlands, and Sweden; and <16, 16–499, 500+ employees in Italy.

To examine the effect of the person's past work life on their present risk of becoming unemployed we entered variables that represent the number of employers, industries, and types of occupations a person has experience of over their life-course up to their present job. An employee's past experience of unemployment is also entered into the statistical model. Since recent unemployment is of interest rather than spells in the more distant past, a variable measuring the months of unemployment in the last five years is used. This type of measure allows us to introduce an assumption of 'discounting over time' for past employment behaviour. That is, we assume that past events are not taken into account by employers after a specific period of time.

A number of variables were introduced to reduce confounding effects. There were grounds for expecting that the region a person lived in might have affected the likelihood that they would become unemployed. In Britain: the Midlands, North West, North East, Scotland, and South Wales all suffered particularly high unemployment rates. Southern Italy and the Italian Islands were particularly badly affected by economic recession for an extended period and differ markedly from the North West and particularly the North East and Central regions of Italy. In The Netherlands, the Western region faired slightly better than the North or East, but regional differences were far less marked than in Britain and Italy.

As well as region, variables are entered to represent the yearly national unemployment rate (in time varying format), and the industry[5] of the job as well as whether the job is part time. Unemployment has been much more common among the young, especially in the 1980s, and especially in Italy, and amongst some ethnic minorities. In Britain, unemployment badly affected the West Indian population, although other minorities, notably those from India, Pakistan and South-East Asia fared rather better. To control for these effects, variables are entered to represent the respondents age and ethnic background.

THE DISTRIBUTION OF THE RISK OF UNEMPLOYMENT

To examine the risk that an employee ran of becoming unemployed in each month from 1975, we use a statistical model called the 'piecewise constant exponential hazard rate model' (Blossfeld and Rohwer 1995). As the section on the national context and unemployment suggested, we are interested in how the risk of unemployment changes with the length of time the person has been in a job, since we expect different patterns in the four countries. The piecewise constant model allows us to control for the length of the employment spell whilst also examining the changing risk of unemployment. In this way, we get to examine how the processes underlying the risk of unemployment unfold through time.

Before examining the effect of particular variables on the risk of unemployment, we can shed light on the processes underlying the move from employment to unemployment in our four countries by examining the way the risk of unemployment changes over time. Although the actual coefficients for each model are shown in the appendices, the pattern of risk is better grasped graphically.

Figure 8.1 shows the 'hazard rate' or risk of moving from employment to unemployment by the length of the respondent's job amongst British men

[5] Unfortunately, the HIN survey did not contain information on industry thus this variable is not used in the Dutch models. Similarly, without this variable we cannot calculate the number of industry changes in the persons employment history, thus this variable is also omitted from the Dutch models.

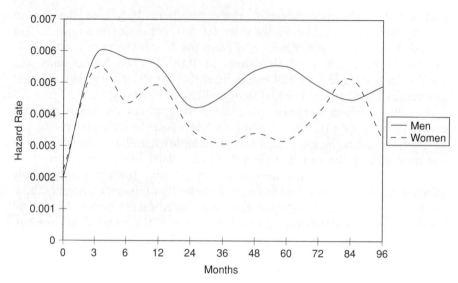

FIG. 8.1. Hazard of exit from employment to unemployment in Britain, by sex
Source: The Employment in Britain Survey, 1992.

and women controlling for the covariates previously mentioned. As can be seen, women in Britain have a generally lower risk reflecting the lower unemployment rates amongst women in the period from 1975 to 1992. More importantly, we do not observe a decreasing risk over time for either men or women. Generally, the risk is inversely related to tenure as individuals accumulate job-specific investments and companies gain information on employee productivity. However, this relationship is also a function of labour market regulation in an economy through employment legislation and trade union activity, as well as being affected by macro-economic conditions. As already discussed, levels of employment protection in the UK are rather low. Although the costs of dismissal increase with length of service, no statutory protection is obtained for the first two years, or five years for part-time workers, and severance pay is relatively low: one week per year of service after age 22 up to a maximum of twenty weeks. The period covered by the data was also one in which there were two major recessions, both of which affected those in mid-career with medium to long term employment tenure. The outcome of weak protection and bad economic conditions is clear from the meandering, but basically flat pattern of risk in Fig. 8.1.

If we turn to Fig. 8.2, we see a different pattern emerging for Sweden. Here, although unemployment rates between men and women were about the same, and low from 1975 to 1992, controlling for other factors, women have a higher risk of moving into unemployment. However, unlike Britain,

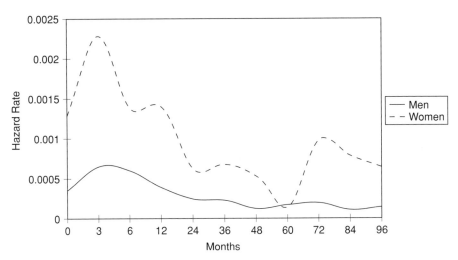

F IG. 8.2. Hazard of exit from employment to unemployment in Sweden, by sex
Source: Swedish Level of Living Survey, 1991.

both men and women exhibit a generally negative relationship between tenure and risk, except for an initial increase in the hazard in the first six months of employment. Our hypothesis was that the use of six-month screening contracts in Sweden after 1982 should lead to an increased risk of unemployment between three and six months of employment and this seems to be apparent in Fig. 8.2.

Turning to Italy, our hypothesis was that employment legislation and trade union power coupled with a relatively immobile labour market would mean that we should observe a slow and uniform decrease in the risk of unemployment for Italians. This does seem to be the case amongst Italian men, but amongst Italian women there is a pronounced increase in risk in the first three months of a job. This is interesting in the light of differences in the levels of trade union coverage between men and women in Italy, and may reflect the weaker position female workers find themselves in. But there is no ready explanation for the pronounced peak at three months tenure. Similarly, the results displayed in Fig. 8.3 also show that Italian women have a consistently higher risk than Italian men. Since we are controlling for industrial sector, region, and employment status, this large difference suggests that there is another, sex-specific process that may be shaping the risk of unemployment for Italian women. Until recent changes in legislation, vacancies in Italy had to be awarded to main earners in households, usually men (Emerson 1988), and it may be that this practice of differential recruitment is extended to the use of lay-off and dismissal procedures.

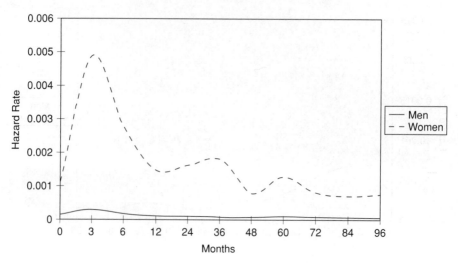

F<small>IG</small>. 8.3. Hazard of exit from employment to unemployment in Italy, by sex
Source: Italian Household Longitudinal Survey, 1997.

Figure 8.4 shows the pattern of risk over ninety-six months of tenure for Dutch men and women. As with Italy, our hypothesis was that we should see a shallow downward slope in risk in these models, but unlike Italy, we may also see an initial rise amongst Dutch respondents in the first twelve months, which is the maximum duration of fixed-term contracts in The Netherlands. Figure 8.4 shows some support for both these hypotheses in the Dutch models. Both the male and female 'hazard rates', or risk of unemployment rise to an initial high at six months and fall quickly after a year before following the slow downward course expected of a highly regulated labour market. The risk for women tends to be higher than for men, reflecting the generally higher unemployment rates among women after 1980.

Having established the basic differences in the risks of unemployment both within and between countries, we can now examine the effects of different covariates and assess the different explanations of labour market vulnerability. Table 8.1 shows the coefficients and levels of significance of the variables representing the Erikson/Goldthorpe class schema in the male country specific models controlling for both other structural variables and individual level variables. As expected given their 'labour contract' employment terms, unskilled manual employees are most at risk of entering unemployment. But among British male employees this risk is also shared by some categories of employees who are closer to a 'service' type contract, such as routine non-manual workers. It is clear that the risk of unemployment

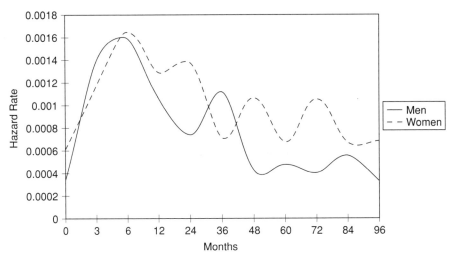

FIG. 8.4. Hazard of exit from employment to unemployment in
The Netherlands, by sex

Source: Households in The Netherlands Survey, 1995.

TABLE 8.1. *Risk of entry into unemployment for men, coefficients and significance of selected variables (final piecewise constant exponential model)*

	Britain	Sweden	Italy	Netherlands
EGP Class				
Service	*ref.*	*ref.*	*ref.*	*ref.*
Routine non-manual	0.46***	0.37	−0.14	0.15
Petty-bourgeois	0.53**	0.34	−0.83***	−0.70
Technical & supervisory	0.27	−0.81	0.36	0.00
Skilled manual	0.51***	0.91***	−0.05	0.48*
Unskilled manual	0.87***	0.97***	0.36*	0.33
Organization Size				
Large	*ref.*	*ref.*	*ref.*	*ref.*
Small	0.47***	0.85***	0.41**	1.29***
Medium	0.25**	0.40	0.29	0.89**
Log likelihood	−7859.47	−1738.38	−3611.43	−1039.99
N	36156	17423	37113	12802

Notes: * = P < 0.05, ** = P < 0.01, *** = P < 0.001.

Layte, Levin, Hendrickx and Bison

TABLE 8.2. *Risk of entry into unemployment for women' coefficients and significance of selected variables (final piecewise constant exponential model)*

	Britain	Sweden	Italy	Netherlands
EGP Class				
Service	*ref.*	*ref.*	*ref.*	*ref.*
Routine non-manual	0.10	0.19	0.08	0.46
Petty-bourgeois	−0.26	0.65	−0.54*	−0.32
Technical & supervisory	0.35	−10.5	0.38	*n.a.*
Skilled manual	0.12	0.26	0.49*	0.85
Unskilled manual	0.29**	0.82**	0.34**	1.00**
Organization Size				
Large	*ref.*	*ref.*	*ref.*	*ref.*
Small	0.28*	0.64*	0.05	0.52
Medium	0.20	0.33	0.18	0.20
Log likelihood	−5284.43	−1264.97	−3783.03	−817.253
N	31444	17834	24749	11259

Notes: * = P < 0.05, ** = P < 0.01, *** = P < 0.001.

is spread far more widely amongst British employees compared to the Swedes, Dutch, and Italians. Interestingly, Table 8.1 shows that only the skilled manual class in The Netherlands is significantly different from the service class in terms of the risk of unemployment. This may be due to the fact that a large proportion of middle-aged, male, unskilled manual workers claimed sickness benefit rather than unemployment benefit after the onset of recession in The Netherlands in the 1980s.

Amongst Italian men, the difference between service class workers and unskilled manual workers is much smaller and the effect less significant than in either Britain or Sweden, which suggests that processes of segmentation are far weaker. This is unsurprising given the strong position of Italian employees, be they in professional or unskilled manual positions. A smaller, less significant effect for Dutch skilled manual employees may also be evidence that where all class groups are protected by employment regulation, this decreases the segmenting processes that would otherwise occur within organizations.

Table 8.2 has the results for the women's models in the four countries. What is immediately apparent is the much smaller difference between service class and unskilled British women compared to British men. Being in an unskilled job does increase the risk of unemployment, but to a much lesser degree than amongst the men. This reflects the stability of much female employment in expanding sectors. On the other hand, unskilled Dutch women have a far higher risk of entry into unemployment than either skilled, or unskilled male Dutch manual workers. As in the model for Italian men, self-employed Italian women are at a lower risk of unemployment than service class women, but overall, it seems that being in an unskilled position increases the risk of unemployment for both men and women in all four countries.

Was there any evidence of an 'external' segmentation of the economy into more or less stable sectors defined by the size of workplaces? Tables 8.1 and 8.2 show that being an employee in a small organization of less than twenty-five employees makes it far more likely that the job will end in unemployment, compared to being in a large organization of 500 plus employees. This is as true for men as it is for women, except in Italy and The Netherlands where organizational size seems to be a less important variable in women's employment. Amongst men at least, there is also support here for the hypothesis that the application of employment protection legislation to organizations over a certain size leads to differential insecurity between organizations. If we look at the effects for Sweden and Italy in Table 8.1, both countries with exclusions for small organizations, it is clear that jobs in medium size organizations are not significantly more likely to end in unemployment than those in large.

Overall then, Tables 8.1 and 8.2 show that there are distinct processes of dualism within all of the countries in this paper, though to a greater or lesser extent depending on the legislative environment and union presence. This is true even after controlling for a number of confounding variables: unemployment rate, persons age, ethnicity, geographical region, and industrial sector.

Lastly, what effects do we see from the variables that represent past work life experiences? Previous research (Payne and Payne 1992; Gallie *et al.* 1998; Gershuny and Marsh 1994) has suggested that a spell of unemployment can make it more likely that a person will experience further unemployment in the future. However, our hypothesis was that the cumulative disadvantage associated with unemployment may not be as significant a factor in Sweden compared to Britain and Italy because of the active labour market policies in Sweden. Similarly, the albeit it more limited active labour market policies in The Netherlands may also reduce the effect of past unemployment. Tables 8.3 and 8.4 show the coefficients and significance of these variables for each country and for men and women.

The insignificant effects for Sweden in both the male and female models are evidence in favour of the hypothesis, as is the substantially smaller effect for The Netherlands compared to Britain and Italy. However, there is some mixed evidence for Swedish women in the form of a significant positive effect for the number of occupations. In the British and Italian models on the other hand, there is strong evidence of a cumulative effect resulting from

TABLE 8.3. *Risk of entry into unemployment for men, coefficients and significance of past work-life variables (final piecewise constant exponential model)*

	Britain	Sweden	Italy	Netherlands
Past work-life variables				
Months unemp. last 5 yrs	0.07***	0.06	0.07***	0.03***
Number employers	0.06**	0.12	−0.24***	0.01
Number occupations	0.00	0.13	0.15	−0.18**
Number industries	0.05	0.00	0.15	*n.a.*
Log likelihood	−5284.43	−1264.97	−3783.03	−1039.99
N	31444	17834	24749	12802

Notes: * = P < 0.05, ** = P < 0.01, *** = P < 0.001.

TABLE 8.4. *Risk of entry into unemployment for women, coefficients and significance of past work-life variables (final piecewise constant exponential model)*

	Britain	Sweden	Italy	Netherlands
Past work-life variables				
Months unemp. last 5 yrs	0.08***	0.03	0.08***	0.05***
Number employers	0.10***	−0.09	−0.23***	0.02
Number occupations	0.05	0.23**	0.12	−0.12
Number industries	−0.03	−0.07	0.17	*n.a.*
Log likelihood	−5284.43	−1264.97	−3783.03	−817.253
N	31444	17834	24749	11259

Notes: * = P < 0.05, ** = P < 0.01, *** = P < 0.001.

past unemployment for both men and women. In both countries, a month of unemployment raises the odds multiplier by 7 per cent for men and 8 per cent for women.

How should we explain this effect of past unemployment? It may be, as underclass theorists (Murray 1992; Willetts 1992) suggest that this relationship is a consequence of the attitudes and general instability of particular individuals, but it may also be due to the discriminatory practices of employers (Calender and Metcalf 1991; Maguire 1992) who see any unemployment in the past of potential employees as a mark of unreliability and/or low productivity. In the second scenario, we return to the 'structural' explanation of unemployment via the greater vulnerability of particular occupational positions and the actions of employers in discriminating against those affected. Using the results from the hazard analyses alone it is difficult to decide between these explanations. But if it were the case that unemployment makes it more likely that a person will move into a vulnerable structural location, and conversely, that it also makes it more difficult to leave it, the evidence would tend to favour an explanation based upon employer discrimination rather than personal instability.

UNEMPLOYMENT AND MOVEMENT
BETWEEN CLASSES

To examine the factors that predict downward occupational mobility we have used an ordered logit regression model. This allows us to examine the relationship between a dependent variable which is categorical, but which nonetheless has a particular order to it, and a set of independent variables.[6]

Our model of movement between classes shares many of the variables from previous models. We still control for characteristics that may confound the effect of other more theoretically interesting variables, thus age, sex, region, and ethnicity are entered. Most importantly for our present purposes, variables representing the respondent's previous class location and work-life experiences are used as predictors of their destination. Once again then, we take into account past changes in employer, occupation, and industry. We also enter a variable representing whether the respondent experienced a spell of unemployment immediately before moving to the destination class.

Table 8.5 gives the effects of selected variables for class destination in the four countries. Previous class position has a great deal of influence upon the next position attained. With the self-employed class positions removed, there is a steady negative growth in the estimates of effect in all four countries as we move from routine non-manual positions to the unskilled manual class. A history of frequent moves between different employers also has a negative effect on the level of the social class position attained in all four countries.

But, is there an effect for having experienced an unemployment spell prior to entry into the destination class? Table 8.5 shows that unemployment has a very significant negative effect on the level of destination class in all four countries. We have already seen in the last section that manual workers tended to be more vulnerable to becoming unemployed, but the results in Table 8.5 show that mobility out of these positions is difficult, and moreover, that unemployment exerts a strong negative effect on mobility. This suggests that the cumulative effect that we saw for past unemployment experience in previous models is likely to be due to exposure to vulnerable class

---

[6] Because we are assuming that the classes have an underlying linear scale, we will drop movements to and from the petty-bourgeois EGP categories which do not sit easily on a labour/service contract scale.

TABLE 8.5. *Coefficients and significance of selected variables on EGP class destination (ordered logit regression)*

Variable	Britain	Sweden	Italy	Netherlands
Prev. EGP class				
Service	*ref.*	*ref.*	*ref.*	*ref.*
Routine non-manual	−2.22***	−2.14***	−2.41***	−1.26***
Technical & supervisory	−3.53***	−2.57***	−3.77***	−1.87***
Skilled manual	−4.11***	−3.60***	−4.55***	−2.95***
Unskilled	−5.10***	−4.64***	−5.62***	−3.29***
Unemployed last event	−0.64***	−0.77***	−0.50***	−0.31**
Number employers	−0.03***	−0.05***	−0.15***	−0.015***
Number occupations	0.07	−0.36	−0.02	0.08***
Number industries	−0.24	0.84	0.08	*n.a.*
Log likelihood	−24632.77	−8953.91	−7693.49	−7983.05
N	21770	8949	7623	6270

Notes: Year, sex, age, region, and ethnicity entered but not shown.
Significance: * = P < 0.05, ** = P < 0.01, *** = P < 0.001.

locations in the past, rather than to personal characteristics that lead to work life instability.

Although unemployment has a general negative effect on class destination, can we detect a specific increase after unemployment in the probability of moving directly into unskilled manual working class locations? We can examine this question directly by using a logistic regression to analyse the probability of entering the unskilled manual class compared to any other destination. As in the ordered logit model, we control for a number of factors such as sex, age, and year that may confound the effect, whilst focusing on the direct effect of being unemployed in the previous spell. Table 8.6 gives the coefficients and significance of selected variables from the logit regression. What is immediately clear is that all class categories stand an increased chance of entering the unskilled manual class after unemployment and, as in Table 8.5, there is a distinct, positive gradient to the effect as we move from the routine non-manual employees to the unskilled manual employees.

The large positive and significant effects for the unskilled employees in all the countries confirms our previous finding that once in this class it is difficult to leave. However, Table 8.6 also shows that having experienced a spell of unemployment before the move significantly increases the probability of entering the unskilled manual working class. As in Table 8.5, the number of employers that a person has worked for in the past also increases the probability of entering the unskilled manual class in all the countries.

TABLE 8.6. *Coefficients and significance of selected variables on probability of entry into unskilled manual class (logit regression)*

Variable	Britain	Sweden	Italy	Netherlands
Prev. EGP Class				
Service	*ref.*	*ref.*	*ref.*	*ref.*
Routine non-manual	0.61***	1.19***	1.25***	0.56***
Technical & supervisory	1.46***	1.46***	2.11***	0.96***
Skilled manual	1.66***	1.74***	2.14***	1.35***
Unskilled	3.33***	3.44***	3.74***	2.60***
Unemployed last event	0.68***	0.85***	0.48***	0.40**
Number employers	0.03***	0.04*	0.11*	0.07**
Number occupations	−0.21	−0.44	−0.01	−0.01
Number industries	0.38	−0.12	−0.01	*n.a.*
Log likelihood	−10358.98	−4343.59	−3933.91	−2731.17
N	21948	8954	7631	6270

Notes: Year, sex, age, region, and ethnicity entered but not shown.

Significance: * = $P < 0.05$, ** = $P < 0.01$, *** = $P < 0.001$.

Overall, Tables 8.5 and 8.6 lend weight to the view that the cumulative effect of past unemployment that we saw in the earlier analyses is a product of past occupational position rather than personal employment instability. Unemployment increases the probability of entering the unskilled manual working class and decreases the probability that one will change class categories into a more secure position.

CONCLUSIONS

Whilst accepting that the risk of unemployment is a function of the economic cycle and the rise and fall of particular industries, this chapter has used empirical evidence to examine several other possible explanations for the distribution of this risk. Drawing on aspects of dual labour market theory, we examined the differential risk attached to being employed in the 'peripheral' sector represented by smaller organizations compared to being employed in large organisations. The results showed that the size of the organization in which a person is employed is a very important predictor of their risk of entering unemployment. It seems probable that the size of an organization is a proxy for level of unionization and organizational stability, which have important effects for vulnerability to unemployment. We also examined whether different types of employees within organizations face differential risks of unemployment as predicted by class theory. The evidence showed clearly that employees in different class positions faced differential risks of unemployment and insecure work.

However, these characteristics of jobs and sectors affect individuals differentially depending on the structure and extent of national employment protection. Where legislation on dismissal is limited, collective bargaining fragmentary, and the cost of dismissal to the employer low, the risk of unemployment is spread far more widely across the population of employees. In Britain, results show that even routine non-manual men run a significantly higher risk of unemployment compared to service class groups, whereas the higher risk is confined to skilled manual or unskilled manual groups in the other three countries. The national employment regime also shapes the nature of the risk of unemployment over the tenure of jobs. For Britain, the models showed that the risk of unemployment is relatively constant, irrespective of tenure, whereas this risk decreased over time in Italy, The Netherlands, and Sweden. In Sweden and The Netherlands, another indicator of the effect of legislation appeared in the form of an increased entry into unemployment between three and six months or six and twelve months of tenure. In The Netherlands this coincides with the end of the period allowed for fixed-duration contracts, whereas in Sweden, it reflects the end of the six month period allowed by the legislation aimed at increasing labour market flexibility.

In general, both past unemployment and frequent employer changes increase the probability of experiencing unemployment in the future. Vulnerability to repeated unemployment is likely to result from entrapment within a more insecure work location. The experience of unemployment significantly increased the probability of downward occupational mobility, and reduced the chances of moving to less vulnerable positions. In particular, unemployment increases the probability of moving into the unskilled manual class, the most vulnerable of labour market locations. We had hypothesized that the Swedish and Dutch systems of active labour market policies may ameliorate the longer-term effects of unemployment and this did indeed seem to be so. The models for Sweden revealed no significant effect for past unemployment and the effects were substantially reduced in The Netherlands compared to Britain and Italy.

APPENDIX

TABLE 8A. *Coefficients and significance of a piecewise constant exponential model of transition to unemployment from employment, British men and women, 1975–1992*

		Men		Women	
Variable		Model 1	Model 5	Model 1	Model 5
Time Period	0	−7.13***	−6.21***	−6.55***	−6.10***
(months)	3	−6.13***	−5.14***	−5.75***	−5.21***
	6	−6.27***	−5.16***	−6.07***	−5.43***
	12	−6.51***	−5.20***	−6.11***	−5.31***
	24	−6.96***	−5.46***	−6.60***	−5.64***
	36	−7.01***	−5.38***	−6.88***	−5.79***
	48	−6.97***	−5.22***	−6.87***	−5.68***
	60	−7.01***	−5.20***	−7.02***	−5.75***
	72	−7.20***	−5.32***	−6.85***	−5.51***
	84	−7.34***	−5.41***	−6.67***	−5.26***
	96	−7.33***	−5.32***	−7.30***	−5.75***
Service		ref.	ref.	ref.	ref.
Routine non-manual		0.58***	0.46***	0.32**	0.10
Petty-bourgeois		0.81***	0.53**	0.29	−0.26
Technical & supervisory		0.46**	0.27	0.73**	0.35
Skilled manual		0.95***	0.51***	0.59***	0.12
Unskilled manual		1.38***	0.87***	0.73***	0.29**
Large organization		ref.	ref.	ref.	ref.
Small organization		0.61***	0.47***	0.37***	0.28*
Medium organization		0.35***	0.25**	0.24*	0.20
Full-time		ref.	ref.	ref.	ref.
Part-time		0.58***	0.47***	−0.55***	−0.42***
Finance			ref.		ref.
Mineral & agriculture			0.15		0.40
Manufacture			0.27		0.50**
Construction			0.39*		0.94**
Dist. & catering			0.18		0.61***
Transport			−0.34		0.39
Public			0.00		0.06
Other service			0.46*		0.55**
Months unemp. last 5 yrs			0.07***		0.08***
Number employers			0.06**		0.10***
Number occupations			0.00		0.05
Number industries			0.05		−0.03
		N: 36156		N: 31444	
Log likelihood		−8259.18	−7859.47	−5551.38	−5284.43

Note: Coefficients for age, region, ethnicity, yearly unemployment rate are entered but not shown. * = P < 0.05, ** = P < 0.01, *** = P < 0.001.

TABLE 8B. *Coefficients and significance of a piecewise constant exponential model of transition to unemployment from employment, Swedish men and women, 1975–1991*

		Men		Women	
Variable		Model 1	Model 5	Model 1	Model 5
Time Period	0	−7.56***	−7.95***	−7.67***	−6.66***
(months)	3	−6.96***	−7.32***	−7.13***	−6.08***
	6	−7.12***	−7.42***	−7.70***	−6.59***
	12	−7.66***	−7.87***	−7.79***	−6.57***
	24	−8.20***	−8.33***	−8.72***	−7.39***
	36	−8.34***	−8.40***	−8.72***	−7.29***
	48	−8.99***	−8.97***	−9.03***	−7.52***
	60	−8.74***	−8.67***	−10.4***	−8.83***
	72	−8.69***	−8.54***	−8.58***	−6.93***
	84	−9.36***	−9.16***	−8.87***	−7.14***
	96	−9.24***	−8.84***	−9.34***	−7.34***
Service		ref.	ref.	ref.	ref.
Routine non-manual		0.28	0.37	0.38	0.19
Petty-bourgeois		0.55	0.34	1.15*	0.65
Technical & supervisory		−0.64	−0.81	−6.77	−10.5
Skilled manual		1.19***	0.91***	0.47	0.26
Unskilled manual		1.30***	0.97***	1.18***	0.82**
Large organization		ref.	ref.	ref.	ref.
Small organization		0.98***	0.85***	0.68**	0.64*
Medium organization		0.42	0.40	0.37	0.33
Finance			ref.		ref.
Mineral & agriculture			1.52**		0.50
Manufacture			1.05*		0.09
Construction			1.52**		0.16
Dist. & catering			1.16*		−0.04
Transport			0.76		0.26
Public			1.50**		−0.15
Other service			1.41*		0.88*
Months unemp. last 5 yrs			0.06		0.03
Number employers			0.12		−0.09
Number occupations			0.13		0.23**
Number industries			0.00		−0.07
		N: 17423		N: 17834	
Log likelihood		−1787.17	−1738.38	−1306.0991	−1264.9717

Note: Coefficients for age, region, ethnicity, yearly unemployment rate are entered but not shown. * = P < 0.05, ** = P < 0.01, *** = P < 0.001.

TABLE 8C. *Coefficients and significance of a piecewise constant exponential model of transition to unemployment from employment, Italian men and women, 1975–1997*

		Men		Women	
Variable		Model 1	Model 5	Model 1	Model 5
Time Period	0	−6.94***	−8.81***	−6.26***	−6.77***
(months)	3	−6.27***	−8.09***	−4.96***	−5.32***
	6	−6.94***	−8.70***	−5.71***	−5.92***
	12	−7.39***	−9.06***	−6.44***	−6.51***
	24	−7.62***	−9.20***	−6.46***	−6.41***
	36	−7.85***	−9.37***	−6.46***	−6.31***
	48	−7.81***	−9.28***	−7.35***	−7.14***
	60	−7.79***	−9.24***	−6.87***	−6.63***
	72	−7.99***	−9.40***	−7.36***	−7.09***
	84	−7.94***	−9.33***	−7.54***	−7.22***
	96	−8.42***	−9.68***	−7.70***	−7.16***
Service		ref.	ref.	ref.	ref.
Routine non-manual		0.19	−0.14	0.10	0.08
Petty-bourgeois		−0.44*	−0.83***	−0.68**	−0.54*
Technical & supervisory		0.55	0.36	0.24	0.38
Skilled manual		0.49**	−0.05	0.64***	0.49*
Unskilled manual		0.88***	0.36*	0.51***	0.34**
Large organization		ref.	ref.	ref.	ref.
Small organization		0.71***	0.41**	0.14	0.05
Medium organization		0.45***	0.29	0.26*	0.18
Full-time		ref.	ref.	ref.	ref.
Part-time		0.80***	0.56*	0.04	0.01
Finance			ref.		ref.
Mineral & agriculture			1.23		0.26
Manufacture			2.01***		0.16
Construction			2.39***		0.44
Dist. & catering			2.26***		0.30
Transport			2.51***		0.50*
Public			1.79**		0.35
Other service			2.10***		0.10
Months unemp. last 5 yrs			0.07***		0.08***
Number employers			−0.24***		−0.23***
Number occupations			0.15		0.12
Number industries			0.15		0.17
		N: 37113		N: 24749	
Log likelihood		−3760.47	−3611.43	−3990.94	−3783.03

Note: Coefficients for age, region, ethnicity, yearly unemployment rate are entered but not shown. * = $P < 0.05$, ** = $P < 0.01$, *** = $P < 0.001$.

TABLE 8D. *Coefficients and significance of a piecewise constant exponential model of transition to unemployment from employment, Dutch men and women, 1975–1995*

Variable		Men		Women	
		Model 1	Model 4	Model 1	Model 4
Time Period	0	−8.73***	−8.0***	−7.77***	−7.38***
(months)	3	−7.30***	−6.57***	−7.17***	−6.74***
	6	−7.21***	−6.44***	−6.85***	−6.40***
	12	−7.66***	−6.86***	−7.21***	−6.65***
	24	−8.06***	−7.21***	−7.22***	−6.59***
	36	−7.67***	−6.8***	−7.96***	−7.25***
	48	−8.68***	−7.78***	−7.60***	−6.84***
	60	−8.57***	−7.64***	−8.11***	−7.29***
	72	−8.78***	−7.82***	−7.73***	−6.85***
	84	−8.49***	−7.5***	−8.23***	−7.30***
	96	−9.19***	−8.04***	−8.44***	−7.28***
Service		ref.	ref.	ref.	ref.
Routine non-manual		0.13	0.16	0.46	0.46
Petty-bourgeois		−0.82	−0.7	−0.57	−0.32
Technical & supervisory		−0.17	0.00	n.a.	n.a.
Skilled manual		0.64**	0.48*	0.97	0.85
Unskilled manual		0.37	0.33	0.95**	1.00**
Large organization		ref.	ref.	ref.	ref.
Small organization		1.45***	1.3***	0.73*	0.52
Medium organization		0.94**	0.89**	0.21	0.20
Full-time		ref.	ref.	ref.	ref.
Part-time		0.58	0.58	−0.79***	−0.70**
Months unemp. last 5 yrs			0.03***		0.05***
Number employers			0.01		0.02
Number occupations			−0.18**		−0.12
		N: 12802		N: 11259	
Log likelihood		−1058.09	−1039.99	−844.67	−817.25

Note: Coefficients for age, region, ethnicity, yearly unemployment rate are entered but not shown. * = $P < 0.05$, ** = $P < 0.01$, *** = $P < 0.001$.

9

Lone Mothers' Poverty and Employment

Lisbeth Pedersen, Hanne Weise, Sheila Jacobs, and Michael White

INTRODUCTION

All European countries have experienced a rise in the number of lone mothers and several analyses have pointed to their exposed position in the society (Lewis 1997; Bradshaw *et al.* 1996). The crucial dilemma of the lone mother is her situation as a sole caregiver and a sole breadwinner. Variations in welfare state regimes may lead to significant divergence in the employment possibilities and income poverty of lone mothers in Europe. The classification of four types of welfare regimes would point to the universalistic regime, with high level of cash benefit, as a regime that offers lone mothers protection against poverty. In the employment-centred regime the income level of the lone mother will depend on employment status, and—for those not participating—may well be lower than for married mothers and women who are included in the labour market. However, active employment policy— as in the universalistic regime—should make it relatively easier for the mothers to participate. In the liberal/minimal regime, income for those lone mothers not in employment will be depressed because of the low welfare cover, and the weakness of active employment policy will accentuate this problem. The sub-protective welfare regime offers hardly any welfare support to lone mothers, and since active employment policy is also virtually non-existent, the mother's income will depend on herself and her family.

It seems likely, however, that the simple four-regime typology will not by itself give a satisfactory explanation of the differences in poverty rates and labour market attachment among lone mothers. This is because the care-regime for children does not play a sufficiently central role in the typology. Lewis (1997) makes a distinction between care-regimes that differ in their attitude to the mother mainly as a caregiver or as a worker and in the sources available to reward the mothers for their care-work. Countries with traditionally strong male-breadwinner regimes usually consider the mother as a caregiver and therefore make some provision to treat the lone mother as such. On the other hand the lone mothers in these countries often have a stronger incentive to work than married mothers since the absence of the father means the loss of an important source of income. In the countries that have generally higher participation rates among women and among mothers, the lone mother is also expected to take care of herself and her children. Therefore the state is also more engaged in providing social services that make participation in the labour market possible. In its ideal form the mother in the care-giving regime is not expected to be active on the labour market and will be given social support that substitutes for the wages from paid work. Conversely a lone mother in the parent-worker regime will be offered a care service that is available and affordable for all working parents.

This chapter is concerned with the living conditions and the labour market attachment of lone mothers in European countries that belong to different welfare and care-regimes. It is in two main sections. The first consists of a comparative analysis of the characteristics and circumstances of lone mothers across eleven countries of the European Union, for which data were available in the European Community Household Panel (ECHP) survey, or Europanel. This part of the paper presents the problems of lone mothers in Europe in terms of measures of their prevalence and poverty rate. Next the lone mothers' income packages are studied, their attachment to the labour market is described, and some possible explanations for the differences that are seen are suggested. The second part focuses upon two of these countries, Denmark and Great Britain, in order to analyse more intensively the institutional explanations for differences in the employment of lone mothers.

PREVALENCE AND LIVING CONDITION OF LONE MOTHERS IN THE EU COUNTRIES

In Fig. 9.1 the number of lone mothers in the eleven European countries is shown as a percentage of all mothers in the ECHP, aged 16–60 years. Lone mothers are defined as female respondents who are mothers of at least one resident child aged less than 18 years and are without a resident partner. They may, or may not, head their own households. By this definition lone motherhood is seen to be most prevalent in the UK, with 16.3 per cent of all mothers, followed by Denmark at 15.4 per cent, and Ireland at 13.8 per cent. The proportions are particularly low in Greece with 5.3 per cent, and Spain with 6.6 per cent. It is noteworthy that lone motherhood is most prevalent in countries of two different welfare regimes and less prevalent in the sub-protective Southern European countries.

While separation/divorce is the norm for most lone mothers, marital status shows striking international variation. It is apparent from Fig. 9.1 that in the Southern European countries, or sub-protective regimes, there is a greater proportion of widowed lone mothers than in the other countries. The employment-centred countries can be divided into two groups. The

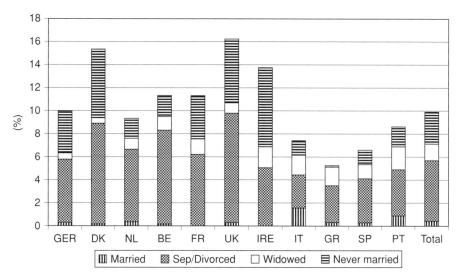

Fɪɢ. 9.1. Lone mothers and their marital status (% of all mothers)
Source: ECHP 1994.

Netherlands and Belgium have a preponderance of separated or divorced lone mothers while Germany, France, the UK, and Ireland together with Denmark have a more substantial proportion of lone mothers who have never married. This indicates that the last mentioned group of countries has the least traditional pattern of family life.

Table 9.1 shows the percentage of mothers and of women without children who are in poverty in selected EU countries. Poverty is defined as household income below the 50 per cent mean poverty line[1] for the entire national sample. In every country lone mothers are more likely to be in poverty than are non-lone mothers or women without children. The variation in the poverty rate for lone mothers to some extent reflects the variation in the countries' poverty, but the correlation is far from perfect. Denmark and Germany have relatively low poverty rates among lone mothers, but the poverty rates are still a lot higher than for married mothers in these countries. Considerable problems of absolute poverty are seen in the UK, Ireland, Spain, and Portugal. In these countries the poverty rates for lone mothers are substantially higher than for married mothers. Though Italy, Greece, and The Netherlands have a non-trivial rate of poverty for lone mothers, it is only a little higher than the poverty rate for married mothers.

In terms of absolute poverty rates for lone mothers, the two extremes were Denmark and the UK, the two countries with the highest rates of lone

---

[1] The mean poverty line is here equivalized by the new OECD Scale.

TABLE 9.1. *Lone mothers and non-lone mothers in poverty* (%)

	All lone mothers*	Indep. lone mothers*	Dependent lone mothers~	Married/ cohabiting mothers	Women no children aged <18
Belgium	19.7	18.7	—	8.1	9.7
Denmark	13.8	14.3	—	2.4	6.0
France	23.3	22.1	41.3	13.8	15.5
Germany	16.8	17.2	—	6.6	6.7
Greece	21.1	19.1	32.5	15.9	17.5
Ireland	31.1	36.9	13.0	18.4	13.0
Italy	24.6	25.1	23.1	19.5	18.9
Netherlands	21.4	21.4	—	15.2	11.9
Portugal	36.9	37.1	36.5	20.6	23.0
Spain	33.6	32.7	35.3	18.8	17.6
United Kingdom	45.3	47.2	21.3	18.8	12.1

Notes: * Lone mother includes dependent single mothers; ~ Countries with >14 dependent single mothers; Women respondents aged 16–60.
Source: European Community Household Panel, 1994.

motherhood, where respectively 14 per cent and 45 per cent of lone mothers were in poverty. Germany and Belgium were similar to Denmark, in having lone mother poverty rates below 20 per cent, while Portugal, Spain, and Ireland were more similar to the UK, in having rates above 30 per cent. The Netherlands, France, Italy, and Greece had lone mother poverty rates between 21–25 per cent.

THE INCOME PACKAGE FOR EUROPEAN LONE MOTHERS

Four main sources of income are potentially available for the lone mother: labour income, benefit from the state, alimony or maintenance from the father, and financial support from other family members. The way in which the income of lone mothers is composed varies from country to country. We have no information on maintenance payments in the ECHP, but from Lewis (1997) it appears that in all countries, contributions from the father consti-tute the least important source of income. The most important income sources are paid work and cash benefit. Only in the Southern European countries do the contributions from other family members constitute a substantial income source.

Table 9.2 summarizes the main income sources for lone mothers. It appears that lone mothers in the Southern European countries only receive

TABLE 9.2. *Lone mothers: social benefits and employment status* (%)

	Social benefits main income source	In employment	In full-time employment
Belgium	32.0	66.5	51.8
Denmark	32.1	77.6	70.8
France	Missing	71.7	59.4
Germany	24.1	74.8	54.0
Greece	3.6	63.3	54.8
Ireland	69.9	22.1	14.6
Italy	1.1	62.5	46.4
Netherlands	66.3	42.7	22.6
Portugal	5.5	74.3	66.2
Spain	9.8	54.7	45.0
United Kingdom	65.6	37.6	18.4

Notes: * Lone mother includes dependent single mothers; Women respondents aged 16–60.
Source: European Community Household Panel, 1994.

a minor part of their income as social benefit. By contrast two-thirds of lone mothers in the UK and Ireland, who have a high rate of poverty, and also in The Netherlands with its much lower poverty rate, rely on social benefit as their main source of income. Social transfers were also the most important source of income for one-third of lone mothers in Belgium and Denmark, and for one-quarter in Germany. Data on this question were absent for France. The majority of countries have a high labour market participation rate among lone mothers. In only the three countries—The Netherlands, the UK, and Ireland—where the majority of lone mothers had social transfers as their main income did lone mothers have a low participation rate. In these countries only between 15–20 per cent of the lone mothers have a full time job.

On the basis of Tables 9.1 and 9.2 the countries can be divided into four groups:

1. Germany, Denmark, Belgium, and France where the poverty rates are relatively low and the majority of lone mothers are wage earners. In this group Denmark stands out with a high rate of full time workers while part-time work is more common in the three other countries.
2. The Netherlands constitutes its own group by having both a relatively low poverty rate and a very low employment rate. The Netherlands has historically paid generous benefits to replace male breadwinners' earnings (Lewis 1997) and still seems to support lone mothers with more adequate benefits than many other welfare states.
3. The UK and Ireland have high poverty rates and low employment rates. Social benefit, which constitutes a major part of the income, is not sufficient to prevent poverty among lone mothers.

4. In the Southern European countries—Italy, Greece, Spain, and Portugal—state benefit is only a very minor income source, and there is a high participation rate. Whereas in Italy and Greece the poverty rate of lone mothers is similar to that of North European countries with relatively high employment rates, the poverty rate is substantially higher in Spain and Portugal. The anomalous result for Portugal, with very high employment and a high poverty rate, may reflect a problem of low wages, discussed below.

LABOUR MARKET PARTICIPATION

Women's labour market attachment is most likely influenced both by attitudes towards women as workers and by incentives to work. Variations in the lone mothers' participation rate for countries in different care and welfare regimes are therefore to be expected. As mentioned in the first section the care-giving regime is in its ideal form characterized by low labour market participation among women and a high level of social support that substitute wages from paid work for lone mothers. Conversely in the parental-worker regime the participation rates among women and mothers will generally be high and the lone mother is expected to take care of herself and her children. Therefore the state will be offering a care service that is available and affordable for all working parents.

As is evident from Table 9.3, women with children have *general* participation rates varying from more than 90 per cent in Denmark to less than

TABLE 9.3. *Participation rate of lone mothers and non-lone mothers* (%)

	Non-lone	Lone
Belgium	77.2	85.2
Denmark	91.6	90.5
France	69.8	90.0
Germany	61.7	80.6
Greece	43.5	81.9
Ireland	37.1	35.1
Italy	52.7	77.4
Netherlands	66.0	61.6
Portugal	72.0	82.6
Spain	48.9	79.6
United Kingdom	68.6	44.8

Notes: * Lone mother includes dependent single mothers; Women respondents aged 16–60.
Source: European Community Household Panel, 1994.

40 per cent in Ireland. Besides Ireland, the participation rate is generally low in the Southern European countries, except Portugal, and in Germany and The Netherlands. *Lone mothers* have as high a participation rate as non-lone mothers in Denmark, and it is equally low for lone mothers and non-lone mothers in The Netherlands and in Ireland. The low labour-force participation of lone mothers in these countries is not due to the special behaviour of this group, rather it is the same among all mothers.

The eleven countries can be divided into two groups on the basis of relative employment rates. One group consists of Denmark, The Netherlands, and Ireland, where lone mothers have a labour-market attachment quite similar to non-lone mothers. The other group consists of the remaining countries, where the attachment of lone mothers differs from other mothers. In the countries where the labour market attachment is almost the same for lone mothers and non-lone mothers, that attachment can be explained by the care regime. In Denmark all mothers have a high participation rate because of the parental-worker regime, and in The Netherlands and Ireland the care-giving regime results in a very low degree of participation for all mothers. In contrast to this, in the countries where labour market attachment for lone mothers and non-lone mothers differs, the welfare regime seems to be the explanation. In Germany, Belgium, and France, countries belonging to the employment-centred regime, lone mothers have a stronger incentive to supply labour. In these countries lone mothers who have to resort to state support only get second class social benefits, and this puts them in an unfavourable position compared to married mothers who get insurance-based benefits through their husbands (Lewis 1997). In the Southern European countries, where only widows are entitled to benefits, divorced and never-married lone mothers have to provide for themselves through support from other family members and through paid work. In the sub-protective regime, the family provides care that makes it possible for the mother to work. Moreover the lone mothers' labour supply is made easier by their own family structure with fewer and older children. Finally, the UK is the only country where lone mothers have a much lower labour supply than other mothers. We will return to this in the section comparing Denmark and the UK.

Incentives to work are affected both by wages and by cost of work. The anomalous results for Portugal, demonstrated by Table 9.2 in the former section, indicate the importance of considering influences on wages, and this points particularly to education, which works both through labour supply and labour demand. Higher education usually results in a higher wage and thereby in higher incentives to work. In addition, education can have an effect on the productivity level and on labour demand.

There were wide variations in national levels of educational attainment. The proportion of lone mothers with no, or only minimal, educational

TABLE 9.4. *Educational qualifications of lone mothers* (column %)

	GER	DK	NL	BE	FR	UK	IRE	IT	GR	SP	PT
Highest educ. qualification											
Higher	14.0	35.5	**12.8**	23.5	23.4	11.9	**5.5**	**8.3**	**27.6**	**13.7**	**5.1**
Intermed	53.6	37.6	53.3	36.8	33.3	33.4	26.9	44.6	**22.3**	17.5	**9.7**
Minimum	32.4	26.9	34.0	39.7	43.3	54.6	67.5	47.1	50.1	68.9	85.2

Notes: Lone mother includes dependent single mothers; Women respondents aged 16–60;
Bold = count <30.
Source: European Community Household Panel, 1994.

qualifications was 55 per cent in the UK, 68–69 per cent in Ireland and Spain, and 85 per cent in Portugal (Table 9.4). Thus, the four countries with the highest levels of lone-mother poverty had the lowest levels of educational qualification of lone mothers. The very low level of educational attainment in Portugal goes some way to explaining why that country had a high level of lone-mother poverty in spite of a high participation rate. The higher rates of lone-mother poverty in Spain and Portugal, relative to Italy and Greece, may in part have resulted from the lower levels of educational attainment in the former pair. In the northern group of countries, also, the national proportions with only minimum qualifications accorded fairly closely with poverty rates.

We have earlier emphasized the importance of childcare as an integral part of the welfare regime. The ECHP data do not contain information about the availability and cost of childcare services, so this issue cannot be directly addressed by the analysis. However, the type of family is likely to affect the childcare requirements of the lone mother and this, in turn, will be relevant to participation. Table 9.5 shows that lone mothers in all countries, except Portugal, on average had fewer dependent children than did non-lone mothers. The three countries with the highest proportions of lone mothers with three or more children were Portugal, the UK, and Ireland, all of which had high poverty rates for lone mothers. The proportion in Ireland, at 27 per cent, was exceptionally high, but this in part is an artefact caused by the presence of two or three mothers in the one household. At the other extreme, only 2 per cent of lone mothers in Greece had more than two children. The variation in the proportion was not large among the remaining countries. The figures indicate a connection between poverty and the number of children that may both be due to a reduced labour supply because of childcare costs, and to increased family needs which are not compensated for by social or family transfers.

TABLE 9.5. *Number of children of lone and non-lone mothers* (column %)

	GER	DK	NL	BE	FR	UK	IRE	IT	GR	SP	PT
Lone mothers											
Number of children in household											
1 child	65.0	66.4	50.1	56.2	59.2	46.1	46.2	66.2	72.1	60.2	51.0
2 children	27.7	27.6	39.8	32.1	28.5	38.2	26.6	25.0	**25.7**	32.5	34.6
3 or more	**7.2**	**6.0**	**10.1**	**11.6**	12.3	15.7	27.2	**8.8**	**2.2**	**7.3**	**14.4**
Non-lone mothers											
Number of children in household											
1 child	48.4	45.3	31.0	45.1	41.0	38.2	25.6	47.8	41.7	49.6	50.4
2 children	39.6	42.5	48.4	36.5	40.3	43.5	34.0	39.0	47.7	40.5	36.6
3 or more	12.0	12.2	20.6	18.4	18.7	18.3	40.3	13.2	10.6	9.9	13.1

Notes: Lone mother includes dependent single mothers; Women respondents aged 16–60;
Bold = count <30.
Source: European Community Household Panel, 1994.

TABLE 9.6. *Age of youngest child of lone and non-lone mothers* (column %)

	GER	DK	NL	BE	FR	UK	IRE	IT	GR	SP	PT
Lone mothers											
Age of youngest child in household											
Less than 6 years	35.5	30.3	**21.9**	31.3	34.6	49.4	47.9	33.4	**17.8**	**28.9**	**28.0**
6 to 11 years	31.5	31.1	36.6	34.1	31.9	30.8	24.8	26.3	**25.3**	32.1	39.0
12 to 17 years	33.0	38.6	41.6	34.6	33.5	19.8	27.3	40.3	56.8	39.0	33.0
Non-lone mothers											
Age of youngest child in household											
Less than 6 years	42.3	46.3	43.8	48.0	49.0	47.6	49.2	37.3	39.1	42.0	39.2
6 to 11 years	31.0	23.1	29.3	26.8	27.3	27.0	28.9	29.4	27.3	27.1	31.3
12 to 17 years	26.7	30.5	26.9	25.2	23.7	25.4	22.0	33.3	33.6	30.9	29.5

Notes: Lone mother includes dependent single mothers; Women respondents aged 16–60;
Bold = count <30.
Source: European Community Household Panel, 1994.

Table 9.6 shows the proportions of lone mothers with a youngest child in various age groups. Having a pre-school-age child is likely to be associated with high potential childcare costs, and in most countries young children were more often present for non-lone than for lone mothers. Ireland and the UK once more stood out from the other countries, with nearly half of their lone mothers having a child under 6 years old. Greece was again at the other extreme, with a proportion of 18 per cent, and The Netherlands, with

22 per cent, was the next lowest. The remaining countries were clustered in the range 28–36 per cent.

Overall, the number and age of children did not display a simple relationship to lone mothers' poverty rates or employment rates across the eleven countries. However, they may help to explain the especially low participation rates in Ireland and the UK, taken in conjunction with relatively low levels of public childcare provision in those countries.

LONE MOTHERS IN DIFFERENT CARE AND WELFARE REGIMES

As mentioned in the first section, the eleven countries can be divided into four welfare regimes and two care regimes that together provide very different living conditions for the lone mothers of Europe. With the aid of this schema, the pattern that emerges from the Europanel's information on poverty, income, and labour market attachment can be summarized as follows:

Denmark belongs to the universalistic welfare regime and to the parental-worker care regime. The percentage of lone mothers is very high compared to other countries, which to some extent might reflect a change in family life induced by the care/welfare regime itself. On average, lone mothers in Denmark are similar to non-lone mothers with respect to labour market attachment and family structure. Even though the poverty rate for lone mothers is lowest among the eleven countries, it is significantly higher than for non-lone mothers. The reason may be that reflections about the average disguise the fact that a minor group of low-educated long-term unemployed mothers are not well off. However, the majority of lone mothers in Denmark are well-educated and live by their market work, which is made possible by the childcare service offered by the state.

Germany, Belgium, and France belong to the employment-centred welfare regime and are all more traditional male-breadwinner countries than Denmark. The lone mothers that are relatively well-educated have higher incentives to work than do non-lone mothers in these countries. This is due, first of all, to the unfavourable financial position of lone mothers without attachment to the labour market. Especially in Germany, the incentive to work is strengthened by better pay in the labour market compared to, for instance, lone mothers in the UK labour market (Lewis 1997). On the other hand lone mothers in Belgium and France are to some extent excluded from the labour market by the high rate of unemployment.

The Netherlands also belongs to the employment-centred welfare regime, but the care-giving regime provides sufficient benefit to keep the poverty rate relatively low. However it also keeps the well-educated lone mothers out of the labour market.

Lone mothers in *Ireland* and the *UK*, as in The Netherlands, have a low labour market participation rate, but the poverty rate is much higher than in The Netherlands. In these countries the care-regime is that of the care-giving mother, with welfare support provided unconditionally to lone mothers, and little active policy to draw lone mothers into employment. However, the welfare regime is liberal/minimal, and this restricts the amount of welfare support provided to a level which is insufficient to prevent poverty in many cases.

Italy, Greece, Spain, and Portugal all belong to the care-giving regime where women's labour supply typically is very low. However, lone mothers have a much higher participation rate than do non-lone mothers. The reasons are both that most of them get no benefit from the state and that the families offer childcare that makes it possible for lone mothers to supply their work. However, severe poverty problems exist in Spain and Portugal, which may be due in part to low wages, and in part to insufficient support from the families that may be poor in themselves.

The two extremes among the eleven countries are Denmark and UK which, with over 15 per cent of mothers being without resident partners, have the highest proportions of lone mothers. In both countries lone mothers are most likely to be separated, divorced, or never married. But there the similarities end. In Denmark, where lone mothers show high levels of both education and employment, only a minority are below the poverty line. In the UK, where most lone mothers are young, have few qualifications, are not in the labour-force, and live on benefits, almost every second lone mother is in poverty. The next section will take a closer look at these differences.

EMPLOYMENT OF LONE MOTHERS IN DENMARK AND GREAT BRITAIN

In most cases, lone mothers in Denmark seem to be living under conditions which are very different from those of lone mothers in the UK. In the rest of this paper, a more intensive analysis will be made concerning these two countries, which seem to represent two extremes in the EU. This analysis will focus upon the difference in the employment rate between the two countries, which is likely to be a crucial factor in the different levels of income poverty experienced. For this purpose, two special sets of data are used. For the UK—or more precisely, for Great Britain, since Northern Ireland is not included—a national sample survey of lone mothers was conducted in 1991, and this sample was followed with repeated interviews to 1995. For

Denmark, the analysis is based on a 5 per cent test sample from administrative registers for the period 1988–1993, providing a comparable range of information to the British survey.

Hypotheses about Influences on Employment for Lone Mothers in Denmark and Great Britain

The main hypothesis proposed is one which has frequently been suggested before, for example by Bradshaw *et al.* (1996), namely that the higher participation rate in Denmark results from the wider availability and lower cost of childcare in comparison with Britain. An additional hypothesis, however, is that the different employment rates result from differences in the structure of welfare benefits for lone mothers in the two countries. In Denmark, the majority of lone mothers have acquired rights to insurance-based unemployment benefits, with entitlement related to earnings. In Britain, on the other hand, lone mothers have means-tested support, which has a fixed maximum amount based on family needs.

The Hypothesis of Differential Childcare Systems

The decision of whether to enter paid employment—the participation decision—has usually been analysed within an economic framework of consumer choice theory. Within this framework, the main factors influencing a woman's participation are generally assumed to be her own potential wage or earnings capacity, and the other income available to the woman which is independent of her employment, such as her spouse's earnings. The economic theory in its simplest form predicts that the probability of participation increases with the woman's own wage and falls with the other income available.

It has been recognized that this standard framework does not correctly represent the situation with respect to childcare. This arises because of the interdependence of women's participation and childcare decisions. Total income for a mother can be expressed as:

$$\text{Income} = \text{Non-wage income} + (\text{Labour hours} \times \text{Wage rate})$$
$$- (\text{Paid childcare hours} \times \text{Childcare cost}).$$

Similarly, the mother's hours can be expressed as:

$$\text{Total hours} = \text{Leisure} + \text{Labour hours} + \text{Own childcare hours}.$$

Paid childcare hours will be a function of labour hours and the availability of other, non-paid carers, whether family or friends (Heckman 1974). Unless a mother has non-paid childcare support, she cannot increase her labour hours without increasing paid childcare. At the same time, childcare is itself a consumption good, desired for its beneficial effects on the development of the child as well as for its value in releasing the time of the mother, or of both parents, for other activities (Duncan *et al.* 1995). Thus, as income rises, the probability of purchasing childcare also rises, irrespective of female participation. It is, therefore, incorrect to consider childcare simply as a cost of employment. The mother's utility involves not only consumption and leisure, but the quality of the child's development and the value of the mother's own time with the child. A *childcare subsidy* reduces the cost of paid childcare and thereby increases the net income from paid work. Other things being equal, this should have a positive effect on participation. Conversely a relatively high price of childcare will reduce the capacity to purchase childcare, other things being equal, and this will reduce participation.

In Denmark, the majority of paid childcare is provided through public services such as day nurseries, with about two-thirds of childcare for under-school-age children taking this form. All such childcare is subsidized. The value of the subsidy is not less than 70 per cent of the full cost (Hansen *et al.* 1995; Mabbett 1996), although this varies, with some municipalities providing a substantially higher subsidy. Additionally, families with very low incomes obtain childcare free of any charge. In 1987, 22 per cent of children in public daycare obtained reductions—below the already subsidized standard level—and about one-half of these paid nothing (Fridberg 1988). It should be noted that the subsidy rate is not increased in any way for lone mothers as such. None the less, they are likely to be among the major groups of beneficiaries because they have at most one family earner, and because of their high need for childcare support if in work. It also appears that there may be some degree of rationing of places, which works to the advantage of lone mothers. Fridberg (1988) points to the practice, in many municipalities, of giving priority for places to the children of lone mothers.

In Britain the supply of public day-care is targeted on a very small number of children 'in need' (European Commission Network on Childcare 1996a). Local authorities have no duty to provide day-care for children because their parents work, and in practice coverage is at a low level. This 'reflects a basic concept of public policy that providing care for children with employed parents is a responsibility of parents' (ECNC 1988: 118). Tax allowances for lone mothers in work, to set against childcare costs while income is sufficiently low, were introduced in the UK in 1994, but do not apply to the period being analysed.

Because of the lack of subsidy, paid childcare is much more costly in Britain than in Denmark. According to Ditch *et al.* (1996), day-care for a pre-school child costs twice as much, while, according to Bradshaw *et al.* (1996), who base comparisons on the most widely used type of paid childcare, the cost is nearly four times as great in Britain. These figures will understate the differential in childcare costs between low-income families in the two countries, because of the additional subsidies to such families in Denmark.

In Denmark, the high availability of public childcare, coupled with a high subsidy which is available to all whether in or out of employment, will increase the net value of paid employment. On the other hand, the additional childcare subsidy available to low-income mothers in Denmark would increase the net value of welfare income when out of work, and increase the availability of child development activities. These could reduce participation. In the case of Britain, high childcare costs would in general reduce the net value of paid work and thereby reduce the probability of participation. However, if mothers value child development activities, and these are costly, this could also create some compensating incentives for participation.

Although the theoretical predictions are not entirely clear, it seems likely that the dominant influence will be one of higher work incentives through lower childcare costs in Denmark. Furthermore, in Britain lone mothers' participation will be reduced, other things being equal, the greater are their childcare requirements. In Denmark, on the other hand, the impact of higher childcare requirements will be reduced by the presence of subsidization. It has frequently been observed that both the probability of using childcare, and the unit cost of childcare, vary inversely and to a marked degree, with the age of the youngest child. Accordingly, in studies of women's participation, a commonly used proxy for childcare costs is the age of the youngest child. Using this proxy, our operational hypothesis is that in Britain participation will be positively related to the age of the youngest child, while in Denmark there will be either no such relationship or a weaker relationship.

The Hypothesis of Differential Income Support Systems

The Danish and British income support systems for lone mothers, when they are not employed, differ in a number of major respects. In Denmark, there are two main forms of support for working-age individuals who lack employment, excluding those not working for reasons of sickness or disability: insurance-based unemployment benefit (UI), and means-tested social assistance (SA). Lone mothers receive these on the same basis as others, and have no special entitlement arising from lone parenthood. Under the UI system, those who have a sufficient previous employment record and have also joined an unemployment insurance fund, are able to draw unemployment benefits which are related to the amount of their prior earnings but are unrelated to their other sources of current income. In the late 1980s and early 1990s, the period being considered here, it was necessary only to have worked for twenty-six weeks in the previous three years, in order to obtain, for two-and-a-half years, a payment amounting to 90 per cent of the prior earnings. As with most unemployment insurance systems, however, there was a payment ceiling, which reduced the value of benefits at average earnings and above. According to Hansen *et al.* (1995), the net replacement rate for a Danish lone parent with two children was over 90 per cent at two-thirds average earnings but about 70 per cent at average earnings. As Mortensen (1977) demonstrated, if jobs are of limited duration, then a job-seeker's choices must also take into account the value of future periods of unemployment. A lower-paid worker in Denmark gains by being employed, not only from the differential between wages and out-of-work benefits, but also because she will accrue new UI rights which will provide generous benefits in the event of a future spell out of work. The higher-paid worker has less to gain from employment in this respect. Accordingly, the overall balance of financial advantage in resuming work between higher-paid and lower-paid workers is ambiguous.

If a Danish worker does not have entitlement to unemployment insurance benefits—for instance, because she has not been working in recent years— then she will usually receive social assistance (SA) on losing work. For low-paid workers, SA appears a reasonably attractive alternative to unemployment insurance, and Hansen *et al.* (1995) report replacement rates for SA which differ only slightly from those under UI. In practice, however, it appears that the majority of Danish workers prefer to join UI schemes. One reason for this would be that SA is means-tested whereas UI benefit is not. If for example a lone mother enters a new partnership, the earnings of the partner would be offset against SA, but not against UI. Women increase their financial independence from present or potential partners through UI.

Turning to the UK, one finds a system in many respects the antithesis of the Danish one. Most lone mothers—about 75 per cent of those not employed—rely on means-tested income support, which they are entitled to receive without any work test or active job search. The basic rate is at a low level but varies substantially, in the case of a lone mother, with the number and ages of the dependent children. It also carries with it an entitlement to free housing. There are also housing subsidies in Denmark, but they generally cover only part of housing costs. Hansen *et al.* (1995) estimated that the net replacement rate for a British lone parent with two children was about 70 per cent at half average earnings—fairly typical of many such lone mothers—falling to about 45 per cent at average earnings.

There is an unemployment insurance (UI) system in the UK, but its terms are very different from those in Denmark, or indeed any other European country. The payment under UI is similar to SA, in that it does not vary with prior earnings, and until 1996 was payable for up to one year, a shorter time than in Denmark. Many low-paid workers are not required to take part in UI. Very few lone mothers in Britain receive UI benefits.

The main factor for work incentives in Britain is likely to be the replacement ratio between SA levels and potential earnings. SA will be relatively high for those lone mothers who have several children, making participation relatively unlikely, other things being equal. Further, participation will be less likely when there is no partner and more likely when there is a partner. When there is a partner, because of means-testing, the expected value of not working will decline sharply, while the expected value of working will increase sharply. This assumes that the partner is either employed or is likely to become employed.

In the light of this discussion, we formulate two hypotheses about the effects of the out-of-work income systems as follows. First: in Great Britain, the probability of participation for lone mothers will be reduced by the presence of additional children as a proxy for higher income support levels, whereas this will not apply, or will apply less strongly, in the case of Denmark. Second: in Great Britain, getting a new partner will increase the lone mother's rate of participation, whereas in Denmark there will be no such effect, or only a weak effect confined to the minority of lone mothers dependent on social assistance.

Data and methods of analysis

The sources of data have been described earlier in the section. In each country, data were available for a number of successive years: in the case of Denmark, six years from 1988 to 1993; in the case of Britain, four years from 1991 to 1994. In each country, the sample is nationally representative of lone mothers in the first of these years. The sample ceases to be representative of lone mothers in the following years since women may exit from lone-mother status because they re-partner or cease to have any dependent children. Thus, the analysis relates to the participation decisions over several years, of an initial one-year sample of lone mothers in each country.

Since the Danish data have been taken from administrative sources, they are unaffected by non-response and attrition: $N = 2544$ for each year. The British data on the other hand came from a 1991 sample survey which had an initial response rate of 82 per cent, and was affected by some sample attrition at follow-up—see Bryson *et al.* (1997), for further details. Only those with responses for all the years 1991–93 are included; the resulting N is 649 for 1991, 1992, and 1993, falling to 563 in 1994.

Participation was defined, in this analysis, to mean being in an employed status for 90 per cent or more of the year. For the great majority of Danish lone mothers, regular employment is the normal state. Even in the British sample, there was a marked polarization between those who were in employment all the time or nearly all the time, and those who were never, or scarcely ever, in employment.

As far as possible, the variables have been defined in the same way for both samples, but some differences were unavoidable either because of data limitations, or because they reflect genuinely distinctive features of the two societies. In education, the Danish data distinguishes between higher and basic education only, with 'apprentice' as an additional intermediate category. For Britain, however, it is important to distinguish between advanced and basic education, corresponding to qualifications at ages 18 and 16 respectively, as well as higher education. Also, the nearest to the apprentice category in Britain is vocational education, which does not have such a clear status as in Denmark.

The variable causing most difficulty for the analysis was 'other, non-wage, income'. We wished to define other income to include all income sources which were independent of employment status. In Britain, this was straightforward, and the variable consisted mainly of child benefits and maintenance payments from a former partner, together with interest payments from savings for a small minority. For Denmark, a variable of this type could only be constructed by subtracting earned income and unemployment benefits, including social assistance, from total taxable income. Maintenance payments were not included because in Denmark they are not taxable. It is thought that interest payments and imputed rents were major elements in the derived variable but this cannot be directly confirmed. Because of these uncertainties, it was decided to conduct all the analyses both with, and without, the 'other income' variable.

With a series of annual observations on the same sample, one possibility is a panel data analysis method, which tests time-related changes and models bias due to unobserved variables. However, in the present case the dependent variable (participation) is binary, and panel estimation with qualitative data leads to a number of technical complications (Hsiao 1986; Blundell and Bond 1995; Orme 1996). It was therefore decided, in the interests of simplicity, to analyse each year of data separately. Accordingly, we cannot claim to have modelled the dynamics of labour participation for lone mothers in these countries, and our specification runs the risk of bias from unobserved variables. However, the analysis offers at least an initial exploration of the changing influences on participation over several years, which will be useful for the subsequent development of more complete models.

For both countries, the potential wage of the lone mother is represented, in the reduced form specification which was adopted, by age proxying experience, educational level, and locational differentials, as a set of regional dummies. For Denmark, UI or SA entitlements are also represented by the same variables, since such benefits are, subject to income ceilings, proportional to previous earnings. In Britain, income support or UI entitlements are represented by the number of dependent children, which is also included in the Danish models for comparison. The models also include a dummy variable to indicate whether the woman has re-partnered, and this variable is an indicator of partner's earnings being available. Finally, the age of the youngest child is included to proxy the cost of childcare. The variables are further defined in the Appendix Tables 9A and 9B. The analytical model adopted is the probit, as customary for the analysis of participation—for further details, see Maddala (1983).

Results

The results of the participation models for the two national samples are shown in full in the Appendix Tables 9A and 9B. For both countries, the variables which determine the predicted wage generally acted to raise the probability of participation, consistent with the labour supply theory. Age, here interpreted as a proxy for experience, was consistently significant in Denmark and always had the expected positive sign in Britain, where it became significant only in years 3 and 4. Furthermore, regional dummies were always significant in both countries, which we interpret as indicating the effect of higher regional wages or job vacancies in encouraging women's participation. The most interesting results in this group concerned educational qualifications. Except for basic qualifications in Denmark, all qualifications in each country were associated with a significantly higher probability of being employed. But the effects of qualification on participation were considerably greater in Britain. For example, the estimated coefficients for a basic-level qualification varied in Denmark between 0.02–0.22, but in Britain between 0.29–0.53; similarly, for an apprentice qualification the range in Denmark was 0.21–0.38, and in Britain 0.53–0.82. This suggests that the returns to education were higher in Britain than in Denmark, or equivalently, that the economic disincentive of being a lone mother without qualifications was particularly severe in Britain.

When included in the models, the effect of 'other non-wage income' on the probability of participation was always positive, and usually highly significant, although falling below significance in two years in Britain. The magnitudes of the coefficients were broadly similar in the two countries, although the significance levels were higher in Denmark partly because of larger sample size. These results are contrary to the customary assumptions of labour supply theory, but have been reported in Britain. One interpretation for Britain, advocated by Duncan *et al.* (1995), is that non-wage income makes it possible for mothers to increase the purchase of childcare as a consumption good, and this in turn increases the probability of participation. Another interpretation is that under the UK tax-benefit system, maintenance payments are more advantageous to lone mothers when in work than not in work (Bryson *et al.* 1997). However, neither of these explanations appears applicable to Denmark. A possible explanation for Denmark

TABLE 9.7. *Influence of age of youngest child on lone mothers' participation, Britain and Denmark*

	Years					
	1	2	3	4	5	6
Britain						
with 'other income'	0.14	0.14	0.09	0.06	—	—
	***	***	***	***		
without 'other income'	0.13	0.14	0.09	0.07	—	—
	***	***	***	***		
Denmark						
with 'other income'	0.01	0.02	0.02	0.02	0.01	0.02
	n.s.	*	**	**	n.s.	*
without 'other income'	0.02	0.02	0.03	0.03	0.02	0.03
	*	n.s.	***	**	*	***

Notes: *Significance*: * = $P < 0.05$, ** = $P < 0.01$, *** = $P < 0.001$, n.s. = not significant.
Sources: Statistics Denmark and PRILIF (GB).

is that social assistance is not available for those who have positive net wealth excluding housing (Hansen *et al.* 1995). Income from investments—which may be the main element in the Danish variable—may be less likely to exist for those with significant amounts of unemployment. The relationship could then be one of reverse causation, with 'other income' in Denmark determined by employment status. This result confirmed the need for caution with this variable, and accordingly the remaining results are reported both for the models including the variable, and for those excluding it. In fact, despite the high significance level of the 'other income' variable, the other results were little affected by its inclusion or exclusion.

The effect of the age of the youngest child, interpreted as a proxy for child-care costs, was predicted to differ for the two countries. In Britain, it should be positively related to participation, while in Denmark it should either be unrelated to participation or related to a smaller degree than in Britain. As Table 9.7 shows, the effect in Britain was always positive, as hypothesized, and highly significant, although the magnitude of the coefficient declined somewhat after the second year. In Denmark the coefficient was also sig-nificantly positive in most years. None the less, the coefficient on this variable was always considerably smaller than in Britain, which is consistent with the hypothesis.

Turning next to the predictions concerning the income support systems, we consider the effect of number of dependent children and of re-partnering. The results concerning number of children were reasonably consistent with

TABLE 9.8. *Influence of number of dependent children on lone mothers' participation, Britain and Denmark*

	Years					
	1	2	3	4	5	6
Britain						
with 'other income'	−0.14	0.00	−0.16	−0.39	—	—
	n.s.	n.s.	*	***		
without 'other income'	−0.03	0.02	−0.13	−0.30	—	—
	n.s.	n.s.	*	***		
Denmark						
with 'other income'	0.00	−0.03	0.00	0.08	−0.01	−0.04
	n.s.	n.s.	n.s.	n.s.	n.s.	n.s.
without 'other income'	0.00	−0.02	0.01	0.06	−0.01	−0.04
	n.s.	n.s.	n.s.	n.s.	n.s.	n.s.

Notes: Significance: * = P < 0.05, ** = P < 0.01, *** = P < 0.001, n.s. = not significant.
Sources: Statistics Denmark and PRILIF (GB).

TABLE 9.9. *Influence of re-partnering on lone mothers' participation, Britain and Denmark*

	Years				
	2	3	4	5	6
Britain					
with 'other income'	0.15	0.56	0.53	—	—
	n.s.	**	**		
without 'other income'	0.16	0.56	0.54	—	—
	n.s.	**	**		
Denmark					
with 'other income'	−0.17	0.05	−0.15	0.14	−0.09
	*	n.s.	n.s.	n.s.	n.s.
without 'other income'	−0.21	0.03	−0.15	0.10	−0.11
	*	n.s.	n.s.	n.s.	n.s.

Notes: Significance: * = P < 0.05, ** = P < 0.01, *** = P < 0.001, n.s. = not significant.
Sources: Statistics Denmark and PRILIF (GB).

predictions. In Britain, the number of children was always negatively related to participation, although this was significant only in years 3 and 4. In Denmark, on the other hand, the number of children took positive and negative signs in different years, and was never significantly related to participation. These findings are summarized in Table 9.8.

This pattern of differences between the two countries was largely repeated in the case of re-partnering. Year 1 cannot be used for this analysis since by construction the sample members are without partners at this point. In years 2, 3 and 4, re-partnering was, as predicted, positively associated with participation in Britain, although significantly so only in years 3 and 4. In Denmark, re-partnering took positive and negative signs in different years; only in year 2, when re-partnering was associated with a lower probability of participation, rather than a higher probability as in Britain, was the relationship significant. These results are summarized in Table 9.9.

CONCLUSION

The earlier part of this chapter showed that there were large differences among countries in the incidence of income poverty among lone mothers. The eleven countries are divided into four welfare regimes and two care regimes that in combination provide very different living conditions for the lone mothers of Europe. *Denmark* belongs to the universalistic welfare regime and to the parental-worker care regime. The percentage of lone mothers is high compared to other countries, but the majority of lone mothers in Denmark are well-educated and live by their market work—made possible by the childcare service offered by the state. *Germany, Belgium, and France* belong to the employment-centred welfare regime and to the parental-worker care regime; they are more traditional male-breadwinner countries than Denmark. The lone mothers that are relatively well-educated have a much higher incentive to work than do non-lone mothers in these countries. This is due, first of all, to the unfavourable financial position of lone mothers without attachment to the labour market, coupled with active support for those who wish to participate. *The Netherlands* also belongs to the employment-centred welfare regime, but to the care-giving care regime: consistent with this, it provides sufficient benefit to keep the lone mother poverty rate relatively low and the relatively well-educated lone mothers from the labour market. The lone mothers in liberal/minimal *Ireland* and *the UK* also have a very low labour market participation rate but the poverty rate is much higher than in The Netherlands. Though these countries belong to the care-giving care regime, their liberal/minimal welfare stance restricts benefit levels and makes them insufficient to keep lone mothers from poverty. *Italy, Greece, Spain, and Portugal* all belong to the sub-protective welfare regime and to the care-giving regime. The combination of almost no benefit from the state, and families that offer childcare and other forms of support, makes it possible for lone mothers in these countries to supply their work to the labour market. Still, severe poverty problems exist in Spain and Portugal, which may be partly due to low wages.

The two extremes among the eleven countries are Denmark and UK—having the highest proportions of lone mothers but very different living standards. In the second half of this paper, a more intensive study of labour market attachment in Denmark and Great Britain has been attempted. In broad terms, this analysis has suggested that institutional factors, especially with respect to childcare systems and welfare support systems, may account for at least part of the observed wide differences in employment and income poverty between the two countries.

Women's participation was very much reduced in Britain by the presence of a young child, and this can be attributed to the higher costs of paid childcare in that country. This influence however had been reduced to a much lower level in Denmark, although it still remained significant. Denmark provides substantial childcare subsidies but these fall short of completely free provision, except in the case of those on the lowest incomes. These features of the Danish system are sufficient both to explain the lower level of impact of the age of the youngest child on participation, and also the fact that some residual impact remains.

Most lone mothers in Britain who are not in employment depend on means-tested income support which varies with number of children, and is withdrawn when other sources of income, such as the earnings of a new partner, become available. These considerations apply much less to Danish lone mothers, since the majority of them are likely to be eligible for non-means-tested unemployment benefits. As predicted, there was little sign of the number of children or re-partnering influencing the participation of the Danish sample. But the relations of these variables to participation were also not wholly consistent in Britain, since they only became significant there in years 3 and 4. This suggests that the income support system became an increasingly important influence on lone mothers' participation in Britain as time went on, but its influence was initially suppressed by other factors. Notably, the age of the youngest child, which is indicative of childcare costs, had a particularly large effect on participation at the beginning of the study period, and this may suggest that initially lone mothers' choices in Britain were primarily dominated by childcare issues.

Overall, the analysis, which was conceptualized chiefly in economic terms, was more successful in explaining the employment of lone mothers in Britain than in Denmark. The analysis tended to show that the factors important in Britain have been neutralized or weakened in the Danish system. But it remains difficult to explain why such a large proportion of lone mothers in Denmark is employed, when net replacement rates are so high, and when subsidized childcare is available both in and out of employment.

Smith *et al.* (1993) commented on this issue, and suggested that Danish lone mothers might continue to participate for longer-term financial reasons, such as access to promotion opportunities. The operation of social norms might also be important, in view of the exceptionally high participation rates which prevail throughout Danish society. These are issues which should be pursued in future research.

Finally, how does the analysis concerning Britain and Denmark relate to the material of the first part of the paper? At a general level, it illustrates the importance of welfare state regimes in influencing the capacity of lone mothers to participate in employment, which is likely to be one of the most effective safeguards against poverty and exclusion. It also illustrates the value of detailed knowledge of each national system, in order to derive testable hypotheses about the differential effects of welfare regimes. Finally the analysis has confirmed the importance of incorporating childcare policies in cross-national comparisons of welfare regimes and their effects.

ACKNOWLEDGEMENTS

The British analysis for the second half of the chapter made use of data from the Programme of Research into Low Income Families (PRILIF), and the assistance is gratefully acknowledged of the UK Department of Social Security and of Alan Marsh at the Policy Studies Institute, in providing access to this dataset. The Danish analysis for the second half of the chapter made use of administrative records from Statistics Denmark. The analysis of the Danish data by Mohammad Azhar Hussain is gratefully acknowledged.

Appendix

APPENDIX

TABLE 9A. *Analysis of Danish data on lone mothers*

Year	1988		1989		1990		1991		1992		1993	
Model	1	2	1	2	1	2	1	2	1	2	1	2
Constant	-1.25	-1.08	-1.13	-1.22	-1.41	-1.44	-1.34	-1.17	-2.30	-1.89	-1.58	-1.43
	(1.91)	(1.69)	(1.68)	(1.90)	(2.07)	(2.18)	(1.89)	(1.69)	(3.17)	(2.66)	(1.97)	(2.17)
Age	0.098	0.098	0.081	0.070	0.078	0.075	0.083	0.073	0.109	0.100	0.110	0.092
	(3.09)	(2.59)	(2.48)	(2.25)	(2.39)	(2.39)	(2.60)	(2.33)	(3.33)	(3.14)	(3.22)	(2.88)
Age-squared	-0.108	-0.063	-0.081	-0.049	-0.080	-0.062	-0.085	-0.063	-0.108	-0.087	-0.123	-0.085
	(2.56)	(1.58)	(1.90)	(1.20)	(1.93)	(1.55)	(2.13)	(1.62)	(2.71)	(2.26)	(3.04)	(2.25)
Higher qual.	0.336	0.411	0.593	0.493	0.495	0.530	0.456	0.463	0.406	0.416	0.448	0.486
	(3.98)	(4.99)	(6.90)	(5.87)	(5.66)	(6.17)	(5.32)	(5.46)	(4.79)	(4.95)	(5.14)	(5.73)
Apprentice	0.332	0.377	0.267	0.307	0.267	0.294	0.262	0.283	0.215	0.216	0.210	0.206
	(4.66)	(5.45)	(3.78)	(4.52)	(3.81)	(4.29)	(3.78)	(4.13)	(3.14)	(3.20)	(2.99)	(3.07)
Basic qual.	0.044	0.098	0.021	0.117	0.221	0.158	0.057	0.063	0.012	0.012	-0.021	0.010
	(0.37)	(0.86)	(0.18)	(1.03)	(1.89)	(1.38)	(0.49)	(0.55)	(0.10)	(0.11)	(0.18)	(0.08)
Youngest	0.024	0.016	0.019	0.106	0.029	0.024	0.026	0.023	0.016	0.012	0.027	0.019
	(2.69)	(1.86)	(2.17)	(1.88)	(3.46)	(2.85)	(3.16)	(2.91)	(2.10)	(1.60)	(3.41)	(2.51)
Nchildren	0.000	-0.003	-0.033	-0.018	-0.003	0.010	0.063	0.076	-0.011	-0.014	-0.040	-0.038
	(0.01)	(0.01)	(0.66)	(0.37)	(0.07)	(0.20)	(1.24)	(1.51)	(0.21)	(0.28)	(0.76)	(0.75)
Re-partner	—	—	-0.212	-0.171	0.030	0.036	-0.145	-0.149	-0.102	-0.138	-0.113	-0.087
			(2.61)	(2.19)	(0.29)	(0.35)	(1.38)	(1.43)	(0.86)	(1.17)	(0.98)	(0.79)
Non-wage	0.013	—	0.012	—	0.009	—	0.005	—	0.005	—	0.010	—
	(12.44)		(13.04)		(10.97)		(8.52)		(8.67)		(13.43)	
Log-likelihood	-1261	-1362	-1255	-1366	-1255	-1330	-1290	-1330	-1308	-1351	-1237	-1356

Estimated effects on employment each year. Probit coefficients (with absolute values of t-statistics in parentheses).
Notes: Variable labels: Age = age of mother in years, Higher qual. = has educational qualification above the basic level (dummy), Apprentice = has apprenticeship qualification (dummy), Basic qual. = has basic educational qualification (dummy), Youngest = age of youngest child in years, Nchildren = number of dependent children, Re-partner = has a partner (dummy), Non-wage = non-wage income excluding benefits in 1000 kr./year. Reference category for education dummies = has no qualification. 5 regional dummies, not shown; N = 2544 for all years.
Sources: Statistics Denmark.

TABLE 9B. *Analysis of British data on lone mothers*

Year	1991		1992		1993		1994	
Model	1	2	1	2	1	2	1	2
Constant	−2.73	−3.16	−3.31	−3.35	−3.68	−3.75	−4.35	−4.54
	(3.64)	(3.70)	(2.07)	(2.18)	(4.16)	(4.24)	(4.32)	(4.50)
Age	0.051	0.080	0.069	0.070	0.113	0.117	0.170	0.179
	(1.36)	(1.39)	(2.39)	(2.39)	(2.37)	(2.46)	(3.23)	(3.40)
Age-squared	−0.001	−0.001	−0.001	−0.001	−0.001	−0.001	−0.002	−0.002
	(1.49)	(1.98)	(1.74)	(1.75)	(2.33)	(2.41)	(3.19)	(3.33)
Degree qual.	0.884	1.034	1.317	1.347	1.187	1.236	0.840	0.950
	(4.29)	(5.16)	(6.27)	(6.50)	(5.83)	(6.19)	(3.89)	(4.48)
Vocqual	0.580	0.653	0.801	0.818	0.800	0.820	0.528	0.562
	(3.29)	(3.77)	(4.58)	(4.70)	(4.73)	(4.86)	(2.89)	(3.09)
Advqual	0.982	1.049	1.539	1.561	1.253	1.279	1.081	1.093
	(3.85)	(4.16)	(5.66)	(5.79)	(4.89)	(5.10)	(3.90)	(3.97)
Basic qual.	0.298	0.404	0.506	0.526	0.506	0.534	0.285	0.333
	(1.98)	(2.76)	(3.41)	(3.59)	(3.56)	(3.85)	(1.91)	(2.25)
Youngest	0.138	0.133	0.139	0.139	0.086	0.087	0.062	0.067
	(6.97)	(6.85)	(6.89)	(6.93)	(5.23)	(5.30)	(3.57)	(3.84)
Nchildren	−0.139	−0.030	−0.003	0.023	−0.160	−0.128	−0.393	−0.297
	(1.81)	(0.42)	(0.04)	(0.31)	(2.30)	(1.99)	(5.01)	(4.15)
Re-partner	—	—	0.148	0.162	0.558	0.561	0.533	0.537
	—	—	(0.69)	(0.75)	(3.11)	(3.13)	(2.87)	(2.91)
Non-wage	0.012	—	0.002	—	0.003	—	0.007	—
	(4.02)	—	(0.82)	—	(1.16)	—	(3.17)	—
Log-likelihood	−310	−319	−310	−311	−343	−344	−292	−297

Variable labels: Age = age of mother in years, Degree qual. = has educational qualification at tertiary level (dummy), Vocqual = has vocational qualification (dummy), Advqual = has advanced school qualification (dummy), Basic qual. = has basic school qualification (dummy), Youngest = age of youngest child in years, Nchildren = number of dependent children, Re-partner = has a partner (dummy), Non-wage = non-wage income excluding benefits in £/week. Reference category for education dummies = has no qualification. 8 regional dummies, not shown.
Notes: Estimated effects on employment each year. Probit coefficients (with absolute values of t-statistics in parentheses); N = 649 for 1991–1993, and 563 for 1994.
Sources: PRILIF (GB).

10

Social Capital and Exits from Unemployment

Paolo Barbieri with Serge Paugam and Helen Russell

INTRODUCTION

The job matching process is one of the most important characteristics of Western European societies. In most of the countries of continental Europe, entering the labour market is a crucial step in an individuals' life history: given strong labour market segmentation, the high level of unemployment and labour market exclusion, and slow economic growth, the moment when job supply meets job demand strongly influences an individual's work history and consequently his or her overall life opportunities. For this reason, the manner in which job matching processes are institutionally regulated can be considered as a way of regulating and redistributing social inequality. This chapter will examine the role played by a person's social capital in finding a job, and subsequently in determining the type and quality of employment obtained.

It will show that the role and importance of social capital are affected by two crucial institutional factors: the extent of job creation in each national labour market, and the degree of public regulation of such labour markets. We shall use the term *'public institutional regulation'* to denote the role of the state in managing the match between job seekers and vacancies. With respect to the literature on the redistributive effects of different welfare regimes, our study suggests that the public regulation of the job matching process is as important as the welfare regime *per se*. As we shall see, 'public' redistribution can take place both through active labour market policies and through the efficient working of the 'traditional' public employment office. These two different kinds of public intervention, the former more actively concerned to help the unemployed find jobs, the latter impartially redistributing occupational vacancies, can be considered jointly since their effects on social inequalities are similar. Both methods are therefore referred to as 'public institutional', or, more generally, as 'state' regulation.

INSTITUTIONAL ARRANGEMENTS AND LABOUR MARKET FEATURES: AN OVERVIEW

A well-established body of socio-economic literature has summed up the European experience of unemployment in the term *eurosclerosis*. The core problem—it has been argued by the supply-side economic literature—is the dualism created by European systems of job security legislation. These systems have produced a core group of primary secure workers, guaranteed in their jobs by labour laws and by an industrial relations system which prevents any sort of labour market clearing. Standing in contrast to these core workers is a large population of the jobless, who, depending on the country concerned, are forced to rely either on the welfare system or on the family for support (OECD 1990, 1994, 1997; Soskice 1990; Ichino and Bertola 1995). The high degree of protection given to the former group is claimed to be one of the main causes for the lack of turnover between insiders and outsiders in continental Europe, and as a result for the prolonged exclusion of outsiders. The personal characteristics of those excluded from employment —and thereby from full citizenship rights—are not homogeneous across countries. Specifically, in central and northern European countries, being out of work is generally not so closely coupled with specific gender or demographic characteristics as it is in the southern part of Europe—see Chapter 1 this volume.

The degree of segregation between insiders and outsiders also differs among countries, as shown by the data in Table 10.1. Some countries, Italy and France in particular, clearly demonstrate a stronger degree of segmentation in their labour markets. This means greater difficulties in hiring and firing practices, stronger protection for those in employment, longer tenures and, more importantly, higher indirect labour costs, which constitute a disincentive to job creation.

Table 10.2 shows that Italy and France also have higher average tenures, and a larger quota of the working population with long records of employment. Such labour market conditions are usually conducive to a situation in which the 'employed' are to various degrees 'protected' against the economic cycle and its variations. A large body of empirical research in labour economics allows us to regard the Italian and the French labour markets as typically 'insider-outsider' in nature (Ichino and Ichino 1994; Ichino and Bertola 1995; Reyneri 1996b; Abowd *et al.* 1994; Abowd *et al.* 1995; Kramarz *et al.* 1995).

Table 10.3 shows employment responsiveness to output variations in the period 1970–91. Employment responsiveness differs greatly among the five countries analysed; the lowest exposure to change occurs, once again, among the Italian and French employed, while the highest exposure is

TABLE 10.1. *Employment protection regimes and other labour market regulations*

	Italy	France	Ireland	UK	Denmark
Individual firing					
Required notice for individual dismissal (months)	2.2	2	2	2.8	5
Compensation (no. monthly salaries)	18	2.7	3.9	4.6	1.5
Maximum duration of fixed-term contracts (months)[a]	12	24	no limits	no limits	no limits
Procedures to be followed for dismissal (index)[b]	1.5	1.5	1.5	1	0.5
Reinstatement after unfair dismissal (index)[c]	3	0	1	0	1
Hiring/firing practices					
Cost of hiring as perceived by employers (%)[d]	29	25	25	16	n.a.
Degree of flexibility in hiring/firing practices, as perceived by employers[e]	2.6	4.0	5.5	7.0	8.1
Indirect labour costs					
Social cost of labour, quota charged on employers (as % of gross wage)	45.1	38.0	12.2	10.2	0.3
OECD rankings for strictness of employment regulation and working practices					
Strictness of protection against dismissals	9.0	5.5	3.0	1.0	2.0
Regulation of fixed-term contracts	10.0	8.0	2.0	2.0	2.0
Restrictions on normal weekly hours	6.0	7.0	2.0	1.0	11.0
Restrictions on overtime, week-end, night work	3.5	7.5	3.5	1.0	2.0
Bertola's Job Security index[f]	1	3	n.a.	7	9

[a] Refers to the maximum duration of fixed-term contracts offered to unemployed people taking account of the possibility that the contract will be renewed.
[b] The index for the 'procedures to be followed for dismissal' scores 1 when only written notification to the worker is required; 2 when a third actor (trade unions or public employment office) is notified; 3 when formal approval by these third actors is necessary. Decimals refer to intermediate situations.
[c] The index for 'reinstatement after unfair dismissal' scores 0 if reinstatement is never guaranteed to the worker; 1 if it is rare; 2 if it is possible; 3 if the worker is always offered such a possibility.
[d] 'Cost of hiring' is the percentage of employers who regard the cost of hiring as an important reason for not hiring.
[e] Degree of flexibility in hiring/firing practices' ranges from 0 = nil flexibility to 10 = max flexibility. Both figures refer to 1994.
[f] From most (1) to least (10) restrictive.
Sources: Bertola 1990; Grubb and Wells 1993; OECD 1994, 1997.

TABLE 10.2. *Distribution of employment by employee tenure, 1995 (%)*

	Under 1 year	Under 2 years	Under 5 years	Under 10 years	10 to 20 years	20 years and over	Average tenure	Median tenure
Denmark	25.1	36.5	52.7	70.9	17.7	11.4	7.9	4.4
France	15.0	23.0	40.6	58.0	23.3	18.7	10.7	7.7
Ireland	17.8	28.8	48.8	66.9	21.2	11.9	8.7	5.3
Italy	8.5	15.5	33.6	54.4	26.1	19.5	11.6	8.9
UK	19.6	30.3	49.8	73.3	17.3	9.4	7.8	5.0

Source: OECD Employment Outlook, 1997.

TABLE 10.3. *Main economic indicators*

	Index of responsiveness	Econometric estimates of average tenure	Outflow rates from unemployment	Active L.M. policies (% GDP)	Tot. empl. policies (% GDP)	Net employment change
	(a)	(b)	(c)	(d)	(d)	(e)
Denmark	0.59	−1.52***	20.9[1]	1.56	6.53	2.2
France	0.38	0.59***	5.7	1.00	3.00	−0.2
Ireland	0.54	−0.34	n.a.	1.48	4.31	n.a.
Italy	0.15	1.51***	2.3	0.75	1.42	−0.1
UK	0.68	−2.04***	9.5	0.56	1.91	2.4

(a) The index of responsiveness (a measure of variation in economic cycle) refers to variations from 1970 to 1991 in real GDP. For further specification of the index of employment responsiveness to variations in GDP trends, see OECD Economic Studies 21/1993.
(b) Econometric estimates of average tenure as reported in: OECD Employment Outlook (1997: 158) (*** indicate significance at 1%).
(c) CEPR, 1995. [1] δ ECHP, 1994: for Sweden—which has an employment regime reasonably comparable with Denmark's—the CEPR index of outflow from unemployment ranks 30.4. Similar data are reported in Esping-Andersen (1999) and Rhodes (1997).
(d) Source: EC Employment Observatory, Tableau de Bord, 1994. Total employment policies comprise both active and passive labour market policies.
(e) Net Employment Change, as reported in The OECD Jobs Study Working Paper No. 1, Tables 1 and 2; OECD 1995.

experienced by UK workers. This appears to be related to the length of tenure, to the outflow from unemployment, and to the quotas of public spending on employment policies. The picture of very different national employment systems is confirmed.

It is not our intention to enter the debate on the causes of 'euroscler-osis', in which these views of labour market structure have been elaborated (see CEPR 1995; Jackman, Layard and Nickell 1996; Simonazzi and Villa 1997; Michie and Grieve Smith 1996; Freeman 1994; Nickell 1997). But in assessing the effects of social capital on job acquisition, it may also be use-ful to view European employment structures as characterized by different degrees of labour market closure. More closed, segmented labour markets and more rigid employment structures exist in Italy and France.[1] More heterogeneous labour markets conditions prevail in the UK, Ireland, and Denmark: as we shall see, both the UK and Denmark produce more job chances for people out of work, but in very different ways.

The labour economic literature (OECD 1994; CEPR 1995) has shown that in continental European countries the great majority of core, 'insider' workers who lose their jobs re-enter secure employment rapidly and easily: they 'change jobs' without experiencing any serious spells of unemployment. The picture changes, however, if we consider the rates of outflow from unemployment instead of work turnover rates. As clearly shown by Table 10.3, outflow rates are quite heterogeneous among the countries analysed. Two countries exhibit the largest degree of outsider exclusion from the labour market: Italy, with only a 2.3 per cent outflow from unemployment, and France, with 5.7 per cent. At the opposite end of the scale, Denmark achieves the largest re-insertion of the unemployed into the labour market. In these conditions, social capital may thus be of great importance not only in enabling people to find jobs but also in determining the type and quality of the employment to which they gain access (Granovetter 1973, 1974; Coleman 1991). To clarify the point it is advisable to give more precise definition of the concept of social capital, since it is central to this paper.

SOCIAL CAPITAL: AN OVERVIEW

The starting point is a classical tenet of sociological theory: individuals are embedded in networks of social relations. These relations, it is argued, 'create' social capital, a real resource which people utilize to achieve their goals. The concept was first developed by Pierre Bourdieu (1980), and was subsequently elaborated by James Coleman, who, within a framework inspired by rational action theory, regarded social capital as the key concept to establish an individualist approach to sociological analysis (Coleman 1988, 1990, 1991). In Coleman's view, actors committed to pursuing their own aims rationally weave together a network of social relations and mobilize their social capital. The latter is to be treated and analysed like any other sort of capital—economic and human—at an actor's disposal.

---

[1] Note that a segmented labour market can coexist with high levels of average job turnover and, even more so, work turnover. Labour market segmentation, in fact, gives rise to a situation in which 'insiders' simply change their jobs, without any serious 'competition' from people out of work, because the latter have insufficient skills or qualifications to compete with the former. This is exactly what happens in Italy, which has turnover rates similar to the US—about 24 per cent for the mid-1980 to mid-1990s period—and very high levels of long-term unemployment among low-skilled young people.

Social capital has become a key issue in job acquisition and status attainment research, and has been operationalised in various ways—for a survey see Lin (1999):

(1) with class of origin, or a correspondent status score (Lin 1986);
(2) with attained occupational position, again measured with a status score;
(3) with the contact-person status score (Marsden and Hurlbert 1988; Lin *et al.* 1981a,b; Lin and Dumin 1986);
(4) by combining different indicators of social activity, like club affiliations or shared membership in voluntary organisations (Boxman *et al.* 1991; Beggs and Hurlbert 1997);
(5) by using the partner's educational level as an indicator of the amount of social resources available to individuals involved in coupled careers (Bernasco *et al.* 1998).

The dual origin of social capital—family and social relationships—has recently been recognized (Furstenberg and Hughes 1995; Teachman *et al.* 1997). However, none of the different solutions proposed seems sufficiently generalizable. Contact-person status is a good proxy for the social resources utilized by an actor. In an analysis of job search processes, though, it can be used only for people who seek jobs via networks. Furthermore, the total number of work contacts or club affiliations is peculiar to specific professional categories. Class of origin, like destination class, may also be misleading because it superimposes two concepts: class and social capital. These two concepts are very close, but they do not coincide and therefore should be kept separate. Even Coleman's concept of social capital probably does not avoid this conflation. In any case, both from a theoretical and empirical point of view, this double 'identity' of social capital—ascription and achievement— in the job matching process should be emphasized.

When Coleman operationalized social capital with reference to young people's educational attainment chances, he used a combination of predictors like parents' socio-economic status, the presence in the household of both parents, the existence of siblings, household composition, parents' expectations with respect to the child's educational results, ethnic membership, and the kind of school attended (Coleman 1988). He employed a wide variety of 'status' covariates, refusing to operate with only formal or descriptive attributes of networks, such as number and frequency of contacts. Other kinds of indicators that could be used as proxies for the relevance of social capital in job attainment processes are variables such as having sought a job through personal or formal channels; the number of household members in employment, and their occupational status; the total length of residence in a specific area as a rough proxy for the possibility of network creation; the length of spells of unemployment/precarious employment as negative indexes of social capital; partner's employment situation; and the proportion of friends and network members in employment. Finally, for women, the presence of young children has been proposed as a negative index of social capital, since it reduces women's chances of cultivating useful employment contacts (Russell 1997).

Notwithstanding the debate surrounding the conceptual status of social capital, one common starting point can be identified. Social capital is something between a social resource and a social mechanism, which operates throughout a person's life course, and which must be analysed as an intervening variable between family, economic and human capital to explain the amount of 'social rewards' obtained by actors. This perspective is the one from which we start and which has been formalized in the analyses.

RESEARCH HYPOTHESES

In this section we present a number of research hypotheses to be verified empirically. These hypotheses concern: the type of social capital that can be expected to constitute a real resource for individuals, the conditions determining the efficacy of social capital in facilitating work entry, and the influence of social capital on the type and quality of employment found, or in other words, its influence in defining the social status attained. These are aspects that, although interconnected, should be kept conceptually and analytically distinct.

Social Resources

The first hypothesis is that the social resources expected to be efficacious for work entry are those which consist of direct, strong status ties, since these provide a job seeker not only with information about available vacancies but also, and especially, with influence and support for the purpose of gaining employment and subsequent occupational status (Grieco 1987; Marsden and Hurlbert 1988; Lin 1982, 1999; Barbieri 1997b; Breen 1998).

Obtaining Work

The efficacy of social resources in gaining employment, we suggest, is primarily a function of the degree of openness of the national labour market and the amount of job creation realized. A closed and excessively rigid labour market inevitably depresses labour demand, hampering or entirely obstructing job creation. In this case, no form of social capital is able to 'force' the narrow entry ports of a restricted labour market reserved for insiders (Althauser 1989; Althauser and Kalleberg 1990).

On the basis of the observations and macroeconomic data set out in the first section, it is possible to divide the countries analysed between those with 'flexible' and open labour markets—Denmark, the UK, and Ireland—and those with more protected labour markets in which jobs are scarce and more difficult to obtain—Italy and France. Accordingly, we may expect the effect of social resources on the chances of finding a job to be high in the UK—the country which represents the ideal type of a deregulated labour market.[2] A positive effect of social capital is also to be expected for Ireland, which has a degree of labour market flexibility similar to the UK's.

Denmark currently has one of the most flexible labour markets in Europe, but at the same time it embodies the ideal type of the universalistic welfare system (Esping-Andersen 1990), as evidenced in its high level of investment in active employment policies which should have positive effects on the employability of the long-term unemployed; in its regulation of the job matching system, and in its substantial investments in vocational training. For this reason, we do not expect the effect of social capital to be as important in defining the chances of finding employment in Denmark as in the UK and Ireland. The influence of the welfare system on labour market regulation should lead to the predominance of universalistic conditions in the job matching process.

Finally, one would expect the role of social capital to be decidedly minor for the unemployed in France and Italy, since these countries have the highest degree of job security and labour market closure of those analysed. One can therefore predict that the barriers to employment deriving from strong institutional protection greatly reduce the effect of social networks on the chances of the unemployed gaining work. The low level of job creation and the institutionally engendered absence of competition between insiders and outsiders are the principal features of the Italian and French labour markets—markets in which a substantial proportion of work turnover consists of 'job swaps' between insiders.[3] For this reason the 'insider effect', or the increased chances of re-entering work enjoyed by the previously employed, will be maximized in those two countries.

The Process of Status Attainment

Assessment of the causal importance of social capital in the process of status attainment requires the introduction of a further factor affecting the

[2] Research conducted, using panel data, in the UK, confirm that status connections have a utility in helping people to exit from unemployment (Hannan 1998).

[3] We should note that the outsiders' chances of being competitive with respect to the insider, on the labour market, are enhanced not only by deregulation policies, but, and probably more, by active labour market policies and training and re-training programmes, which are still quite underdeveloped both in Italy and in France.

extent to which individual social resources act as genuine social capital. This involves the contrast between, on the one hand, the universalistic and transparent regulation performed by the public system of job allocation, and on the other, the private, personalistic and 'non-transparent' regulation of the job matching process based on individual and familial social capital. In the absence of universalistic and transparent job allocation systems, one may expect status attainment to be heavily influenced by people's status resources. In these conditions, personalistic social ties reduce transaction costs, providing the trust required for performance of the 'exchange' undertaken when job seekers and vacancies are matched, while also ensuring that the parties to the exchange share the same meanings and values (Bourdieu 1979; Coleman 1990). Social capital thus transmits ascribed privileges through the labour market. Hence the effect of social capital on the social position attained by individuals will be higher in labour markets without a universalistic, efficient, and transparent public system of job allocation, such as the UK, Ireland, and Italy.

A large body of empirical research (Cobalti and Schizzerotto 1994; Barbieri 1997b) reports the substantial importance in Italy of personal and ascribed factors in determining social position in labour market entry. Moreover, the inefficiency of Italy's public job placement system, as well as its scant investment in active labour market policies, are factors which work in favour of the personalistic regulation of status attainment processes performed by social capital.[4] For the same reasons, the role of social capital in the status attainment of 'insiders', who are better able than the unemployed to exploit their personal and familial resources during their work careers, should be more influential in the UK, Ireland, and Italy.

EMPIRICAL FINDINGS

Data and Variables

This study uses data from the first wave of the European Community Household Panel (ECHP) conducted in 1994. In order to estimate the chances of finding employment, we selected individuals who had obtained jobs or had begun new ones in 1994. These individuals were compared with those who had been unemployed in 1993 and were still unemployed in 1994. In this way—that is, controlling for the temporal dimension—it was possible to assess the chances of workers who were unemployed or formerly employed in 1993, of finding a job in 1994 rather than remaining unemployed, taking account of socio-personal features, previous occupational

---

[4] In Italy, about 1 per cent of people find jobs via public employment services (ECHP 1994).

status, and the amount of social capital possessed by each subject. The variables employed in this preliminary analysis were: sex, age in years, educational qualification, civil status, occupational status in the previous year in order to control for the 'insider effect', being in long-term unemployment, as well as total household income.

Previous research (Furstenberg and Hughes 1995; Barbieri 1997b; Lin 1999) suggests that social capital cannot be defined uniquely; rather, it requires a plurality of measurement indices, each of which must be tested on the dependent variable. For this reason, we used two different indices, each of them intended to be an operationalization of a specific perspective on an individual's social resources. The first can be termed a status index of social capital and was realized using a confirmatory factor analytical model. The factor score 'adds' together the household members' occupational status, net of the respondent's own status, and the household members' total years of education, net of the respondent's years of schooling—the effect of which is measured separately. The second index is a network measure of social capital which combines information about network relations and contacts gathered by questions in the ECHP questionnaire. These questions concerned membership of organizations or clubs, frequency of contact with neighbours, and frequency of contact with friends/relatives outside the household.[5]

Social Capital and Job Attainment

Table 10.4 addresses our first hypothesis, which we could define as the 'structural embeddedness' of social capital in the given assets of national political economies. The model we present links macro-, or national indexes of job creation, and micro-, or individuals' social capital, characteristics in order to estimate the probability of the subjects finding work between 1993 and 1994. The degree of job creation within each country has been operationalized with the net employment change index for the mid-1980s–mid-1990s period, as reported by OECD official data. This 'macro' index has been matched to the pooled individual data file by recoding each single national dummy variable to its corresponding 'macro' value (OECD 1995).

As expected, the effectiveness of status social capital is associated with the degree of openness of the different labour markets, that is with their ability to create job opportunities, so that unemployed people seeking work do not have to queue for a long period before a position. We see that the more

---

[5] The social capital indices refer to all the individuals considered in our analyses, regardless of whether they subsequently found jobs via networks. It seems, in fact, correct to assume that people seeking jobs try to obtain them by using and mobilizing all the personal, familial, and relational resources at their disposal, thereby making use of a broad spectrum of job search channels.

TABLE 10.4. *Multiplicative parameters (odds) of the logistic regression model estimating individuals' chances of becoming employed*[a]

Net Employment Change	
France	*ref.*
UK	1.72***
Denmark	1.78***
Italy	0.40
Status social capital	1.06*
Network social capital	0.95
Net Employment Change* Status social capital	
UK	1.14***
Denmark	1.15**
Italy	1.09
Model Chi-Square (8 df)	619.3***

[a] Ireland is excluded because of lack of employment change data.
Notes: *** = sign. 1%; ** = sign. 5%; * = sign. 10%. The constant term is included in the model.

job creation there is, the more social capital can act in matching job offers and job seekers.

Table 10.4 shows that the UK and Denmark are the two countries which succeed in creating most job opportunities. The interaction terms also demonstrate that status social capital has a significant effect only in the two countries which have a large and positive increment of employment opportunities—we have no data on net employment change for Ireland. Italy, and France, the reference category, which are both characterized by closed labour markets, score at the lowest levels. In the next section we will see how the effect of social capital differs among countries and how it is also affected by individuals' characteristics.

Table 10.5 sets out the multiplicative parameters (odds) of the logistic regression models used to estimate, in each country, the probability of the subjects' finding work between 1993 and 1994.[6] One notes, with respect to socio-personal features, that men have a better chance of finding a job than women in Italy and France—the countries with stronger insider/outsider occupational structures. In the other countries, this comparative advantage of males reaches the 10 per cent significance threshold only in Denmark. In all the countries analysed, age tends to be negatively associated with the chances of finding a job, while there is a comparative advantage for married people. As regards educational qualifications, with the sole exception of Italy, human capital is of increasing value for employability, although it is not equally significant in all countries. The distinctiveness of the Italian case

[6] Excluded from the model are people out of the labour market in both years and those who were employed in 1993 and 1994, but did not change job.

TABLE 10.5. *Multiplicative parameters (odds) of logistic regression models estimating individuals' chances of becoming employed, by country*[a]

	UK	Ireland	Denmark	France	Italy
Sex					
Female (ref.)					
Male	0.99	0.84	1.42	1.73**	1.68***
Age	0.97**	0.98	0.96***	0.96***	0.98**
Education (CASMIN)					
General elementary (ref.)					
Intermediate qualification	1.41*	1.68**	1.47*	0.85	0.87
Maturity certificate	1.44*	2.08***	1.90*	0.91	1.18
Tertiary education	1.77**	2.81***	1.88**	1.39**	0.66
Civil Status					
Not married (ref.)					
Married	1.86**	1.28	1.56	1.12*	1.22**
Previous year (93)					
occupational status					
Unemployed (ref.)					
Employed	1.34	1.05	0.92	3.27***	2.79***
Long-term unemployed	0.36***	2.94***	3.67***	0.30***	0.29***
Ln Household income	1.04	1.02	0.95	0.96	1.15*
Status social capital	1.35***	1.49***	1.24	1.05	1.07
Network social capital	0.91	0.95	1.00	0.92	0.88
Model Chi-Square (11 df)	102.78***	131.34***	109.29***	55.53***	138.31***
N	736	977	491	448	1033

[a] Excludes those outside the labour market in 1993 and 1994 and those continuously employed with the same employer.
Notes: *** = sign. 1%; ** = sign. 5%; * = sign. 10%. The constant term is included in the model.

can probably be explained in terms of a composition effect—for a more detailed discussion see Chapter 11.

As expected, the impact of previous occupational status, or the 'insider' effect, is greatest and highly significant only in Italy and France. It does not reach significance in the UK and Ireland, and it has no influence in Denmark. This finding should be considered jointly with the odds of being in long-term unemployment. Consistent with the view that there is a 'welfare' effect, the chances of individuals unemployed for more than twelve months re-entering employment are positive and highly significant in the two countries which invest most in active labour market policies: Denmark and Ireland.[7] Total household income proves to have an effect only in Italy. This may be due to the large proportion of independent workers in that

[7] The Irish result is likely to be due to government sponsored, direct employment schemes for the unemployed. Between April 1994 and April 1995 the Irish Labour Force Surveys showed that long-term unemployment fell dramatically by 25,000 units. This coincided with an substantial expansion in the Community Employment Scheme from 20,000 to 40,000 places targeted at the long-term unemployed.

country—around 28 per cent of the labour force—and to the economic support provided by the family for those opting for self-employment.

We now turn to the variables of greatest interest: the two different forms
of social capital. The empirical results confirm our initial hypotheses. Network social capital has no influence. In none of the countries considered,
it seems, do relational resources provide individuals with a valid and efficacious form of social capital which they can exploit to gain employment. This is
not to imply that network resources do not constitute supportive resources
for individuals—moral, counselling, psychological, and more generally
socialization resources—only that their efficacy for the specific purpose of
finding work is meagre.[8] It is worth noting that the network index of social
capital represents the degree of 'extensiveness' of the network itself, that is
the mere number of contacts, independently of any kind of evaluation of
the effective 'quality' of such connections. Moreover, it should be remembered that the original theory of the strength of weak ties (Granovetter 1973,
1974)—which considered the frequencies of the contacts with others—was
originally devised to study a specific population of managers and profes-
sionals, and was subsequently revised to take into account the social status
dimension of the ties analysed (Granovetter 1982).

Social status seems to be the form of social capital that positively influences job acquisition. But, in accordance with our initial hypothesis, it has
a significant effect only in those countries, like the UK and Ireland, with
particularly open and deregulated labour markets. In Denmark, once main
individual characteristics have been controlled, the effect of social capital,
although of the expected sign, is no longer statistically significant. In this
case, the extreme flexibility of the Danish labour market, and the value placed
on human capital, together with the efficiency of the Danish public welfare
state and the system of job allocation,[9] make the use of personalistic channels to find employment substantially pointless. Denmark, in effect, demonstrates that a flexible labour market and open employment relations can easily
coexist with an advanced welfare regime and close public involvement in
management of the labour market, both through investment in active
employment policies and through direct intervention in the job matching
process. Finally, and again confirming our hypotheses, the role of status social
capital is irrelevant in both Italy and France.

The data therefore confirm our expectations concerning the role of
status social capital in the job acquisition process. We shall now see what
happens when we move from job acquisition processes to an examination
of the status of the occupational position acquired by individuals.

---

[8] With respect to Italy, these results confirm previous research conducted in northern
Italy (Barbieri 1997a, b). In France, Paugam (1997) found that unemployment is frequently
coupled with loss of social contacts and relations, even in the same household.

[9] Denmark is the country with the largest investment in public employment services in Europe:
5.3 per cent of the total amount of social protection expenditure in 1994 (Eurostat 1996a).

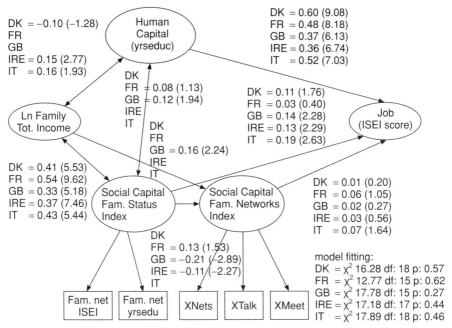

FIG. 10.1. Social capital and status attainment models

Note: t-values in brackets.

Social Capital and Status Attainment

To analyse the role of social capital in status attainment processes, we have elaborated different kinds of structural equation models (SEM), using ECHP 1994 data, selecting only individuals who obtained their jobs via networks in 1994. The analyses (see Fig. 10.1 and Table 10.6) have substantially validated our hypothesis that the ability of social capital to distribute occupational rewards is related to the degree of public intervention in the job matching process. The causal path between status social capital and the International Socio-Economic Index (ISEI) (Ganzeboom and Treiman 1996) of the work position attained is notably higher and highly significant in Italy (0.19) UK (0.14), and Ireland (0.13), countries in which the percentage of people allocated by the public employment services is extremely low; while the social capital effect is lower and not significant in France and Denmark, countries with stronger systems of job matching regulation.[10]

---

[10] Note that in the specific case of Ireland, the high percentage of people who obtain jobs via networks (about 73 per cent) is likely to limit the effectiveness of public investments in active labour market policies, which are also quite high.

TABLE 10.6. *Direct effect of social capital on status attainment:*
summary of results from the SEM

	Network social capital (all individuals)	Status social capital (all individuals)	Employed in 1993 status social capital	Unemployed in 1993 status social capital
	(a)	(b)	(c)	(d)
Denmark	0.01	0.11	0.13	0.05
France	0.06	0.03	0.00	0.08
Great Britain	0.02	0.14***	0.26***	0.00
Ireland	0.03	0.13***	0.25***	0.00
Italy	0.07	0.19***	0.32***	0.15

*** = significance 1%.

The effect of personal ties is greatest in Italy, which displays a combination of strong labour market closure and the virtual absence of public allocation. In Italy and Ireland the lack of public intervention is also revealed by the high percentage of job seeker/vacancy matches achieved through networks—respectively 71.8 per cent and 72.8 per cent, according to Eurobarometer 1994 data—while in the UK it is 26 per cent, and two-thirds of matches apparently take place via 'market' channels. Nevertheless, the notable impact in the UK of status social capital on attained occupational position reveals that status social resources are influential even in a market-driven system of labour market regulation. This is a clear example of market failure, demonstrating that the market in itself cannot effectively substitute for the informal regulation performed by networks.

The Insider/Outsider Effect as a Problem of Social Inequality

To assess the ways in which labour market outcomes can produce or reproduce social inequality, we need to examine the relevance of social capital among different types of individuals: 'privileged' and disadvantaged. We therefore looked at the possible differences in the quality—measured as causal weight in the status attainment process—of social capital and resources between people who were regularly and continually employed more than fifteen hours per week during 1993,[11] and people who were unemployed as defined by ILO or not in the labour force in 1993. We define as 'insiders' all the subjects who worked continually and full time in 1993. In contrast, 'outsiders' refers to people not employed in 1993. 'Insiders' and 'outsiders', therefore, are used here merely as labels to define the two different groups in the labour market.

[11] This restriction regarding the limit of fifteen worked hours per week is imposed by the ECHP questionnaire.

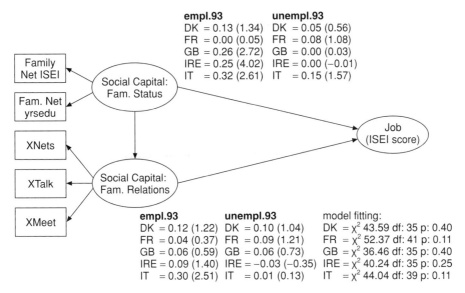

FIG. 10.2. Social capital and insider-outsider status attainment sub-models

Notes: t-values in brackets.

To compare the effect of social capital among these two groups we used multi-sample models. These models were structured in the same way as the previous ones, but were applied to the two subsamples of people who, in 1993, were insiders, and had continuous regular jobs, and outsiders, being unemployed or not in the labour force. In so doing, we could directly compare these two categories, and look at the total value of their social resources. They all found jobs in 1994, but how much did their social resources matter in terms of status attainment? The results of our analysis are presented in the submodels shown in Fig. 10.2,[12] and reported in columns (c) and (d) of Table 10.6.

The status index of social capital again proves to be a better measure of social inequality, revealing that former workers have a greater amount of social resources to 'spend' in the job attainment process. This is especially the case for Italy, the UK and Ireland, countries in which—controlling for the effects of respondents' educational attainment and household incomes —the greater 'amounts' of social capital possessed by insiders enables them to find better jobs. By contrast, Denmark and France display a more marked 'equity effect', which is particularly evident in France, a country in which, notwithstanding its closed labour market—the reason for the insiders'

[12] Fig. 10.2 just illustrates the paths of interest, but the SEM models are identical to that one shown in Fig. 10.1.

advantage in obtaining jobs—the large-scale job allocation performed by pub-lic employment offices and public services closes the gap between insiders and outsiders with respect to the processes of status attainment.[13]

CONCLUSIONS

Our results can be summarized in two main findings. The first regards the concept of social capital, and its utilization in empirical social research. As we have shown, a status measure of social capital which directly refers to the individual's household and familial background is a more useful indicator of the social resources at an individual's disposal because it is a better measure of the qualitative nature of an actor's resources. Size of net-works, and frequency or quantity of contacts, are often merely 'noise'. They depend on too many situations and local characteristics to be taken as a 'robust' indicators of social resources, and are therefore of little use in inter-national comparisons.

Previous studies on social capital conducted in individual countries (Forsé 1996; Barbieri 1997b) have demonstrated the relevance of status social resources to status attainment, while casting doubt on the 'network' re-sources. Gallie *et al.* (1994) have shown that unemployment does not lead to a decline in the frequency of social contact, finding instead that the social networks of the unemployed differ qualitatively from those of the em-ployed, in that they lack contacts in employment and are less supportive. Our paper confirms these findings within a comparative framework. Gen-erally, of greatest relevance is the 'quality' of the social relations that an individual can 'spend' on the labour market, and not the mere 'quantity' of social relations. For all the countries analysed, the social capital effect, measured in terms of 'contacts', 'relations', and 'network activities' is close to zero. The quality of social resources, measured by the social status index, proves to be a better measure of social capital, and it varies considerably among the countries analysed. What makes the difference with respect to 'networks as a resource' is not the number of connections available to an individual, but the type of person with whom they are connected.

Our second finding concerns the usefulness of status social capital in job acquisition, and, after that initial hurdle, in status attainment. Social capital proves itself to be a valuable resource for finding employment in open and flexible labour markets—that is, in employment structures which foster a large amount of job creation. Closed labour markets, tight employment

---

[13] 28 per cent of people in France and 12.5 per cent in Denmark obtained their jobs in 1994 via public channels (ECHP 1994).

relations, and markedly insider-outsider occupational regimes, strongly depress labour demand, thereby restricting job opportunities and making it much more difficult for the unemployed to find jobs. In this situation, even people endowed with valuable social resources must patiently 'queue' for their turn to enter the world of work.[14] However, the Danish case demonstrates that we are not caught between the horns of a deregulated labour market regime on the one hand and a closed, insider-outsider regime on the other. Broad flexibility, greater job creation, and high outflows from unemployment are not only compatible with a good welfare system; but they greatly benefit from it when it is able to ensure a flexible and widely accessible labour market.

With respect to social capital's usefulness for status attainment, we have found that the state and networks, as ways of regulating the process, substitute for each other: that is, a trade-off takes place between them. The weaker the role of the state in allocating people to jobs, the more personal social capital becomes the regulatory institution (North 1990). This has been found to be true even in the most deregulated labour markets, thereby revealing the failure of the market itself as a criterion of labour market regulation. Social capital, in fact, introduces elements of ambiguity, non-transparency, and particularism into the status attainment process—elements which counteract meritocracy and therefore reduce both the efficacy and efficiency of hiring decisions. Since individual social capital relates primarily to an individual's strong ties, that is, to his/her social origin and background, it tends to reproduce social inequality. For this reason, lack of transparency in the way in which people are allocated to jobs is one mechanism by which social differences are not only established but maintained. Since occupational position is one of the main gateways to better life opportunities, it follows that the way in which the labour market is regulated, and the way in which it structures access to occupational position, is central to the issue of social justice.

---

[14] With respect to Italy, we should note that even Bernardi *et al.*, in Chapter 11 of this volume, find that family characteristics, as indexed by class position, had very little impact on the duration of time it took for Italians to get their first job.

11

Who Exits Unemployment? Institutional Features, Individual Characteristics, and Chances of Getting a Job. A Comparison of Britain and Italy

Fabrizio Bernardi, Richard Layte, Antonio Schizzerotto and Sheila Jacobs

INTRODUCTION

In recent years numerous scholars have taken up the challenge of explaining the variations in unemployment rates in Western countries. The debate on the causes of unemployment has focused on the institutional regulation of the labour market and on how this regulation hinders market clearing (Grubb and Wells 1993; Siebert 1997). In spite of these efforts, no conclusive and coherent results have emerged. In particular, it seems that there is no simple relationship between the institutional regulation of the labour market and the *level* of unemployment, that is how many unemployed there are (Alogoskoufis *et al.* 1995; Scarpetta 1996; Reyneri 1996b; Nickell 1997). However, the institutional regulation of the labour market does affect the *structure* of unemployment, or who is unemployed. In other words, the regulatory structure seems to produce unemployment among some socio-demographic groups and not others.

The aim of this chapter is to investigate the mechanisms by which differences in the structure of unemployment in Italy and Britain come into being. In our analysis we focus on the process of *exit* from unemployment using event history analysis to study transitions from unemployment to employment. Therefore, our analysis can be seen as complementary to the analyses on *entry* into unemployment conducted in Chapter 8 in this book, by Layte, Levin, Hendrickx, and Bison, and in previous studies (Gershuny and Hannan 1997). Moreover it enables us to study the duration of unemployment and to address the policy-relevant question of who runs the higher risk of entrapment in unemployment.

Two additional features characterize our study. First, we widen the debate on the effect of the institutional regulation of unemployment beyond the narrow confines of the labour market. Thus, we refer to the wider institutional context defined by welfare measures for the unemployed, the workings of the educational system, and the role of the family (Esping-Andersen 1997; Saraceno 1997; Müller and Shavit 1998). In order to gain a firmer grasp on the interaction among these elements, we contrast the very different systems of Italy and Britain. Second, we distinguish between transitions into first occupation, and those from unemployment after some labour force experience. This distinction allows us to focus on a crucial type of unemployment that is of particular importance in southern European countries: young people in search of their first occupation.

In sum we address two main questions: first, which groups of the population run a higher risk of entrapment in unemployment in Italy and Britain? Second, how is this risk affected by the institutional contexts of the two countries?

The chapter is organized in the following way. In the next section we discuss the main features of the institutional context in Italy and Britain. In the third section we present our hypothesis with regard to the relationship between the institutional context and the mechanisms that account for exit from unemployment. In the fourth section we describe the data, variables, and methods used in the analysis. In the fifth section we present the empirical results of our research. Finally we summarize the principal findings and draw some tentative conclusions.

ECONOMIC AND INSTITUTIONAL FEATURES OF BRITAIN AND ITALY: A SHORT OVERVIEW

Before turning to the institutional context of the two countries, we should first briefly discuss the main features of the two economies which have a direct bearing on the structure of unemployment. By and large, in comparison with the Italian economy the British economy has:

(1) a broader private tertiary sector;
(2) a lower proportion of small firms with fewer than 10 employees, and of self-employed individuals;
(3) less pronounced regional variations in the degree of economic development and unemployment rates;
(4) a smaller informal and black economy.

Turning to labour market regulation, Italy and Britain are often juxtaposed in the current debate on unemployment as representative examples of, respectively, high rigidity and high flexibility (Bertola 1990; Grubb and Wells 1993; Siebert 1997). Historically, Britain has never had strict labour market regulation. Moreover, that regulation which did exist has been progressively weakened since the mid-1970s. On the other hand, the Italian labour market can be considered as an example of strict regulation produced by legal measures, contractual bargaining and informal norms.

Employment protection in Italy was very stringent until the late 1980s. Strict legal rules prevented firms with sixteen employees or more from selecting employees to be hired or fired on an individual basis. Collective dismissals, which were mainly regulated by contractual bargaining, were rather difficult to carry out. In fact, permanent jobs on a full-time basis were the main form of employment allowed by the law and by contractual norms, while non-permanent positions and part-time jobs were regarded as absolutely exceptional. The main effect of these measures was to protect the jobs of adult males against both employers' decisions and competition from 'outsiders'—usually young people and women—looking for employment. The effectiveness of these forms of employment protection was reinforced by the behaviour of trade unions at firm level. The extremely influential Italian trade unions systematically differentiated their local protective action for dependent workers by following gender, age, and position within the family. In other words, they provided much greater protection for adult married men than other categories of workers—both married and unmarried women and young unmarried men—against the risks of dismissal. And it is worth noting that the idea and practice of considering adult married males as the last category of dependent workers to be fired was also widespread among Italian employers.

Since the beginning of the 1990s, some of these rigidities have been weakened, and both hiring and dismissal procedures have been slightly relaxed (Samek Lodovici 1997). More specifically, new types of contract have been introduced in the form of fixed-term, work-training and temporary contracts. However, these measures have not greatly reduced the amount of social contributions paid by firms, they are not generally supported by public funds, and the law restricts their use. These kinds of contract are therefore relatively uncommon, and are restricted mainly, though not entirely, to young people in their first jobs. Part-time jobs, though more widespread than in the past, are still uncommon. As a consequence, the level of unemployment and the degree of segmentation by age and sex in the Italian labour market has been almost unaffected by the new forms of employment relation.

The same holds for the procedures currently governing the dismissal of Italian workers. Although, following an EU directive, legislation on collective dismissals was introduced in 1991, in several cases this legislation has not been applied and *de facto* replaced by the use of either '*Cassa Integrazione Guadagni Straordinaria*' (special wage supplementation fund)[1]

---

[1] Redundant workers in CIGS maintain their employment contract with the firm and can receive almost their entire salary for an extended period. Further information on CIGS appears later in this section.

or early retirement measures. Moreover, the workers involved in the application of the 1991 legislation on collective dismissals are usually placed on a 'Lista di Mobilità' (mobility list) which entitles them to high unemployment benefits and re-employment facilities. Finally, it should be stressed that since 1990 restraints on individual dismissals have been extended to small firms as well. Clearly, all these measures are intended to continue the protection of 'insiders', rather than accelerate the integration of those searching for a job (Faini, Galli and Rossi 1996; Samek Lodovici 1997). Trade unions still continue to believe that adult men should be laid off after young people and women (Reyneri 1996b).

In Britain, wage levels usually depend on workplace agreements between employers and employees. By contrast, in Italy they are fixed by industry-level collective contracts, where, to date, an egalitarian approach has prevailed in wage negotiations. As a result, variations in wage by age and educational level are far less pronounced in Italy than in Britain (OECD-Ceri 1997; Esping-Andersen 1998). One consequence of the more egalitarian distribution of wages in Italy is that employers find it more convenient to hire adult workers with previous work experience, rather than young first-time job seekers who require several months' training.

Strong legal, contractual, and informal regulation of the labour market can often have the unintended effect of producing informal sources of flexibility. In Italy, the spread of an informal economy and 'black' jobs has been interpreted as also being a consequence of the rigid rules governing the official economy and labour market. Given the topic of this paper, we concentrate here on irregular dependent jobs. Several attempts have been made to estimate the number of black market jobs. Istat (1994) recently estimated the number of irregular jobs in 1992 as 12.1 per cent of Italian employees. In Britain, the absence of real labour market regulation means that the distinction between official and informal jobs is less meaningful.

Besides the regulation of the labour market and the importance of black market jobs, the two countries also differ in terms of their unemployment welfare regimes, as shown in the Chapter 1. Benefits guaranteed by the 'liberal/minimal' unemployment welfare regime of Britain, though of low level, are universalistic in character. Eligibility is general and the only significant sources of variation in benefit levels are the claimant's age and the number of dependent children. However, under-eighteens can only claim income support in special circumstances. In the Italian 'sub-protective' unemployment welfare regime on the other hand, subsidies are offered on a rather particularistic and restrictive basis. Only people who were employees are eligible to any benefits, while those looking for their first job and the self-employed are not. The amount and duration of benefits varies greatly, depending on the kind of job, the sector of employment and, above all, the size of the firm (Dell'Aringa and Samek Lodovici 1996; Negri and Saraceno 1996; Samek

Lodovici 1997). By and large, workers from firms with more than fifteen employees are the most favoured by the Italian system of income support. The measures in their favour guaranteed by '*Cassa integrazione guadagni straordinaria*', '*Cassa integrazione guadagni ordinaria*' or '*Lista di mobilità*' amount to at least 75 per cent of the previous salary and last, on average, for two years, although in some cases duration can be extended to four years or more. In short, only a small minority of Italian unemployed workers obtain some form of economic support—see Chapter 1. Of those who receive it, about one-half obtain the very generous benefits of either ordinary or supplementary '*Cassa Integrazione Guadagni*' or '*Lista di mobilità*', while the other half mainly receive the very low ordinary benefits, which amount to 30 per cent of the last wage and last at most, for six months.[2]

In contemporary societies, the education system is an important mediating institution between supply and demand within the labour force (Halsey *et al.* 1997). A country's educational system thus may play an important role in shaping its unemployment structure. According to the typology proposed by Allmendinger (1989), the Italian educational system is more standardized and stratified than the British one (Müller and Shavit 1998). The Italian system is more nationally organized than the British system partly because of the division between private and state secondary schools in the latter, although more homogeneity of educational certificates has been achieved in Britain in recent years (Heath and Cheung 1998). As regards the stratification of education, the proportion of the population obtaining university degrees in Britain is twice as large as in Italy, and the proportion of British individuals with higher secondary school educations is almost 30 points higher than in Italy (OECD-Ceri 1997). As a consequence, the effect of school qualifications on the occupational level of a person's first job appears to be much stronger in Italy (Shavit and Müller 1998; Schizzerotto and Cobalti 1998; Heath and Cheung 1998). However, despite the differences just listed, there is an interesting similarity between the two countries: their post-compulsory schools pay little attention to the requirements of the economy, and both lack an effective system of vocational training. Moreover, in both countries, attending vocational courses instead of the regular school system, is usually considered to be a sign of educational failure.

The family too is an important mediating agency between individuals and the labour market in the sense that the structure of a family, its pattern of relations between parents and children and husbands and wives can influence its members' labour market activities (Saraceno 1997). In Italy and Britain, as in other Western countries, the patterns of family structure have undergone significant change since the 1960s. The most notable changes are

---

[2] For more detailed discussion of the types of income support for unemployment in Italy, and of the criteria required to qualify for them—see Dell'Aringa and Samek Lodovici (1996).

in the increasing age of marriage, the spread of non-marital cohabitation, the increase in divorce and separation, and the decrease in fertility. However, the rate of change is very different in the two countries. Britain has one of the highest rates in Western Europe of divorce, births outside marriage, teenage births and cohabitation (Ringen 1997). As a consequence, post-nuclear families are much more frequent in Britain, and the family as an institution seems to play a weaker role, compared to the past, in shaping the life chances of individuals. Italy on the other hand has experienced a much lower rate of change: thus the standard nuclear family still represents the dominant pattern and has not lost its role as a central and stable institution within Italian society (Bettio and Villa 1996). Moreover, the traditional pattern of the division of domestic labour between men and women, though attenuated compared with the past, is still widespread among Italian families. Italy also has one of the highest proportions of young people aged 18–29 years still living with the family of origin (Cavalli and Galland 1995), whereas in Britain not only do young people leave home earlier, but they are encouraged to be economically independent within the parental household (Jones 1992).

However, the differing behaviour towards children of the Italian and British family does not depend entirely on a different cultural pattern. It is also a consequence of differences in the regulation of both the labour market and eligibility to unemployment benefits, of different degrees of fluidity in the house rental market, and of different types of welfare state.

Italian families are often compelled to take long-term care of their sons and daughters because, as stressed earlier, the strong protection afforded to insiders by the official labour market prevents many young men and women from finding jobs, and because first-time job seekers are, as previously noted, not eligible for unemployment subsidies. Neither can the presence of a large informal labour market effectively alleviate the economic dependence of young Italians on their parents. 'Black' jobs are unstable and poorly paid, and do not represent a sound basis for an independent life. Even young Italians with permanent, full-time and regular jobs may find it difficult to leave their family of origin. In fact, the strict regulation of the Italian house rental market, originally intended to defend the lower classes against exploitation by landlords, has had three markedly negative effects:

(1) a dramatic decline in the numbers of rentable apartments;
(2) the practical impossibility of renting accommodation at the legal price;
(3) an increase in the real, though illegal, cost of renting accommodation to almost unsustainable levels for young people at the beginning their work careers.

In Britain, the absence of mechanisms to protect the jobs of adults against competition by young people, the greater fluidity of the house rental market, and the universalistic character of unemployment benefits, enhance the likelihood that young British men and women will become independent of their parents much earlier than their Italian counterparts.

In a very real sense, the workings of the Italian welfare state and the structure of the family unit are intertwined and symbiotic. To be more precise, we should say that cultural patterns and structural need reinforce each other. And as we will argue in the next section, because the structural dependence of young Italians on their families of origin complies with a traditional cultural pattern, this dependence has different consequences on the chances of getting jobs of young men and young women.

RESEARCH HYPOTHESES

On the basis of these differences in the economic structure and institutional arrangements of Britain and Italy we would expect to find very different patterns of exit from unemployment between the countries. We would also expect to find a longer duration of first or new job search in Italy compared with Britain.

Due to the strict regulation of the labour market and the protection granted to insiders in Italy, we hypothesize that the process of exiting unemployment among first-time job seekers will be very different from the parallel process among in-career people looking for a new job after a job loss. In Britain we expect the two processes to be quite similar, in the sense that individual characteristics should have the same net effect on the attainment of first job and subsequent jobs.

Perhaps the most important implication of the above hypothesis is the differential effect of educational qualifications and vocational training on the chances of finding one's first job in Britain compared to Italy. In Italy the effect of these variables on duration of first job search will be negligible, while they may be influential among those with previous work experience. In Britain, we expect that education and vocational training to have the same effect on both processes. This is not to say that in Italy there are no occupational returns to education. On the contrary, as said in the second section, they are stronger than in Britain. We are simply suggesting that in Italy the process and the duration of first job search, though not the kind of job finally attained, is largely independent of level of schooling.

This hypothesis is quite unusual, given that most research shows that the level of education is usually inversely related to the risk of unemployment (Schizzerotto and Cobalti 1998). But, as we suggested above, in a labour market that closely protects insiders, first-time job seekers experience a very different process. Educational credentials are of no help to them in moving closer to the front of the job queue as they are for those looking for a new occupation, because insider protection gives rise to a collectivist form of exclusion which acts against younger job seekers. This effect is exacerbated by the 'loose fit' between the skills taught in the Italian post-compulsory education and vocational training system, and the requirements of firms.

The hypothesis can also be extended to the effect of class of origin on duration of first job search in Italy. Even though in Italy, as in most contemporary societies, the risks of unemployment are higher among people in the intermediate and working classes, first-time job seekers from service class households will not gain any advantage from this characteristic in terms of the duration of their search because of the general segmenting effect of the insider market.

These hypotheses do not imply that in Italy educational qualifications and social origin do not affect the social position of the occupation that young first-time job seekers finally achieve. On the contrary, it has been shown elsewhere that Italy is one of the countries in which educational credentials and class of origins display the strongest direct and indirect effects on the class of a person's first occupation (Cobalti and Schizzerotto 1994; Müller and Shavit 1998). But in this chapter we are not concerned with occupational destinations of individuals, neither with the risk of entering unemployment. Instead we are interested in the rapidity of exiting unemployment, and it is exclusively this variable that our hypotheses refer to.

One explanation of this effect is that the children of the high and middle classes, and university graduates are only interested in filling particular occupational vacancies. As suggested by Breen and Goldthorpe (1997), they are concerned not to fall below their parents' social position, or below the position usually associated with a university qualification. Therefore they continue to wait—and their families strongly support them in doing so—until a job that they and their parents deem to be appropriate becomes available. Despite the current occupational upgrading in contemporary Italy, service class positions are still less common than those for the working class or routine non-manual employees. However, there is a second and more important explanation for this apparent paradox. At a time of high aggregate unemployment and fiscal contraction, the higher social classes cannot artificially create new jobs for their offspring.[3] As a consequence, the descendants of the higher classes are unable to by-pass the exclusionary effect

---

[3] In Italy during the mid-1970s, members of the service class did manage to induce the state to artificially create new intellectual and professional positions in the public administration, in order to provide suitable jobs for their children, otherwise condemned to an exhausting first job search (Barbagli 1974; Cobalti and Schizzerotto 1994). But because of the fiscal crisis of the Italian state and the current weakness of the Italian economy, this strategy is no longer practicable.

of insider protection in the Italian labour market, and must wait as long as those from the lower classes before they obtain their first jobs.

We turn now to the effect of unemployment benefits in the two countries. There is little empirical evidence, and even less agreement, in the economic and sociological literature on the direction of these effects. Sometimes income support for the unemployed is viewed as a negative work incentive; sometimes this effect is denied because unemployment subsidies usually allow only a very low standard of living (Esping-Andersen 1998; Chapter 3 in this book). Our hypothesis on this matter differs from both the above alternatives and follows the discussion on flexibility in job search conducted by Gallie and Alm in the Chapter 6. We contend that, under certain conditions, unemployment benefits may slow the speed of exiting unemployment, not because they allow a comfortable lifestyle without working, but because they may encourage a more thorough job search and, as a consequence, a better match between job and individual characteristics. High subsidies enjoyed for a long period can effectively raise the reservation wage, but where the level of benefits is low they are unlikely to have this effect. Hence it is our view that, in Britain, income support to the unemployed facilitates the match between jobs and skills, while in Italy it operates as a negative work incentive.

As mentioned earlier, the structure and role of the family in Britain and Italy differs quite markedly. In the case of women we expect it to exert almost opposite influences in Britain and Italy. Starting with first job seekers, we hypothesize that living with one's own parents has a negative effect on the chances for Italian young women of exiting unemployment. For the reasons given in the previous section, both young Italian males and females stay longer with their family of origin. But while young Italian men are not required to share domestic duties with their mother during their first job search, this is not the case of many young women (Bettio and Villa 1996). Moreover, according to a traditional model of the division of labour within the household, in Italy every man is expected to become, sooner or later, a family breadwinner, so that young males are not kept in their family of origin—though they are not pushed out of it either. By contrast, housekeeping is still the expected main adult role for a large proportion of young girls, who therefore encounter an additional constraint in finding a first job while they are living in the family of origin.[4] In Britain, the dependence of children on their parents is weaker, and housekeeping is a less likely destination for girls. Thus we hypothesize that, for British men and women, living with the family of origin should not be a disincentive against exit from first job search and unemployment, and that gender differences should be smaller.

---

[4] Among married Italian women aged 20 to 50 years, a quarter become housewives without having had any work experience, and another quarter become housewives after marriage (Bernardi 1999).

In our opinion, the more traditional Italian pattern of the division of domestic labour, together with the familialistic character of the Italian welfare state system, also gives rise to different effects of marriage on exit from unemployment among Italian men and women. In Britain, high rates of participation among women mean that men and women may be equally anxious to leave unemployment. In Italy, on the other hand, having a spouse should increase the propensity to find a new job only among unemployed men, because, as stressed above, married men are still perceived as the main breadwinner in the household. Italian women are largely expected to be full-time housewives when married. We thus hypothesize that, once unemployed, they will have a very low probability of obtaining a new job.[5] Alternatively, we could hypothesize that Italian married women are restricted in the types of jobs that they can accept because of the prevailing pattern of the division of domestic labour between the genders in Italian households. Either way, the outcome is the same: Italian women should have a lower propensity to exit unemployment than Italian men. Moreover, given this and the scarcity of part-time jobs allowing women to combine domestic chores with work, we should expect Italian women to have a lower probability of exiting unemployment than their British counterparts.

DATA, METHODS AND VARIABLES

The analysis for Italy is based on data from *Indagine Longitudinale sulle Famiglie Italiane* (ILFI), the Italian Household Longitudinal Survey, carried out in 1997 by the University of Trento, *Istituto Trentino di Cultura* and ISTAT (Italian Statistics) on a national representative sample of 10,423 individuals belonging to 4,714 households throughout Italy. The analysis for Britain is based on data from the waves 1 (1991) to 6 (1996) of the British Household Panel Study (BHPS), involving a nationally representative sample of over 5,000 households.

We have analysed unemployment episodes that started after 1991, up to 1996, for Britain, and from 1990 to 1997 for Italy. However, before describing the structure of the data sets and the methods and variables used in the analysis, we should briefly discuss the key issue of the reliability of retrospective data on unemployment. It has been argued that retrospective event history data under-report short employment and unemployment spells (Elias 1996). On the other hand, inter-wave accounts of unemployment

---

[5] We have shown elsewhere (Bison, Pisati and Schizzerotto 1996) that the chances of being employed among Italian women strictly depend on their marital status, while this feature does not show any influence on the occupational condition of Italian men.

episodes collected with a panel design have shown a fair degree of reliability. It may be then, that while under-reporting of unemployment does not affect the data from the BHPS, it might do so for data from the ILFI, collected retrospectively in 1997. One of the possible sources of bias is that the more distant the episode, the more likely short episodes are forgotten altogether (Gershuny and Hannan 1997). To control for this bias, in the analysis for Italy we have introduced a dummy equal to 1 for the episodes that started after 1994.[6] This dummy allows us to check whether there is any under-reporting or over-reporting of short or long spells in the past: if this is the case, the effect of the dummy should be positive.

As stated in the above sections there are good reasons, at least in the Italian case, to suspect that the mechanisms underlying exit from unemployment vary according to whether a person is looking for his/her first job, or for a new occupation after a job loss. We therefore carried out separate analyses for these two categories of individuals, and we built two separate event-oriented data sets. The dependent variables of the event history analysis are the transition rates from being a first-time job seeker to employment; and from being unemployed with previous work experience to employment. The statistical model used is an exponential piecewise constant model that allows one to control for the duration dependence of the process without making any prior assumption about it (Blossfeld and Rohwer 1995).

There are two kinds of independent variable: time-constant and time-varying variables that change their state within the episode of first job search and unemployment. To introduce time-varying variables in the transition rate models, we used the method of episode splitting, and each episode has been split in a duration of at most twelve months.

Age is the first time-varying variable considered in our models. It is obvious that age can influence the length of the job search, in the sense that the older a person is, the longer and more difficult his/her job search will be.

In the models of exit from unemployment among first-time job seekers, class of origin is the second variable which was controlled for. This variable refers to the occupational position of the father of each interviewee when the latter was fourteen, in Italy, or sixteen, in Britain. This variable is coded with a collapsed version of Erikson and Goldthorpe's (1992) widely-used class scheme.[7] In the models referring to exit from unemployment after a

---

[6] Three years is the time horizon identified by Elias (1996) in his analysis of the reliability of retrospective data on unemployment, using data from the BHPS and the *Family and Working Lives Survey*: beyond the three-year time limit, bias due to under-reporting emerges.

[7] The six-fold classification adopted is as follows: a) service class (I+II); b) routine non-manual employees, higher grade (IIIa); c) routine non-manual employees, lower grade (IIIb); small proprietors with and without employees (IVab); foremen and skilled manual workers (V+VI), unskilled manual workers (VIIab). For Britain, social origin has a very high rate of missing cases. Therefore the variable is introduced in the analysis but its effects are not substantively interpreted.

job loss, instead of class of origin, we examine the social class of the last occupation before unemployment. As individuals' working lives proceed over time, the social privileges—comprising the chances of finding a new job quickly—that they enjoy increasingly, not to say completely, depend on their own social position rather than on that of their family of origin.

Level of schooling is a time-varying variable, because during the period of job search individuals are able to improve their educational qualifications. The level of schooling is coded according to a variant of the CASMIN scheme (König, Lüttinger, and Müller 1988). The six levels are as follows: uncompleted lower secondary school (1a); completed lower secondary school (1b); basic vocational qualification (1c); vocational and technical higher secondary qualification (2ab); general higher secondary qualification (2c); tertiary certificate (3abc).[8] As comprehensive schooling is widespread in Britain, no distinction is made between tracks of higher secondary education.

Vocational qualification—also time-varying—is usually viewed as a device to improve the match between the general knowledge of individuals, deriving from their educational level, and the specific skills required to efficiently perform a job. Yet, as mentioned, in Britain and Italy attendance on vocational courses before entering the labour market may be socially perceived as a stigma denoting educational failure. We have separated attendance on vocational programmes before and after entering the labour market. In the case of the unemployed looking for their first jobs we only consider pre-employment vocational courses attended after leaving, either definitely or for the first time, the educational system. In the case of unemployed persons with previous work experience we refer only to vocational programmes attended while employed or during spells of unemployment.

In order to detect the influence of the family on the chances and the speed of exiting unemployment, both among first-time job seekers and interviewees with previous work experience, we use three time-varying variables: living with the family of origin, marital status, and number of children.

Unemployment benefits are also introduced as a time-varying covariate. For Britain they include unemployment benefit/income support, later job seeker's allowance; for Italy payments from the *Cassa Integrazione Ordinaria*, the *Cassa Integrazione Straordinaria* or the *Lista di Mobilità*. The very low amount and very short duration of the Italian ordinary unemployment benefits explain why those receiving them are not included. Note also that unemployment benefit is only a meaningful variable for Italy in the analysis of exit from unemployment by people with previous work experience.

---

[8] In Italy basic vocational schools (1c) are post-compulsory schools that last 2 or 3 years, while all tracks (vocational, technical and general) of higher secondary school last 5 years.

Regional unemployment rate on a yearly basis is included in our analyses in order to detect how the macroeconomic conditions in a specific time
and context affect an individual's chances of obtaining a job. It is a time-
varying covariate which refers to the yearly average unemployment rate of
the region in which the subject was living in that year.

The last variable appearing in the models for Italy is the dummy to control for the above-mentioned possible recall bias in the Italian data set. Our
models show that this variable never displays significant effects. This means
that the Italian data are not affected by recall bias, and we shall not com-
ment upon it further.

EXITS FROM UNEMPLOYMENT IN ITALY
AND BRITAIN

Descriptive Results

A first finding is that Table 11.1 shows that exit from first-time job search
unemployment is more rapid in Britain than in Italy. After three months
only one in four British men or women have failed to obtain their first jobs,
whereas in Italy the ratio is one in three men and one in two women. Likewise,
the percentage of those who remain trapped in this search for their first
position is much lower in Britain than in Italy. One in four Italian women

TABLE 11.1. *Kaplan-Meir estimation of the median duration (in months) and
of the survival function for exit from unemployment among first-time job seekers and
among unemployed with previous work experience*[a]

		First-time job seekers					
	Median duration	S(3)	S(6)	S(12)	S(24)	S(48)	N
Italian men	0.9	0.37	0.31	0.24	0.20	0.18	581
Italian women	3.2	0.50	0.43	0.33	0.27	0.25	611
British men	0.7	0.28	0.23	0.16	0.10	0.06	935
British women	0.7	0.25	0.21	0.15	0.11	0.06	786
		Unemployed with previous work experience					
Italian men	14	0.77	0.65	0.54	0.41	0.31	349
Italian women	15	0.85	0.70	0.53	0.41	0.32	341
British men	7.1	0.70	0.53	0.37	0.23	0.13	1456
British women	6.3	0.67	0.51	0.36	0.25	0.16	1031

[a] S(x) refers to the proportion of the subjects that have survived in the original state after
x months, i.e. to the percentage of the subjects who are still searching for their first job or
are still unemployed after x months.
Sources: For Italy ILFI 1990–1997, for Britain BHPS 1991–1996.

has not managed to enter the labour force after four years of search. This leads to a second important result, again in accordance with the hypotheses discussed in the third section: whilst in Britain there is no gender difference, in Italy women face greater difficulty and need more time to enter the labour force.

The same pattern of results is also found for exit from unemployment by individuals with previous work experience. In Britain, the median duration of unemployment spells after a job loss is almost half that for Italy. Moreover, in Italy the risk of entrapment in unemployment is higher: one in three is still searching for a new position after forty-eight months, whilst in Britain, the figure is less than one in six. Again, the gender differences are more pronounced in Italy. However, the initial disadvantage of Italian women tends to disappear after the first year.

Overall the results of Table 11.1 confirm the hypotheses drawn from the discussion on the differences due to labour market regulation and institutional arrangements in Italy and Britain. The high level of insider protection in Italy, the mismatch between school curricula and the requirements of the economy, the lack of effective pre-employment vocational training, and the workings of the family make finding an occupation more difficult. Accordingly, the risk of entrapment in long term unemployment is much higher in Italy than in Britain. This being so, it is important to identify the mechanisms that produce this outcome.

The Transition from Unemployment to Employment among First-time Job Seekers

Starting with the results for Italy, Table 11.2 shows that, as expected, class of origin does not have a clear and systematic impact on the chances of finding one's first job. Members of the most privileged classes (I–II and IIIa) encounter the same difficulties in finding their first job as do members of the working class (VIIab). The only significant effects are found for the sons of small proprietors, who are able to create jobs for their children in their own firms;[9] and for the daughters of the lower middle class (IIIb) and skilled working class (V–VI), who are likely to have more resources than those belonging to the working class and yet have lower occupational expectations than daughters of the higher classes. Hence, even these two exceptions confirm the validity of our arguments regarding the general lack of effects of class of origin on the speed of exiting unemployment among Italian first-time job seekers.

---

[9] The reason why this effect does not appear among daughters of small proprietors is that the latter tend reproduce themselves as a social class by mainly following a male lineage (Schadee and Schizzerotto 1990; Cobalti and Schizzerotto 1994).

232   *Bernardi, Layte, Schizzerotto, Jacobs*

TABLE 11.2. *Effects on the transition rate from unemployment to employment among first job seekers, piecewise constant model*

	Italy		Britain	
	Men	Women	Men	Women
Duration				
<3 months	−0.21	−1.53**	−0.39	−0.37
3–12 months	−1.84**	−2.88**	−2.03**	−2.24**
12–24 months	−2.15**	−3.30**	−2.24**	−2.65**
>24 months	−2.55**	−3.63**	−2.52**	−2.65**
Age	−0.00	0.03**	−0.001**	−0.002**
Class of origin (EG)				
Service class (I+II)	0.22	0.07	−0.03	0.12
Routine n. m. employees higher grade (IIIa)	−0.26	−0.10	0.29	0.13
Routine n. m. employees lower grade (IIIb)	0.22	0.44**	0.08	0.16
Small proprietors (IVabc)	0.32**	0.19	0.32	−0.02
Skilled m. workers (V+VI)	0.04	0.30**	−0.07	0.02
Missing			0.02	0.11
Education (CASMIN)				
Tertiary (3abc)	−0.37	−0.15	0.59**	0.66**
General secondary (2c)	−0.29	0.01		
Vocational and technical secondary (2ab)	−0.41	0.00	0.53**	0.59**
Basic vocational (1c)	−0.10*	0.02	0.49*	0.36
Complete lower secondary (1b)	−0.13	−0.01	0.43*	0.34
Vocational training				
Yes	0.12	0.05	−1.25**	−1.04**
Living with parents				
Yes	−0.03	−0.30**	−0.11	0.25*
Civil status				
Married/consensual union	0.52	−0.44**	−0.38*	0.20
Number of children	−0.19	0.09	0.12	−0.17
Unemployment benefits				
Yes			−1.12**	−0.97**
Yearly regional unemployment rate	−0.07**	−0.07**	−0.06**	−0.08**
Dummy episodes started after 1994	−0.06	−0.01		
Number of events	482	466	830	713
χ^{2a}	347	270	432	463
Degrees of freedom	17	17	17	17

[a] The χ^2 value refers to likelihood ratio test statistic obtained comparing the loglikelihood of the present model with the loglikelihood of the base model without covariates (Blossfeld & Rohwer 1995).
Notes: ** $P <= 0.05$; * $P <= 0.10$.

As hypothesized, neither level of education nor pre-employment vocational training have effects on the likelihood of exiting from the search for a first job, among either men or women in Italy. This means that, regardless of the educational qualifications achieved, young people in Italy face similar difficulties in entering the labour market for the first time. In other words, the data on the cultural capital of Italian first-time job seekers confirm the result obtained when looking at their social origins: in seeking his/her first job no young Italian is able to overcome the negative effects of labour market segmentation.

On the other hand, and again in accordance with our hypothesis, in Britain education is an important resource for those seeking to enter the labour market for the first time. The effect of education increases almost linearly for British men, while for British women the effect is significant for the higher levels of qualification. Transition into the labour market is more problematic for the less-educated in Great Britain. Moreover, those who have attended vocational training programmes encounter more difficulties in finding their first jobs. As mentioned in the third and fourth sections, this result can be explained by the fact that in Britain, vocational programmes consist of government training schemes attended by people who have experienced educational failures and previous periods of unemployment. The paradoxical outcome is that attending a vocational training programme may have a stigmatic effect on young and unskilled people, and this further reduces their chances of finding their first job (Calender and Metcalf 1991; Brynner and Roberts 1997).

With regard to family effects, living with the family of origin and being married have different implications for Italian men and women. The search for first job takes longer for women still living with their parents, and the same applies to married women. A traditional model of the domestic division of labour between genders, and within families, is involved here: household responsibilities in the family of origin or in a new family reduce the time that women can devote to their job search, and their willingness to accept any kind of job. Accordingly, the family has different implications for Italian men and women in that it acts as a constraint on the first job search only for women. These results completely match our hypothesis.

A quite different pattern emerges from the British model. Living in the family of origin improves the chances of finding their first jobs for young British women, while being married does not make any real difference. On the other hand, living with parents has no influence for British men.[10] One may therefore state that, in Britain, men's and women's behaviour in the process of gaining their first job is largely independent of family relations, in accordance with our hypothesis.

Taking the results of both models together, we can therefore conclude that only in Italy does the family negatively influence the likelihood and speed of exiting unemployment among first-time job seekers. And, as expected, this negative influence affects only women. In other words, only Italian women are morally obliged, either by the family of origin or by the family of arrival, to assume domestic responsibilities which constrain their first job searches.

---

[10] The negative effect of the variable 'being married' is not substantially interpreted for British men, as it is significant only at 10 per cent level and refers to a small number of cases.

By contrast, their British counterparts, even though they are not completely free from domestic obligations, are far less bound by them when looking for their first job.

As we suspected, receiving unemployment benefits has a negative effect on the speed of exiting unemployment for British first-time job seekers, both male and female. And we continue to maintain that this result does not imply that transfers from the state reduce the willingness of the unemployed to look for jobs. Rather, they increase the chances of a good match being achieved between employer requirements and potential employee characteristics by allowing a more thorough, and therefore longer, job search. Our model does not provide any direct evidence for this statement. Yet our data do give some indirect support to our hypothesis that the chances of finding a job are not depressed by unemployment benefits. The parameters of the above models expressing the effect of unemployment benefits on the duration of first job search have similar values for men and women. Nevertheless the rate of unemployment among British women is lower than that among British men—see Table 1.1 in the Introduction to this book.[11]

The general condition of the labour market and economic system, as expressed by the yearly regional unemployment rate, has the same effect in both countries, for men and women: the higher the level of unemployment, the longer it takes for people who have never worked to find their first jobs.

The Transition from Unemployment to Employment among Individuals with Previous Work Experience

We have argued that, contrary to the patterns observed among those looking for their first job, those with previous work experience will derive some benefit from their educational qualifications and occupational experience during their job search in Italy. Table 11.3 provides some support for this hypothesis, since for Italian men, having attended a basic vocational post compulsory school (1c), a vocational or a technical high school (2ab), or a training programme outside the school system—mainly formal training on the job—enhances their likelihood of exiting unemployment. Moreover, those employed in some specific occupational classes appear to be at an advantage in leaving unemployment. The positive effects found for service class (I–II), routine non-manual employees of lower grade (IIIb) and skilled working class (V–VI) mean that exit from unemployment is faster for people whose previous occupation is placed at the top of social ladder, is an unskilled job belonging to the expanding tertiary sector, or is linked to technologically advanced productive processes in the industrial sector.

[11] The same result is yielded by the model regarding British men and women looking for new jobs after a job loss.

TABLE 11.3. *Effects on the transition rate from unemployment to employment among individuals with previous work experience, piecewise constant model*

	Italy		Britain	
	Men	Women	Men	Women
Duration				
<3 months	−2.25**	−1.21**	−1.72**	−1.75
3–12 months	−1.87**	−0.40	−1.49**	−1.52**
12–24 months	−2.55**	−0.97	−2.13**	−2.14**
>24 months	−2.90**	−1.58**	−2.44**	−2.93**
Age	−0.04**	−0.03**	−0.003**	−0.002**
Last occupational class (EG)				
Service class (I+II)	0.55*	0.28	0.37**	0.41**
Routine n. m. employees higher grade (IIIa)	0.48	0.14	0.37**	0.24**
Routine n. m. employees lower grade (IIIb)	0.58**	0.43*	0.24	0.44**
Small proprietors (IVabc)	−0.01	−0.30	0.19*	0.30
Skilled m. workers (V+VI)	0.35*	0.30	0.23**	0.16
Education (CASMIN)				
Tertiary (3abc)	−0.29	0.25	0.40**	0.49**
General secondary (2c)	0.26	0.42		
Vocational and technical secondary (2ab)	0.60*	0.01	0.22**	0.15
Basic vocational education (1c)	0.89**	−0.35	0.13	0.02
Complete lower secondary (1b)	0.34	−0.16	0.10	−0.10
Vocational training				
Yes	0.46**	0.09	−0.20**	−0.04
Living with parents				
Yes	−0.11	−0.86**	−0.14*	0.31**
Civil status				
Married/consensual union	−0.13	−0.65**	0.20**	0.27**
Divorced, widowed	−0.09	−1.11**		
Number of children	0.11	0.12	0.00	0.05
Unemployment benefits				
Yes	−0.60**	−0.77*	−0.94**	−1.15**
Yearly regional unemployment rate	−0.03**	−0.13**	−0.01	−0.08**
Dummy for episodes started after 1994	0.12	0.11	—	—
Number of events	195	188	1433	803
χ^{2a}	85	99	278	206
Degrees of freedom	19	19	16	16

[a] The χ^2 value refers to likelihood ratio test statistic obtained comparing the loglikelihood of the present model with the loglikelihood of the base model without covariates (Blossfeld and Rohwer 1995).
Notes: ** P < = 0.05; * P < = 0.10.

However, none of these school qualifications and work experience effects—with the exception of the positive effect found for class IIIb—is significant for Italian women. As found in the analysis of exit from first search, it is the family situation that makes a difference: living with parents or being married substantially reduces the likelihood of exiting from unemployment.[12]

[12] Being divorced also reduces the chances of exiting unemployment. The proportion of divorced women, however, is very small: hence we do not interpret substantively the size of this effect.

Turning to Britain, these gender differences are, overall, less pronounced than expected. For British men it is higher education, more than vocational education, which improves their chances of escaping unemployment. Again, as found in the analysis of the transition from first search to employment, training programmes outside the educational system act as a negative signal to employers and thus have a negative effect on exit rates. In spite of some differences, the same results are found for British women. Moreover, considering the impact of family situation, the effect of being married is positive and significant for both men and women. This more symmetrical pattern found for Britain can be explained by reference to the higher incidence of unemployment among both members of the couple in comparison with Italy: if the spouse is also unemployed his/her income cannot be relied upon, and hence there is stronger financial pressure to re-enter the labour market—see Chapter 13. However, an unexpected difference between British men and women concerns the effect of living with the family of origin on the chances of exiting unemployment: this effect is positive for British women as was also found for the analysis of exit from the search for first occupation, while it is negative for British men.

The hypothesis of a negative effect on the speed of exiting unemployment related to unemployment benefits is also confirmed in the case of people seeking new jobs after a job loss. Those who have claimed income support in Britain exit unemployment less rapidly. The same applies to individuals in 'Cassa Integrazione Guadagni Straordinaria', 'Cassa Integrazione Guadagni Ordinaria' or 'Lista di Mobilità' in Italy. Once again we would repeat that, in Britain, these effects on the duration of job search must be considered positive factors leading to a better match between jobs and skills, rather than as negative elements leading to long-term unemployment. On the contrary, we suspect that the Italian CIGS, CIGO and LM actually increase long-term unemployment. As previously noted, there are three main reasons for this suspicion: the high replacement rate of individual salaries, the long duration of benefits, and the permanence of the contractual relation between those receiving CIGS and CIGO benefits and the firm in which they were employed.

CONCLUSIONS

This paper has studied the role played in Britain and Italy by labour market regulation, the economic conditions, the family, educational system, vocational training policies, and unemployment subsidies, in the processes of exiting unemployment.

One of the main findings regards the effects of different legal, contractual, and informal labour market regulations on the chances of obtaining a job and the amount of segmentation by age, of unemployment. We have demonstrated that in Italy the process of exiting unemployment among young first-time job seekers differs greatly from the corresponding process among older people who have lost their former jobs, while in Britain the two processes are identical. In Italy, first entry into employment is mainly constrained by the close regulation of the labour market, and more precisely by the strong protection against dismissal afforded to insiders. We have observed a collectivist mechanism of exclusion which operates against young first-time job seekers in that individual characteristics like class of origin, level of education, and attendance on vocational training courses do not influence the duration of the job search. However, in the search for a new job after a job loss, the social class of last occupation, the level of education, and the attendance of vocational courses do matter. On the other hand, our models have shown that in Britain, education is a key resource which enhances the chances of gaining a job both among first-time job seekers and people looking for a new job after a job loss. Hence we could summarize all the above remarks by stating that the more rigid a country's labour market regulation and the more it protects insiders, the stronger are generational inequalities in the transition from unemployment to employment.

Of course, the actual impact of labour market regulation is either reinforced or weakened by the features of a country's economy and its level of aggregate unemployment. Results from the hazard rate models showed that the latter has a somewhat stronger impact among the Italian than among British job seekers.

However, family and education are as important as the economic and regulative factors in shaping the social and economic, features and consequences of unemployment. Where a traditional pattern of the domestic division of labour between genders prevails, women are the most disadvantaged social group in exiting unemployment. To be more precise, our models have shown that the family has different implications for Italian and British women looking for jobs. In Italy, the burden of household responsibilities reduces the amount of time that women can devote to job search, and restricts the types of job that they can accept. On the other hand, British women have greater economic responsibilities within the household and are therefore encouraged to exit unemployment in order to contribute to the family income. It is worth adding that, in Italy, family constraints do not only operate on married women with children; they also apply to young women living with their parents. The latter, too, are expected to carry out domestic work, and as a consequence they have fewer opportunities than their brothers of finding a job. By contrast, British parents do not seem to expect strong commitment by their daughters to domestic responsibilities. Rather, they appear to push them into the labour market. We would stress, however, that the negative discrimination suffered by Italian women—looking for both first and new jobs—in their rapidity of exiting unemployment does not depend entirely on the familialistic character of Italian culture. The cultural pattern is reinforced, in fact, by the informal, contractual and legal regulations of the Italian labour market. We have pointed out that trade unions and employers tend to protect the jobs of adult men more than those of women; that the lack of part-time jobs increases the difficulties of women in combining work with family duties. The strong protection and long leave usually accorded to working mothers in Italy also dissuade employers from hiring women rather than men.

The familalization of protection within Italian households partly explains the longer job search of the children of the more affluent. However, we have also seen that part of the reason for this long job search is the comparative difficulty of entering the labour market in Italy compared to Britain. Families are also compelled to take care of their children because of the complete absence of unemployment subsidies for first-time job seekers and the difficulties usually encountered by young people in renting accommodation, even when they are working on a full-time basis and with permanent positions. In sum, at least in the case of men, the very long residence of young Italians with their parents should be interpreted as mainly a response to the institutional arrangements of the Italian society and, above all, as a response to the lack of any income support for young first-time job seekers, rather than as the effect of a propensity of most Italian parents to provide permanent protection for their children.

Turning to education, our research has demonstrated that post-compulsory education produces limited reductions in the length of job search. It has been argued that this is partly because of the 'loose fit' between the structure of education and the labour market. Nonetheless, educational qualifications can act both as signaling and screening device. The models show that this happens among all British job seekers and Italians looking for a new job after a job loss. But in that case schooling is little effective—or less effective than it could be—in offsetting the negative influences of a labour market regulation which strongly protects insiders. As we have already noticed, educational qualifications seem not to have any effect on the duration of the first job search in Italy. Similar remarks can be made with reference to vocational training programmes. When they are intended to transmit specific skills they can accelerate the exit from unemployment as observed among the Italian unemployed with previous work experience. On the contrary, if vocational courses are mainly addressed to school dropouts and long-term unemployed like in Britain, they display a definite stigmatizing effect and slow the job search process.

Our final point is that the unemployment welfare regime plays a crucial role in determining the social consequences of unemployment and shaping the workings of the family and of the labour market itself. On one side, the sub-protective Italian welfare state compels families to take long-term care of their children who are often engaged in a rather exhausting first job search that can lead to poverty among the unemployed receiving the very low ordinary benefits. However, a few unemployed do enjoy very generous and long-lasting benefits that dramatically raise their reservation wage. By contrast, the British liberal/minimal unemployment welfare regime, though suboptimal, seems to be less inefficient than the Italian system because it reduces the need of protection of the young first-time job seekers by the family of origin, and probably allows a more flexible job search which could enable a better match between the individual's skills and the technical characteristics of the job.

PART 3

Unemployment and Social Integration

12

The Effects of Employment Precarity and Unemployment on Social Isolation

Serge Paugam and Helen Russell

INTRODUCTION

The effect of unemployment on the level of participation in social life has already been the subject of numerous studies. As early as the 1930s Paul Lazarsfeld and his research team analysed the impact of unemployment on social isolation in the Austrian town of Marienthal after the closure of the main factory (Lazarsfeld, Jahoda, and Zeisel 1933). Before the crisis, participation in the life of clubs and associations was very active in this little town, but the study showed a collapse of social links in the unemployed community when a great part of the working population was suddenly without employment. Work was the basis of social integration, the main reference for men and women in the every day organization of life. All other activities, such as theatre, culture, sport and leisure depended upon work. The social life around school, public library, and public garden maintenance collapsed. The unemployed community became tired and lethargic in spite of the fact that everyone now had more than ample time to take up all of these activities.

More than sixty years after this classic study, it is possible to begin a comparative analysis on the effects of employment insecurity and unemployment on social networks in European countries, in particular with the ECHP data source. The question we wish to answer is whether Lazarsfeld's results are stable in time and homogeneous across countries. Several analyses on this subject have been undertaken in recent years, in particular in the UK and France (Gallie, Marsh, and Vogler 1993; Paugam 1991; Paugam, Zoyem, and Charbonnel 1993) and some preliminary national comparisons have been carried out (Paugam 1996; Gallie 1999).

The objective of this chapter is to improve this analysis of the dynamics of social networks with the ECHP data source. Four questions were posed concerning social links, two of which concern social relations: How often do you talk to any of your neighbours? How often do you meet friends and relatives who are not living with you? Another question deals with the receipt of basic support: Did you personally receive in 1993 any financial support or maintenance from relatives, friends, or other persons outside your household? The final question deals with membership of associations or clubs: Are you a member of any club or organization, such as a sport or entertainment club, a local or neighbourhood group, or a party? Taken on their own the questions are not sufficient to study the nature of social links. Such questions can only indicate a general direction of inquiry and must be complemented by other sources, particularly more qualitative and descriptive ones. However the questions can be asked in the same form in every European country and hence can serve as the basis of a comparison at the macro-sociological level.

For each one of the questions, a logical process of reasoning was undertaken in order to calculate the link between the strength of the relationship to regular work and the strength of social links. Five separate categories of employment status are identified: stable job, insecure job, precarious job, unemployed for less than one year, unemployed for more than one year.[1]

This chapter analyses successively the impact of employment precarity and unemployment on three different spheres of sociability. The primary sphere involves immediate family and household relations; the secondary sphere concerns interactions with neighbours, encounters with friends and relatives outside the household; and the tertiary sphere relates to participation in organizational and associative life. These three spheres of sociability are not cumulative in most European countries. As we shall show, sociability is more based on close relationships in Southern countries and more organized around social participation in Northern countries. For this reason, it is most appropriate to study the impact of employment precarity and unemployment separately on each of them.

THE PRIMARY SPHERE OF SOCIABILITY

The most important factor with respect to primary sociability is whether people are living on their own. The probability of living alone is not in itself an indicator of social network weakness. It can be a sign of an individual's choice to live with more self-sufficiency in relation to the family. This autonomy does not prevent close ties with relatives and friends. It is

---

[1] The different levels of job stability were established by a question concerning the satisfaction of the employed with the stability of work. Those who were satisfied were put into the stable job category. Those not satisfied but who had held their job for more than a year were classed as having an insecure job. Those not satisfied and who had held their job for less than a year were classified as precarious.

TABLE 12.1. *Living alone according to labour market situation, by country* (%)

	Stable job	Insecure job	Precarious job	Unempl. <1 y	Unempl. >1 y	All active (18–65)
Belgium	9.3	10.2	9.8	10.0	7.9	9.4
Denmark	15.2	12.7	19.0	29.9	30.2	16.5
France	10.6	8.7	8.6	13.0	10.3	10.3
Germany	15.1	15.0	13.1	21.1	17.2	15.4
Greece	5.8	4.8	6.4	4.5	3.7	5.3
Ireland	8.2	8.1	3.5	5.0	7.1	7.6
Italy	6.3	6.6	1.5	2.5	2.4	5.6
Netherlands	13.2	17.9	22.3	19.3	23.5	15.0
Portugal	2.4	2.6	1.6	1.4	1.1	2.4
Spain	3.7	3.3	1.8	1.7	1.5	3.0
UK	7.9	9.1	10.2	15.0	15.7	9.1

Note: Coverage: population 18–65 years of age.
Source: ECHP (1994) wave 1.

not incompatible with a dense and varied social network. However, if the unemployed living alone also have little contact with their circle of friends and do not participate in any club or organization, the risk of isolation is stronger and there is a danger of a cumulative process of disadvantage leading to social exclusion, defined here as the last phase of the social disqualification process.

Demographers and specialists of the family have frequently noted in recent years that the probability of living alone varies considerably from one European country to another. Taking the population as a whole, the figures range from 4 per cent in Spain to 22 per cent in Denmark (Middlemans, and Paserman 1996).

It is striking to observe that people under the poverty threshold more frequently live alone in Northern countries than in Southern countries. Among the unemployed under the poverty line—50 per cent mean, new equivalent scale, OECD modified—we find almost 46 per cent live alone in Denmark, 37.3 per cent in Germany, and only 2.2 per cent in Spain and 1.6 per cent in Italy.

We can also observe that the probability of living alone increases with the degree of precariousness of employment status in several countries: 30.2 per cent of the long term unemployed are in this situation in Denmark, compared to 15.2 per cent of the securely employed: a gap of 15 points. The proportion of the long term unemployed living alone is also high in The Netherlands, at 23.5 per cent, in Germany at 17.2 per cent, and in the UK at 15.7 per cent—see Table 12.1 and Fig. 12.1. The gap between the long-term unemployed and those in a stable job is around 10 points in The

TABLE 12.2. *Effects of employment insecurity and unemployment on the likelihood of living alone (logistic regression)*

	Insecure job		Precarious job		Unempl.<1		Unempl.>1	
	B	Sig.	B	Sig.	B	Sig.	B	Sig.
Belgium	0.04	n.s.	0.31	n.s.	0.39	n.s.	−0.08	n.s.
Denmark	−0.36	*	0.05	n.s.	0.60	***	0.75	***
France	−0.04	n.s.	−0.12	n.s.	0.23	(*)	0.21	n.s.
Germany	0.07	n.s.	−0.14	n.s.	0.46	*	0.26	n.s.
Greece	−0.17	n.s.	−0.11	n.s.	−0.45	*	−0.95	**
Ireland	0.32	(*)	−0.21	n.s.	0.02	n.s.	0.64	*
Italy	0.35	**	−0.77	n.s.	−0.30	n.s.	−0.52	(*)
Netherlands	0.53	***	0.58	**	0.65	**	0.81	***
Portugal	0.09	n.s.	0.53	n.s.	−0.01	n.s.	−1.33	n.s.
Spain	0.22	n.s.	−0.01	n.s.	−0.08	n.s.	−0.37	n.s.
UK	0.15	n.s.	0.51	*	0.84	***	0.85	***

Notes: Reference: stable job with controls for age, gender, level of education.
Coverage: population 18–65 years of age; (*): $P < 0.1$, *: $P < 0.05$, **: $P < 0.01$, ***: $P < 0.001$.
Source: ECHP (1994) wave 1.

Netherlands and 8 points in the UK. This is in sharp contrast with the countries of Southern Europe, where the proportion of the unemployed living alone is very low: less than 2 per cent in Spain and Portugal, and less than 5 per cent in Italy and Greece. In these countries, the unemployed, particularly the young, continue to live with their families, often for a long period before they have a stable job and start a family. It could be termed an 'extended dependence model' (see Chapter 1).

These differences between Northern and Southern European countries are confirmed by the results of a logistic regression—see Table 12.2. The likelihood of living alone is high and significant both for the long-term unemployed and for the short-term unemployed in relation to the securely employed in the UK, The Netherlands, and Denmark when we control for age, gender, and level of education. The likelihood of living alone is negative for the same categories in Italy, Spain, Portugal, and Greece and strongly significant in this last country.

This can be seen as reflecting two factors. First in these countries there is a tradition of solidarity organized by relatives and reinforced within the household by a strong division of labour. The head of the family has the role of assuring the financial autonomy of the family though paid employment, while the woman has the central role in the organization of domestic life, and in providing care for the children even after they have reached adulthood. The normative obligation of prolonged cohabitation affects both parents and children, thereby considerably reducing the risk of social

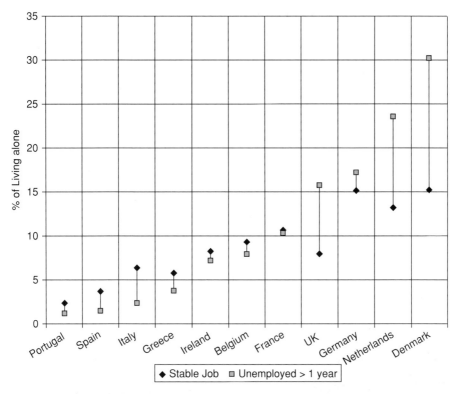

FIG. 12.1. Frequency of living on own for stable job and unemployment, by country
Source: ECHP (1994) wave 1. Coverage: population 18–65 years age.

isolation when the latter are confronted by difficulties on the labour market. In Italy especially, researchers have noted that family values, notably
parent-child relationships, are of paramount importance (Saraceno 1988).
From this it can be deduced that in countries where the family unit is the
foundation of social integration, unemployment does not lead to a weakening of family ties.

Another complementary explanation is that Southern countries are characterized by a weaker development of the welfare state than in Northern
countries. As we saw in the introduction of this book, Southern Europe
is characterized by a sub-protective unemployment regime which therefore creates a greater reliance on the family, in particular for those who
have never worked. Young people are more likely to live with their parents when they have little chance of receiving unemployment benefit or
if the benefit they receive is so low that there is no possibility of financial
autonomy.

THE SECONDARY SPHERE OF SOCIABILITY

This sphere relates to sociability in the local community. We use three different indicators: neighbourhood sociability, encounters with friends and relatives, and social and family support from persons outside the household. The relations between neighbours are often less intensive than the relations with friends and relatives, but they express both the same idea of conviviality in the immediate networks where strong and affective ties are usually developed.

Neighbourhood sociability

An important question that emerges is the following: does the social life which centres around neighbourhood ties decrease in strength with a decrease in the regularity of work? In Table 12.3, we have indicated the proportion of people who talk to neighbours on most days according to their labour market situation and nationality, and we added the results for two specific cases: the first case is people who declared that they were living in an area characterized by vandalism or crime, the second is people who live alone. These two cases correspond to two hypotheses: we have tried to confirm if living in a dangerous and socially disqualified area could lead people to withdraw into themselves. In previous research carried out at Saint-Brieuc in France, the unemployed who inhabited 'la Cité du Point du Jour' admitted that they often entered their own houses via the cellar in order to avoid contact with the other inhabitants either in the courtyard or through the windows. They positively avoided their neighbours and took no part in communal life (Paugam 1991). We also wanted to confirm whether unemployed and precariously employed people living alone are more likely to be isolated.

First, it is striking to observe that neighbourhood relationships are, on the whole, more developed in Southern countries. The percentage of people of working age who talk to neighbours on most days is less than 20 per cent in The Netherlands, less than 40 per cent in Belgium, Denmark, and Germany, and increases to 57 per cent in Portugal, 58 per cent in Spain, and 75 per cent in Greece—see Table 12.3. This strong difference may be partially explained by the configuration of living spaces in Mediterranean towns in which the housing concentration and narrow streets make exchanges and conversations easier. In towns or areas where housing is less dense and conceived to allow a greater autonomy, neighbourhood relationships are likely to be weaker. However, further research is needed to confirm this hypothesis.

Looking at the results for the whole population, the decrease of neighbourhood sociability during the experience of unemployment would not seem

TABLE 12.3. *People talking to neighbours on most days according to labour market situation, by country* (%)

	Stable job	Insecure job	Precarious job	Unempl. <1 y	Unempl. >1 y	All active (18–65)
Denmark						
Total	**32.1**	**29.0**	**33.9**	**36.9**	**41.7**	**32.4**
Case 1	31.9	28.3	36.3	27.4	31.7	31.4
Case 2	33.1	23.9	35.5	44.7	35.9	33.8
*France**						
Total	**42.7**	**40.4**	**31.0**	**38.6**	**43.0**	**41.4**
Case 1	38.7	39.5	34.4	36.1	45.4	38.8
Case 2	25.8	32.7	19.4	24.9	39.5	27.3
Germany						
Total	**34.5**	**34.4**	**25.1**	**42.1**	**49.7**	**35.1**
Case 1	34.3	35.0	28.3	41.1	50.5	35.2
Case 2	24.3	23.1	29.4	34.1	27.3	25.0
Netherlands						
Total	**18.2**	**17.4**	**20.7**	**34.9**	**25.7**	**19.0**
Case 1	19.0	14.9	24.1	38.1	23.4	19.5
Case 2	14.4	18.4	19.9	57.6	34.3	18.8
Belgium						
Total	**27.5**	**28.4**	**31.9**	**39.4**	**50.6**	**29.4**
Case 1	30.7	24.9	36.3	51.6	56.8	32.5
Case 2	24.6	29.6	n.s.	n.s.	58.5	27.4
UK						
Total	**39.4**	**43.2**	**43.8**	**52.4**	**55.5**	**42.1**
Case 1	39.6	45.3	42.0	57.8	54.7	43.5
Case 2	31.2	40.0	47.4	42.1	65.5	38.2
Ireland						
Total	**53.0**	**51.7**	**60.1**	**62.2**	**62.5**	**54.9**
Case 1	51.8	49.0	53.5	46.9	55.1	51.5
Case 2	54.1	41.9	n.s.	n.s.	83.1	57.2
Italy						
Total	**45.5**	**45.6**	**41.5**	**55.4**	**56.6**	**47.2**
Case 1	36.5	39.1	30.1	45.2	51.1	39.8
Case 2	42.9	41.7	n.s.	n.s.	n.s.	43.1
Spain						
Total	**54.1**	**53.4**	**55.0**	**69.8**	**67.5**	**57.6**
Case 1	50.6	47.0	50.3	63.2	66.9	53.5
Case 2	54.4	41.4	23.9	67.8	63.4	51.9
Portugal						
Total	**55.9**	**55.1**	**59.0**	**66.7**	**59.3**	**56.4**
Case 1	43.2	39.4	60.0	58.7	49.3	44.1
Case 2	57.2	63.1	n.s.	n.s.	n.s.	60.3
Greece						
Total	**73.9**	**77.3**	**69.2**	**78.0**	**79.3**	**75.5**
Case 1	55.0	55.7	52.4	56.7	69.3	56.0
Case 2	50.4	38.4	15.3	49.0	81.8	45.6

Notes: Coverage: population 18–65 years of age; Case 1: Vandalism or crime in the area; Case 2: People living on own; n.s. = non significant; * The item is 'often' and not 'on most days'.
Source: ECHP (1994) wave 1.

TABLE 12.4. *Effects of employment insecurity and unemployment on relations with neighbours (ordered logistic regression)*

	Insecure job		Precarious job		Unempl.<1		Unempl.>1	
	B	Sig.	B	Sig.	B	Sig.	B	Sig.
Belgium	−0.04	n.s.	0.16	n.s.	0.34	*	0.58	***
Denmark	−0.16	(*)	−0.06	n.s.	−0.14	n.s.	0.30	(*)
France	−0.18	**	−0.28	**	−0.01	n.s.	0.01	n.s.
Germany	−0.22	***	−0.62	***	0.01	n.s.	0.32	*
Greece	0.01	n.s.	−0.15	n.s.	0.28	**	0.40	**
Ireland	−0.33	***	0.04	n.s.	0.21	n.s.	0.35	**
Italy	−0.18	***	−0.10	n.s.	0.27	**	0.39	***
Netherlands	−0.15	*	−0.28	*	0.12	n.s.	−0.08	n.s.
Portugal	0.01	n.s.	0.29	*	0.43	**	0.20	n.s.
Spain	−0.22	***	−0.17	*	0.35	***	0.29	***
UK	−0.01	n.s.	−0.01	n.s.	0.44	***	0.36	**

Notes: Reference: stable job with controls for age, gender, level of education, household composition, vandalism or crime in the area. Coverage: population 18–65 years of age; (*): $P < 0.1$ *: $P < 0.05$, **: $P < 0.01$, ***: $P < 0.001$.
Source: ECHP (1994) wave 1.

to be confirmed. Most countries show an opposite tendency, particularly for the long-term unemployed. In Belgium, for example, 50 per cent of the long-term unemployed and only 27 per cent of the regularly employed talk to their neighbours.

This tendency is confirmed by the ordered logistic regression: the long-term unemployed talk significantly more often to their neighbours than the securely employed in Germany, Belgium, Ireland, The Netherlands, Italy, Spain, and Portugal—see Table 12.4. The coefficient is also positive in Denmark but not significant. France is an exception with a negative and significant coefficient.

However, there exists a negative correlation for those in precarious jobs in several countries: France, Germany, Italy, Spain, and Greece. We are presently unable to fully explain this phenomenon, perhaps those in precarious jobs are more likely to be geographically mobile than other groups in these countries. Greater detail about the nature and duration of residency and the size of the community is necessary before we can further establish the reasons for such coefficients.

On the whole, vandalism or crime in the area has an impact on the neighbourhood sociability. We observe that people living in a dangerous area are significantly less likely to talk with their neighbours on most days than people living in a quiet area, in particular in France and in Southern European countries. In Greece, for instance, neighbourhood sociability is weaker for the long-term unemployed when they live in an area characterized by vandalism: 59 per cent against 77 per cent for the long-term unemployed as a whole. However, we can note too that neighbourhood sociability stays very high for the unemployed in Southern European countries even if they live in an area affected by vandalism. The hypothesis of a collapse of neighbourhood relations when people live in a disqualified and dangerous area is not confirmed in a systematic way. We can explain this by the progressive adaptation to living in an insecure area and the ability of people to find their own protection against risks, especially among those who do not move away.

Living alone can have an impact on neighbourhood sociability. In Denmark, France, and Germany, for example, the unemployed living alone are less likely to have frequent contact with neighbours than the unemployed on the whole. Only 30 per cent in Denmark, 35 per cent in France and 32 per cent in Germany of the long-term unemployed living alone talk to their neighbours on most days.

Meeting Friends and Relatives

The experience of unemployment has often been analysed as a withdrawal from social and family life. The process of losing your position in society can be humiliating and this can change relations with others and lead to a self-imposed isolation. Even close family relations can suffer if a person no longer appears to be able to fulfill the role he/she wished to play for his/her family. Several qualitative surveys have already shown that people who do not attain their professional goals, especially if they are in good health and could work, feel that they have failed to meet the expectations of their family. Many people may prefer to accept a reduced level of contact with their wider family until such time as they have gained a job which, in their eyes, renders them more respectable. This process has been confirmed in France: when the unemployed find a job, they simultaneously reinforce their family sociability (Paugam 1993). The financial hardship that usually accompanies unemployment can also affect certain types of sociability with friends and relatives. Gallie *et al.* (1994) found that in the UK unemployment led to a decrease in more expensive sociability such as going to the pub or cinema, however, this is often substituted with cheaper informal sociability within people's homes (Russell 1999).

Our second indicator concerns the sociability in the local community with relatives or friends. The survey question was worded: 'How often do you meet friends and relatives who are not living with you?' An initial feature of the results is that the unemployed in the Southern European countries are more likely than those in the Northern countries to report that they meet people that they are close to on most days. This is the case for more than 60 per cent of the long-term unemployed in Spain and Italy and more than

Serge Paugam and Helen Russell

TABLE 12.5. *People meeting friends and relatives who are not living in the household on most days, according to labour market situation, by country (%)*

	Stable job	Insecure job	Precarious job	Unempl. <1 y	Unempl. >1 y	All active (18–65)
Denmark						
Total	**24.9**	**21.7**	**29.6**	**42.4**	**39.3**	**26.4**
Case 1	29.1	23.0	30.2	26.5	49.6	29.2
Case 2	40.5	40.4	29.5	53.9	48.4	41.8
*France**						
Total	**65.8**	**63.4**	**62.3**	**63.4**	**55.2**	**64.5**
Case 1	62.6	61.5	56.5	60.2	54.7	61.4
Case 2	68.5	67.9	58.2	60.4	58.2	66.6
Germany						
Total	**23.3**	**20.7**	**31.3**	**29.5**	**30.4**	**23.6**
Case 1	23.1	18.9	11.9	25.7	30.9	22.0
Case 2	30.7	28.9	65.0	26.3	37.4	31.3
Netherlands						
Total	**17.6**	**17.9**	**22.5**	**42.4**	**31.1**	**19.3**
Case 1	20.4	20.3	24.3	40.6	39.1	22.5
Case 2	28.4	30.8	33.5	60.7	51.7	32.2
Belgium						
Total	**30.6**	**32.0**	**36.8**	**45.3**	**41.9**	**32.1**
Case 1	37.5	36.5	50.6	38.8	42.8	37.9
Case 2	42.4	54.9	n.s.	n.s.	60.8	46.0
UK						
Total	**36.4**	**32.3**	**39.3**	**42.9**	**48.4**	**36.4**
Case 1	36.4	35.4	45.1	44.5	55.9	38.3
Case 2	44.4	40.9	50.1	41.6	54.8	44.4
Ireland						
Total	**73.9**	**71.6**	**73.1**	**67.9**	**59.0**	**71.3**
Case 1	67.9	66.4	80.6	65.0	49.7	64.7
Case 2	71.6	83.5	n.s.	n.s.	82.6	76.4
Italy						
Total	**38.7**	**40.7**	**59.5**	**61.8**	**62.0**	**43.7**
Case 1	33.5	41.3	63.8	61.4	62.6	42.8
Case 2	49.3	51.0	n.s.	n.s.	n.s.	50.9
Spain						
Total	**60.3**	**59.5**	**67.0**	**76.9**	**67.4**	**63.7**
Case 1	56.5	59.4	57.5	76.6	60.9	60.7
Case 2	62.6	52.7	41.3	96.2	88.5	63.6
Portugal						
Total	**35.5**	**40.5**	**44.2**	**46.4**	**39.3**	**37.6**
Case 1	29.8	37.0	59.8	36.5	46.3	34.0
Case 2	44.7	46.9	n.s.	n.s.	n.s.	44.2
Greece						
Total	**57.7**	**56.6**	**56.6**	**63.7**	**55.8**	**57.8**
Case 1	40.3	42.5	41.5	42.2	35.8	41.0
Case 2	45.1	48.9	47.7	n.s.	n.s.	48.5

Notes: Coverage: population 18–65 years of age; Case 1: Vandalism or crime in the area; Case 2: People living on own; * The item is 'often' and not 'on most days'.
Source: ECHP (1994) wave 1.

TABLE 12.6. *Effects of employment insecurity and unemployment on relations with friends and relatives (ordered logistic regression)*

	Insecure job		Precarious job		Unempl.<1		Unempl.>1	
	B	Sig.	B	Sig.	B	Sig.	B	Sig.
Belgium	0.01	n.s.	−0.26	n.s.	0.16	n.s.	0.16	n.s.
Denmark	−0.21	*	−0.22	n.s.	0.30	*	0.38	*
France	0.01	n.s.	−0.29	*	−0.24	**	−0.41	***
Germany	−0.20	**	−0.31	*	−0.18	n.s.	−0.41	**
Greece	−0.09	(*)	−0.16	n.s.	0.06	n.s.	−0.27	*
Ireland	−0.06	n.s.	−0.16	n.s.	−0.09	n.s.	−0.30	*
Italy	−0.13	**	0.01	n.s.	0.22	**	0.24	**
Netherlands	−0.20	**	−0.45	**	0.19	n.s.	−0.15	n.s.
Portugal	0.10	(*)	0.06	n.s.	0.12	n.s.	0.07	n.s.
Spain	−0.15	**	−0.06	n.s.	0.36	***	−0.04	n.s.
UK	−0.19	**	−0.15	n.s.	−0.20	(*)	0.02	n.s.

Notes: Reference: stable job with controls for age, gender, level of education, household composition, vandalism or crime in the area. Coverage: population 18–65 years of age; (*): $P < 0.1$, *: $P < 0.05$, **: $P < 0.01$, ***: $P < 0.001$.
Source: ECHP (1994) wave 1.

55 per cent in Greece—see Table 12.5. The proportion is similar in Ireland and in France, although in France interpretation must be cautious given that there was a difference in the response set. In contrast, the proportion fell to around 30 per cent in Germany and The Netherlands. In the other countries, it hovers between 39 per cent, for Denmark, and 48 per cent for the UK.

What is the specific effect of unemployment on this kind of sociability? In most countries, a higher proportion of the unemployed meet relatives and friends on most days than is the case for people in work. This is likely to be explicable in terms of amount of time available to people. An employed person working throughout the week will have less time to spend for meeting people in the local community than an unemployed person.

When account is taken of factors such as sex, age, level of education, household composition, and vandalism in the area, it turns out that unemployment has a negative effect on sociability in several countries—see Table 12.6. The long-term unemployed have significantly less contact with friends and relatives outside the household than those in stable jobs, in particular in four countries: France and Germany, Ireland, and Greece. In contrast, in Denmark and Italy, the long-term unemployed are significantly more likely to meet regularly with friends and relatives than those who have a stable job. In the other countries, the results are not significant.

The conclusion of these figures is that the unemployed are significantly more isolated in some countries than others. We can also observe that the negative impact of a precarious job on encounters with friends and relatives is confirmed for several countries, especially France, Germany, and The Netherlands.

Living in an area characterized by vandalism and crime can have a negative impact on the encounters with friends and relatives. However, for the long-term unemployed in Denmark, the UK, The Netherlands, Belgium, and Portugal, we have an inverse effect: those living in such areas meet more often with their friends and relatives than the long-term unemployed population as a whole. We can probably explain this phenomenon through a mechanism analysed by social psychologists (Tajfel 1978): when people live in an area where the whole population is strongly socially stigmatized, they try to avoid regular relations with the part of the population the most disadvantaged and the most stigmatized, creating a sort of internal segregation (Elias and Scottson 1965). In doing so, they reinforce their relations with the others or, sometimes, with relatives or friends outside the area. It could be termed 'compensation effect': a strategy based on social distinction.

Finally, we can observe, in general, that living alone has a positive effect on sociability with friends and relatives. The unemployed living alone have more contact with their close circle than the unemployed as a whole. We have to conclude that the collapse of the relationships with friends and family during unemployment is only confirmed in a minority of European countries. The social disqualification process is not as marked in other countries.

Social and Family Support

The discussion so far has focused on the frequency of contact, however in order to estimate the *effectiveness* of social networks we will take into account the availability of social and family support—see Table 12.7. Examining the help given by family and friends is a way of measuring the strength of the social links that exist. Our information is limited to the question of financial support. The need for such support is likely to be greatest among the long-term unemployed, since we know that resources are reduced progressively with the length of unemployment.

In Southern Europe—Italy, Spain, Portugal and Greece—the coefficient for the long-term unemployed is significantly positive whereas it is weaker in Belgium and is not significant in France, Denmark, the UK, and Ireland—see Table 12.8. The division between Northern and Southern Europe found in the previous Eurostat survey (Paugam 1996) is found to be even stronger here. The case of The Netherlands provides a particular point of interest: the coefficient for the long term unemployed is approximately of the same size as in the Southern European countries, which is surprising owing to the fact that social welfare help is higher than in the south. It would be natural to assume that the overall efficiency of the social

TABLE 12.7. *Receiving financial support or maintenance from relatives, friends, and other persons outside the household (%)*

	Stable job	Insecure job	Precarious job	Unempl. <1 y	Unempl. >1 y	All active (18–65)
Belgium	6.0	6.9	11.5	8.3	11.5	6.8
Denmark	8.1	8.0	11.5	8.7	7.4	8.3
France	3.2	2.6	7.2	5.9	4.2	3.6
Germany	6.6	5.2	10.2	5.8	9.9	7.5
Greece	3.4	3.6	9.1	6.5	14.4	4.7
Ireland*	0.3	0.4	1.0	2.1	0.7	0.5
Italy	2.6	3.7	6.4	6.5	9.7	3.6
Netherlands	0.6	0.4	4.9	0.8	0.9	0.8
Portugal	0.9	1.5	1.2	2.4	3.2	1.2
Spain	1.9	2.3	3.7	4.0	5.3	2.6
UK	5.3	3.9	9.9	6.1	7.9	5.5

Notes: Coverage: population 18–65 years of age. The question asks if respondents received any financial support or maintenance from relatives, friends or others outside the household in 1993; * In Ireland the question asked if respondents received *regular* financial support.
Source: ECHP (1994) wave 1.

TABLE 12.8. *Effects of employment insecurity and unemployment on likelihood of receiving financial support or maintenance from relatives, friends, and other persons outside the household (logistic regression)*

	Insecure job		Precarious job		Unempl.<1		Unempl.>1	
	B	Sig.	B	Sig.	B	Sig.	B	Sig.
Northern Countries								
Belgium	0.10	n.s.	0.50	(*)	0.02	n.s.	0.69	**
Denmark	−0.03	n.s.	0.25	n.s.	0.17	n.s.	0.04	n.s.
France	0.03	n.s.	0.50	*	0.52	*	−0.00	n.s.
Germany	−0.06	n.s.	0.13	n.s.	−0.54	(*)	0.35	(*)
Ireland	0.02	n.s.	0.84	n.s.	1.43	*	0.48	n.s.
Netherl.	−0.33	n.s.	1.23	**	−0.28	n.s.	1.60	**
UK	−0.27	n.s.	0.54	**	−0.10	n.s.	0.17	n.s.
Southern Countries								
Greece	0.19	n.s.	0.94	***	0.68	*	1.59	***
Italy	0.23	(*)	0.94	***	1.09	***	1.40	***
Portugal	0.45	n.s.	0.53	n.s.	1.38	**	1.34	**
Spain	0.28	n.s.	0.64	**	0.72	**	1.20	***
Regions in Italy								
North	0.14	n.s.	0.62	n.s.	−0.06	n.s.	0.86	*
Centre	0.24	***	1.24	***	0.35	***	1.66	***
South	0.38	***	1.27	***	1.87	***	1.84	***

Notes: Reference: stable job with controls for age, gender, household composition, level of education, household income. Coverage: population 18–65 years of age;
(*): $P < 0.1$, *: $P < 0.05$, **: $P < 0.01$, ***: $P < 0.001$.
Source: ECHP (1994) wave 1.

TABLE 12.9. *Effects of age on likelihood of receiving financial support or maintenance from relatives, friends and other persons outside the household (logistic regression)*

	18–24		25–29		30–39		> = 55	
	B	Sig.	B	Sig.	B	Sig.	B	Sig.
Belgium	0.86	**	1.10	***	0.82	***	−0.85	*
Denmark	0.63	**	0.42	*	0.24	(*)	−1.20	***
France	1.15	***	0.12	n.s.	0.22	n.s.	−0.75	(*)
Germany	2.33	***	1.20	***	0.68	***	−0.64	*
Greece	1.15	***	1.07	***	0.98	***	−0.07	n.s.
Ireland	−0.22	n.s.	n.s.	n.s.	0.16	n.s.	−0.61	n.s.
Italy	−0.05	n.s.	0.62	**	0.56	***	−1.20	***
Netherlands	3.78	***	1.95	**	0.31	n.s.	n.s.	n.s.
Portugal	0.32	n.s.	0.05	n.s.	0.15	n.s.	−0.39	n.s.
Spain	0.13	n.s.	0.52	*	0.62	**	−1.02	**
UK	1.46	***	0.78	***	0.74	***	−0.85	*

Notes: Reference: 40–54 years old with controls for gender, employment situation, household composition, level of education, household income. Coverage: population 18–65 years of age; (*): $P < 0.1$, *: $P < 0.05$, **: $P < 0.01$, ***: $P < 0.001$.
Source: ECHP (1994) wave 1.

welfare system would reduce the need for private help or at least restrict it to areas of fundamental need. However, the overall level of financial support received by the long-term unemployed in The Netherlands is less than 1 per cent. The *relatively* higher support received by the unemployed may be because they remain close to their families and are often more fixed, geographically speaking. It is also interesting to observe that the coefficient is positive for the short-term unemployed in Italy, Spain, Portugal, and Greece.

In Italy, the differences between regions stand out sharply. In the North, the effect of employment precarity and short-term unemployment are not significant on support. In contrast, there is a high and positive significant effect in the Centre and in the South for each of the four precarious employment situations in relation to the stable job situation. The coefficients are always stronger for the South. These results can be explained both by the lower economic level of development in this region and the local organization of the poor families to fight against poverty and unemployment—see Chapter 3 in this volume.

Age is an important explanatory factor of the level of financial support from the family—see Table 12.9. People under 25 years old are much more likely to receive support in cases of difficulty whereas the probability is lower and decreases for those over 30 years old. The age impact is, first of all, the result of a simple mechanism: the progressive reduction in the number of older relatives during the life-cycle. This decrease in support in relation to age is also explained by the social habit of helping young people at the start of their adult life. In some cases, this form of solidarity is spontaneous. Those who provide it want to help the young, while those who benefit have no qualms, knowing that the social definition of the parents' role towards their children in difficulties justifies it. Things are different in the next age group where collective expectations have changed. Whereas a young adult who experiences difficulties in settling down might expect to get help from her family, an older adult is more likely to be suspected of inadequacy. The latter will also find asking for help more embarrassing. However, this phenomenon is not confirmed in Portugal[2] where none of the age coefficients are significant. We can also see that in Italy and Spain, the coefficient is not significant for people under 25 years old, but it becomes significantly positive for people aged 25–29 and 30–39. We can explain this result by the tendency for young people to live with their parents, therefore receiving direct help from within the household.

If a great part of family support is directly given *inside* the household in Southern Europe where many of the unemployed live with their parents, it is interesting to know that this solidarity continues when the unemployed live alone. We have calculated the proportion of the unemployed living alone who receive financial support or maintenance from relatives, friends, and other persons and the same frequency for people living alone but not unemployed. It is striking to see again that the unemployed are more likely to be helped in Greece, Spain, and Italy. In Greece, more than 50 per cent receive support in this case.

Although familial solidarity in the Southern countries plays a major part in decreasing the risk of hardship arising from unemployment, the role played by state benefit in the Northern countries in no way leads to a break down of familial support. This is, first of all, the result of a social system. When a large part of the population shares the same unfavourable social conditions, familial solidarity does not arise from a logic of compensation nor from the logic of emancipation—it becomes a collective fight against poverty. Reciprocity in the exchanges is then functional. In order to face adversity, everyone gives and gives back, therefore everyone gives and receives. This is why we are more likely to find examples of lasting familial solidarity in those regions where unemployment and hardship are higher, because it is based on a reciprocity imposed by the need to resist collectively. One can talk here of combined hardship.

Although familial solidarity has not altogether disappeared in the more economically developed regions, it does not play such a vital role. Individuals' need for autonomy and the less homogeneous character of the family lead to a kind of familial solidarity which is at the same time more

---

[2] This is also true in Ireland but the results must be treated with caution because of the difference in question format.

flexible and less formal, but also more fragile. Once the exchanges taking place in the family have become deeply unbalanced, there is a risk that these exchanges will decline.

THE TERTIARY SPHERE OF SOCIABILITY

The final type of sociability considered is membership of clubs and associations, that is to say interaction in organized groups with formalized objectives. This type of sociability is probably less important than sociability with relatives or friends if the concern is to measure the strength of affective ties, but it nonetheless reflects a form of interaction into the wider social life. It is possible that unemployed people who participate regularly in associative structures are less likely to be stigmatized due to their lack of a job, and are likely to have better chances of finding a job again than those people who have withdrawn into the domestic sphere. However, since this type of social involvement often involves costs such as membership fees, it is potentially more susceptible to income loss during unemployment.

The first thing to note about involvement in clubs and organizations is that the differences between countries again stand out sharply. The frequency of participation is clearly higher in Northern than Southern European countries—see Table 12.10. The two extreme cases are Denmark with a rate of 59 per cent and Greece with only 13 per cent. This difference reveals that participation in social life is more institutionalized as a dimension of citizenship in Northern countries, and more informal and organized around close relationships in Southern countries, as we saw before. So, participation in a club or organization does not have the same sociological meaning in every country.

The participation of the long-term unemployed in associative life is highest in Denmark where the proportion is above 45 per cent. It is also quite high in The Netherlands with 39 per cent and in the UK and France, each with 33 per cent. In contrast, participation is much lower in Portugal, Greece, and Italy where it lies between 9 and 12 per cent. In the other countries, it ranges between 18 and 30 per cent.

Moreover, the long-term unemployed have a significantly weaker link with clubs or associations than the regularly employed in most countries: Germany, Belgium, France, the UK, The Netherlands, Ireland, Italy, and Spain. The coefficient is also negative, but not significant in Portugal and Greece either for the short- or the long-term unemployed—see Table 12.11. This tendency for social interaction in the institutionalized sphere of social life to diminish with unemployment points to a significant risk of social isolation. It confirms the results of Lazarsfeld and his research team in the

TABLE 12.10. *Participation in any club or organization according to labour market situation, by country* (%)

	Stable job	Insecure job	Precarious job	Unempl. <1 y	Unempl. >1 y	All active (18–65)
Denmark						
Total	**61.1**	**57.5**	**56.2**	**43.0**	**47.6**	**58.8**
Case 1	58.6	54.5	69.6	36.4	45.7	56.8
Case 2	59.8	64.7	64.2	43.8	44.7	57.8
France						
Total	**49.3**	**51.8**	**40.2**	**44.2**	**33.0**	**48.5**
Case 1	30.8	27.7	19.6	26.7	18.6	28.4
Case 2	36.6	30.2	40.1	26.2	10.3	33.3
Germany						
Total	**57.3**	**46.3**	**36.5**	**27.3**	**29.5**	**51.8**
Case 1	44.7	39.7	39.2	22.9	13.5	40.8
Case 2	53.8	42.0	59.8	19.3	9.0	47.4
Netherlands						
Total	**51.2**	**50.4**	**41.5**	**46.1**	**39.0**	**50.0**
Case 1	46.2	44.4	34.9	26.9	37.2	44.1
Case 2	49.1	53.6	31.2	44.3	55.0	49.1
Belgium						
Total	**38.1**	**32.1**	**30.7**	**32.6**	**18.7**	**35.5**
Case 1	32.7	31.9	18.4	29.0	18.1	30.9
Case 2	36.7	33.2	n.s.	n.s.	36.1	35.6
UK						
Total	**49.3**	**51.8**	**40.2**	**44.2**	**33.0**	**48.5**
Case 1	48.1	52.1	41.5	46.6	25.4	47.4
Case 2	50.4	57.7	51.2	46.1	22.0	49.6
Ireland						
Total	**53.2**	**50.3**	**48.0**	**37.1**	**21.0**	**47.5**
Case 1	54.9	49.9	25.5	29.5	21.0	43.8
Case 2	45.2	60.3	n.s.	n.s.	11.5	43.4
Italy						
Total	**21.5**	**16.3**	**13.5**	**12.7**	**11.8**	**18.4**
Case 1	20.6	12.0	12.7	11.2	9.5	15.9
Case 2	20.7	15.1	n.s.	n.s.	n.s.	18.3
Spain						
Total	**34.5**	**31.3**	**27.2**	**22.8**	**21.6**	**30.4**
Case 1	34.5	27.7	26.0	21.0	20.0	28.9
Case 2	27.9	32.8	31.5	23.2	21.6	28.4
Portugal						
Total	**20.1**	**16.4**	**14.2**	**11.6**	**9.3**	**18.3**
Case 1	22.2	23.6	21.8	13.1	12.6	21.6
Case 2	27.3	10.9	14.6	n.s.	n.s.	21.3
Greece						
Total	**14.9**	**11.3**	**12.5**	**10.5**	**10.4**	**12.9**
Case 1	12.9	12.3	2.9	12.9	17.5	12.3
Case 2	21.6	11.0	10.6	n.s.	n.s.	15.9

Notes: Coverage: population 18–65 years of age; Case 1: Vandalism or crime in the area; Case 2: people living on own.
Source: ECHP (1994) wave 1.

TABLE 12.11. *Effects of employment insecurity and unemployment on social participation (logistic regression)*

	Insecure job		Precarious job		Unempl.<1		Unempl.>1	
	B	Sig.	B	Sig.	B	Sig.	B	Sig.
Belgium	−0.24	**	−0.33	n.s.	−0.14	n.s.	−0.79	***
Denmark	−0.12	n.s.	−0.10	n.s.	−0.62	***	−0.30	n.s.
France	−0.03	n.s.	−0.09	n.s.	−0.21	*	−0.37	*
Germany	−0.42	***	−0.73	***	−1.05	***	−0.96	***
Greece	−0.08	n.s.	0.03	n.s.	−0.08	n.s.	−0.01	n.s.
Ireland	0.24	**	0.17	n.s.	0.05	n.s.	−0.57	***
Italy	−0.24	***	−0.47	**	−0.50	***	−0.50	***
Netherlands	0.04	n.s.	−0.40	**	−0.20	n.s.	−0.43	**
Portugal	−0.13	n.s.	−0.29	n.s.	−0.09	n.s.	−0.10	n.s.
Spain	−0.08	n.s.	−0.06	n.s.	−0.19	**	−0.26	**
UK	0.09	n.s.	−0.27	(*)	−0.12	n.s.	−0.51	***

Notes: Reference: stable job with controls for age, gender, level of education, household composition, vandalism or crime in the area. Coverage: population 18–65 years of age; (*): $P < 0.1$, *: $P < 0.05$, **: $P < 0.01$, ***: $P < 0.001$.
Source: ECHP (1994) wave 1.

1930s in Marienthal. Sixty years after, in most European countries, participation in the life of clubs and associations still decreases in the local community when a great part of the working population is suddenly without employment. But its is important to recognize that the impact will vary between countries. A low level of participation in associative life will not have the same social significance in a country where associative life is generally weakly developed as it does in a country where it had become a normal aspect of social relationships and hence an important dimension of social integration. For example, if participation in associative life concerns only 10 per cent of the unemployed in Greece, the impact of unemployment is not significant because the percentage is also very low for the overall working-age population. In this country, participation in associative life is not in itself a factor of social integration. In contrast, in Germany, the impact of unemployment is higher, even if participation in associative life involves around 30 per cent of the unemployed, because membership of a club or a formal organization can be considered as an important dimension of social integration: 52 per cent of the working age population participates in associative life.

It must also be noted that association with clubs is also significantly weaker for the employed with an insecure job or a precarious job, than for the regularly employed in several countries: Germany, The Netherlands, Belgium, and Italy. Perhaps those in insecure or precarious jobs feel the need to work longer hours to maintain their position and so have less time for social activities.[3] Alternatively social participation might be affected by greater geographical mobility among this group. These are questions which warrant further research.

We have to emphasize that participation in clubs or social life organizations is, on the whole, less developed in areas where vandalism and crime are prevalent. There are, however, some exceptions for the unemployed. In Greece and Portugal, for example, the unemployed are proportionally more likely to participate in such activities when they live in a dangerous area. In Greece, 17.5 per cent of the long-term unemployed participate in clubs or organizations when they live in an area characterized by vandalism, when only 10 per cent of the unemployed as a whole are involved in this kind of social activity.

Europe-wide, people living alone are not significantly less isolated from clubs or organizations than others. However, in some countries, the social participation of the unemployed is lower when they live alone. This is the case in particular in Germany and France: only 9 per cent in Germany and 10 per cent in France of the long-term unemployed participate in such organizations when they live alone. The frequency goes to 29 per cent in Germany and 33 per cent in France among the long-term unemployed as the whole. Therefore in these countries, living alone has an aggravating effect on weak social participation.

THE STIGMA EXPLANATION

Taking the overall pattern for the unemployed, we will argue that unemployment is less of a stigma in Southern Europe than in some of the Northern countries, in particular in France and Germany. In order to explain these cross-national differences in sociability, the social status of precarious workers and the unemployed is taken into account. In societies where mass unemployment has persisted for many years and is linked to weak economic development, as is the case in several countries and regions in Southern Europe, unemployment is unlikely to deeply affect social relations. Because precarious wage earners and the unemployed form a broad social class, rather than a strictly defined underclass, they are not heavily stigmatized. Their standard of living is low, but they remain part of social networks which stem from family and the immediate neighbourhood. Moreover, unemployment does not lead to a concomitant loss of status. In fact, its effects are sometimes compensated for by resources available from

---

[3] However, evidence from the ISSP 1997 survey suggests that this tendency would be counteracted by a lack of organizational commitment among the insecurely employed.

TABLE 12.12. *People who completely agree with the statement*
'unemployment is very distressing' (%)

	France	UK	Belgium	Germany	Netherlands	Italy
Unemployed	82.1	76.9	68.9	63.8	59.2	47.1
Total	76.6	80.4	60.8	55.4	69.1	50.5
Gap	5.5	−3.5	8.1	8.4	−9.9	−3.4

Source: Eurobarometer 21, *Political Cleavages in the European Union*, April 1984.

the underground economy, and furthermore, such activities play an integrating role for those who participate.

In countries which have seen a big increase in unemployment after a period of full employment, the unemployed are more likely to experience social disqualification. Social status is more dependent on direct participation in a professional activity. The unemployed exist outside the productive sphere and become more dependent on social welfare institutions as they encounter greater and greater problems. Qualitative surveys in France provide an understanding of this process. Both dismissal, which is often interpreted as professional failure, and the failure to obtain a first job cause an increasing consciousness of the distance between the individual and the large majority of the population. The unemployed develop an overriding sense of failure accompanied by the belief that their everyday behaviour will be interpreted as an indication of social ineptness or inferiority, and in extreme cases as a social handicap. The unemployed often feel that they are perceived as carriers of a 'social plague' when they try to explain their problems openly in public (Paugam 1991).

It is striking to observe, from the results of a Eurobarometer (Table 12.12), that the proportion of people completely agreeing with the proposal 'Unemployment is very distressing' are particularly numerous in France, with 76.6 per cent and in the UK with 80.4 per cent, and clearly less numerous in Italy with 50.5 per cent. A wide gap between the perceptions of the unemployed and the whole population suggests a lack of integration of the former.

Furthermore, if the gap between the employed and unemployed is negative, that is the unemployed are less likely to say that unemployment is distressing, this suggests that the unemployed have developed a rationalization to resist stigma. A high positive gap indicates a weak ability among the unemployed to rationalize their situation. A high positive gap occurs for France, Belgium, and Germany. In these countries, the unemployed appear to have internalized the public perceptions of unemployment and the unemployed. In contrast, the gap is large and negative in The Netherlands.

TABLE 12.13. *Some friends look down on you for not having a paid job* (row %)

	Agree Strongly	Agree Somewhat	Neither Agree nor Disagree	Disagree Somewhat	Disagree Strongly	N
Belgium	9.3	30.0	15.9	21.1	23.8	227
Denmark	3.6	17.6	8.8	11.1	58.8	306
France	8.2	15.1	16.2	25.1	35.4	291
W Germany	10.0	26.4	25.8	22.6	15.2	341
E Germany	13.7	26.2	26.0	23.1	11.0	527
Greece	3.8	11.7	19.0	34.0	31.5	326
Ireland	13.7	24.1	17.0	25.9	19.3	336
Italy	3.7	7.4	9.8	25.2	54.0	176
Netherlands	8.8	12.0	4.9	13.2	61.1	409
Portugal	7.7	23.7	21.4	24.4	22.7	299
Spain	2.6	9.0	9.6	43.9	34.9	344
UK	8.1	18.8	9.2	34.2	29.8	272

Source: Eurobarometer 44.3 (ILO Unemployed).

The 1996 Eurobarometer provides interesting results on the stigmatization of the unemployed (Table 12.13). This survey asks if people agree with the following proposal: 'Some friends look down on you for not having a paid job'. The results confirm the hypothesis that stigmatization is less important in Southern European countries, but also in Denmark, but is particularly strong in Ireland, East and West Germany, and Belgium.

CONCLUSION

Taking the overall pattern of sociability for the unemployed, the major difference is between the Southern and Northern European countries. Primary and secondary types of sociability are considerably stronger in Italy, Spain, Portugal, and Greece. In these countries, the tertiary sphere of sociability is, however, less developed. Denmark and The Netherlands represent the sharpest contrast with this pattern: a high proportion of people living alone, relatively low levels of informal sociability, and high levels of participation in associative life. Social participation in formal organizations usually needs resources. While the welfare system in general permits people to maintain the pattern of sociability characteristic of the wider society, it is somewhat more disruptive of the more expensive forms of sociability of people in the Northern countries than of the largely informal sociability of the Southern countries.

Overall, the sharpest impact of employment precarity and unemployment on social isolation is in France, where it affected all three spheres of sociability we defined. But, in absolute terms, the social isolation of the unemployed is most marked in Germany. In this country, a relatively high proportion of the unemployed are isolated in terms of position in the household; they are the least likely to meet friends and relatives most days, and their participation in associative life is also very low in comparison to the regularly employed.

The differences that emerge between the European countries have several theoretical implications. The strength and the nature of the social links are different from country to country and from this we can deduce that the process of social disqualification is not equally probable in all countries. Sociability and private networks of help offer varying degrees of support in the struggle to find work, to achieve financial stability, and to prevent the process of social disqualification.

Any analysis of the process of social disqualification must take account of the differences of scale—the qualitative differences—without isolating them from the social structures of which they are a product. A similarity of appearance in the behaviour of similar groups in the populations of similar countries does not imply that the phenomenon in question has the same social meaning and importance, nor that it affects the same groups in each country. These first results open the way to further investigations not only of the social links concerning the underprivileged populations, but also the wider issue of the regulation and fluctuation of social links in European societies, taking into account economic development, the role of the state and also of non-institutionalized help. The combination of these three elements might explain both the relations hips that each society develops with that segment of its population which it labels as poor, and also the national characteristics of the process and experience of unemployment.

13

United in Employment, United in Unemployment? Employment and Unemployment of Couples in the European Union in 1994

Paul M. de Graaf and Wout C. Ultee

INTRODUCTION

The impact of the high levels of unemployment in the European Union is more severe when unemployment does not only hit younger people, who are still living with their parents, but threatens the employment opportunities of breadwinners as well. The social consequences of high levels of unemployment in a country will be particularly severe if it is associated with the occurrence of double unemployment in couples.

Some economic theories have argued that the unemployment of one spouse will increase the probability for the other spouse to be employed, because of the financial incentives. Other things being equal, when one spouse is doing well on the labour market, and has high earnings, this may create a negative incentive for the other spouse to be employed. When one spouse is not earning a satisfactory income, the other spouse will have incentives to find a job. The 'additional worker' hypothesis reflects this view.

But there are reasons to doubt that the association between the employment positions of husbands and wives is negative. Data taken on a regular basis from labour force surveys conducted in Canada and the United States (Statistics Canada 1986; US Department of Labor 1986), show a positive relation between the labour market positions of husbands and wives. If a husband is employed, his wife is more likely to be employed than when her husband does not hold a job, and when a wife is not employed her husband is more likely to be unemployed or outside the labour market as well. For The Netherlands the same positive relationship has been established by Bernasco (1994). As yet, the labour force surveys of the European Union do not establish on a regular basis whether the positive relationship found in North America and in The Netherlands, can also be observed for other European countries—the exception is Sexton (1988).

Apparently pertinent factors were missing from this simple economic theory. So why does a positive relation obtain between the labour market position of husbands and wives? One factor obviously missing from economic search theory, is the opportunity to find a job. It is well known that countries differ in their unemployment rate, and that the regions within a country do so too. Since couples live in the same region, they face the same more or less favourable regional labour market. When the regional unemployment rate is high, the chances that both halves of a couple will be unemployed are higher than when regional rates are lower. This explanation of double unemployment amounts to what might be called a by-product explanation. There is nothing particular in the bond between the members of a couple that makes for double employment or double unemployment, this phenomenon is simply there because regional labour markets differ in the opportunities they present to people to find jobs.

Other explanations are possible, too, that do not postulate that there is a direct relationship between spouses' unemployment probabilities. A well-supported finding in the sociology of marriage is the existence of educational homogamy: persons with a higher level of education tend to be married to persons who also have a higher level of education. Indeed, this tendency prevails in all industrial countries, although its strength differs somewhat between countries (Ultee and Luijkx 1990). Now it is known too that the higher a person's level of education, the lower a person's chances of unemployment. These statistical regularities imply some positive relationship between the employment rates of husbands and wives, because level of schooling is positively related to labour market performance (Ultee, Dessens and Jansen 1988).

However, apart from these by-product explanations, other explanations are possible which postulate effects of the resources of one's spouse (De Graaf and Ultee 1991). We note that a high level of education is not only an indicator of productivity as desired by employers, but also resembles a large set of labour market resources. Educational attainment may be an indicator of knowledge of the labour market, the capacity to look for jobs, and the motivation to work. Education not only enhances an individual's own labour market opportunities, but also stands for resources which are transferable to other persons close to that person. People may be helped when looking through newspapers for the proper job to apply for, and may be provided information on jobs not advertised. The higher-educated also have less strong norms against working wives, especially against working mothers. This observation leads to the hypothesis that the level of schooling of husbands affects the labour market participation of women. Educational homogamy then means that the highly-educated especially will have ample employment opportunities.

It remains to be seen whether the regional unemployment rate explanation, the educational homogamy and spouse's education explanations, and the negative economic explanations account for the association originally found between the labour market position of husbands and wives. Several scenarios are possible. In the first place the direct relationship between the labour market positions of husbands and wives might disappear completely. Such an outcome would make the search for inter-country explanations superfluous. The same would be true, if the remaining direct relationship would be equal for all twelve EU countries. Without variation, there is nothing to explain. However, if there remains a direct association between the unemployment rates of husbands and wives, after the appropriate individual and contextual characteristics have been controlled for, and if this remaining association varies significantly between countries, we need additional hypotheses.

Both institutional and structural hypotheses can explain inter-country differences. The structural hypothesis argues that the larger the proportion of working women in a country, the stronger the association between husband's and wife's labour market positions will be. For a woman it is more difficult to find a job if more women aim to participate in the labour market, and differences between women with resources and women without resources will become salient. In countries in which married women's labour market participation is not governed by a standard, differences in resources will not be decisive. The hypothesis, then, is that the husband's labour market participation has stronger effects on wife's labour market participation in countries where more married women are employed.

Institutional hypotheses focus on the effects of social security and tax systems. In some countries the eligibility to unemployment benefits strongly depends on the spouse's income. No unemployment benefits will be granted if the spouse has an income, and thus spouses of the unemployed have an incentive to stop working. In such a country, the same is true the other way around: a person who is not working, doesn't have many incentives to start working when his or her spouse receive unemployment benefits. Indeed, after a comparison of Britain, Ireland, the USA, Sweden, and Denmark, Dex *et al.* (1995) argue that in countries where unemployment schemes provide wholly individual benefits, the labour force participation of wives of unemployed men does not differ from the labour market participation of wives of employed men. In contrast, in countries where the unemployment benefits for men do take a wife's earnings into account, there is a significant and negative effect of a husband's employment on his wife's labour force participation. It should be pointed out however that Dex *et al.* do not take into account in their analysis the characteristics of both spouses with respect to level of education, age, and region.

A second institutional hypothesis deals with the effects of tax systems. When husband's and wife's incomes are summed for the purpose of taxation, and when this total income is taxed progressively, the wife might be reluctant to accept a job, because her contribution to the family income is taxed with a higher percentage than when she would be taxed individually.

Of course, under such a tax regime, it is not the wife's income *per se* which is taxed strongest, but when couples see it this way, only the labour market participation of the wife will be affected. In countries in which income tax is assessed on a strict individual basis women's labour market participation does not affect the tax rate.

In the Introduction to this book, it was pointed out that countries vary not only in the extent to which the welfare regime provides coverage to the inhabitants, but also in their model of family residence and the extent to which the social security regime treats generations within a family as autonomous. At one end of both dimensions are the countries of Southern Europe—Italy, Spain, Portugal, and Greece—which are both sub-protective and patriarchal. At the other end are Denmark and Sweden. Their welfare systems are universalistic with respect to social rights and are based on individual autonomy. Further, there are countries which stress inter-generational autonomy, but whose welfare regime is in the middle between sub-protective and universalistic social rights: the UK, The Netherlands, and Germany. But for our purposes a crucial factor is the degree to which spouses are treated as independent from one another by a country's welfare regime. There also needs to be a typology of 'spousal autonomy'.

In this chapter we aim to answer three research questions. The first is the size of the association between the labour market positions of husbands and wives in the member countries of the EU. The second is whether significant association remains when we account for educational and age homogamy, for regional variation in unemployment rates, and for the propensity for a person to work less if his or her partner earns more. The third is whether the remaining association varies between the twelve 1994 EU countries. If we find variation between countries, we will explore structural and institutional explanations.

LABOUR MARKET PARTICIPATION AND MARITAL STATUS

We investigate the labour market participation of couples and its determinants by using the first wave of the European Community Household Panel study (ECHP 1994) for twelve EU countries.[1] This panel interviews all adult members of a household. Thus, comparable data are available for husbands and wives. The most important variables we employ in the analysis are labour market participation, educational attainment, personal income, and regional unemployment rate.

---

[1] German data are not included in the ECHP data file, but the relevant tables and models were computed separately by the German EPUSE members. In the combined analysis of Table 13.3 Germany could not be included.

Labour market participation has three categories: employed, unemployed, and inactive. We use the ILO (International Labour Organisation) definition of employment. According to this definition, the employed hold jobs of fifteen or more hours a week. The unemployed do not hold jobs of fifteen hours or more a week, seek employment, are available to take up employment in the next two weeks, and have taken steps during the past four weeks to find employment. The inactive do not hold jobs of at least fifteen hours per week and do not meet the other criteria to be defined as unemployed. Additionally, we have some information on the unemployment history of the respondents. We know whether the respondent has experienced unemployment in the last year, and in the last five years.

The important contrast to be investigated in this paper is the one between employment and unemployment, as defined above. However, the disadvantage of focusing on this contrast only, is that the inactive part of the population is neglected. Indeed, it is known that, especially for women, the distinction between unemployment and inactivity is rather vague. When the general unemployment rate goes down, the proportion of formerly inactive women looking for jobs increases. This points to hidden unemployment among women who are classified as housewives. Therefore, we will use a second contrast to investigate accumulation in couples, the contrast between employment and non-employment. Non-employment combines unemployed and inactive persons. Of course, this approach has a disadvantage as well, because in this broad category of non-employment, persons looking for a job and persons not looking for a job are grouped together. Yet, the second contrast enables us to see to what extent couples have a foot in the labour market.

Educational attainment is measured in four categories: primary education only, secondary education lower level, secondary higher level, and tertiary education. This crucial variable is directly available in the ECHP panel study, but its standardization does not seem to be fully reliable, making it difficult to compare the educational distribution in the twelve countries. However, we can safely assume that the measurement of educational attainment warrants the assumption of ordinal measurement *within* each country, although caution is needed in comparing effects of educational attainment on labour market participation between countries.

Personal income is measured by the personal disposable income in the calendar year 1993. The income of both spouses is measured in quartiles. For each country separately, and for husbands and wives separately, we have computed the percentile of their personal income. These percentile scores are categorized into quartiles, and a fifth category is constructed for persons without income. Quartile 1 is the lowest income group, and quartile 4 the highest. This gives us the possibility to test whether one spouse's income produces a negative incentive for the other spouse's employment status, and whether there are differences in this negative effect between countries.

Regional unemployment rates were found in Eurostat Statistics in Focus Regions (1995). For Denmark, Ireland, and Luxembourg, only national unemployment rates were available. The national unemployment rate is lowest for the Luxembourg, at 3.4 per cent and highest for Spain with 24 per cent. Within the countries for which regional information is available, there is strong variation in regional unemployment rates as well.

Table 13.1 classifies all couples with respect to the labour market position of both spouses. We have limited the sample to married and cohabiting persons between 25 and 54 years old; the age interval applies to both respondent and spouse. In the remainder of this paper we will refer to persons living as common law couples as spouses too. We impose the upper age limit of 54 years because we do not wish to focus on differences between countries with respect to the timing of early retirement. The lower age limit of 25 years is chosen for two reasons. First, in this way most respondents have finished their educational careers. Second, we regard youth unemployment as a research topic to be addressed separately from our question. We distinguish four states for the employment status of both spouses: full-time employed for 30 hours or more weekly, part-time employed for less than 30 hours weekly, unemployed, and inactive with regard to labour market participation: housewives, retired persons, and those who are unable to participate due to disability.

Large differences between the twelve countries can be observed, which seem to stem mainly from the labour market participation of women. Denmark is the one extreme: in 83.5 per cent of all couples both spouses have jobs, and in the majority of the couples both spouses have full-time jobs. In 14.5 per cent of all Danish couples only one of both spouses has a job, and only 10.3 per cent of all couples in which spouses are between 25 and 54 years old can be categorized in the traditional family model with a male provider and a housewife. Belgium with 74.5 per cent, the UK with 63.9 per cent, Germany with 63.2 per cent, and France with 62.5 per cent come closest to the Danish pattern of both spouses having jobs. However, in the UK, and to a lesser extent in Belgium, a higher proportion of women in employment are in part-time jobs than is the case in France.

The most traditional countries with respect to the division of labour between husbands and wives are to be found in Southern Europe—Greece, Italy, and Spain—together with Ireland. In these four countries, in almost half of all couples only the husband has a job, and in only about 40 per cent of all couples both spouses hold jobs. Luxembourg, The Netherlands, and Portugal are countries which take middle positions when compared to the modern and the traditional countries. Due to the remarkably high proportion of married women working in part-time jobs, the case of The Netherlands is special. In 57 per cent of couples both husband and wife have jobs, but only in 22 per cent of the couples do both have full-time jobs.

TABLE 13.1. *Labour market positions of couples in twelve European countries, both spouses 25–54 years old* (%)

	Belgium	Denmark	France	Germany	Greece	Ireland	Italy	Luxembourg	Netherlands	Portugal	Spain	United Kingdom
Both spouses employed	74.5	83.5	62.5	63.2	43.7	41.1	45.8	47.8	57.0	60.8	32.3	63.9
One spouse employed, one spouse unemployed	4.7	6.1	10.4	4.9	11.0	3.8	5.9	2.8	5.6	4.8	12.4	5.1
One spouse employed, one spouse inactive	18.5	8.4	24.4	30.1	41.8	47.1	44.1	47.3	34.8	31.2	48.0	23.3
Both spouses unemployed or inactive	2.3	2.0	2.7	1.8	3.5	8.0	4.1	2.0	2.7	3.3	7.3	7.7
Husband *Wife*												
Unemployed unemployed	0.4	0.6	0.8	0.3	0.9	0.8	0.4	0.3	0.2	0.3	1.8	0.9
Unemployed inactive	0.8	0.2	0.8	0.8	1.6	5.1	1.3	0.8	0.9	0.8	3.1	3.9
Inactive unemployed	0.0	0.0	0.2	0.1	0.2	0.1	0.2	0.0	0.2	0.1	0.4	0.2
Inactive inactive	1.1	1.2	0.9	0.6	0.9	2.0	2.2	1.0	1.4	2.1	2.1	2.7
Number of couples with complete information	1416	1054	2330	1720	1764	1381	2760	393	1313	1572	2504	1710

Source: ECHP (1994).

272 Paul de Graaf and Wout Ultee

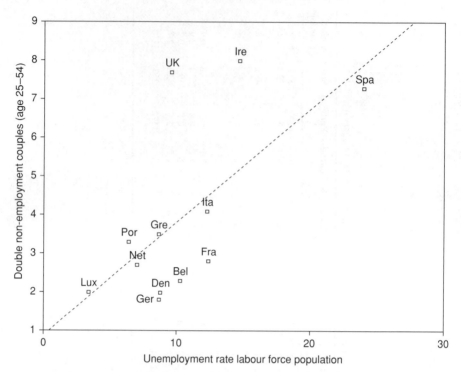

FIG. 13A. The relationship between a country's overall employment rate
and the occurrence of double non-employment in couples

Note: Correlation = 0.65.

The proportion of couples in which both spouses are unemployed is very low in most countries. Spain has the highest proportion of couples in which both husband and wife are unemployed with 1.8 per cent, and in all other countries this proportion is less than 1 per cent. More couples can be characterized by dual non-employment. In most of these cases the unemployment of one spouse, mostly the husband, goes together with the inactivity of the other spouse, mostly the wife, although sometimes the pattern is reversed, and it also occurs that both spouses are inactive. Germany has the smallest proportion of couples in which both spouses do not have jobs— only 1.8 per cent. Other countries with less than 3 per cent of couples without jobs are Belgium, Denmark, France, Luxembourg, and The Netherlands. In Greece, Italy, and Portugal the proportion of jobless couples is between 3 and 5 per cent. Ireland, Spain, and the UK have the largest proportions of jobless couples, between 5 and 8 per cent. The proportion of jobless couples is strongly related to the overall unemployment level, as is shown in Fig. 13A. The relationship is linear with a correlation coefficient of $r = 0.65$, although there are two important outliers. In the United Kingdom and in Ireland double non-employment occurs more often than in the other countries.

THE ASSOCIATION BETWEEN THE EMPLOYMENT STATUS OF HUSBANDS AND WIVES

In Table 13.2 we display the strength of the association between the employment statuses of husbands and wives in the twelve 1994 EU countries. The *odds ratio* is our measurement of this association.[2] When the odds ratio is 1 there is no association, and the higher the odds ratio, the stronger is the association. An odds ratio lower than 1 refers to a negative association between spouses' employment statuses. In Belgium the odds ratio is 3.8, which stands for a moderate to strong association.

The first panel of Table 13.2 gives an overview of the association between husband's non-employment and wife's non-employment. According to the odds ratios three groups of countries can be distinguished. In Denmark, Belgium, Ireland, and the UK there is a rather strong association between the employment statuses of husbands and wives with odds ratios between 3.2 and 5.1. In The Netherlands and Portugal the association is moderate with odds ratios 1.8 and 2.0. In the other countries the association is weak or non-existing: in France, Germany, Greece, Italy, Luxembourg, and Spain a person's probability of being non-employed is hardly affected by the non-employment of his or her spouse.

The second panel of figures in Table 13.2 refers only to couples in which both spouses are either employed or unemployed only, and focuses on the contrast of employment against unemployment: the odds ratios here are considerably higher than for non-employment against employment. However, in some countries, the odds ratios are still rather low. In France, Greece, Italy, and Spain the odds ratios are 3.2 or lower. In Belgium, Denmark, and Luxembourg the odds ratios are very strong, between 5.7 and 12.1. The countries in between are Germany, Ireland, The Netherlands, Portugal, and the UK.

We conclude this descriptive section by noting that not many couples are characterized by double non-employment or double unemployment. In all

---

[2] An odds ratio is computed by the formula $(p/(1 - p)) / (q/(1 - q))$, in which p is the probability that the spouses of an employed spouse is employed, and q is the probability that the spouse of a non-employed spouse is employed.

TABLE 13.2. *Association between spouses' employment status in twelve European countries, both spouses 25–54 years old*

	Belgium	Denmark	France	Germany	Greece	Ireland	Italy	Luxembourg	Netherlands	Portugal	Spain	United Kingdom
Non-employment vs. employment												
Odds ratio	3.8	3.9	1.2	1.1	1.0	3.2	1.4	0.9	1.8	2.0	1.0	5.1
Unemployment vs. employment[a]												
Odds ratio	5.7	5.7	2.4	3.5	2.8	4.7	3.2	12.1	2.2	4.1	3.1	4.3

[a] inactive persons omitted.
Source: ECHP (1994).

twelve 1994 EU countries the lion's share of people who live in couples and who are between 25 and 54 years old are strongly attached to the labour market, either themselves or via their partners. Nonetheless, we must acknowledge that a small proportion of couples with double unemployment may reflect a serious social problem. Double non-employment may not happen very often to couples, but at the same time it is clear that the labour market positions of spouses are moderately to strongly associated. In times with higher unemployment rates, like the double-digit period of the 1980s, double unemployment or double non-employment may be an even stronger social problem than it is today. If one spouse is not employed, the probability that the other spouse is not employed is relatively large. How this association occurs will be the focus of the next section of the chapter.

THE ASSOCIATION BETWEEN THE EMPLOYMENT STATUS OF HUSBANDS AND WIVES EXPLAINED

In order to test the hypotheses that homogamy, income, and regional unemployment rates explain the association between the employment statuses of husbands and wives, we need to estimate multivariate statistical models. The statistical models predict a person's employment status from a set of variables. This set of variables includes an individual's own and spouse's level of education, spouse's income quartile, and the regional unemployment rate.[3] If the hypotheses hold, and offer a complete explanation for the association between the employment statuses of husbands and wives, the multivariate regression models would display no differences in the employment status of persons with employed spouses, unemployed spouse, or inactive spouses. The absence of differences would show up in our multivariate models as insignificant effects of spouse's employment status.

In Table 13.3 a combined regression analysis of couples in eleven countries is performed. Germany is excluded as the data were not available as part of the 'pooled' data set (see note 1). The outcomes of this analysis give a first impression of the tenability of our hypotheses. In Table 13.3 four regression models are presented (logistic regression equations). In the first model we investigate whether husband's non-employment can be predicted by the

---

[3] The model also includes controls for own and spouse's age and for the family cycle. Three age groups are distinguished: 25 to 34 years old, 35 to 44 years old, and 45 to 54 years old. Family cycle refers to the age of the youngest child. It has four categories: youngest child younger than 4 years old, youngest child between 5 to 12 years old, youngest child between 13 to 16 years old, and no child younger than 17 present.

TABLE 13.3. *Effects of personal characteristics, partner's characteristics, and regional unemployment on non-employment and unemployment, for husbands and wives*

	Husband		Wife	
	Non-employment	Unemployment	Non-employment	Unemployment
Country	**	**	**	**
(reference) Belgium	0	0	0	0
Denmark	0.72**	0.82**	−0.62**	0.06
France	0.27	0.48*	0.13	0.71**
Greece	0.31	0.62**	1.12**	1.48**
Ireland	0.34	0.68**	0.76**	−0.06
Italy	0.17	−0.06	0.72**	0.51**
Luxembourg	0.12	−0.12	0.99**	0.16
Netherlands	0.46*	0.33	0.67**	0.51*
Portugal	0.06	−0.27	0.03	0.22
Spain	−0.01	−0.10	0.55**	0.85**
United Kingdom	1.12**	1.25**	0.24**	0.08
Educational attainment	**	**	**	**
(reference) primary	0	0	0	0
low secondary	−0.29**	−0.33**	−0.22**	0.11
high secondary	−0.57**	−0.51**	−0.83**	−0.34**
tertiary	−1.09**	−1.05**	−1.73**	−0.58**
Partner's employment status	**	**	**	**
(reference) employed	0	0	0	0
unemployed	1.00**	1.14**	0.44**	0.98**
inactive	0.54**	0.32**	0.51**	0.04
Partner's educational attainment	**	**	**	*
(reference) primary	0	0	0	0
low secondary	−0.27**	−0.24*	−0.14*	−0.03
high secondary	−0.69**	−0.67**	−0.27**	−0.16
tertiary	−0.65**	−0.53**	−0.27**	−0.38**
Partner's income	**	**	**	
(reference) first quartile	0	0	0	0
second quartile	0.03	−0.03	0.08	0.04
third quartile	−0.01	−0.18	0.23**	0.02
fourth quartile	0.11	−0.11	0.54**	−0.13
missing	−0.59**	−0.69**	−0.02	−0.49*
Regional unemployment rate	0.05**	0.08**	0.05**	0.05**
Constant	−2.86**	−3.52**	−1.44**	−2.92**
−2 log likelihood	9145.46	6090.41	21926.54	6817.99
chi-square improvement	793.61	612.79	3439.51	751.62
df	30	30	30	30
prob	0.000	0.000	0.000	0.000
improvement for effects per country	414.35	350.65	677.24	299.53
df	197	197	197	197
prob	0.000	0.000	0.000	0.000

Notes: Data for Germany was not available for this analysis. Additional controls: age, partner's age, family cycle.
* = $P < 0.05$, ** = $P < 0.01$.
Source: ECHP (1994).

wife's employment status, after we have statistically accounted for educational homogamy, spouse's income, and regional unemployment. In the second model we do the same, but focus on the husband's unemployment. In an analogous way, the third and fourth models predict the wife's employment status. All four models also include an indicator for each of the eleven countries to which our data refer.

We have three hypotheses on factors—own and spouse's educational attainment, spouse's income, and regional unemployment—which add to a positive relationship between the employment statuses of husbands and wives. The results of the combined analysis of Table 13.3 suggest that all three of them have significant and interesting effects.

To begin with, the models of Table 13.3 show that both a person's own educational attainment and his or her spouse's educational attainment have the expected negative effects on non-employment and unemployment. At the level of secondary education the effect of the wife's level of schooling on her husband's employment status is equal to the effect of the husband's own level of schooling; and at the tertiary level, the effect of the wife's education is about half of the effect of her husband's own level of schooling. The negative effects of the husband's schooling on his wife's unemployment are considerably smaller. Apparently, wives affect their husbands' employment status more strongly than husbands affect their wives' employment status. The effects of a spouse's educational attainment are a remarkable result. Often, educational attainment is seen as just a human capital variable which affects the occupational career because it represents productivity, but it is an important resource for the furtherance of the spouse's career as well. All the effects of educational attainment together mean that educational homogamy gives an important contribution to the positive relationship between the employment statuses of husbands and wives.

In the second place Table 13.3 focuses on the impact of the spouse's financial situation. For all eleven countries together, the husbands' employment status is not affected by the size of the wife's personal income, but only by the question of whether she has an income or not. When his wife has no income, the probability that a man has a job is significantly higher than when she has an income. The third and fourth regression models focus on the wife's employment position. The spouses of men with more than median incomes have a higher probability to be inactive. This points towards the persistence of traditional roles: when the husband is able to make a decent living, his wife can withdraw from the labour market. Indeed, this finding was predicted by our economic hypothesis: if the husband is doing well on the labour market, the wife has less incentive to participate, and if the husband is not making enough money, she has a stronger tendency to have a job.

In the third place, Table 13.3 shows that the regional unemployment rate adds to double employment in couples. The regional unemployment rate has a positive effect on the probability to be non-employed or unemployed, again both for husbands and for wives, and because husbands and wives live in the same household, and thus in the same region, this will contribute to the positive association as well.

However these various factors do not fully explain the association between the employment statuses of husbands and wives in this combined eleven-country analysis. Table 13.3 shows that after controlling for the effects of homogamy, income, and region, husbands of unemployed or inactive wives still have a smaller probability to be employed, and also wives of non-employed husbands work less frequently than wives of employed husbands. This raises the question how the remaining association is to be explained. The combined analysis of Table 13.3 cannot address the question of differences between countries; it just gives an overall impression of the tenability of our assumptions.

Now we proceed to a more detailed analysis at the country level. In Tables 13A, 13B, 13C, and 13D in the appendix to this chapter, the results of the same four regression equations are displayed, but this time separately for each country, and thus we can include Germany in the analysis again. These tables give country-specific numbers for the four regression models in the four columns of Table 13.3.

We will first concentrate on the various effects on husband's non-employment, in Table 13A. Husband's own educational attainment has negative effects on the non-employment of men in all but three countries: Denmark, Greece, and Portugal. Although the wife's educational attainment has negative effects, reducing the probability that the husband will be non-employed, in all twelve countries, the effect is significant only in France, Ireland, and Spain. In this country-specific analysis, the wife's income situation has a significant negative effect only in Italy and Spain. The regional unemployment rate has the predicted positive effects on husband's non-employment in four countries, Germany, Italy, Spain, and the UK. According to Table 13A, in a majority of the countries the wife's employment has a direct positive effect on her husband's participation, after all explanatory variables have been accounted for. The remarkable exception is Spain, where the relationship is significantly negative. These direct effects show that men of inactive and unemployed wives have significantly higher probabilities to be non-employed as well.

Focusing on husband's unemployment instead of non-employment in Table 13B, we observe the same pattern. Own educational attainment affects the unemployment probability of men significantly in most countries, but wife's level of schooling has only direct negative effects in France, Ireland, and Spain. Wife's income has negative effects in Greece and Italy only. Regional unemployment has significant positive effects in Germany, Italy, and Spain only. After controls for educational homogamy, wife's income, and regional unemployment, wife's employment has effects in all countries except Germany, Italy, and Luxembourg.

Next, we move on to the determinants of wives' labour market participation. This is a more informative analysis than the analysis for men. The inter-country variation in married women's participation rates is much

higher than the inter-country variation in men's participation rates, and institutional differences will affect women more strongly than men. This becomes
immediately visible when we inspect the figures in Tables 13C and 13D: there
are more significant effects to be found than in Tables 13.3 and 13A, both
of the wife's own characteristics and of the husband's characteristics.

Table 13C focuses on the determinants of wife's non-employment. Own
educational attainment has strong effects in all countries. The higher a
married or cohabiting woman's level of schooling, the higher the likelihood
that she is employed. We expect that the wives of higher-educated men will
participate more frequently in the labour market than the wives of lower-
educated men, but this expectation is supported by the data only in France,
Greece, and Portugal. The personal income of the husband increases a
wife's chances of non-employment in most countries. Only in Denmark and
Portugal do we not find that the wives of husbands with the higher incomes
tend to refrain from participating in the labour market. It is in only in Greece
and Spain that the wives of the husbands in the lowest income quartile are
more likely to participate than the wives of the men who belong to the one
but lowest quartile. In Belgium, France, Italy, and Spain, effects of the regional
unemployment rate are significant and as expected.

After controlling for own and husband's education, husband's income, and
regional variation in unemployment, the husband's employment status still
has its own effect in five out of the twelve countries: Belgium, Denmark,
Ireland, The Netherlands, and the UK.

Table 13D presents the effects on married women's unemployment probabilities in the twelve countries. Broadly speaking, we observe the same effects
as in the analysis of non-employment in Table 13C, although less pronounced.

How are the observed differences between countries to be explained? It
will be clear that the differences in the association between the employment
statuses of spouses cannot fully be accounted for by postulating that patterns of homogamy, spouse's income, and regional unemployment differ
between countries. The effects of one spouse's employment status on the other
spouse's employment status vary between countries, and we must look for
other explanations for the observed country differences. Before we go into
institutional explanations of the variation, we will first address one structural explanation. The hypothesis is that when female employment, or more
specifically, married women's employment, is high in a country, resources
become more important to be successful on the labour market. In Fig. 13B
we get a picture of the tenability of this hypothesis. Fig. 13B displays the
association between the labour market participation of all married women
between ages 25 and 54 in the twelve EU countries; and the association between the non-employment status of spouses, expressed as the gross odds ratio,
not controlled for the three sets of explanatory variables. The association is

Paul de Graaf and Wout Ultee

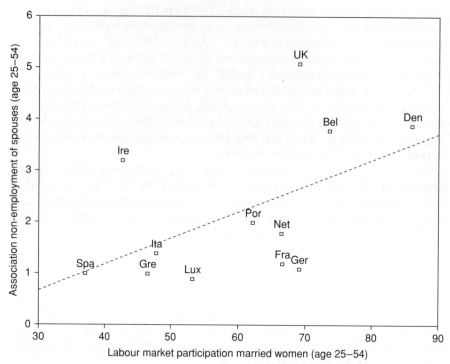

FIG. 13B. The relationship between married women's labour market participation
and the association between spouses' employment positions

Note: Correlation = 0.58.

rather strong, as indicated by the Pearson's correlation coefficient of 0.58. Indeed, the association is stronger if more married women have jobs.

Although the association is rather strong, there are interesting deviations from the general linear relationship. In the first place, Ireland and the UK, and to a lesser extent Belgium, are characterized by a stronger association than expected by the structural explanation. In the UK, eligibility to social security is strongly affected by the spouses' employment status. The unemployed receive higher social benefits if they have a dependent spouse. This additional money destroys the incentive to work for the dependent spouse, because finding a job would lead to losing the extra income. The other way around, employed women whose husbands lose their jobs, will have a relatively strong incentive to become unemployed as well, because then their husbands will receive higher social benefits. The UK seems to be unique as regards these regulations. If our institutional explanation holds, the social security system or tax regime of Ireland and Belgium should also produce more than average negative incentives for the spouses of the unemployed to participate on the labour market.

CONCLUSION

Does unemployment come in couples? Yes, it does. When one spouse is unemployed, there is a relatively high probability that the other spouse is unemployed as well. This holds in all twelve member states of the European Union in 1994. In this way we have shown the effects of what is nowadays called social capital. Yet, we were not able to show which kind of social capital is most important. Is it knowledge about vacancies provided by spouses, help when writing an application, or recommendation?

Does double unemployment vary between countries? Yes, again. Although double unemployment is to be observed in all countries, we find differences between countries as well. They still persist after individual characteristics of both spouses have been taken into account, as well as educational homogamy, spouse's income, and regional unemployment rates. The association is strongest in those countries in which female employment rates, especially married women's employment rates are high. At one end of the spectrum there are countries, to be found in Southern Europe, where the labour market participation of married women is low, and the association between spouses' employment statuses is low as well. At the other end of the spectrum, in countries like Denmark and Belgium, the employment rates of married women are high, and the association between spouses' employment statuses is high as well. It appears that in countries in which employment of married women has become part of the standard lifestyle of couples, the effects of available resources are stronger than in countries where the employment of married women is not part of this standard lifestyle.

Do institutions matter, when explaining differences between countries in double unemployment? Yes, it seems so. Deviations from the hypothesis that double unemployment is stronger when overall female labour market participation is higher, suggest that regulations about eligibility to unemployment benefits contribute to the explanation of inter-country differences. The prime deviation we found was the UK, where spouses are not treated individually by the social security system.

For the future we have established a topic worthy of investigation: the extent to which the countries of the European Union differ in double unemployment. A prime issue in this respect is whether structural explanations can be separated from institutional explanations. After all, the percentage of working wives may be viewed as an institutional outcome. Another issue is the addition of a dimension to current typologies of welfare states. In the 1990s, the dimension of inter-generational autonomy has been added to existing political theories of differences in welfare regimes. Here, we suggest that future research should incorporate the dimension of 'spousal autonomy': the degree to which spouses are treated as dependent or independent by social security systems.

APPENDIX

TABLE 13A. *Non-employment of husbands: effects of own characteristics, wife's characteristics, and regional unemployment rate*

	Belgium	Denmark	France	Germany	Greece	Ireland	Italy	Luxemb.	Netherland	Portugal	Spain	United Kingdom
Educational attainment	**		**			**	**		**		**	**
(reference) primary	0	0	0	0	0	0	0	0	0	0	0	0
low secondary	-1.06*	0.29	-0.36	-1.78**	0.19	-1.31**	-0.36	-0.58	-0.72	0.01	-0.03	-0.63
high secondary	-1.73**	-0.27	-0.76**	-1.97**	0.13	-0.90**	-0.77**	-0.83	-1.11**	0.08	-0.31	-0.85
tertiary	-1.94**	-0.35	-1.05**	-2.33**	-0.42	-1.81**	-1.79**	-2.62*	-1.40**	-0.43	-0.95**	-1.72**
Wife's employment status	**	*	**		*	**	**			**		**
(reference) employed	0	0	0	0	0	0	0	0	0	0	0	0
unemployed	2.10**	0.95	0.55*	0.60	0.73*	1.66**	0.77**	1.94	0.80	1.18*	0.37	1.84**
inactive	1.64**	0.98**	-0.47	0.09	0.49	0.91**	0.18	0.16	0.57	0.75*	-0.40*	1.57**
Wife's educational attainment		*	*			**						**
(reference) primary	0	0	0	0	0	0	0	0	0	0	0	0
low secondary	-0.61	-0.27	-0.36	-0.92	-0.13	-0.93**	-0.04	-0.68	-0.48	-0.88	-0.26	0.46
high secondary	-0.01	-0.96*	-0.78**	-0.54	-0.12	-1.40**	-0.32	-1.07	-0.58	-1.10	-0.68**	-0.22
tertiary	-0.12	-0.87	-0.70*	-0.74	-0.22	-1.13*	-0.76	-1.37	-0.87	-0.98	-0.57*	-0.36
Wife's income					**		**	*				
(reference) first quartile	0	0	0	0	0	0	0	0	0	0	0	0
second quartile	0.34	-0.21	0.16	-0.02	1.04**	0.36	-0.53	0.15	0.34	0.19	0.01	-0.39
third quartile	0.49	-0.85*	-0.24	-0.35	0.97*	0.72*	-0.68	1.59	0.13	0.29	-0.05	-0.19
fourth quartile	0.52	-0.69	0.31	0.10	0.32	0.66	0.01	3.37**	0.68	0.11	-0.41	0.23
missing	-0.16	-0.60	0.26		-0.44	0.82*	-0.86**	1.07	0.26	-0.47	-0.42*	-0.20
Regional unemployment rate	0.04	n/a	0.05	0.08**	-0.01	n/a	0.05**	n/a	0.13	0.03	0.06**	0.08*
Constant	-3.85**	-1.14	-2.10**	-0.40	-3.57**	-1.41**	-2.70**	-3.63**	-3.53**	-3.81**	-2.72**	-2.43**
-2 log likelihood	349.67	446.23	1047.62	681.60	796.04	778.42	1203.98	120.08	518.74	675.28	1721.28	1073.78
chi-square improvement	68.57	44.38	65.27	55.68	58.03	158.60	149.83	28.18	45.06	61.30	154.37	199.49
df	20	19	20	20	20	19	20	19	20	20	20	20
prob	0.000	0.001	0.000	0.000	0.000	0.000	0.000	0.080	0.001	0.000	0.000	0.000

Notes: n/a = no regional unemployment rate available; * P < 0.05, ** P < 0.01; additional controls: age, partner's age, family cycle.
Source: ECHP (1994).

TABLE 13B. *Unemployment of husbands: effects of own characteristics, wife's characteristics, and regional unemployment rate*

	Belgium	Denmark	France	Germany	Greece	Ireland	Italy	Luxemb.	Netherland	Portugal	Spain	United Kingdom
Educational attainment	**		**			**	*				*	**
(reference) primary	0	0	0	0	0	0	0	0	0	0	0	0
low secondary	-1.66**	-0.25	-0.35	-2.45**	0.22	-0.99**	-0.78*	-9.89	0.40	-0.20	0.00	-0.53
high secondary	-2.16**	-0.62	-0.80**	-2.93**	0.41	-0.67*	-1.07**	-2.31	-0.56	0.48	-0.24	-0.59
tertiary	-2.34**	-0.52	-1.34**	-2.87**	-0.28	-1.91**	-1.68**	-1.19	-0.46	-7.37	-0.90**	-1.65*
Wife's employment status	**	*	**			**				*	**	**
(reference) employed	0	0	0	0	0	0	0	0	0	0	0	0
unemployed	2.68**	1.31*	0.53	0.71	0.97**	1.76**	0.70	5.09	1.56*	1.65**	0.46*	2.14**
inactive	1.62**	-0.61	-1.01**	0.21	0.43	0.69*	-0.17	0.11	1.05	0.83	-0.56*	1.59**
Wife's educational attainment					**	**						**
(reference) primary	0	0	0	0	0	0	0	0	0	0	0	0
low secondary	0.71	-0.44	-0.19	-1.25	-0.06	-1.13**	-0.42	0.65	0.30	-1.46	-0.14	0.50
high secondary	1.40	-1.02	-0.70*	-0.66	-0.19	-1.61**	-0.80	0.58	-0.03	-1.12	-0.60*	0.08
tertiary	1.26	-0.70	-0.84*	-1.00	-0.05	-1.69**	-0.46	-9.90	0.19	2.43	-0.47	-0.11
Wife's income							**					
(reference) first quartile	0	0	0	0	0	0	0	0	0	0	0	0
second quartile	0.42	-0.15	0.09	0.03	0.86*	0.26	-0.87	0.00	-0.54	0.37	0.15	-0.55
third quartile	0.15	-1.71*	-0.27	-0.62	0.58	0.40	-1.03	10.11	0.09	0.33	-0.01	-0.27
fourth quartile	0.66	-0.74	0.50	0.20	-0.35	0.31	-0.35	11.94	-0.16	-8.12	-0.20	0.10
missing	-0.41	-4.71	0.48		-0.55	0.65	-1.25**	11.07	-0.75	-0.72	-0.24	-0.97
Regional unemployment rate	0.09	n/a	0.08	0.13**	0.00	n/a	0.10**	n/a	0.26	0.14	0.08**	0.05
Constant	-5.25**	-0.83	-2.67**	-1.00	-3.82**	-1.32*	-2.75**	-13.54	-6.38**	-5.92**	-3.43**	-3.03**
–2 log likelihood	218.13	292.50	787.53	389.07	583.16	621.01	602.18	37.66	266.25	274.37	1315.98	740.99
chi-square improvement	44.06	34.13	70.46	56.92	36.23	139.43	95.43	24.76	22.90	40.35	113.13	129.38
df	20	19	20	20	20	19	20	19	20	20	20	20
prob	0.002	0.018	0.000	0.000	0.014	0.000	0.000	0.169	0.294	0.005	0.000	0.000

Notes: n/a = no regional unemployment rate available; * P < 0.05; ** P < 0.01; additional controls: age, partner's age, family cycle.
Source: ECHP (1994).

TABLE 13C. *Non-employment of wives: effects of own characteristics, husband's characteristics, and regional unemployment rate*

	Belgium	Denmark	France	Germany	Greece	Ireland	Italy	Luxemb	Netherland	Portugal	Spain	United Kingdom
Educational attainment	**	**	**		**	**	**	**	**	**	**	**
(reference) primary	0	0	0	0	0	0	0	0	0	0	0	0
low secondary	-0.41	-0.82*	-0.12	-0.86*	0.01	-0.16	-0.41**	-0.16	-0.51*	-0.70**	-0.08	-0.64
high secondary	-0.88**	-0.70*	-0.59**	-0.91*	-0.34*	-1.00**	-1.54**	-0.71*	-0.82**	-0.73**	-0.80**	-0.99*
tertiary	-1.96**	-1.21**	-1.61**	-1.75**	-1.32**	-2.24**	-2.46**	-2.56**	-1.63**	-3.08**	-1.84**	-1.56**
Husband's employment status	**	0	0	0		**			*			**
(reference) employed	0	0	0	0	0	0	0	0	0	0	0	0
unemployed	1.74**	0.61	-0.12	0.48	0.30	0.89**	-0.41	0.73	0.99*	0.53	-0.21	1.68**
inactive	1.42**	1.62**	0.59	0.18	-0.15	1.04*	0.20	-0.29	0.62	0.40	-0.21	1.47**
Husband's educational attainment		**	**	0	*					*		
(reference) primary	0	0	0	0	0	0	0	0	0	0	0	0
low secondary	-0.17	0.00	-0.51**	0.19	0.02	-0.25	0.00	0.38	-0.34	-0.25	-0.05	-0.36
high secondary	-0.20	-0.20	-0.52**	-0.08	0.22	-0.35*	-0.15	0.05	-0.51*	-0.90**	-0.25	-0.32
tertiary	-0.38	-0.62	-0.33	-0.06	-0.22	-0.57*	-0.27	0.12	-0.56*	-0.24	-0.19	-0.10
Husband's income	*		**	0	*	**	**		**		**	**
(reference) first quartile	0	0	0	0	0	0	0	0	0	0	0	0
second quartile	-0.07	-0.20	0.03	0.15	0.34*	-0.01	0.05	0.23	0.25	-0.10	0.31*	-0.14
third quartile	0.31	-0.19	0.28*	0.01	0.40**	0.24	0.30*	0.89*	0.53**	-0.11	0.39**	-0.28
fourth quartile	0.54*	-0.09	0.91**	0.45**	0.52**	0.90**	0.80**	0.83*	0.73**	0.19	0.35*	0.38*
missing	-0.39	-0.37	0.81*		0.47	-1.81*	0.22	-0.20	0.40	-0.91**	-0.47	0.15
Regional unemployment rate	0.05*	n/a	0.13**	-0.03	0.01	n/a	0.07**	n/a	-0.09	0.05	0.03**	0.03
Constant	-1.57**	-0.67	-2.18**	-0.87	0.02	-0.64*	-0.55**	-1.19**	-0.13	-1.06**	-0.11	-1.34*
-2 log likelihood	1186.62	731.99	2661.26	2141.51	2315.37	1721.26	3343.80	487.06	1891.42	1831.52	3141.09	1937.90
chi-square improvement	226.08	68.51	267.25	194.90	164.15	300.62	500.38	88.01	161.86	169.99	372.42	311.06
df	20	19	20	20	20	19	20	19	20	20	20	20
prob	0.000	0.000	0.000	0.000	0.000	0.000	0.000	0.000	0.000	0.000	0.000	0.000

Notes: n/a = no regional unemployment rate available; * P < 0.05; ** P < 0.01.
Source: ECHP (1994).

TABLE 13D. *Unemployment of wives: effects of own characteristics, husband's characteristics, and regional unemployment rate*

	Belgium	Denmark	France	Germany	Greece	Ireland	Italy	Luxemb.	Netherland	Portugal	Spain	United Kingdom
Educational attainment	**		*			**	**		*			
(reference) primary	0	0	0	0	0	0	0	0	0	0	0	0
low secondary	0.10	-0.60	0.25	-1.06	0.14	0.30	0.22	0.40	0.15	0.24	0.12	-0.78
high secondary	0.16	-0.49	-0.10	-0.65	-0.28	-1.18*	-0.56	-1.51	-0.91*	-0.47	-0.19	-0.69
tertiary	-0.82	-0.91	-0.65*	-1.22	-0.42	-1.38	-0.64	-0.58	-0.59	-6.62	-0.46*	-0.51
Husband's employment status	**	**				**	**			*		**
(reference) employed	0	0	0	0	0	0	0	0	0	0	0	0
unemployed	2.49**	1.66**	0.52	0.60	0.79*	1.63**	0.50	3.54	1.31	1.54**	0.45*	2.10**
inactive	-4.30	-5.29	0.38	0.50	-0.37	-4.23	0.29	-8.75	0.75	0.52	-0.16	0.86
Husband's educational attainment					*							
(reference) primary	0	0	0	0	0	0	0	0	0	0	0	0
low secondary	0.19	1.50	-0.63	-0.66	-0.25	0.31	-0.35	-8.87	-0.03	0.69	0.10	4.13
high secondary	0.43	0.79	-0.43*	-1.62	0.27	0.20	-0.42	-0.02	-0.46	-0.48	-0.32	4.08
tertiary	0.15	0.27	-0.45	-1.60	-0.49	0.31	-0.93	-1.22	-0.52	-6.01	-0.34	4.03
Husband's income	**										**	**
(reference) first quartile	0	0	0	0	0	0	0	0	0	0	0	0
second quartile	-0.02	-0.89	-0.09	0.36	0.39	0.37	0.00	-9.45	0.09	0.14	0.14	-0.44
third quartile	0.05	-0.53	-0.19	-0.78	0.12	-0.05	-0.04	0.44	0.10	0.12	0.12	0.05
fourth quartile	-1.92*	0.17	0.18	-0.08	-0.05	0.39	-0.23	-0.48	0.15	0.09	-0.64*	0.35
missing	-1.09	-5.59	0.12		0.34	0.35	-0.66	-8.34	-5.38	-7.58	-0.59	0.69
Regional unemployment rate	0.09	n/a	0.06	0.21**	-0.01	n/a	0.10**	n/a	0.05	0.22**	0.03*	-0.01
Constant	-4.23**	-2.86**	-1.81**	-2.92**	-0.97*	-2.91**	-2.37**	-2.19*	-2.24	-3.93**	-1.47**	-6.92
-2 log likelihood	335.57	300.12	1116.49	404.98	914.02	284.04	829.27	56.39	477.47	421.52	1298.88	484.70
chi-square improvement	48.94	34.29	63.00	95.88	47.44	47.06	105.75	25.97	27.08	60.97	97.67	66.56
df	20	19	20	20	20	19	20	19	20	20	20	20
prob	0.000	0.017	0.000	0.000	0.001	0.000	0.000	0.131	0.133	0.000	0.000	0.000

Notes: n/a = no regional unemployment rate available; * P < 0.05, ** P < 0.01.
Source: ECHP (1994).

14

Unemployment and Satisfaction: A European Analysis

Christopher T. Whelan and Frances McGinnity

INTRODUCTION

In this chapter we draw on the first wave of the European Community Household Panel (ECHP) study carried out in 1994 to examine cross-national variation in the impact of unemployment on satisfaction.[1] There is a widespread belief in Western society that paid employment is a necessity and an assumption that most adults want and indeed, need to 'work' in the sense of having paid employment. Of course many people are willing to make exceptions to the view that work is necessary, most notably in the case of women with young children, but also in such cases as older members of the labour force. Such evaluations can obviously vary both across time and between societies. The stigma associated with unemployment may also vary with the extent of the employment opportunities available in a particular location and society. This ideological background provides the context in which evaluations of the impact of employment must take place.

There now exists a substantial body of literature that documents the consequences of unemployment for subjective well-being (Warr 1987; Clark and Oswald 1994). Longitudinal analysis supports the argument that the direction of causality is from job loss to a reduced perception of well-being (Kessler *et al.* 1989; Kasl and Kobb 1979; Liem 1987). Theoretical explanations of the manner in which joblessness may lead to a decline in subjective well being have been dominated by the contributions of psychologists. Jahoda (1988, 1992) has argued that both the manifest and latent consequences of work are essential to the development of a favourable perception of self. The latent or hidden benefits include social contact, activity, status, purposefulness, and time structure. Others have followed Jahoda in making psychological, rather than material deprivation, theoretically central. Warr (1987)

---

[1] The analysis of German data reported in this paper was conducted by Konstanze Möersdorf from Goethe University, Frankfurt on Main.

suggests that psychological well-being is negatively affected by unemployment because, in addition to experiencing the loss of the psychological and material benefits offered by employment, the role of being unemployed also involves a set of tasks which are potentially unpleasant or threatening.

More recently a number of authors have argued that the dominant psychological approaches have underestimated the role which material deprivation plays in mediating the impact of unemployment. Kelvin and Jarrett (1985) noted that while there was widespread recognition that unemployment brings both economic and psychological problems, consideration of the relationship between them was remarkably rare. Similarly Fryer (1986, 1990) in a number of publications drew attention to the fact that while financial hardship was frequently referred to in the literature, it was seldom allocated a central role. Despite the evidence that unemployment in the 1980s still involved the manifest consequences of a substantial reduction in income, sight was lost of the potential impact of declining economic resources on psychological functioning. Notwithstanding the plausibility of this argument, a number of studies employing both cross-sectional and panel designs have failed to establish any significant mediating role for income (Clark and Oswald 1994; Clark 1998; Winkelman and Winkelman 1998). However, other work focusing on lifestyle deprivation has provided evidence for the psychological consequences of economic hardship (Pearlin 1989; Whelan 1992, 1994). Our analysis will address both types of relationship.

CROSS-NATIONAL VARIATION IN THE PSYCHOLOGICAL IMPACT OF UNEMPLOYMENT

While substantial progress has been made in developing our knowledge of the psychological consequences of unemployment, we know very little about the extent to which such impact varies across countries. Is the distress that unemployment brings broadly similar across societies, or is its impact much sharper in some societies than in others? Gallie and Russell (1998) identify four types of factors that might be expected to lead to marked differences between countries. The most important from the perspective of this volume is related to the nature of the welfare system

1. *The relative generosity of welfare systems.* Does the impact of unemployment vary across welfare regimes and if so what are the mediating factors? In the opening chapter to this volume it was stressed that our central concern was with those aspects of welfare regimes that provide protection from the misfortunes of the labour market, in particular the system of financial support for the unemployed. The most crucial aspect is the degree of coverage. Dependence on 'assistance' rather than 'benefit' is likely to be

associated with a perceived loss of status. The second element of financial support relates to the level of financial compensation. Provision of a high replacement rate over a relatively long period enables the unemployed to maintain their lifestyle, and the absence of visible signs of their changed employment status would seem likely to minimize the degree of stigmatization to which they are exposed. As the discussion in the opening chapter makes clear, these considerations would lead us to expect the psychological impact of unemployment to be weakest in universalistic welfare regimes where coverage is comprehensive, and the level and duration of cover is high. The next most favourable situation relates to employment-centred regimes where a more heterogeneous situation is observed in that coverage is variable, and the level and duration of provision are unequal. In the liberal/minimal regime coverage is incomplete, and the level and duration of cover of provision are weak. Finally in sub-protective regimes coverage is very incomplete, and the level and duration of cover very weak. To the extent that material deprivation is a major factor in determining life satisfaction, we would expect the impact of unemployment to vary systematically across regime types by the relative generosity of welfare systems: displaying its weakest effect in universalistic regimes and being most damaging in sub-protective regimes. In particular we might expect a contrast to emerge between high and low welfare regimes. Gallie and Russell (1998) identify six of the twelve countries included in our analysis as low welfare regimes: Italy, Greece, Portugal, and Spain fall into this category due to their poor coverage as do the UK and Ireland because of the exceptionally low income they provide.

2. *The level of unemployment.* High levels of unemployment, and in particular, significant levels of long-term unemployment, could heighten levels of psychological distress, reduce levels of self-esteem, and minimize satisfaction. Alternatively, the existence of widespread unemployment could encourage a process of adaptation, and a reduction in the extent to which joblessness is experienced as stigmatizing. On this basis we might expect high unemployment countries like Spain, Ireland, and Italy to contrast sharply with low employment countries such as Portugal, Germany, and The Netherlands.[2]

3. *The composition of the unemployed.* There are significant variations across societies. From the point of subjective well-being perhaps the most important differences relate to age and gender. Much available evidence suggests that the psychological consequences of unemployment are different for men and women and for different age groups. Such differences may arise because of the variable economic and cultural consequences of unemployment, the degree of cross-national variation in the composition of the

---

[2] For further details see Gallie and Russell (1998: Table 6).

unemployed in terms of age and gender, the extent to which the impact of unemployment on satisfaction varies across age-groups, and the degree to which any such interaction between age and unemployment varies across countries. The second and third conditions will be considered in our subsequent analysis. With regard to the first, while in all of the countries in the EU, unemployment is disproportionately located among the younger groups, this is particularly so in the Southern countries and in Ireland. There is also significant variation in gender composition with a majority of the unemployed being women in Belgium, Greece, Italy, France, and Portugal, and men in Ireland.[3]

4. *The cultural importance attached to work*. Marsh and Alvaro (1990) in a comparative analysis of Spain and the United Kingdom explored the possibility that variation in the strength of the work ethic might be an important mediating factor. Gallie and Russell (1998) in a recent analysis subjected the hypothesis to further examination, with respect to a much wider range of European countries. Both of these studies draw on specific measures of the work ethic of individuals that are unavailable to us. It is still possible to interpret cross-natural differences in cultural terms, although, in the absence of appropriate measures, there are dangers involved in any such enterprise with the ever-present risk that explanation may collapse into tautology.

DATA

In what follows we endeavour to test the hypotheses that have been outlined up to this point by making use of the first wave of the ECHP panel study for eleven counties.[4] In conducting our analysis we employ the individual and household weights designed to ensure representative samples within countries. The results we report are therefore based on an overall sample of 58,143, comprising 51,199 employees and 6,944 unemployed.[5] In pursuing the issues we have outlined we are constrained by the data available in the ECHP survey. At this point we wish to document the key variables to be employed in our analysis.

---

[3] See Gallie and Russell (1998:14–18) for a more detailed discussion.

[4] Data for twelve countries were available as part of the joint ECHP data set. The German data set was analysed separately by the German team. As a consequence cross-national multivariate analysis reported later in this paper will not include the German data. We will, however, draw on the German analysis in order to consider the implications of this omission. Luxembourg has been excluded because its unique situation makes comparisons problematic.

[5] Where Germany is excluded from the analysis the relevant figures are 52,034, comprising 45,334, and 6,700.

Unemployment

In the present paper our analysis is restricted to employees and those who are unemployed using the International Labour Organisation (ILO) definition of employment. The unemployed are therefore not at present or normally working in a job or business, have not done any work in a job or business during the past seven days, are at present seeking employment, are available to take up employment in the next two weeks, and have taken steps during the past four weeks to find employment. One disadvantage of the ECHP data set is that we do not have a measure of length of unemployment available to us. We do, however, have some information on unemployment for each month in 1993 and an indication of whether the individual has been unemployed at any time in the previous five years.

Satisfaction

Up to this point we have talked in overall terms of psychological well-being, but in fact the measure available in the ECHP relates very specifically to satisfaction. The determinants of satisfaction are likely to be somewhat different than those for psychological distress. It easy to imagine, for example, many people who will be dissatisfied but not distressed. The measure we employ is based on the responses to three items dealing with: satisfaction with work or main daily activity, financial situation, and housing situation. Each item was allocated a score ranging from 1 to 6 on a continuum running from 'not satisfied at all' to 'fully satisfied'. A reliability analysis showed the three-item scale to have an alpha of 0.67.[6] The satisfaction score is computed as an average of these three items. In our multivariate analysis, scores are standardized for each country by taking the deviation from the mean and dividing by the standard deviation. Therefore, we are not attempting to explain country differences in average levels of satisfaction, but instead trying to assess the extent to which the *relative* impact of employment varies across countries. Standardization has the advantage that it controls for biases arising from country-specific effects that may arise from factors such as translation of terms. For ease of presentation we employ the unstandardized measure in our more descriptive analysis but will concentrate on relativities rather than absolute differences.[7]

[6] A further item dealing with satisfaction with leisure time was excluded because of the low level of correlation it exhibited with the other items.
[7] The distinction between relative and absolute satisfaction is one which is conceptually unambiguous. In practice, however, for the range of countries in our analysis a correlation of 0.9 between the standardized and unstandardized measures means that the choice of measure is one which must be made an conceptual rather than empirical grounds.

Income

Our measure of income is net monthly income at the time of interview in 1994. This is based on an overall estimate by the relevant member of the household, and is a cruder measure than those available for the calendar year 1993. While the former measures would be expected to be superior in terms of precision, the 1994 measure has significant advantages if one wishes to study the impact of current labour force status. Since our analysis suggests that our conclusions would not be significantly altered by inclusion of the 1993 measure, in what follows we make use of the 1994 measure which clearly relates to current employment status. Our analysis is based on the assumption that satisfaction will be influenced by relative income position in the national distribution rather than by absolute income or relative position in the European distribution. We therefore follow the same procedure as with our satisfaction scores.

Lifestyle Deprivation

This index is calculated from twenty-one items dealing with a range of household deprivations ranging from rather basic ones relating to heat food, clothing, and housing to less essential items such as a car, video recorder, microwave oven, and telephone. It was constructed so as to reflect as deprivation only enforced absence rather than lifestyle choice.[8] Once again our focus is on within-nation relativities. This index has an alpha coefficient of reliability of 0.79.

CROSS-NATIONAL VARIATION IN SATISFACTION

Table 14.1 shows the extent of variation in satisfaction across the eleven countries. It must be remembered that these differences are of a gross nature and do not take account of the complicating factors discussed earlier. The absolute level of satisfaction varies across countries in a manner which broadly follows a North-South continuum. However, our interest is in the relativities between employees and the unemployed. For our present purposes we summarize these by taking the ratio of the scores of the latter to the former. Perhaps the most notable feature of these results is the relatively modest range of variation in the index. Its value varies from a high of 0.81 for Denmark to a low of 0.63 for Italy. However, there is no clear North-

---

[8] For further discussion of the rationale underlying such indices see Callan *et al.* (1993) and Nolan and Whelan (1996).

TABLE 14.1. *Life satisfaction, by unemployment and country*

	Employees	Unemployed	Ratio of unemployed to employees
Belgium	4.48	3.21	0.68
Denmark	4.95	4.04	0.81
France	4.25	2.93	0.69
Germany	4.35	2.99	0.69
Greece	3.70	2.69	0.72
Ireland	4.36	2.93	0.67
Italy	3.89	2.44	0.63
Netherlands	4.75	3.80	0.80
Portugal	3.61	2.37	0.66
Spain	3.91	2.84	0.73
United Kingdom	4.23	3.02	0.71

Source: ECHP (1994).

South gradient as there was in the case of the absolute scores. Denmark and The Netherlands show the weakest effect of unemployment and Italy the strongest, but it is the constancy across nations which is most striking with the remaining eight countries having ratios which fall between 0.66 and 0.73.

It is immediately clear that there is no relationship between the extent of the relative disadvantage enjoyed by the unemployed and the national level of unemployment. Portugal and The Netherlands with low levels of unemployment are located at different ends of the spectrum.

SATISFACTION AND THE COMPOSITION OF THE UNEMPLOYED

Gender

In Table 14.2 we break down the impact of unemployment on satisfaction by gender. In every country the effect is stronger for men. In some countries, such as Portugal, Italy, and Belgium it is modest, but in others such as Germany, the UK and Ireland it is quite substantial. Therefore, the strongest effects are observed for countries where the interaction of unemployment rates and labour market participation rates ensure that women constitute a significantly lower percentage of the unemployed than in any of the other nine countries. The overall picture of a stronger impact of unemployment for men is consistent with the argument that paid employment is more crucial for male identities. However, before reaching this conclusion it will be necessary to allow for differences in the material consequences of unemployment for men and women.

TABLE 14.2. *The impact of unemployment on satisfaction,*
by gender and country

	Ratio of unemployed to employees	
	Women	Men
Belgium	0.72	0.71
Denmark	0.85	0.80
France	0.73	0.64
Germany	0.74	0.63
Greece	0.77	0.68
Ireland	0.74	0.63
Italy	0.64	0.61
Netherlands	0.83	0.77
Portugal	0.67	0.65
Spain	0.77	0.68
UK	0.80	0.67

Source: ECHP (1994).

TABLE 14.3. *The impact of unemployment on satisfaction, by age-group and country*

	Ratio of unemployed to employees		
Country/Age	Less than 30	30–49	50+
Belgium	0.75	0.71	0.73
Denmark	0.86	0.79	0.85
France	0.69	0.69	0.71
Germany	0.65	0.68	0.74
Greece	0.74	0.72	0.73
Ireland	0.69	0.66	0.68
Italy	0.65	0.60	0.68
Netherlands	0.80	0.82	0.77
Portugal	0.70	0.66	0.60
Spain	0.75	0.72	0.67
UK	0.73	0.70	0.74

Source: ECHP (1994).

Age

In Table 14.3 we break down the relationship between unemployment
and satisfaction by age-group. Contrary to the expectations arising from
our earlier discussion we find that the consequences of unemployment are
rather similar across age-groups. However, since older employees are more
satisfied than younger ones, a broadly similar impact of unemployment means
that the older unemployed are also somewhat more satisfied than their younger
counterparts.

TABLE 14.4. *The economic situation of the unemployed, by country*

	Household monthly equivalent income 1994 (in Euros)	Lifestyle deprivation (average score)	Difficulty in making ends meet (%)	Deteriorating economic situation (%)
Belgium	599	3.82	32.6	33.6
Denmark	748	3.48	26.6	40.0
France	596	4.81	41.0	52.4
Germany	498	3.95	26.7	59.0
Greece	378	7.85	72.6	63.0
Ireland	403	5.40	55.4	45.9
Italy	439	4.98	44.8	52.5
Netherlands	784	2.88	30.6	40.4
Portugal	367	8.35	53.1	67.4
Spain	421	6.39	56.1	58.5
UK	626	5.12	45.0	49.3

Source: ECHP (1994).

UNEMPLOYMENT AND ECONOMIC CIRCUMSTANCES

Economic Circumstances

The ECHP contains a variety of indicators of economic circumstances. In our multivariate analysis we will operate with standardized measures of income and deprivation, but for present purposes we continue to use the absolute measures while focusing our attention on the relativities between employees and the unemployed.[9] For descriptive purposes, Table 14.4 shows the absolute economic circumstances of the unemployed and in Table 14.5 we proceed to summarize the situation of the unemployed relative to employees in their own country.

Table 14.4 sets out monthly household equivalent disposable income at the time of interview for the unemployed.[10] The highest levels of income are observed in Denmark and The Netherlands, the next group of countries includes the UK, France, Belgium, Ireland, and Italy. The second indicator of economic standards is lifestyle deprivation where the number of items lacking runs from a low of 2.88 in The Netherlands to a high of 8.35 in Greece. The ECHP also contains a number of subjective indicators of

[9] Once again the strategy of distinguishing between absolute and relative approaches is somewhat easier in principle than in practice given the magnitude of the correlations between the indicators. For personal income it is 0.97, for equivalent income 0.94, and for lifestyle deprivation 0.90.

[10] The measure also takes into current housing benefits.

TABLE 14.5. *The impact of unemployment on economic circumstances, by country*

	Ratio of unemployed to employees			
	Household equivalent income 1994	Lifestyle deprivation	Difficulty in making ends meet (odds ratio)	Deteriorating economic situation (odds ratio)
Belgium	0.67	1.96	3.76	1.90
Denmark	0.75	2.19	2.59	3.74
France	0.72	1.76	3.27	2.04
Germany	0.68	1.91	2.18	1.72
Greece	0.76	1.31	3.23	1.83
Ireland	0.56	2.25	3.22	2.86
Italy	0.58	1.74	4.53	2.25
Netherlands	0.74	2.69	4.84	3.48
Portugal	0.80	1.24	2.93	2.87
Spain	0.65	1.46	3.09	1.95
UK	0.65	2.33	4.65	2.25

Source: ECHP (1994).

economic well-being. The first concerns the extent to which households have difficulty in making ends meet, where the percentages range from 27 per cent in Denmark to 73 per cent in Greece and Portugal. The final indicator is the perceived deterioration of economic situation in the previous year. Since the item is by definition a relative one, we would expect less variation across countries. This is indeed the case but the relative percentage still varies from 33 per cent in Belgium to 67 per cent in Portugal. The broad pattern of economic circumstances across these variables gives us four groupings of countries:

(1) Denmark, The Netherlands;
(2) UK, France, Belgium, and Germany;
(3) Ireland and Italy;
(4) Greece, Spain, and Portugal.

In Table 14.5 we turn our attention to the impact of unemployment on economic circumstances. For household equivalent income the ratio of the unemployed to employees varies from a high level of between 0.72 and 0.80 in Portugal, Greece, Denmark, The Netherlands, and France to a somewhat lower level of approximately 0.66 in Belgium, Spain and the UK; with the lowest levels of 0.58 and 0.56 being found in Ireland and Italy respectively. There is no evidence that country differences in the impact of unemployment on satisfaction are mediated by cross-national variations in the relationship between unemployment and equivalent income. The countries with the highest income ratios are located at different ends of the satisfaction spectrum.

Moving from income measures to lifestyle deprivation, France and the 'Mediterranean' countries show a significant improvement in their relative position while The Netherlands, Ireland, and the UK show deterioration. Cross-national variation in the differential impact of unemployment on income and lifestyle deprivation is something that clearly merits further investigation. However, for the moment, the important fact is that the change in pattern is not one that appears to offer further insight into the manner in which unemployment differentially impacts on satisfaction across countries.

In dealing with subjective indicators of well-being, in order to control for substantial cross-national variation in absolute percentages, we summarize our results in terms of odds ratios which are unaffected by such marginal differences and can therefore serve as valid measures of inequality. Any prospect that shifting from objective measures of economic well-being to subjective evaluations might hold the key to the relationship between unemployment and satisfaction, does not survive much beyond the observation that, for the item concerning perceived difficulty in making ends meet, the two countries exhibiting the lowest odds-ratios—Denmark and Portugal—are those where the weakest and strongest impact, respectively, of unemployment on satisfaction are observed.[11] In the light of these findings, it is hardly surprising that the item relating to deteriorating economic situation in the previous year offers no additional insights into the interaction between unemployment, satisfaction, and nationality.

A MULTIVARIATE ANALYSIS OF COMPARATIVE SATISFACTION

In our multivariate analysis of comparative satisfaction set out in Table 14.6[12] we have adopted the following procedure:[13]

1. For the analysis for which the final results are presented in equation (i) we initially allowed the impact of unemployment to vary by country.
2. We also permitted the unemployment coefficient to vary by gender, age-group and by whether or not the respondent had a partner. These effects in turn were allowed to vary across country. With regard to age-group we distinguish between those aged less than 30, those between 30 and 50, and those 50 or over. In this equation we also control for the physical health variable described below.

---

[11] Responses were dichotomized between those reporting financial difficulty and those that did not.

[12] Germany is not included in this analysis.

[13] The purpose of introducing health as a control variable is to remove any association between unemployment and satisfaction which arises not from the causal impact of the former but because poor health is likely to lead to both unemployment and lower satisfaction.

3. In equation (ii) we introduce a series of control variables relating to material circumstances:
   (a) *Health.* Where the contrast is between those who perceive their health as 'bad' or 'very bad' and all others.
   (b) *Deterioration in Economic Situation.* Comparing those who thought deterioration had occurred with all others.
   (c) *Lifestyle Deprivation.* We employ the standardized version of the variable.
   (d) *Monthly Household Equivalent Income.* At time of interview in 1994 in standardized form.
   (e) *Non-Manual versus Manual Social Class for Employees.*

The dependent variable is the standardized version of the satisfaction measure. Our analysis therefore seeks to examine the relative satisfaction of employees and the unemployed within each country. In attempting to explain country differences we explore the possibility that such differences in the impact of unemployment might be explained by:

1. Variation in the relationship of unemployment to health and material circumstances.
2. Differences in composition that could be taken into account by allowing unemployment to interact with variables such as gender, age, and having a partner.
3. Cross-national variation in the manner in which the foregoing variables interact with unemployment.

This approach could result in a highly complex model but, in fact, as is apparent from Table 14.6, our final models are relatively parsimonious. This table reports only the subset of coefficients that are relevant to our current argument. Thus we display only those terms including unemployment and the effects for non-manual employees and those relating to income and living standards.[14] The main findings emerging from equation (i) are as follows:

1. Non-manual employees are more satisfied than manual employees as reflected in the coefficient of 0.26. Although this gap is modest in comparison with differences between the unemployed and employees, the result is consistent with the notion of restricted reference groups whereby the satisfaction of manual workers is arrived at, not by comparisons across the social spectrum, but rather on the basis of what it is 'reasonable' to expect.
2. The impact of unemployment increases with age as indicated by the negative coefficient taking its highest value for the 50+ age group and then displaying a reduction of 0.088 for those aged between 30 and 49, and of 0.266 for those under 30.

[14] The full model includes all the lower order terms necessary to estimate the model, and a term for health.

TABLE 14.6. *Multiple regression of determinants of life-satisfaction*

	B (i)	S.E. (i)	B (ii)	S.E. (ii)
Non-manual employee	0.260	0.009	0.072	0.009
Unemployment	−1.377	0.039	−1.072	0.042
Unemployment*female	0.275	0.026	0.215	0.024
Unemployment*less than 30	0.266	0.037	0.095	0.034
Unemployment*30–49	0.088	0.015	0.044	0.014
Partner*unemployment	0.135	0.028	0.151	0.026
Unemployment*Denmark	0.252	0.062	0.269	0.057
Unemployment*UK	0.004	0.056	0.182	0.051
Unemployment*Ireland	0.003	0.070	0.097	0.052
Unemployment*Greece	0.317	0.038	0.226	0.035
Unemployment*Spain	0.237	0.032	0.201	0.029
Uemployment*Portugal	−0.160	0.052	−0.274	0.047
Unemployment*UK*female	0.293	0.091	0.008	0.083
Unemployment*Ireland*female	0.160	0.085	0.147	0.078
Deterioration in economic situation			−0.164	0.008
Monthly household equivalent income 1994			0.062	0.004
Lifestyle deprivation			−0.367	0.004
Constant	0.140		0.214	
R²	0.195		0.324	

Note: N = 52,171.
Source: ECHP (1994).

3. The impact of unemployment is also reduced if one has a partner, as indicated by the coefficient of 0.135.
4. The effect of unemployment is also less for women, as reflected in the coefficient of 0.275.
5. The unemployment coefficient thus represents the difference between the unemployed and employees, for male respondents aged 50 or over, without a partner in unemployment. Unemployment, it can be seen, has a substantial impact on satisfaction. The coefficient of −1.377 is over thirty-five times its standard error. However, this effect applies for our reference group of countries of Belgium, France, The Netherlands, and Italy. Among these countries there is no variation in the impact of unemployment. This group includes a low welfare country together with three high welfare countries. Furthermore, as we shall see, the deviations from this reference group offer even less support for the notion that the impact of unemployment on satisfaction can be accounted for by the role of welfare regime.
6. The effect of unemployment does not differ significantly from the reference group set of countries, for men in the UK and Ireland. However, since the gender difference in the impact of unemployment is strongest

in these countries, as demonstrated by the positive coefficients of 0.293 and 0.160 for the relevant three-way unemployment-gender-country inter-actions, the impact for women is weaker.[15] Thus for men, six countries which encompass high and low welfare regimes produce a constant effect for unemployment.

7. The impact of unemployment is less than in our reference countries in Greece, Denmark, and Spain, with positive coefficients of respect-ively 0.317, 0.252, and 0.237; but is somewhat stronger in Portugal with a negative coefficient of –0.160. There is nothing in our understanding of welfare regimes which suggests such a pattern.

In equation (ii) we introduce the additional set of variables, all of which are significantly related to satisfaction. By far the strongest relationship is with lifestyle deprivation where the coefficient of –0.367 is ninety times greater than its standard error. It is followed in precedence by deterioration in eco-nomic situation in the previous twelve months, which has a coefficient of –0.164 that is over twenty times its standard error, and household income whose coefficient of 0.062 is fifteen times its standard error.

The set of variables relating to economic circumstances appears to play a crucial role in determining satisfaction. They also contribute in a significant way to an understanding of the processes through which unem-ployment impacts on satisfaction since they lead to a reduction in the coefficient for unemployment for the reference group of countries and respondents from –1.377 to –1.073, a proportionate reduction of just above one-fifth.[16] However, the additional set of variables plays no significant role in accounting for the country effects observed in equation (i). The three-way interaction between unemployment, gender, and the UK becomes insignificant but otherwise the pattern of country effects remains much as before.

In order to illustrate the role of material circumstances in mediating the impact of unemployment, in Table 14.7 we set for each country separately, the reduction in the unemployment effect brought about by the introduc-tion of these variables.[17] This implies a model that is a good deal less par-simonious than that underlying our cross-national regression. It also averages effects within countries across subgroups such as men and women, and

---

[15] For Germany the separate analysis suggests that the impact of unemployment is weaker than average for women but not for men. The age pattern also seems to be slightly different with the highest coefficient being observed in the youngest age-group.

[16] The reduction will be somewhat less for those groups where the impact of unemploy-ment is stronger than for the reference group and somewhat greater than where the impact is weaker. A similar result is observed for Germany.

[17] Thus for each country we first run an equation regressing satisfaction on unemployment, gender, and the interaction of gender and unemployment; and then in the second equation we introduce the set of variables relating to material circumstances.

TABLE 14.7. *Gross and partial effect of unemployment, by country*

	Gross effect: controlling only for health and class	Net effect as proportion of gross effect after controlling for income	Net effect as proportion of gross effect after controlling for deprivation and deterioration in economic circumstances
Belgium	−1.155	0.96	0.82
Denmark	−1.043	0.95	0.55
France	−1.211	0.97	0.83
Greece	−0.614	0.93	0.58
Ireland	−1.019	0.97	0.73
Italy	−0.977	0.91	0.77
Netherlands	−1.117	0.99	0.67
Portugal	−1.334	0.98	0.98
Spain	−0.807	0.94	0.77
UK	−1.046	0.93	0.64

Source: ECHP (1994).

age-groups. It does, however, allow us to convey the important substantive findings in a more intuitive fashion.

In the first equation we control for health and social class only in order to estimate the difference in level of satisfaction between the unemployed and manual employees. The breakdown of this effect is done in two stages. In the first we control for the income variable only. At the second stage we also include lifestyle deprivation and perception of economic deterioration in the previous twelve months. What is striking is how modest is the degree of reduction in the gross effect achieved by the introduction of the income variables. The ratio of the net to gross effect lies between 0.91 and 0.99. Clearly, current household income offers relatively little insight into the impact of unemployment on subjective well-being. The addition of the lifestyle deprivation variable and perception of economic deterioration produces a substantial further reduction. For four cases—those of the Denmark, The Netherlands, the UK, and Greece—the effect is reduced to two-thirds or less of its original size. For Italy, Ireland, and Spain, the net coefficient is approximately three-quarters or less of the gross, and for France and Belgium it is just above four-fifths. Portugal is the outlier with hardly any reduction being achieved. The vast bulk of the additional reduction in the impact of unemployment achieved in the final equation is produced by the introduction of the lifestyle deprivation variable.

While significant country effects have emerged in our analysis, one might be more inclined to be impressed by the fact that unemployment has a powerful effect on subjective well-being in all of the countries. Variations around this central tendency are modest and an analysis that omitted country effects would not seriously undermine our understanding of the impact of unemployment on subjective well-being. While many of the variables by which we might have hoped to explain cross-national variations in the impact of unemployment on satisfaction have been proved to be powerful predictors of satisfaction, there is no evidence that they underlie cross-national variation in the impact of unemployment. Unemployment has a powerful influence in all countries that is only partially accounted for by material circumstances. Current household income plays only a modest role. Our findings here support the conclusion of earlier work, primarily by economists, relating the modest role of income in mediating the impact of unemployment (Clark and Oswald 1994; Clark 1998; Winkelman and Winkelman 1998).

Taking lifestyle deprivation into account allows us to reduce the gross effect by approximately one-third to one-quarter. These findings suggest that there is need for more detailed exploration of the relationship between household income and living standards. Hopefully, the availability of panel data will encourage such analysis. But accounting for the remaining two-thirds is likely to require a focus on non-economic factors.

EMPLOYMENT EXPERIENCE AND SATISFACTION

One limitation of our analysis, up to this point, is that in assessing the impact of unemployment on satisfaction, we have implicitly assumed that there is no internal differentiation between employees and the unemployed other than those captured by the socio-demographic variables included in our models. In what follows, drawing on additional information contained in the ECHP, we attempt to rectify this by drawing on information relating to unemployment experience.

In measuring the former we make use of two pieces of information contained in the ECHP data set. The first concerns whether the individual has been unemployed at any time in the previous five years. The second records the employment status of the individual for each calendar month in 1993. Combining these pieces of information with present employment status we create the following fivefold classification:[18]

(1) Unemployed currently and for more than six months in 1993;
(2) Unemployed currently and for six months or less in 1993;
(3) Employee currently and unemployed at some point in 1993;
(4) Employee currently and unemployed at some time in the previous five years;

---

[18] The categories are defined to be mutually exclusive. Unfortunately due to data problems it was necessary to exclude The Netherlands from this analysis.

TABLE 14.8. *Experience of unemployment, by country* (row %)

	Unemployed currently and for more than six months in 1993	Unemployed currently and for six months or less in 1993	Employee currently and unemployed in 1993	Employee currently and unemployed in previous five years	Employee currently not unemployed in previous five years
Belgium	4.0	3.6	5.4	14.4	72.6
Denmark	3.2	3.7	12.3	13.5	67.3
France	5.1	11.5	4.9	10.5	68.0
Germany	1.9	2.1	5.1	10.9	80.9
Greece	10.1	13.6	7.8	9.7	58.9
Ireland	8.3	7.9	7.7	10.2	65.9
Italy	9.6	6.6	4.9	10.9	68.1
Portugal	3.3	4.3	5.6	11.2	75.6
Spain	12.0	12.1	13.0	13.3	49.6
UK	4.1	5.6	6.4	13.0	70.8
All countries	6.8	8.0	7.0	12.0	66.3

Note: Figures in 'All countries' row do not include Germany.
Source: ECHP (1994).

(5) Employee currently and not unemployed at any time during the previous five years.

In Table 14.8 we set out the distribution of unemployment experience across countries employing this definition. Among the unemployed, Italy has almost two-thirds of its unemployed in the category representing those who have been unemployed for more than six months in the previous year, while the situation is reversed for France. For the other countries, the numbers are fairly evenly balanced.

The overall percentage represented in the category most insulated from unemployment ranges from 50 per cent in Spain to over 80 per cent in Germany. It is particularly low in Greece at less than 60 per cent. For the remaining countries it ranges between the mid-sixties and the low seventies. The group of employees who have been exposed to unemployment constitutes almost 30 per cent of employees. The group who had no experience of unemployment in the previous year outnumbers those who had been exposed to unemployment by two to one. However, this ratio varies across countries. For Denmark, Spain, and Greece the two subgroups are of almost equal size, while elsewhere the least precarious are significantly more numerous. Variations by unemployment experience do not appear to be patterned in a manner which offers any possibility for accounting for corresponding variation in the impact of unemployment on satisfaction.

Within countries, however, unemployment experience proves to be a powerful explanatory factor. In Table 14.9 we look at the relationship between unemployment experience and equivalent disposable household

TABLE 14.9. *Household equivalent income in 1994, by experience of unemployment*

	Unemployed currently and for more than six months in 1993	Unemployed currently and for six months or less in 1993	Employee currently and unemployed in 1993	Employee currently and unemployed in previous five years	Employee currently not unemployed in previous five years
Belgium	0.59	0.63	0.79	0.85	1.00
Denmark	0.70	0.82	0.90	0.91	1.00
France	0.60	0.70	0.78	0.89	1.00
Germany	0.68	0.71	0.67	0.78	1.00
Greece	0.48	0.65	0.79	0.84	1.00
Ireland	0.46	0.56	0.75	0.95	1.00
Italy	0.48	0.64	0.67	0.85	1.00
Portugal	0.57	0.62	0.60	0.82	1.00
Spain	0.48	0.56	0.68	0.80	1.00
UK	0.44	0.67	0.80	0.91	1.00
All countries	0.47	0.63	0.73	0.87	1.00

Note: The 'All countries' row does not take account of the German figures.
Source: ECHP (1994).

income at the time of interview in 1994. Those who are currently unemployed and were also unemployed for more than six months in 1993 have household incomes which are less than half those of the group who are currently in employment and have not been unemployed in the previous five years. This figure rises to over 60 per cent for those currently unemployed but unemployed for less than six months in 1993. Those currently in employment but who have experienced unemployment in the previous year have household incomes that are almost three-quarters of those of the most secure group. Finally, the income level of those employees who not experienced unemployment in 1993 but had experienced a spell of unemployment in the previous five years came close to nine-tenths of the most favoured group.

In Table 14.10 we look at the relationship between lifestyle deprivation and unemployment experience. The overall results here are slightly different from income in that there is a gradual increase in the level of deprivation as one goes from the reference category to the most insecure group of the unemployed. There is also a good deal more cross-national variation. Denmark, which showed modest variation in relation to income, displays somewhat more for lifestyle deprivation. Similarly Ireland and the UK which were unexceptional in terms of income inequality display particularly sharp variations in living standards. One of the main factors contributing to variation is that unemployment experience has a good deal less effect on deprivation in the 'Mediterranean' countries than in the others.

As we might have anticipated from our earlier regression analysis, unemployment experience is significantly related to both income and lifestyle

TABLE 14.10. *Lifestyle deprivation by employment experience*

	Unemployed currently and for more than six months in 1993	Unemployed currently and for six months or less in 1993	Employee currently and unemployed in 1993	Employee currently and unemployed in previous five years	Employee currently not unemployed in previous five years
Belgium	2.15	1.53	1.53	1.41	1.00
Denmark	2.86	2.47	1.90	1.67	1.00
France	2.18	1.66	1.58	1.33	1.00
Germany	2.29	1.09	1.79	1.51	1.00
Greece	1.51	1.33	1.35	1.28	1.00
Ireland	2.81	2.23	1.77	1.40	1.00
Italy	2.05	1.69	1.71	1.36	1.00
Portugal	1.38	1.27	1.38	1.35	1.00
Spain	1.80	1.52	1.53	1.29	1.00
UK	3.18	2.15	1.60	1.45	1.00
All countries	2.39	1.86	1.76	1.39	1.00

Note: The 'All countries' row does not take account of the German figures.
Source: ECHP (1994).

deprivation. However, the pattern of cross-national variation is not such as to suggest that the effect of unemployment documented earlier can be accounted for by our failure to take such variation in account. However, it is still possible that correlates of unemployment experience other than income and living standards might explain our earlier findings. As our earlier discussion indicated, experience of unemployment has its impact not just through change in one's material circumstances but also by denying one access to the range of latent functions, which paid employment provides.

In Table 14.11 we document the relationship between unemployment experience and satisfaction. With only very minor deviations, satisfaction declines steadily as experience of unemployment increases. For the most vulnerable group taken across ten countries, we observe a mean satisfaction score of 2.53.[19] This rises to 3.05 for those unemployed less than six months in 1993. For the most insecure employees it rises to 3.69, for the intermediate category it increases to 3.86, and for the most secure group it climbs to 4.2. What is striking about Table 14.11 is the remarkable similarity in patterns across the countries. For the most disadvantaged group the ratio involving the reference group lies between 0.56 and 0.66 for eight of the ten countries. For the most advantaged segment of the unemployed, nine countries are found between 0.70 and 0.76. Turning to the group of employees most exposed to unemployment, we find that eight countries are located between 0.82 and 0.89. Finally, among the intermediate group of employees, all ten countries

[19] Again, Germany is not included in these calculations.

TABLE 14.11. *Satisfaction, by unemployment experience*

	Unemployed currently and for more than six months in 1993	Unemployed currently and for six months or less in 1993	Employee currently and unemployed in 1993	Employee currently and unemployed in previous five years	Employee currently not unemployed in previous five years
Belgium	0.69	0.73	0.92	0.95	1.00
Denmark	0.80	0.81	0.93	0.94	1.00
France	0.61	0.70	0.88	0.93	1.00
Germany	0.66	0.70	0.86	0.91	1.00
Greece	0.63	0.75	0.82	0.86	1.00
Ireland	0.59	0.72	0.87	0.91	1.00
Italy	0.56	0.70	0.84	0.91	1.00
Portugal	0.60	0.65	0.84	0.91	1.00
Spain	0.64	0.75	0.87	0.91	1.00
UK	0.62	0.76	0.89	0.92	1.00
All countries	0.60	0.73	0.88	0.92	1.00

Note: The 'All countries' row does not take account of the German figures.
Source: ECHP (1994).

are located between 0.84 and 0.94. In particular there is nothing to set Spain and Greece apart from the modal pattern.

CONCLUSIONS

In this chapter we have attempted to develop our rather limited knowledge regarding the extent to which the impact of unemployment on well being varies across countries. Drawing on a large literature dealing with particular countries, and a more limited body of comparative work, we have followed Gallie and Russell (1998) in identifying four factors which might mediate observed cross-national variation, the relative generosity of welfare systems, the level of unemployment, the composition of the unemployed, and the cultural importance of work.

Our concern has not been with absolute differences in well-being across countries. Instead we have attempted to assess the extent to which the relative impact of unemployment varies across nations. The adoption of a relative framework extended to the assumption that, in relation to income and living standards what is crucial to individuals is their relative position within their own national context.

Our analysis shows that unemployment has a powerful effect on satisfaction across all twelve countries in our sample. It is important to stress that this finding, relating to the central role of unemployment in each country, is the key finding of our analysis. Cross-national variation in the relative impact, where it exists, tends to be relatively modest when viewed in this context. This is true not just of the relationship between unemployment and satisfaction but also in the impact of the former on income, living standards, and economic strain. There is a general tendency for unemployment to have a less severe impact for women, for those aged under 30 and those with partners.

The cross-national variation that we have observed suggests that the impact of unemployment is somewhat less severe in Denmark, Greece, and Spain and for women in Ireland and the UK. This is not a pattern that appears to be explicable by reference to the relative generosity of welfare systems. Neither does it bear any clear relationship to overall unemployment rates, although women do form a comparatively small proportion of the unemployed in the UK and Ireland. Unemployment is significantly related to material circumstances in all countries. In turn, personal income, household living standards, and perception of recent deterioration in economic situation are highly significant predictors of subjective well-being. Controlling for these factors accounts for a significant, although modest component of the relationship between unemployment and satisfaction. Our analysis supports earlier findings that lifestyle deprivation is a more powerful mediator than income of the employment-subjective well-being relationship and suggests the need for further exploration of the relationship between these variables. However, the introduction of both factors into the analysis leaves the pattern of cross-national variation largely unaffected.

The ECHP data set does not contain the type of measures that would allow us to assess the role of cultural differences. However, both the particular pattern of cross-national effects we have observed and the fact that the manner in which unemployment interacts with age, gender, and having a partner is constant across countries, leads us to think that this is unlikely to be a fruitful avenue of exploration.

Our analysis was extended to take into account differences in unemployment experience within both the unemployed and employees. The findings strengthened our convictions regarding the broadly similar relative outcomes across countries that result from labour market disadvantage. Once again, however, cross-national differences in unemployment experience within the employee and unemployed groups did not seem to offer the key to explaining corresponding variations in the impact of unemployment on satisfaction.

Taking an overall view of our findings we find that, in relation to the cross-national impact of unemployment, we are confronted with a situation not entirely dissimilar to that in the comparative analysis of social mobility regimes. (Erikson and Goldthorpe 1992). Here, as there, the challenge lies more in explaining the constancy of social processes, rather than in the relatively modest cross-national variation.

15

Gender and the Experience of Unemployment

Helen Russell and Paolo Barbieri

INTRODUCTION

It is widely thought that the experience of unemployment will differ for men and women. First, it is argued that women do not have the same financial responsibilities as men and therefore will be protected from the direct financial impact of unemployment, and from the strain that arises from the inability to provide for dependants. Second, it is argued that women do not have the same commitment or attachment to the labour market as men and therefore will be less psychologically and socially affected by job loss. The strong version of this argument suggests that much female unemployment is voluntary: the restrictions women place on their employment because of caring responsibilities are interpreted as an indication that joblessness involves an element of choice. It is has also been argued that women's domestic roles can provide them with an alternative source of fulfilment, activity, and status which is unavailable to unemployed men, and that this will provide a further buffer against the psychological impact of unemployment:

even if women prefer to have a job, unemployment hits them less hard than men psychologically speaking because an alternative is available to them in the return to the traditional role of housewife that provides some time structure, some sense of purpose, status and activity even though it offers little scope for wider social experiences. (Jahoda 1982: 53)

These arguments have been applied in a universalistic way and it is not recognized that their validity might vary within different cultural contexts. The arguments outlined above also view women's unemployment as a homogenous experience despite wide variation in male unemployment experiences. Within Europe there is considerable variation in women's patterns of participation in the labour market, in the distribution of unemployment, the composition of households, and in societal attitudes towards women's employment. This diversity may well lead to differences in the financial importance of women's employment and in the importance of employment for women's self-identity. Furthermore, although commitment to employment cannot be read-off behavioural measures such as participation rates or part-time employment, the longer term attachment to employment of women in some countries may mean that unemployment is more disruptive to women's lives and well-being.

In this chapter we will investigate gender and the experience of unemployment in four countries with distinct patterns of female labour market participation and contrasting social welfare systems: Italy, the UK, France, and Denmark. By undertaking comparative research it is possible to assess financial factors, access to employment compensation, labour market attachment, and the gender culture, as possible sources of gender differences in unemployment experience. We use the term *gender culture* in the sense defined by Pfau-Effinger as 'common assumptions about the desirable, "normal" form of gender relations and the division of labour between women and men.' (1998: 178).

A cross-national comparison of unemployed women can also contribute to the debate about the experience of unemployment and welfare regimes. The four countries addressed in this study have been identified as having very different welfare regimes both within mainstream typologies and in gender-sensitive analyses of welfare states. They have also been shown, in Chapter 1, to have different protection regimes for the unemployed. Conventional approaches to the welfare state recognize that different regimes have important implications for the well-being of the unemployed in general and have important *side-effects* for women's employment. For example Esping-Andersen (1990: 159) argues that the social-democratic welfare states enable women to work via the creation of a large public sector, which both provides the necessary support services, such as childcare, and creates a demand for female labour. In contrast, the Conservative welfare regimes, which include France, are believed to discourage female employment—as outlined in Chapter 1.

Feminist welfare typologies have placed a more central emphasis on the fate of women within different welfare regimes. Both Lewis (1992) and Daly (1996) have attempted to assess how far welfare states support traditional male-breadwinner household forms and whether women are treated primarily as mothers or workers. There is little disagreement on the classification of Denmark and other Scandinavian countries which are believed to encourage *male and female breadwinning* through generous leave schemes, individualized tax and benefit systems, and the provision of public services. Daly classifies Italy as belonging to a Mediterranean Model[1] in which the *family is breadwinner*. Large gaps in welfare provision are assumed to be covered by the family and the underdevelopment of personal social services means that women in the home are the major source of care. The benefits that are available are strongly linked to labour market status rather than need.

---

[1] Lewis does not include Italy or any of the southern European countries in her analysis.

There is less agreement on the classification of the UK and France within gendered welfare regime typologies. Much depends on the weight given to what we might call family policies and the weight given to the tax and benefit policies. Lewis (1992), focusing on pro-natal policies which have had indirect benefits for women, classifies France as a *modified male-breadwinner* country and argues that 'state policy has recognised the reality of women's roles as both mothers and workers' (1992: 167). This standpoint is reinforced by Gornick *et al.*'s (1997) study of policies that support the employment of mothers. In a ranking of fourteen OECD countries based on childcare, maternity and leave policies available for the parents of children under 6 years old, France was ranked first, Denmark second, Italy sixth, and the UK twelfth. However, Daly (1996) who concentrates on social security systems classifies France as a *male breadwinner state*. Daly argues that the risks covered are male risks, and the strong social insurance principle means that benefits are strongly tied to employment record and wage levels, which can lead to sex inequalities in outcomes. Furthermore, unlike the other three countries considered here, France operates a joint taxation system which discourages married women's employment, particularly part-time employment.

Similar discrepancies arise over the classification of the UK. Lewis (1992) classifies Britain as a *strong male breadwinner* state because of the provision of dependants' allowances to maintain non-working wives, and the lack of support for working mothers. However, Daly (1996) argues that low social payments mean that everyone is encouraged to work, and that the lower reliance on social insurance benefits means that the UK system may have less potential for gender inequality than some continental European systems.[2]

These disagreements between typologies highlight the difficulties of trying to capture all dimensions of welfare regimes within a typology. As the authors themselves recognize, these regime-type classifications are simplifications of very complex systems incorporating a wide range of policies. Concentrating on a single policy issue in ostensibly different welfare regimes may shed light on the operation of gender within social policy, which wide-ranging typologies may gloss over. Comparing the provision and outcomes of unemployment for women and men can provide an important insight into the gendered nature of welfare regimes in these four countries. Whether an unemployed woman is treated as a displaced worker or a housewife who requires neither compensation for her joblessness nor support for labour market re-entry, provides an example of policy position on the 'mother versus worker' dichotomy.

[2] Daly's full classification is: 1) Nordic 'Everyone's a breadwinner'—Sweden, Denmark, Finland (NL). 2) Continental European 'Male Breadwinner'—(NL), Germany, Austria, Luxembourg, Belgium and France. 3) Liberal 'More than one breadwinner'—UK (Ireland). 4) 'Family as Breadwinner'—(Ireland), Italy, Spain, Greece, Portugal. The countries in brackets are borderline cases.

In this chapter, we will use data from the 1994 European Household Panel Survey (ECHP) and the 1996 Eurobarometer Survey to examine gender differences in unemployment experiences in Denmark, Italy, the UK, and France. The chapter will begin with a description of the contrasting labour market position of women in these four countries. It will then go on to describe gender differences in access to unemployment compensation in each system. In the third section we examine gender differences in the financial effect of unemployment and how this interacts with the household position of women and the significance of women's employment within a given society. Finally we will examine gender differences in the subjective impact of unemployment, and discuss the extent to which this is influenced by financial responsibilities, previous employment experience, commitment to employment, and societal expectations.

WOMEN IN THE LABOUR MARKET IN DENMARK, ITALY, FRANCE, AND THE UK

Our expectation of national differences in the gendered impact of unemployment is based in part on the recognition that women's roles and involvement in the labour market vary from country to country. Here we will summarize the main features of women's labour market activity and the predominant gender role attitudes in the four societies.

The most basic measure of women's presence in the labour market is the activity rate. Labour force data for 1994 show that only 43 per cent of Italian women aged 16–64 were active participants in the labour market: employed or unemployed. This compares to 61 per cent in France, 67 per cent in the UK, and 76 per cent in Denmark. The EU average in 1994 stood at 57 per cent for women and 79 per cent for men. The country differences change somewhat if we look at the participation rates of mothers. Almost 90 per cent of Danish women aged 25–49 with one child under 15 are in the labour market, in France 80 per cent of this group are in the labour market, in the UK the figure is around 70 per cent and in Italy it is less than 50 per cent.[3] This reversal in the French and UK positions is likely to reflect the extensive childcare provision and leave schemes provided in France, and the very low provision in the UK mentioned above.

The provision of childcare is also likely to influence the hours that women can work. The high incidence of part-time work among British women—44 per cent in 1994—is linked to poor childcare provision. However, 34 per cent of Danish women work part-time despite well-developed

---

[3] The figures date from 1991 and are reported in Employment in Europe (1993: 159).

childcare services—down from 44 per cent in 1985. These high levels of part-time work in Denmark and the UK are also associated with other factors such as increases in service sector employment and employers' demands for part-time labour. In Italy and France, part-time work is lower than the European average, representing 12 and 28 per cent of female employment respectively. It is argued that high fixed labour costs, due in part to the social insurance system, and strict labour market regulation has restricted the introduction of part-time contracts in both countries, although the restrictions are more acute in Italy (SYSDEM 1995; Esping-Andersen 1996). Whatever their origins, these patterns of participation are likely to have a significant impact on women's access to benefit during unemployment, the financial loss that will result from women's unemployment, and the social impact of women's unemployment.

There is also significant variation in the pay differentials between men and women in the four countries. The female to male ratio in industrial wages is 86 in Denmark, 80 in Italy, 77 in France, and 68 in the UK (Siaroff 1994). These differences may be partly attributable to differences in part-time work and in the extent of public sector employment within the welfare regimes. The size of this pay gap has implications for gender differences in the pay-outs from social insurance benefits and for the income lost when a man or woman becomes unemployed.

Social policies and labour demand can only take us part of the way in explaining cross-national variation in women's labour market participation: we also need to consider attitudes towards gender roles across countries. Some insight into the general levels of support for traditional gender roles in the four societies can be seen in a range of attitudinal statements taken from the 1996 Eurobarometer survey, which are outlined in Table 15.1. A traditionalist score is calculated by giving respondents a score of one for every traditional response,[4] which produces a scale ranging from zero to five.

The Italian public express the most traditional attitudes about gender roles. This is most apparent in responses to questions about the primacy of men's breadwinning role. Over 80 per cent of Italians are resistant to the idea of men becoming full-time homemakers. There is also a strong belief that men's claim to paid work takes precedence over women's claim. This belief is particularly strong among Italian men: 43 per cent believe men have a more legitimate claim to work in periods of high unemployment.

The Danes hold the least traditional gender role attitudes. There is very strong support for women taking on a breadwinning role: the vast majority feel that it is very important for a woman to have a job and her

---

[4] This eliminates differences in the number of response categories for the five questions. Analysis of variance shows that the mean traditionalist score for each country is significantly different from the others ($P < 0.005$).

TABLE 15.1. *Level of support for traditional gender role attitudes*[a] (%)

	Denmark	Italy	Britain[b]	France
Disagree/Disagree strongly that if father earns less he should be the one to stop work and look after the children	53.9	82.4	52.4	62.6
Agree/Agree strongly that a mother must give priority to young child rather than her work	68.1	83.2	86.6	76.6
Disagree/Disagree strongly that it is a must for a woman to have her own income	19.2	41.8	52.5	23.3
'Tend to disagree' that it is as important for woman as for a man to have a job	8.2	8.8	17.0	9.6
'Tend to agree' that when jobs are scarce, men have more right to a job than women	8.6	43.1	30.1	29.0
Traditionalist score	*1.5*	*2.4*	*2.2*	*1.9*
Minimum N	(1218)	(1312)	(1252)	(1193)

[a] Statements 1 to 3 answered on 4 point Likert scale: agree strongly, agree, disagree, disagree strongly. Response categories for statements 4 and 5: tend to agree, tend to disagree, don't know.
[b] The data in this table only refer to Great Britain, not including Northern Ireland, hence use of 'the UK' is not applicable.
Source: Eurobarometer 1996.

own income, and only 8 per cent feel that women's claim to employment is less than men's. There is rather less support for women relinquishing their traditional role as carers.[5] Over 60 per cent of both men and women feel that a mother's main priority is family rather than work, and over half of respondents are against any role-reversal in childcare.

Britain and France fall between the other two countries in terms of gender role attitudes. The mean scores show that French attitudes are closer to the Danes while British attitudes are closer to the Italian responses. The French attach a strong importance to women's entitlement to a separate income, however 29 per cent believe that men have a greater claim to employment in conditions of scarcity, which suggests the view that men should be the principle breadwinner still has considerable support. In Britain there is less resistance to change in men's role than there is in Italy, but the British are much less supportive of women's breadwinning role than the Danes and the French. A particularly high proportion of British men, 55 per cent, disagree that women need an independent source of income, which highlights the continuing strength of the male breadwinner ideology.

These attitudes are likely to influence the participation of women in the economy and frame policies towards women's unemployment. They are

[5] Borchorst and Siim (1987) argue that despite a massive rise in activity rates, women in Denmark and Sweden still have chief responsibility for unpaid work in the family.

also likely to affect women's experience of unemployment. Women's role as worker is most strongly emphasized in Danish attitudes and in the Danish welfare regime, therefore unemployed women are likely to experience more normative pressure to find employment. French attitudes and policies seem more neutral in terms of whether mothers work or stay at home (Lewis 1992)[6]; therefore the individual's past experience may be key. In the UK there may be a strong financial pressure for women to work, but the continuing prominence of the male breadwinner ideology may limit the social pressure on unemployed women. The Italians appear to place greater emphasis on women's role as mother than worker, a stance mirrored in the welfare regime, which may reduce the psychological burden of unemployment. These hypotheses will be examined when we look at the subjective impact of unemployment.

The variations in labour market participation, part-time employment, and attitudes to gender roles between countries described above are likely to influence the impact of unemployment among women. Further complexity is introduced by the structure of unemployment within the four countries.

Distribution of Unemployment

As in the other chapters we use the ILO definition of unemployment. The unemployed are those without employment who have been actively searching for work in the past four weeks and are available to start work in the next two weeks. This avoids the problems of underestimating female unemployment that are associated with unemployment registration figures and measures based on self-classification (Cragg and Dawson 1984; Russell 1996).

Gender differences in unemployment vary across our four study countries. France, Denmark, and Italy follow the general European pattern of higher unemployment rates among women than men (Table 15.2). The over-representation of women amongst the unemployed is most evident in Italy and France. In the UK by contrast, men's unemployment rates are significantly higher than women's. In terms of exposure to unemployment then, women fare best in the UK and Denmark. In a wider examination of female to male unemployment ratios, France, Italy, and the other southern European countries come out worst of twenty-three OECD nations (Siaroff 1994). Siaroff argues that this should be taken into account when considering whether different welfare regimes offer women a real 'work' choice.

Substantial cross-national differences also exist in the age composition of the unemployed, as noted in Chapter 1, which have implications for the financial responsibilities of the unemployed, their position in the life-cycle,

---

[6] However, there are clear incentives for mothers of larger families, with 3 or more children, to stay at home.

TABLE 15.2. *Unemployment rates, by gender 1994 (%)*

	Male	Female
Denmark	7.2	9.0
France	10.4	14.5
Italy	8.8	15.6
UK	11.4	7.4

Source: European Labour Force Survey (1994).

TABLE 15.3. *Entry route into unemployment among men and women 1994 (%)*

	Denmark		Italy		UK		France	
	M	F	M	F	M	F	M	F
Job loser	79.1	76.5	36.8	22.4	72.1	39.3	77.3	68.9
Seeking job after econ. inactivity	17.0	4.6	16.8	23.5	18.7	12.2	10.1	16.3
Seeking first job	3.3	18.8	46.2	54.0	8.7	48.1	9.1	11.2
Missing	0.6	0.1	0.2	0.1	0.5	0.5	3.5	3.6

Source: European Labour Force Survey 1994.

and for their access to benefit. Of particular relevance to this last issue is the proportion of the unemployed who are first-time job seekers and the proportion who are re-entering employment following a break outside the labour market. As we can see from Table 15.3 an extremely high percentage, 78 per cent, of unemployed women in Italy have not entered unemployment from a job; this is also true of unemployed women in the UK. In France and Denmark by contrast, the majority of unemployed women are job losers. Where unemployment compensation systems are linked to prior record of employment, these gender differences can disadvantage women. It is to this issue of unemployment compensation that we turn to next.

GENDER AND ACCESS TO UNEMPLOYMENT BENEFITS

The main features of the unemployment compensation systems in the four countries have been described in Chapter 1; here we will concentrate on aspects of these systems which have particular implications for the gender distribution of benefits. We will consider both insurance-based Unemployment Benefit (UB) and means-tested Unemployment Assistance (UA).

There are three main dimensions of insurance rules which tend to act against women who interrupt their careers to care for children or who work

TABLE 15.4. *Characteristics of national unemployment compensation systems*

	Qualifying period 1995[a]	Duration UB varies with length of emp.[b]	Thresholds for UB	Unit for UA[c]
Denmark	12 months in past 3 years (part-timers 34 weeks in the past 3 years)	No	15 hours per week	Individual
UK[d]	Max. 75 weeks in last 2 years (50 in last year) Average: 16.5 weeks (11 in last year)	No	£57 per week	+ Spouse
France	UB 6 months in past year[e] UA 5 years in last 10 years	Yes	None	+ Spouse
Italy	24 months (12 months in last two years)	Yes	None	+ Spouse + other relatives in household

[a] Source: Rubery *et al.* (1998: Table 5.2); and *Social Security Administration 1995*.
[b] Source: Derived from European Commission (1994).
[c] Eardley *et al.* 1996.
[d] The UK system is based on the value of contributions rather than the length of employment. The average refers to the time it would take to build up eligibility on average production worker earnings (OECD 1991).
[e] *Social Security Administration 1995* reports a qualification period of 91 days or 520 hours paid employment in the preceding 12 months rather than the 6 months reported by Rubery *et al.* (1998).

part-time. First is the length of employment record required to qualify for benefits—the longer the spell of employment required for eligibility the more people with interrupted career patterns will be excluded. Second, is the degree to which benefits are linked to recent employment experience. If very recent contributions are necessary, women re-entering the job market following a period of childcare are extremely unlikely to qualify for benefit. Thirdly, the operation of minimum hours or earnings thresholds can lead to the exclusion of part-timers or other low paid women.

The operation of joint means-tests for Unemployment Assistance can mean that married women and men with working spouses are not entitled to UA, which results in enforced economic dependency within the household. Although, in principle, this rule applies to both married men and women, substantial differences in male and female employment rates in France, Italy, and the UK mean that, in practice, it is more likely to affect married women.

The link between employment record and benefits appears to be least strong in Denmark and the UK where contribution periods are relatively short—except for those on low wages in the UK—and there is no link between benefit duration and the length of previous employment—see Table 15.4. In Italy and France, longer periods of employment are required to establish eligibility for unemployment compensation, and the duration of benefits is affected by claimants' employment record. On this basis those with discontinuous careers are likely to fare better in Denmark and the UK. The wider time-frame over which contributions can be made in Denmark means that those re-entering the job market after a short gap are more likely to retain entitlements than in the UK where very recent contributions are required.

However, this categorization overlooks some important details in the operation of national benefit systems. For example, discounts for time spent caring for children applied in France mean that the system is less unfavourable to women than might otherwise be expected: among those who stop work to care for children the qualification period for UA can be reduced by one year for each dependent child up to a maximum of three years. Other elements of the unemployment benefit systems that have gender implications also complicate the picture. For example, Denmark and the UK both operate thresholds for inclusion in the social security system: in the Danish case it is an hourly threshold, and in the UK, an earnings threshold. The effect of both thresholds is to exclude many part-time workers.[7]

Access to *means-tested* benefits is likely to be least gendered in Denmark where the unit of assessment for benefit is the individual. The inclusion of partner's income in the other two countries and in Italy, the income of certain other relatives within the household (Eardley *et al.* 1996), means that married women are less likely to qualify for means-tested benefits than in Denmark.

In Italy there is no national system of UA and UB plays only a minor role in compensating the unemployed.[8] Here, employment subsidies such as the *Cassa Integrazione Guadagni* and Solidarity Contracts, and redundancy type payments such as Mobility Benefits, play an important role in compensating the unemployed. Unfortunately, there are no national figures on the sex breakdown of the recipients of these benefits. However, the targeting of these schemes on those from traditional industries and the construction sector means that women workers are less likely to be eligible. Women are also less likely to become unemployed through mass redundancies, which makes them ineligible for these benefits.

The general structure of the welfare system and the details of the unemployment compensation system presented here suggest cross-national

---

[7] In 1995 it was estimated that two million women in Britain had earnings below the threshold and therefore do not qualify for any insurance based benefits: this represents approximately 17 per cent of working women (ONS 1996: 346). In Denmark, 20 per cent of female part-timers work less than 10 hours per week and 27 per cent work between 11 and 20 hours. Therefore approximately a third of part-time women fall below the 15 hour threshold.

[8] They made up only 8 per cent of all 'fully subsidised yearly equivalent units of benefits' in 1993 (Rubery *et al.* 1998: 158).

TABLE 15.5 *ILO unemployed who receive unemployment compensation* (%)

	Men	Women
Denmark	68.3	70.4
France	53.5	43.8
Italy	8.5	7.2
UK	75.0	39.2

Source: Labour Force Survey, 1994.

differences in provision for the unemployed and the extent to which access to benefits is gendered. Relatively lenient qualification procedures and the individualized benefit system in Denmark suggests benefits should be equally available to unemployed men and women. In contrast, there is a low level of provision for the unemployed in the UK but the predominance of residual, safety-net benefits may mean unemployed men and women are *equally* poor. The strong social insurance dimension in France suggests that the unemployed with short or interrupted careers such as those with caring responsibilities, and labour market entrants, will be disadvantaged; however this may be tempered by policies that encourage mothers' employment and make allowances for childcare responsibilities. The social insurance based system in Italy, and the targeting of typically male industries also creates a potential for unequal gender outcomes.

Our expectation of gender inequalities in access to unemployment benefits in Italy, France and the UK, and equality of access in Denmark are partly confirmed by the figures in Table 15.5, which presents data on access to unemployment compensation from the 1994 Labour Force Survey.[9] This shows that there is no gender difference in access to benefits in Denmark. The biggest gap between men and women occurs in the UK, followed by France where there is a gap of about 10 percentage points. The ordering of these two countries is opposite to what Daly's typology predicts. Social policies that facilitate full-time work among women with children mean that the conservative social insurance-based system in France is not as detrimental to women as might have been expected. Essentially, many French women's employment patterns do not diverge significantly from the 'model male employee' on whom the insurance system is based. The operation of an hourly threshold in the UK and the disadvantages faced by lower-paid workers lead to strong sex differences in access to unemployment benefits despite the relatively weak link to employment records.

---

[9] The UK figures are not included in the European Labour Force Survey Report therefore the figures are taken from the Employment Gazette (Dec. 1995). This uses the UK LFS as its source.

Contrary to our prediction, levels of benefit coverage are equally low for men and women in Italy. The age composition of the unemployed means that the majority of male and female job seekers have no previous employment record to qualify them for benefits. It is unlikely that these figures have picked up those receiving benefits such as *Cassa Integrazione*. Therefore we are unable to establish the true level of gender differences in access to unemployment compensation among older workers in Italy.

In addition to what these figures tell us about governmental and societal attitudes to women's roles in the workplace and family, and their implications for issues of citizenship, they also influence the day-to-day financial situation of unemployed women. In the next section we will consider how cross-national differences in women's employment and household situation affect the financial impact of women's unemployment.

GENDER DIFFERENCES IN THE FINANCIAL IMPACT OF UNEMPLOYMENT

Those who propose that women's unemployment has less serious financial consequences than men's assume that women are predominantly secondary earners whose wages are more dispensable to the household. This position also assumes that the majority of unemployed women are in households where there is a male breadwinner. Our discussion of national patterns of employment and unemployment suggest that the degree to which households are dependent on women's wages is likely to differ cross-nationally. Furthermore, demographic trends such as the growth in single parent households and single person households will influence the extent to which the assumption of a male breadwinner providing financial protection for unemployed women holds true. A first insight into this question can be obtained by looking at the household situation of unemployed women.

Two groups of unemployed people are likely to have access to financial support from within the household—married or cohabiting people with an employed partner, and those living in the parental home. The ECHP data show that in Italy and France there is no significant difference in proportion of unemployed men and women who have access to alternative support within the household: in Italy this applies to 87 per cent of unemployed women and 80 per cent of unemployed men; in France the figures are 64 and 60 per cent respectively. In Denmark and the UK women are more likely to have access to financial support: 53 per cent of unemployed women in Denmark are supported by an employed partner or by parents, compared to 40 per cent of unemployed men, while in Britain the

TABLE 15.6. *Household situation of the unemployed, by sex* (%)

	Denmark		Italy		UK		France	
	M	F	M	F	M	F	M	F
Married/cohab.	45.6	59.1	23.3	38.5	48.5	48.7	45.1	64.3
partner emp.	28.7	45.3	7.0	32.8	17.3	33.2	24.8	48.1
partner not emp.	13.8	7.5	15.9	5.6	29.6	13.0	19.2	14.0
missing info.	3.1	6.3	0.3	0.1	1.7	2.6	1.1	2.3
Single parent[a]	[3.1]	8.8	[0.3]	3.3	[0.7]	10.4	[0.4]	9.2
Single live with parents	11.3	8.2	73.1	54.4	24.3	21.2	34.8	16.0
Single not with parents	40.0	23.9	3.3	3.8	26.5	19.7	19.6	10.4
	100.0	100.0	100.0	100.0	100.0	100.0	100.0	100.0
Unweighted N	(175)	(169)	(721)	(911)	(409)	(206)	(441)	(571)

[a] Includes all single parents regardless of whether or not they are living in the parental home.
Note: [ ] indicates N < 10.
Source: ECHP 1994.

proportions are 54 and 42 per cent respectively. These statistics show that the assumption that women are more likely to be sheltered from the financial effects of unemployment by their families does not necessarily hold true across countries. Even where it is supported, a high proportion of unemployed women do not live with a male breadwinner.

The arguments about the weaker financial consequences of female unemployment are particularly centred on married women, therefore we shall examine the contribution made by married/cohabiting women to household finances in the four study countries. Our discussion on female activity rates suggests that the proportion of married women making *any* contribution varies cross-nationally. This is confirmed when we examine the breadwinning status of couples in each country. The traditional model of a sole male breadwinner applies to only 16 per cent of Danish couples, 28 per cent of UK couples, and 31 per cent of French couples. Only in Italy is the sole male breadwinner still the most common arrangement. In Danish, French and UK couples, dual earnership is now the norm.

Table 15.7 shows the importance of married/cohabiting women's earnings in numeric terms, however, we can also estimate their contribution in financial terms. The first column of Table 15.8 indicates the mean contribution of married/cohabiting women to household earnings in couples where at least one partner is employed—couples where neither partner is earning are excluded. Italian women's contribution is lowest at 23 per cent on average, largely because of the high proportion of women who have zero earnings. UK and French women both make a mean contribution of 31 per cent. The positive effect of the higher incidence of full-time work in France is

TABLE 15.7. *Earnings profiles of married and cohabiting couples*[a] (%)

	Denmark	Italy	UK	France
No earner	4.3	8.6	10.2	8.8
Male sole breadwinner	16.1	50.7	28.5	31.3
Female sole breadwinner	7.1	6.2	8.5	7.0
Joint earners	72.5	34.5	52.8	52.9
	100.0	100.0	100.0	100.0
N	(1632)	(4450)	(2904)	(3923)

[a] Retired couples are excluded.
Source: ECHP 1994 using 1993 earnings data.

TABLE 15.8. *Contribution of married women to household earnings* (mean %)

	Dual Earner & Sole Earner Couples	Dual Earner Couples
Denmark	39.5	42.3
France	31.4	40.8
Italy	23.0	42.8
UK	30.5	35.7

Source: ECHP 1994 calculated using 1993 earnings data.

cancelled out by a lower participation rate. In Denmark married women's mean contribution stands at 40 per cent suggesting a high reliance on women's wages.

The second column confines the calculation to couples where both partners are employed. Interestingly, in dual earner households Italian women's contribution is high, at 43 per cent and is very similar to that of Danish and French women at 42 and 41 per cent respectively. This is likely to be the result of the high incidence of full-time work and the relatively narrow gender wage gap in Italy. In the UK, where part-time working is very common and wage gaps are high, married working women contribute an average of 36 per cent of joint earnings while their partners contribute 64 per cent.

These figures on the family status of unemployed women and on the financial contribution of married women to household finances—in the limited sense of both partners' earnings—suggest that there are significant cross-national differences in the financial importance of women's earnings, and consequently in the financial impact of their loss. These factors, combined with the features of the benefit system outlined above and in earlier chapters, are likely to produce distinct financial outcomes for men and women across countries.

MEASURES OF FINANCIAL HARDSHIP

Financial hardship among the unemployed will be examined in a number of different ways. Firstly we will use a poverty line measure of hardship which refers to whether or not equivalized household income is less than 50 per cent of the mean household income in that society. Secondly, we will use a measure of perceived difficulty in making ends meet. Using a non-income measure may identify needs and benefits that are not captured by household income, such as savings, debts, and non-cash benefits/services. Both questions refer to the financial situation of the *household.* While using a household measure is necessary to address the wider impact of women's unemployment and to take into account additional resources, it does present a number of problems. Most importantly, it obscures women's financial dependency and the impact this might have on women's material and subjective well-being. Secondly, household measures of poverty are based on the assumption that resources will be shared equally among the household members. Evidence of gender differences in access to personal spending money within the household (Vogler 1989; Rottman 1994) and control over money (Rottman 1994; Vogler and Pahl 1993) suggest that this assumption may be unrealistic. These reservations should be kept in mind when interpreting the results relating to married women and young people residing with their parents.

We first examine the levels of hardship using the 50 per cent mean poverty line. The figures show that there is no significant difference in the proportion of unemployed women and men who are poor in Denmark. In the other three countries, household poverty is substantially higher among unemployed men than unemployed women. In Italy and France this sex difference is attributable to a wide gap in the poverty rates of married men and women. In the UK, however, there are significant gender differences in poverty rates for both single and married unemployed respondents. In each of the countries, unemployed single mothers are found to have a high risk of poverty. Household poverty is lowest for both unemployed men and women in Denmark, confirming the effectiveness of the benefit system for both sexes—see Chapter 5 of this volume—rates of poverty for women are also relatively low in France, while in Italy and the UK the incidence of poverty is significantly higher for both sexes.

Using our second measure of household poverty the national differences in poverty rates among the unemployed are repeated. The unemployed are much more prone to economic hardship in Italy, France, and the UK, than in Denmark. The percentages in poverty in the UK and Italy are fairly similar on both measures, however, in Denmark the proportion of respondents experiencing difficulty making ends meet is much higher than the

TABLE 15.9. *Unemployed in poor households[a], by household type and sex* (%)

	Denmark		Italy		UK		France	
	M	F	M	F	M	F	M	F
Married/cohab.	2.2	2.2	52.3*	26.5	58.3*	31.2	31.7*	18.5
Single parent	[14.3]	35.7	[100]	40.7	[33.3]	45.0	[100]	57.1
Single live with parents	4.5	14.3	40.2	36.7	45.6*	22.0	25.6	29.4
Single not with parents	12.2	17.6	15.8	39.3	51.4*	69.4	39.3	32.1
All	6.8	9.7	42.5*	33.0	53.2*	37.9	31.3*	25.2

[a] Poor households are <50% mean household income, as adjusted by new OECD equivalence scale.
Notes: [ ] = N < 10; * Sig. difference between men and women @ 5% level.
Source: ECHP 1994.

TABLE 15.10. *Unemployed experiencing difficulty/great difficulty making ends meet, by household type* (%)

	Denmark		Italy		UK		France	
	M	F	M	F	M	F	M	F
Married/cohab.	24.7*	13.8	59.7*	38.0	47.8*	36.2	46.0*	36.4
Single parent	[66.7]	35.7	[100]	50.0	[66.7]	61.9	[100]	69.4
Single live with parents	18.2	21.4	44.0	42.1	36.9*	19.5	27.9	28.2
Single not with parents	30.8*	51.3	77.3	64.5	57.1	55.3	63.2*	43.6
All	27.7	25.5	49.0*	41.6	47.8*	39.2	43.3	38.9

Notes: [ ] = N < 10. * = P < 0.05.
Source: ECHP 1994.

percentage below the poverty line, and the same is true of women in France. In both countries the discrepancy between the two measures is widest among married respondents and singles living independently; therefore the measure may be picking up feelings of financial responsibility.

Position within the household continues to have a strong influence on the connection between unemployment and financial hardship: in all four countries single parents and single people living independently have the highest risk of poverty. These groups apparently do not have other household resources to draw upon to keep them out of poverty.

Turning to the question of gender differences, the results show that overall men and women's unemployment carries the same the risk of financial difficulty at the household level in both Denmark and France. Unemployed men are at significantly greater risk in both Italy and the UK. There is a significant difference between married men and married women in both countries and, in UK, the difference is also significant for the single living with parents. In France there are high levels of financial difficulty among single mothers, who make up 9 per cent of unemployed women. Levels are also high for single men not living with parents but this is countered by lower levels of difficulty among those living with parents, who make up a higher proportion of unemployed men. The result, in France, is gender similarity in the risk of financial difficulty.

The high level of reliance on female wages in Denmark—due to the high proportion of women who live independently, the high incidence of dual breadwinning in couples and the fact that women contribute 40 per cent of household earnings on average—coupled with the equal treatment of men and women under the social security system, means that there is no gender difference in the financial effect of unemployment. In the UK, high levels of part-time work among married women and a wide gender wage gap, coupled with the greater proportion of unemployed women than men who have an employed partner, results in significant sex differences in the financial impact of unemployment. An unanticipated gender difference is that unemployed men living with parents face worse economic circumstances than women in the same position.

In France and Italy an equal proportion of unemployed men and women have access to alternative support within the household via an employed partner or parents, therefore the proportions of unemployed women and men experiencing financial difficulty, but not household poverty, were much closer than those found in the UK. However, married women's contribution to household earnings was substantially lower than men's in both countries—31 per cent in France and 23 per cent in Italy. Therefore considerable differences in the poverty rate of married unemployed men and women were observed in both countries.

The gendered impact of unemployment is found to be strongly influenced by national patterns of female employment and household composition among the unemployed. However, the results provide little support for the assumption that female unemployment is financially inconsequential. Even among married unemployed women in the UK and Italy there is a very high risk of household poverty and financial difficulty. The assumption of a male provider whom unemployed women can rely upon for financial support is being overtaken by labour market and demographic developments such as the increase in single parent and one-person households. This is especially the case in Denmark but trends in France and the UK are heading in a similar direction. In Italy the traditional male breadwinner model is better preserved but is challenged by women's full-time participation in the labour market and by the very low birth rates among young Italian women. Where assumptions about the financial dependency of women within households and the primacy of men's breadwinner status are built into unemployment policies, this can lead to the exclusion of women from compensation schemes. Such policies also reinforce the attitude that, in the event of unemployment, women can retreat unproblematically back into the home. In the final section of this chapter we will address the issue of whether unemployment has a less detrimental effect on women's well-being.

GENDER, UNEMPLOYMENT, AND WELL-BEING

The arguments suggesting gender differences in the psychological impact of unemployment are somewhat more sophisticated than those relating to financial effects. The argument has taken three main forms. The first version suggests that women are less committed to employment than men and therefore will be less affected by its loss (Hakim 1982; Ashton 1986). In its stronger forms this argument suggests that the experience of joblessness will be similar for unemployed women and housewives. The second version suggests that women will be less psychologically affected by unemployment because of the availability of the domestic role (Jahoda 1982). This is not necessarily because women are more committed to this role than work, but because it provides them with certain categories of experience essential for psychological well-being which are normally imposed by employment. Thirdly, it is argued that if financial hardship is a major cause of the distress among the unemployed, psychological distress should be lower among women because of their status as secondary earners.

Although the authors mentioned above do not limit their claims to any national context, our discussion so far suggests that there is considerable room for cross-national variation. Firstly, we have seen that both the overall financial consequences of unemployment and the gender differences in economic hardship vary between the four study countries. Secondly, the 'importance' of employment in women's lives, measured in terms of the length of time invested in the labour market, also differs between the countries. In Denmark and France where women tend to participate in the labour market throughout the life-cycle, unemployment may be much more disruptive than in Italy and to a lesser extent the UK where women's employment is more discontinuous. Similarly, it might be argued that in countries where part-time work prevails among women, the personal and psychological impact of female unemployment will be lower. We would argue that it is more valid to tap into women's preferences for differing roles directly, rather than attempting to deduce them from labour market behaviour. We will therefore refer to respondents' attitudes to gender roles outlined in Table 15.1, and assess whether women with more traditional attitudes are less affected by unemployment because it involves a return to a preferred role within the household.

TABLE 15.11. *Employment deprivation among unemployed men and women*

	Denmark		Italy		Britain		France	
	M	F	M	F	M	F	M	F
Agree somewhat/strongly—								
Feel left out without paid job	42.3	42.1	71.5	61.3*	71.3	71.6	52.7	50.3
Get bored at home	38.4	31.3	64.9	52.6*	69.8	76.8	51.9	47.9
Often get depressed if I don't have a job	24.5	25.5	58.9	53.3	55.6	56.8	60.8	49.7
Being out of work leads to arguments about money	26.5	23.4	43.2	42.5	55.9	46.8	48.4	33.5*
Friends look down on you for not having a job	25.3	16.7	10.9	11.2	29.2	22.3	26.2	21.1
Disagree somewhat/strongly—								
Being at home v. satisfying	46.0	41.4	83.9	63.0*	67.6	56.8	65.6	53.0*
Having no job doesn't worry me at all	68.9	68.1	89.4	84.5	82.8	81.1	85.4	82.9
Don't need to work for the money	66.0	72.4	89.3	82.1	90.0	87.2	93.9	94.5
N	(159)	(142)	(145)	(176)	(173)	(94)	(131)	(165)
Mean Emp. Deprivation Score	*16.8*	*15.6*	*21.7*	*19.9**	*21.4*	*21.0*	*20.8*	*19.9*

Notes: * = P < 0.05.
Source: Eurobarometer 1996.

In order to analyse the personal impact of unemployment among women, we refer to a series of questions designed to address 'employment deprivation' (Gallie and Vogler 1994). Jobless respondents to the 1996 Eurobarometer survey were asked to express their level of agreement or disagreement with a series of statements about what it is like not to have a paid job. These questions cover a range of aspects of respondent's lives and well-being: family life, status, boredom, exclusion, depression, and financial need. Responses are placed on a five-point likert scale ranging from 'agree strongly' to 'disagree strongly'. In Table 15.11 we report the percentage of unemployed respondents who expressed the most negative view of joblessness on each of the eight statements.

The responses to these questions were also added together to form a scale. The scale excludes the two items that refer to money. This is done so that we can assess how far subjective well-being is linked to financial circumstances without the danger that our measure of well-being is indirectly measuring financial hardship. The index comprising of the six remaining questions ranges from 6 to 30. The alpha for the scale taking all four countries together is 0.78, which indicates that the scale is reliable.

There is a striking similarity in the responses of unemployed men and women in Denmark and Britain. There is no significant disagreement between the sexes on any of the items, and mean scores on the employment deprivation scale do not differ significantly for men and women.

There is somewhat less agreement between unemployed men and women in Italy and France. In both countries women are less inclined to disagree that being at home is very satisfying. However the difference between men's and women's mean scores are small in magnitude and only statistically significant in Italy. Therefore theories which predict a *general* difference in the impact of unemployment among men and women do not receive a strong endorsement.

Jahoda's theory identifies more specific areas in which women's domestic role can substitute for employment. Firstly, she suggests that the domestic role can provide women with an alternative source of structure, purpose, and activity. However only in Italy were unemployed women less likely to report feeling bored and 'left out' than unemployed men. Secondly, Jahoda suggests that the homemaker role provides women with an alternative social status. The item that most closely relates to this issue is the statement 'friends look down on me for not having a paid job' but there are no significant sex differences in the responses to this item. Therefore, Jahoda's theory finds little support, at least when we take women as a whole.

In the light of our previous analysis it is also of interest that few significant gender differences emerge on the two statements that refer to money. Unemployed women in all four countries resoundingly disagreed that they didn't need to work for the money and nowhere was there a significant sex difference. With the exception of France, arguments about money appear to be as common in the case of female as male unemployment. The high level of family tensions over money in Italy where the majority of the unemployed are young people living with parents, suggests that economic dependency within the household is causing stresses that are hidden in household measures of financial well-being.

The responses of unemployed women were also compared to those of full-time housewives as a test of the 'strong thesis' that women's continued commitment to their caring responsibilities means their experience of joblessness is similar to that of housewives. There are large differences between unemployed women and housewives on almost every statement in all four countries.[10] The mean employment deprivation scores of housewives were 9.3 in Denmark, 14 in Italy, 13.9 in Britain and 12.7 in France. This means that in all four countries unemployed women are much closer to unemployed men than to full-time housewives.

To consider women as an undifferentiated group repeats the error of previous thinking on women's unemployment. Therefore, the next step in

---

[10] The one exception is the experience of stigma among British women. Almost one in five British housewives feel their friends look down on them for not having a job.

our analysis will be to examine employment deprivation among groups of women with different degrees of access to a domestic role, and with different attitudes towards this role.

We use a number of different indicators of involvement in the domestic role. Jahoda's theory suggests that simply by being employed or being a housewife, a person gains access to certain categories of experience that are psychologically beneficial. From this perspective, simple indicators such as presence of children in the household and marital status should reduce employment deprivation among unemployed women. Hakim (1996) has argued that part-time work is an important signifier of whether a woman is committed to family or work, therefore we might expect differences between those who have previously worked part-time and those who have not. Similarly, we might expect differences between those who were full-time housewives and those who have lost jobs. Finally, women's attitudes towards gender roles may give us an insight into their preferences for family and work roles that is less contaminated by practical constraints, therefore this is also included in the model. Gender role traditionalism is measured using the questions outlined in Table 15.1. The relationship between these characteristics and employment deprivation is examined by means of OLS regression models—see Table 15.12.

In addition to the variables relating to the domestic role, the models also include a general measure of work commitment which records whether or not the respondent would want to work if she had enough money to live as comfortably as she would like for the rest of her life. We also include a measure of financial difficulty, which identifies respondents finding it 'very' or 'quite difficult' to make ends meet. The final controls included are years of education, duration of unemployment, and age.

We look first at the 'domestic role' indicators. Neither being married nor having children over the age of 5 years leads to a significant reduction in unemployed women's employment deprivation in the study countries. Indeed in Britain and Denmark some groups of mothers displayed greater employment deprivation than women without children. In France and Denmark however, having a child under 6 reduces employment deprivation among unemployed women. Clearly marriage and motherhood are not straightforward indicators of a satisfying substitute for employment, only women with the most demanding domestic role, those with pre-school children, find joblessness less problematic. However, even this group record substantially higher levels of employment deprivation than full-time housewives in their own country: therefore having access to this alternative role does not put them in the same position as those who are voluntarily jobless.

Women's previous record of employment appears to be a somewhat better predictor of their dissatisfaction with unemployment, but only in Italy and France. Italian and French women who entered unemployment from

Helen Russell and Paolo Barbieri

TABLE 15.12. *Regression models of employment deprivation amongst the unemployed*

	Denmark		Italy		Britain		France	
	M	F	M	F	M	F	M	F
Constant	11.90	17.20	19.50	21.00	14.90	18.70	19.40	21.40
Child <6yrs	1.24	−2.15*	1.39	−0.51	0.56	0.51	0.79	−1.97*
Child 6–15	1.42	−0.29	0.41	−0.62	−0.58	2.98**	0.47	0.79
Child >15	−2.60	2.81*	1.76	−0.36	−0.52	0.92	−2.53	−0.55
Married	−0.13	0.07	0.20	−0.41	0.41	−0.59	−0.76	−0.99
Traditional	−0.30	−1.13*	0.24	−0.93**	0.44	−2.39**	0.62	−0.43
Committed to Emp.	5.68**	3.91*	0.27	0.51	4.43**	1.39	1.64	1.32
Prev. part-time	−4.28*	−0.90	1.48	−2.46**	−3.17	2.79*	0.98	−0.27
Prev. out of lab. mrkt.	−0.77	−0.57	−1.11	−2.54**	−0.53	0.99	0.50	−2.57*
Financial difficulty	2.25*	1.28	2.24**	1.42*	2.99*	2.53*	−0.27	2.22*
Age 25–39	−1.56	−2.93*	−0.21	−0.66	−0.46	−1.59	−0.21	−1.72
Age 40–54	−1.56	−1.27	0.39	0.17	1.31	−1.01	2.56	−1.98
Age 55+	−1.61	−3.84	(6.9**)	—	−0.38	−0.87	−2.73	−3.55*
Yrs in ed.	0.06	−0.14	0.01	0.09	0.04	0.24	−0.14	−0.06
LTU 1yr+	1.55	2.01*	0.30	0.47	−1.17	−0.54	3.21**	0.54
N	144	125	126	167	153	83	115	139
Adj. R Square	0.247	0.245	0.228	0.128	0.127	0.271	0.159	0.143

Notes: * $P < 0.05$, ** $P < 0.005$; ( ) N less than 10; Base categories = no children, single, not committed, previously employed full-time, under 25, unemployed less than 1 year.
Source: Eurobarometer 1996.

economic inactivity, and Italian women who previously worked part-time, were found to experience lower employment deprivation than ex-full-time workers.

Holding traditional gender role attitudes significantly reduced employment deprivation among unemployed women in Britain, Denmark, and Italy. This effect is greatest in Britain where each additional score on the traditionalism scale reduced employment deprivation by two points. These findings suggest that in Denmark and Britain especially, it is an individual's acceptance of the traditional division of gender roles that influences whether or not she will be 'content' with joblessness. Measures which attempt to deduce this 'attitude' from women's current domestic commitments and previous behaviour are much less successful.

Of the control variables, financial hardship has the greatest effect. Those who experience difficulty making ends meet express higher levels of employment deprivation. Financial difficulty appears to be more strongly linked to employment deprivation among unemployed men in Denmark,

Italy, and Britain and among unemployed women in France. Years spent in education has no effect on women's employment deprivation; the positive effect of additional employment commitment might be cancelled out by greater psychological resources to cope with unemployment.[11] The results on unemployment duration suggest an intensification of employment deprivation over time among French men and Danish women, and an adaptation to unemployment among the British long-term unemployed.

The differences between the four countries can be seen more clearly in the joint models presented in Table 15.13. Denmark is used as the base category and it is evident from Model 1 that the unemployed in Italy, France, and Britain experience much higher levels of employment deprivation than the Danes. These country differences remain when financial difficulty, employment commitment, marital status, parental status, duration of unemployment, education, and age are controlled—as shown in Model 2. Given the country differences in poverty rates among the unemployed, and the strong link between financial difficulty and employment deprivation, it is possible that further indicators of the standard of living among the unemployed would reduce the country effects.

The interactions between country and each of the explanatory variables were also tested. The results are presented in Model 3. Here we can see that the link between employment deprivation and work commitment is strongest in Denmark and weakest amongst the Italian unemployed. Long-term unemployment is significantly less detrimental to individual's subjective well-being in Britain and France compared to the other two countries. Entering unemployment from part-time work is found to have a distinctive effect for British women: previously working part-time *increases* employment deprivation amongst British women while it has the opposite effect for all other respondents. This suggests that British women do not work part-time because they place a low value on paid work; it is likely that practical considerations such as the lack of childcare facilities are a major factor.

When all four countries are taken together the gap between unemployed women's and men's deprivation scores is sufficient to register as statistically significant. This suggests, at the wider European level, that there is a tendency for women to experience less employment deprivation than men, but that within countries this difference is small. In the four country model, having a young child is found to significantly reduce unemployed women's employment deprivation. These women are likely to have the most demanding domestic roles and this appears to increase the possibility of a meaningful role outside employment even if joblessness is enforced. With the exception of this 'motherhood effect' and the influence of traditional

---

[11] Whelan *et al.* (1991) found that those with higher educational qualifications were less psychologically affected by unemployment.

TABLE 15.13. *Four country models of employment deprivation among the unemployed*

	Model 1	Model 2	Model 3
Constant	16.78	15.54	12.49
Italy	4.55**	5.03**	9.58**
Britain	4.89**	4.08**	5.41**
France	4.10**	4.04**	5.31**
Female	−1.14**	−0.93**	0.89
Child under 6		−0.46	0.50
Child 6–15yrs		0.14	0.15
Child over 15		−0.58	−0.36
Married		−0.22	−0.25
Traditionalism		−0.31*	0.01
Committed to emp.		2.37**	5.30**
Prev. part-time		−0.53	−1.87*
Previously outside lab. market		−1.44**	−1.30**
Financial difficulty		1.89**	1.86**
Age 25–39		−0.98*	−0.96*
Age 40–54		−0.11	−0.20
Age 55+		−1.74*	−1.67*
Years in education		−0.02	−0.02
Unemp. 1yr+		0.71*	1.71**
Female*Traditionalism			−1.05**
Female*Child under 6			−1.84*
Italy*LTU			−1.53*
GB*LTU			−2.17**
Italy*Commitment			−5.27**
France*Commitment			−3.71**
GB*Commitment			−1.89*
France* Traditional			0.63*
France*Part-time			2.12*
GB*Part-time			−1.25
GB*Female*part-time[a]			5.23*
N	1172	988	988
Adj. R Square	0.17	0.25	0.31

[a] The relevant lower order interactions were included in the model but are not presented here.
Notes: * $P < 0.05$, ** $P < 0.005$. Based categories as in Table 15.2, reference country = Denmark.
Source: Eurobarometer 1996.

gender role attitudes, the determinants of employment deprivation among unemployed men and women are found to be the same.

The differences between unemployed women and men's experience of employment deprivation are much smaller than speculation about the gendered impact of unemployment might suggest; the gender differences are also smaller than those found using more global measures of life satisfaction (Gallie and Russell 1998; Chapter 14 in this volume). It is possible that women's role within the family can have a greater effect on their satisfaction with life in general than on their feelings about joblessness. Previous research has also tended to consider women as one group, whereas this analysis has emphasized the need to distinguish between different groups of unemployed women. The domestic role is found to reduce the subjective impact of unemployment as many have suggested, however, the effect is concentrated among the mothers of very young children, and the effect is mediated through women's attitudes and values. To assume that all mothers and wives are psychologically protected from unemployment is overly deterministic.

CONCLUSION

This chapter has sought to examine women's experience of unemployment in four countries with very different gender cultures and structures. Denmark represents a society in which women are playing an increasing role as breadwinners, although the renegotiation of caring responsibilities between men and women is not as well advanced. The reliance on women's wages within Danish households means that it is untenable to consider women's income as non-essential. The financial importance of women's earnings is reflected in the absence of gender differences in the financial impact of unemployment. The non-traditional gender attitudes of the population are mirrored in social policies which support working mothers, and in a social security system that does not rest upon the assumption of female dependency within the household. The individualization of the benefit system and the operation of relatively short contribution periods for insurance benefits mean that unemployed men and women are found to have equal access to benefit payments. The benefit system means that the financial stress caused by unemployment is *equally low* for men and women. This particular combination of cultural and institutional factors also has implications for the subjective experience of unemployment among women. While Danish women have earned equal status as breadwinners, this has been accompanied by equal levels of employment deprivation when this role cannot be fulfilled.

The Italian labour market and welfare regime combine to offer women a stark choice between full-time participation in employment on relatively equal terms with men, or full-time domesticity. This division is also evident in the treatment of unemployed women: once women have been in employment they have equal claim to the various unemployment compensation schemes notwithstanding their indirect exclusion because of the focus on traditionally male industries; however, support for women returners is non-existent. There is still strong support for the primacy of men's breadwinning role and for the view that men's unemployment is more serious than women's. As a consequence, Italian women, like French women, bear a disproportionate share of unemployment. The age composition of the unemployed plays a major role in shaping the impact of unemployment by gender in Italy. Nevertheless, despite the very high proportion of unemployed men who are under 25 living with parents, the financial differences between men and women are considerable. While household measures of poverty may obscure the individual effect of unemployment among young people, the high levels of economic stress in the households where they reside suggests that we should not overestimate the amount of material support they receive. The continuing support for the traditional division of labour between men and women within Italy may account for the wider gender differences in employment deprivation found here, especially among previous part-timers and returners.

In the UK, gender differences emerge in both access to unemployment compensation systems and in the financial impact of unemployment. The link between benefit payments and recent employment, the operation of an earnings threshold, and the use of a household means-test with low earning disregards means that many women are denied benefits during unemployment, even though there is a relatively short qualification period. These low recipiency rates mean that women's unemployment has an effect on household poverty that is disproportionate to the actual drop in earnings. The low value of benefit provision coupled with the significant proportion of unemployed women who do not have another breadwinner in the household means that, despite the gender difference in the financial impact of unemployment, the link between female unemployment and household poverty is very high in the UK. The high levels of employment deprivation among unemployed women in the UK further suggest that the idea that unemployed women can be easily absorbed back into the domestic sphere is mistaken.

In France, the potential for the strongly insurance-based welfare regime to disadvantage and exclude unemployed women has been moderated by relatively high female participation rates and a high incidence of full-time work among women. These employment patterns have been encouraged by highly developed childcare services and generous maternity leave schemes which are not typical of other employment-centred welfare regimes. The French unemployment protection system has also been adapted to take some account of women's caring responsibilities when deciding eligibility for benefit. However caring is still not given equal status to employment, and these discounts only apply to Unemployment Assistance, which in most other European countries is not linked to employment record at all. Therefore, there remains a considerable gap in unemployed men and women's access to benefits. The French example suggests that the welfare regime should be considered in conjunction with existing employment patterns before assessing its implications for gender equality. The concentration of male unemployment among young men living with parents means that the gender differences in the financial impact of unemployment are not as wide as might have been expected. However, elements of a breadwinner model remain in the differences between married men and women, and in the lower levels of employment deprivation found among labour market returnees and mothers of young children.

This analysis has shown that the social policy framework, and the societal gender role attitudes that are embedded within it, are extremely important in influencing women's experience of unemployment and in establishing whether the economic and subjective impact of unemployment is gendered. However, gender equality in outcomes is not necessarily a 'good' in itself, for example, the equal exclusion of young unemployed men and women from benefit systems in Italy is not a welcome policy outcome. In the four countries that we have analysed it is clear that where more gender-neutral policies towards the unemployed are combined with generous levels of benefits, the financial and non-financial well-being of both unemployed women and men is greatest.

16

Public Attitudes to Unemployment in Different European Welfare Regimes

Torben Fridberg and Niels Ploug

INTRODUCTION

This chapter is concerned to describe public attitudes towards unemployment in a number of European countries, and to examine the relationship between public attitudes and the different welfare regimes in Europe. Public attitudes concern the importance of unemployment as a political problem, welfare benefits, and finally possible solutions to unemployment. We will focus on two main dimensions: first, attitudes to unemployment as a political problem and what to do about it, and second, attitudes to the unemployed themselves, the benefits they are receiving and what they should be expected to do to find work.

The attitudes to unemployment of the wider population may be of central importance for the experience of the unemployed. The more people in work sympathize with those who are unable to find jobs, the more likely it is that the unemployed will find support in their local communities. Conversely, if there is widespread public hostility towards the unemployed, this is likely to lead to sharp stigmatization, which by increasing the sense of social isolation of unemployed people and the difficulty of maintaining a favourable self-identity may contribute to the process of social exclusion. It might also be of importance which groups or classes in society consider unemployment to be an important problem, or not, and it is of interest to see whether there is a difference between classes in the perception of the unemployment problem in different welfare state regimes.

A number of factors could in particular be expected to influence public attitudes to the unemployed. In the first place attitudes may vary depending on *the level of unemployment*. The higher the unemployment rate the more evident it is likely to be that unemployment cannot be attributed to the unemployed themselves. Indeed, this is likely to be reinforced by the fact that a much wider section of the population will either have direct experience of unemployment or know family or friends who are in this situation.

As employment prospects improve, then one might expect a more critical attitude to the unemployed on grounds that jobs are available and those committed to employment should be able to find them.

A second factor that may influence the attitudes of the wider public is the nature of the welfare regime or more specifically *the nature of the welfare regime for the unemployed* as outlined by Gallie and Paugam in the introduction to this book. It is sometimes suggested that there is a built-in conflict of interest between those dependent on welfare benefits and those in work who support them through their taxes. It may be expected that expensive regimes are followed by less favourable attitudes to those benefiting from the system, and it is sometimes claimed that *insurance* based systems might tend to reduce this sense of conflicting interest as people are perceived to be receiving support to which they are entitled on the basis of their own past contributions.

Public support may also be affected by the relative *generosity* of welfare support. Where systems provide sufficient assistance to give reasonable protection of living standards, there may be less sympathy towards the unemployed since they are not seen to be suffering from severe financial hardship. More generous systems may also lead to less sympathetic attitudes in the general public because they impose a higher financial burden on those in employment. Other factors like age, sex, and attachment to the labour market might influence public attitudes, and more subjective factors like self-reported class affiliation and political attitudes might play a role too.

The paper will compare the seven countries which are covered by the Eurobarometer surveys (1984, 1992, 1993)—Denmark, Germany, France, Ireland, Italy, The Netherlands, and the United Kingdom. Of the eight countries included in the EPUSE study, only Sweden has not participated in the Eurobarometer surveys until recently.

PUBLIC ATTITUDES TO UNEMPLOYMENT

Throughout Europe unemployment has been considered a major problem since unemployment rates in many European countries started to rise in the 1970s. It has been a concern and worry not only for politicians and economists and other actors at the policy level, but has certainly also been reflected in surveys on general public attitudes in all the countries.

For comparative use, the Eurobarometer surveys included questions on whether the fight against unemployment is considered to be an important problem in 1984 and again in 1993—see Table 16.1. In 1984, the vast majority in all the countries included in this study considered the fight against

TABLE 16.1. *Public attitude considering fight against unemployment to be a very important problem, 1984 and 1993, (%)*

	1984			1993		
	All	In work	Unemployed	All	In work	Unemployed
Denmark	85	84	88	64	62	70
All Germany	—	—	—	—	—	—
West Germany	79	77	88	76	75	88
East Germany	—	—	—	89	91	92
France	79	76	89	89	86	95
Ireland	87	87	87	93	93	91
Italy	84	84	84	87	87	93
Netherlands	76	73	82	60	58	58
UK	78	78	84	76	76	77

Notes: All includes non-active persons.
Source: Eurobarometers, 20 (1984) and 40 (1993).

unemployment to be a very important problem. The variation was only between 76 per cent agreeing in The Netherlands and 87 per cent agreeing in Ireland. In 1993, most Europeans still considered the fight to be very important, but now differences between the countries had increased. The proportion in Ireland had increased to 93 per cent, but in Denmark and The Netherlands the proportions agreeing had decreased to less than 67 per cent.

Level of Unemployment

The relationship between the importance attributed to unemployment as a social problem and the level of unemployment is shown in Figs. 16.1 and 16.2. The first conclusion to be drawn is that there is not a simple relationship between actual unemployment rates and public attitudes about the importance of the unemployment problem. Certainly this does not mean that the magnitude of the real problem of unemployment is without any relevance for public attitudes. At least in 1993 there was a relationship as expressed by the rather high coefficient for R^2. Ireland, it has been seen, was a country where unemployment was particularly likely to be viewed as an important social problem. And unemployment in Ireland was very high both in 1984 and 1993 compared with the other countries, and was even a little higher in 1993 than in the mid-1980s. Similarly, the proportion considering unemployment to be an important problem in 1993 was somewhat higher in East Germany than in West Germany, which was consistent with their different unemployment rates. But otherwise it appears that the salience of the issue of unemployment is not systematically related to the actual levels of unemployment in the different countries—as shown in Figs. 16.1 and 16.2. In

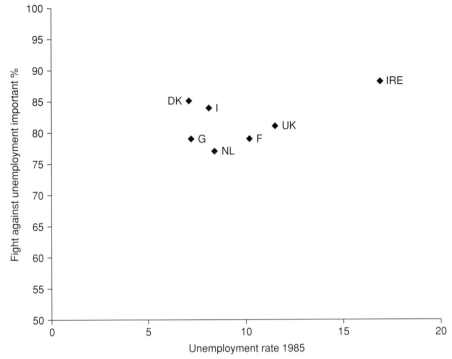

F IG. 16.1. Unemployment rate and those considering the fight against
unemployment to be a very important problem, 1984, (%)

Note: Coefficient of determination R^2 = 0.28. G indicates figures for West Germany
only, East German data being unavailable.

Soure: Eurobarometer, 20 (1984); EC (1996c).

Denmark and The Netherlands, unemployment levels in 1993 were not very
different from the levels in 1984. The changes in public attitudes cannot,
then, be fully explained by changes in level of unemployment.

It is also easy to imagine that the differences in attitudes to the severity
of the unemployment problem might be influenced by the incidence of long-
term unemployment, as the problems created for the individual as well as
for society at large are accentuated by the duration of unemployment. But
differences in long-term unemployment are also not related consistently to
public attitudes about the importance of fighting unemployment—Fig. 16.3.
Certainly, in Ireland, where the incidence of long-term unemployment is
highest, public attitudes show the highest concern in 1993. Conversely,
incidence of long-term unemployment and public worry were relatively low
in Denmark. In The Netherlands, however, the incidence was high and public attitudes show less concern, whereas in France public concern was very

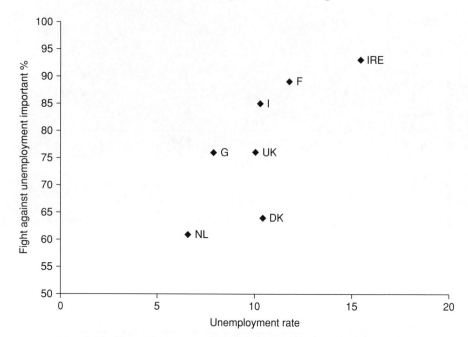

FIG. 16.2. Unemployment rate and those considering the fight against
unemployment to be a very important problem, 1993, (%)

Notes: Coefficient of determination $R^2 = 0.60$. G indicates figures for West Germany
only (also Figs. 16.3, 16.4).

Source: Eurobarometer, 40 (1993); EC (1996c).

high, but the problems of long-term unemployment were less than in most
of the other countries included.

A little more convincing is the relationship between the attitudes to
the importance of fighting unemployment and the subjective perception of
whether the employment situation was worse at the time of questioning in
1993 than it was 12 months before, as can be seen in Fig. 16.4. At one
end was France, where relatively large proportions of the population found
that the unemployment situation had got worse than a year before and considered the fight against unemployment very important, and at the other
end was Denmark with somewhat lower percentages agreeing on both perceptions. The explanation for this may be that changes in the employment
situation bring the problem more sharply into the focus of public debate
and so to the attention of the public at large. In contrast a more stable
situation implies that the issue is inclined to become less publicly visible,
and this again is reflected in the kind of variations which can be observed
in measurements of public attitudes.

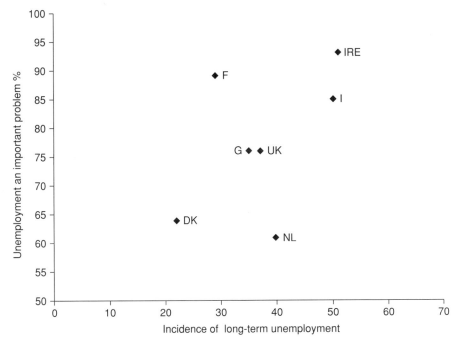

FIG. 16.3. Incidence of long-term unemployment and those considering
unemployment to be a very important problem, 1993, (%)

Notes: Coefficient of determination $R^2 = 0.25$.

Source: Eurobarometer, 40 (1993); EC (1996c).

This indicates that attitudes towards unemployment as a social problem
are related more to subjective factors such as the perception of the situation for the unemployed, than to objective factors like the level of unemployment or the level of long-term unemployment. Therefore one should
look for explanations of the differences in attitudes using more subjective variables. The regression analysis shown in Table 16.2 confirms this.
Whether the person was unemployed or in work at the time of interviewing is not significant, but political affiliation on a left/right scale does have
a significant influence on whether people think that fighting unemployment
is a very important problem in four of the countries. People with left-
wing sympathies are significantly more likely to think of unemployment as
a very important problem than are those with right-wing sympathies. This
is highly significant in the UK and Ireland, and significant in Denmark and
West Germany. The class variable has significant influence on the perception of the importance of unemployment only in France and the UK—which
may come as no surprise as these are the traditional class-societies in the

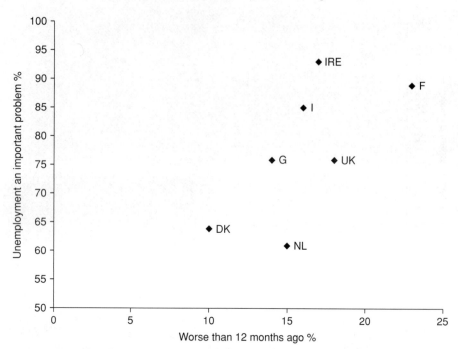

F<small>IG</small>. 16.4. Those finding employment situation worse now than 12 months ago and
considering unemployment to be a very important problem, 1993, (%)

Note: Coefficient of determination R^2 = 0.44.

Source: Eurobarometer, 40 (1993).

T<small>ABLE</small> 16.2. *Regression analysis of variables which significantly influence the perception of
the fight against unemployment as a very important problem, 1993*

	Sex	Age	Class	Political affiliation
Denmark				*
West Germany				*
East Germany		*		
France	*		*	
Ireland				**
Italy		*		
Netherlands		**		
United Kingdom	**		*	***

Notes: * 0.01 < P < 0.05, ** 0.001 < P < = 0.01, *** P < = 0.001; Variables were entered
simultaneously into the regression, together with employment and marital status; employment
status (unemployed/in work) and marital status were not significant.
Source: Eurobarometer, 40 (1993).

analysis. And it is certainly of no surprise that people from the lower classes find the unemployment problem more important than do people from the higher classes. Traditional background variables like sex and age have a significant influence in a number of countries. In France and the UK women worry significantly more about the unemployment problem than do men; and in The Netherlands, Italy, and East Germany young people are more concerned with the unemployment problem than are older people. A separate regression analysis for men and women reveals that political affiliation is especially important for the attitudes of men in the UK, but its influence is also significant for women.

But the main conclusion from this part of the analysis remains that 'politics matters' when it comes to attitudes towards whether unemployment is an important problem. Whether or not a person had experienced unemployment themselves was not significant in any of the countries.

PUBLIC ATTITUDES TO THE UNEMPLOYED

Apart from the general perception that the unemployed have a right to be sufficiently well protected, there is, however, a general perception that they also have some duties—see Table 16.3. Most people in all countries tend to

TABLE 16.3. *Obligations on the unemployed, responses to varying positions*[a]*, by country, 1992, (%)*

	Response			
	a	b	c	d
Denmark	95	50	69	42
All Germany				
West Germany	93	60	65	47
East Germany	95	80	60	14
France	95	49	74	50
Ireland	96	54	67	49
Italy	87	38	71	49
Netherlands	95	42	77	66
United Kingdom	93	68	59	34

[a] Respondents were asked: could you tell whether you tend to agree or disagree with each of the these statements about the unemployed?
a) *The unemployed should accept additional training if they cannot find another job.*
b) *The unemployed should be allowed to turn down a job while still continuing to receive unemployment benefits if the job offer does not match their qualifications and experience.*
c) *The unemployed should not be allowed to turn down a job if it is located within an acceptable distance of the place where they live.*
d) *Fewer people would be unemployed if unemployment benefits were much lower.*
Source: Eurobarometer, 37.1 (1992).

agree that *the unemployed should accept additional training if they cannot find another job*. Also the majority in all countries found that *the unemployed should not be allowed to turn down a job if it is located within an acceptable distance of the place where they live*. Most restrictive in this sense were the French and the Dutch, but the differences in level between the countries are not very large.

The differences between countries are somewhat greater when it comes to views about whether the unemployed should be allowed to turn down a job while still continuing to receive unemployment benefits if the job offer does not match their qualifications and experience. Two out of three people in the UK find that the unemployed should be allowed to turn down a job on these grounds, whereas only one out of three in Italy share this opinion. In The Netherlands a minority considers that unemployed people should be allowed to turn down a job offer if it does not match their qualifications; this corresponds with the fact that most people in The Netherlands think that the unemployed should accept additional training instead. This correspondence is found, but not to the same degree, in Italy.

Most restrictive towards the unemployed is the statement that *fewer people would be unemployed if unemployment benefits were much lower*, as it might imply that there is too little incentive for the unemployed to get work because of unemployment benefits. This attitude most obviously may vary with the generosity of unemployment benefit. It is indeed the case that in The Netherlands, which has exceptionally high benefits, a majority agree with this statement. In Denmark, however, which is close to The Netherlands in level of generosity, the proportion thinking that the benefits are too high is the same as in Italy, which has the most meagre unemployment benefits. Actually, public attitudes on this issue are about the same in Denmark, West Germany, France, Ireland, and Italy. Only The Netherlands has a rather high proportion and the UK a rather low proportion believing that benefits are too high. East Germany comes out with the lowest proportion on this question: only one in seven believes that cutting unemployment benefits will reduce unemployment.

The answers to the four statements have been combined into an overall score of the extent to which people stress the duties of the unemployed, a measure of restrictiveness towards the unemployed, when they are receiving unemployment benefits. The average score in each country is shown in Table 16.4. From this it appears that the most restrictive public attitude towards the recipients of unemployment benefit is found in The Netherlands. This corresponds with the earlier evidence about the attitudes of the public in The Netherlands, which considers that the protection of the unemployed is sufficient, and regards unemployment as a less important social problem than in other countries. So it may be easier for the Dutch to stress that the unemployed themselves have duties in getting work. In the light of such

TABLE 16.4. *Average score of restrictiveness, 1992*

	All	Men	Women
Denmark	2.5	2.6	2.5
All Germany	2.3	2.4	2.3
West Germany	2.4	2.5	2.4
East Germany	1.9	1.9	1.9
France	2.5	2.7	2.7
Ireland	2.6	2.6	2.6
Italy	2.7	2.7	2.7
Netherlands	3.0	2.9	3.0
United Kingdom	2.2	2.1	2.3

Note: Restrictiveness score determined from responses to the questions set out in Table 16.3.
Source: Eurobarometer, 37.1 (1992).

reasoning it should be expected that Denmark would come second in the degree of restrictiveness of attitudes, but public attitudes are not more restrictive towards the unemployed in Denmark than in France and Ireland. Instead it is Italy that is the country with the second most restrictive attitudes, even though the Italians in general are not satisfied with the protection of the unemployed. Least restrictive were the British, who were very dissatisfied with the protection of the unemployed.

Level of Unemployment

Public attitudes concerning the duties of the unemployed in getting into work are not dependent in a simple way on the level of unemployment in the country—see Fig. 16.5. Neither is it correlated to the type of welfare regime or the generosity of unemployment benefits—see Fig. 16.6.

Actually, public attitudes concerning most of the statements included here do not differ much between the European countries. The Netherlands stands out as the country with the most restrictive attitudes, stressing the obligations of the unemployed to get work, and the UK is the least restrictive country in this respect. A regression analysis, shown in Table 16.5, is consistent with the earlier analysis of whether unemployment is an important problem or not—in that political attitudes are also highly significant when it comes to restrictiveness towards the unemployed. This is the case in all countries but Italy and East Germany: the more a person's political sympathies are right-wing the more restrictive they are towards the unemployed.

As was the case in the previous regression analysis the class variable is significant in France, and this time also in Denmark and East Germany. But whereas a person's own experience of unemployment has no significance

Torben Fridberg and Niels Ploug

FIG. 16.5. Unemployment rate and average score of restrictive attitudes towards unemployed, 1992

Note: Coefficient of determination $R^2 = 0.02$.

Source: Eurobarometer, 37.1 (1992); EC (1996c).

for attitudes about whether unemployment in general was an important problem, it is highly significant for attitudes to the duties and rights of the unemployed. People who have not been unemployed during the previous five years are more restrictive towards the unemployed than are people who have experienced unemployment during that period of time. This variable is significant in all countries but West Germany and Italy. Age also plays an important role.

In Germany—with a small difference in the level of significance between West and East—Italy, Ireland, and the UK young people tend to be less restrictive towards the unemployed than do older people. Gender has no effect, except maybe in West Germany. A separate regression analysis for men and women reveals that the strong significance of political affiliation is found for both sexes in all the six countries where political orientation is important. The importance for men and women of a person's experience of unemployment, however, differs between the countries. In France, Denmark, and Italy, it is particularly among women that the experience of unemployment is important for attitudes to the duties of the unemployed. In the other countries the importance of personal experience of unemployment is particularly great for men.

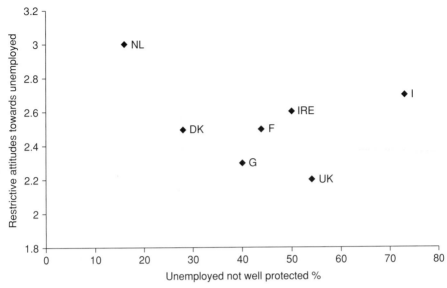

F<small>IG</small>. 16.6. Percentage finding that the unemployed are not sufficiently well
protected and average score of restrictive attitudes towards unemployed, 1992

Note: Coefficient of determination $R^2 = 0.11$.

Source: Eurobarometer, 37.1 (1992).

T<small>ABLE</small> 16.5. *Regression on score of restrictiveness, 1992*

	Sex	Age	Unemployed last five years	Class	Political affiliation
Denmark			***	**	***
West Germany	*	**			***
East Germany		*	**	*	
France			***	*	***
Ireland		**	***		**
Italy		**			
Netherlands			***		***
United Kingdom		***	**		**

Notes: * $0.01 < P < 0.05$, ** $0.001 < P <= 0.01$, *** $P <= 0.001$; Marital status of no significance.
Source: Eurobarometer 37.1 (1992).

So, when it comes to attitudes to the duties of the unemployed, a person's own experience of unemployment is important in all the countries except West Germany. People who have been unemployed within the last five years are less restrictive than those who have not been unemployed during that period. But the most significant correlation in this analysis— as was the case with the analysis of the attitudes towards unemployment as a political problem—is that 'politics matters'. People with right-wing sympathies in all countries, except East Germany, seem to be significantly more restrictive towards the unemployed than do people with left-wing sympathies.

Welfare Regimes and the Unemployment Question

It has been demonstrated before that, in general, the European welfare states enjoy substantial support from their populations (Ferrera 1993; Taylor-Gooby 1995; Svallfors 1996) in spite of discussions around increasing social expenditures, and increasing taxes and contributions. A majority in all countries find that the government must continue to provide everyone with a broad range of social security benefits even if it means increasing taxes and contributions, but the level of the majority varies somewhat between countries. Particularly in the UK, it is very large (Ferrera 1993). Denmark and The Netherlands on the other hand have the highest proportions thinking that governments should provide everyone with only a limited number of essential benefits and encourage people to provide for themselves in other

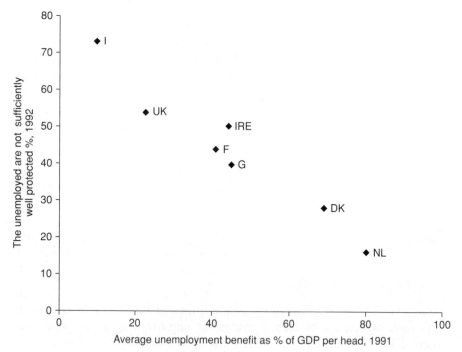

Fig. 16.7. Average unemployment benefit, 1991, and those considering the unemployed not sufficiently well protected, 1992

Notes: Coefficient of determination $R^2 = 0.95$.

Source: Eurobarometer, 37.1 (1992); EC (1993).

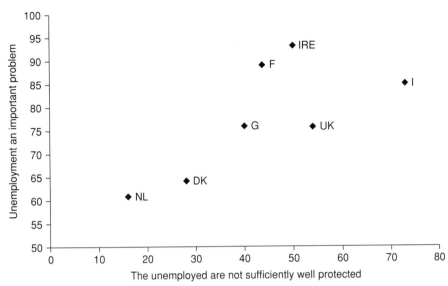

FIG. 16.8. Those finding that the unemployed are not sufficiently well protected, 1992, and considering unemployment to be a very important problem, 1993, (%)

Note: Coefficient of determination R² = 0.53.

Source: Eurobarometers, 37.1 (1992) and 40 (1993).

aspects. These two countries are those with the most generous social security systems. All in all there is a tendency for lower spenders to be more willing to increase expenditure and to pay taxes than higher spenders (Taylor-Gooby 1995).

Although support for expenditure for old age pensions and health care in general is higher than for unemployment benefits there seems to be clear support in all the European countries for a reasonable level of protection for the unemployed. There is a direct relationship between the level of unemployment benefits and the proportions of the population finding that the unemployed are not sufficiently well protected (Taylor-Gooby 1995). As Fig. 16.7 shows, Italy with the most meagre benefits has the highest proportions dissatisfied with the protection of the unemployed; at the other extreme is The Netherlands where the great majority is not dissatisfied in the context of rather generous benefits.

Accordingly the perception of whether the unemployed are sufficiently well protected has some relationship to the public perception of the importance of the unemployment problem—see Fig. 16.8. At least the comparatively lower stress on the unemployment problem in The Netherlands and Denmark might be related to the fact that the protection of the unemployed is perceived to be sufficient. Overall, however, it indicates that an important aspect of the reason why the majority of the citizens of each country consider unemployment to be an important problem, is because they find that people hit by unemployment suffer because they are not sufficiently well protected. This again indicates that the European populations in general are willing to support the unemployed and does not point to any lack of sympathy, which might contribute to a worsening of the situation for the unemployed.

CONCLUSION

The dominant attitude—that unemployment is an important political problem—reflects the fact that all countries included in this analysis are welfare states. They do represent different welfare regimes but there seems to be no sharp difference in attitudes towards unemployment as a political problem, or towards the unemployed between countries or welfare regimes. The security of full employment is a major challenge for all welfare states, and is what is expected by the populations. And this goes for the universalistic type of regime represented by Denmark, for the employment-centred regimes represented here by Germany, The Netherlands, and France, for the liberal/minimal type of welfare regime represented by the United Kingdom and Ireland, and for a sub-protective regime represented by Italy. These welfare systems are very different in their institutional design and in the values upon which they are based; however, their citizens are very much alike with respect to their attitudes and expectations about unemployment.

Across Europe it is political orientation which makes the differences within populations. It has sometimes been argued that social class affiliation is of declining significance in terms of social stratification in the rich post-industrial western societies, whereas gender and age are thought to be of increasing significance—see for example Bradley (1996). But this seems not to be the case when one examines the important issue of people's attitudes towards unemployment. This analysis supports the opposite point of view: that there is a continuing reproduction of old structures and hierarchies—see for example Marshall (1997). Attitudes to unemployment are strongly linked to people's political beliefs, and even though there is huge support about it being an important question, the issue still divides the population along political lines and to some degree also along class lines.

Conclusion

Conclusion

17

The Social Regulation of Unemployment

Duncan Gallie and Serge Paugam

How different was the experience of unemployment in the EU societies that have been examined in this study? And what factors appear to have played the strongest role in affecting this experience? In embarking on this investigation, we noted that there were in particular three types of factor that might affect the severity of the effects of unemployment on people's lives. In the first place, there were the characteristics of the welfare institutions for the unemployed, which reflected distinctive mixes of welfare principles. Second, there were diverse patterns of family life and sociability, which, although possibly influenced by the nature of the welfare institutions, also related to much longer-standing cultural traditions. Finally, there were the specific economic conditions that each society was confronted with, deriving from their level of economic development and the rapidity of economic restructuring. In examining the impact of such differences, we have been concerned with three main spheres of the experience of unemployment: financial deprivation, labour market marginalization, and social integration.

FINANCIAL DEPRIVATION

There are different ways of assessing the financial experience of the unemployed, reflecting distinct dimensions of 'deprivation'. The first, which has been the principal measure used in this study, is an indicator of 'income poverty status'. In particular, we have taken the measure of whether or not people's household income, adjusted for family composition, was below 50 per cent of the average in their own society. This is a measure of *relative* financial deprivation and is often considered a guide as to whether or not people will have the material resources to enable them to participate in the 'normal' activities of their society. It is not, however, a measure of financial hardship, which refers to the ability to meet basic needs of food and living conditions. The relatively poor in a wealthier society may well be in a very different position with respect to absolute measures of hardship than the relatively poor in less economically advanced societies. However, our examination of the association between the different types of measure in Chapter 3, reveals that 'income poverty status' is not a mere statistical abstraction but is consistently related to differences in experiences of financial hardship within countries.

The first issue is whether the nature of state welfare provision for the unemployed has a major impact on financial deprivation. We started from a set of analytical models of 'unemployment regimes', which distinguished between universalistic, employment-centred, liberal/minimal and sub-protective types. While no country exactly corresponded to a pure type, the institutional systems of countries could be seen as closer to or further from the logic of particular types of regime. Denmark and Sweden could be seen as most strongly informed by universalistic principles; The Netherlands, Germany, and France were closer to employment-centred systems; the UK and Ireland to liberal/minimal systems, and Italy to a sub-protective regime. Given the characteristics of different types of regime, our expectation was that countries closest to the universalistic model would be the most effective at ensuring income security and protecting the living standards of the unemployed. These were systems that were implicitly based on the principle that social protection was due to people as citizens, and as such were relatively open in terms of eligibility and generous with respect to the level of compensation. In contrast, the liberal/minimal and sub-protective systems, which provided either low levels of compensation or little guaranteed coverage, could be expected to have the worst financial outcomes for the unemployed.

Our empirical evidence indicated that, in practice, there was a complex relationship between welfare regimes and poverty among the unemployed. It was seen in Chapter 2 that while the universalistic systems did relatively well in providing financial protection, this was also the case with one of the three employment-centred regimes: The Netherlands. It is clear that the Danish system, which came closest to the model of the universalistic regime, was astoundingly successful on virtually all criteria in reducing the level of financial deprivation among the unemployed. It had by far the lowest proportion of the unemployed in poverty—less than 10 per cent on our most conservative estimate for the 50 per cent mean poverty line—a figure that was five times less than in the country in which the unemployed were most vulnerable to poverty. Moreover, our evidence strongly suggests that the relatively low level of poverty among the unemployed in Denmark was the result of the operation of the system of social transfers. As was shown in Chapter 5, if one examines income before such transfers, the poverty rate in Denmark was relatively high compared to most of the other countries examined. It was the effectiveness of social transfers in lifting people out of poverty that explains why poverty was so low once all income was taken into account.

Moreover, not only did Denmark have a low proportion of unemployed in poverty in terms of the relative poverty line, but it also came out well in terms of the measures of financial hardship. It was the country with the lowest proportion of the unemployed reporting immediate financial pressure—finding it difficult to make ends meet at the end of the month—and it had the second lowest score for lifestyle deprivation—the absence of standard household possessions.

Our data for the outcomes of the Swedish system is more limited than for the Danish. But, on the basis of the evidence available, it would appear to have been rather less effective. Some 30 per cent of the Swedish unemployed were below half average household income. While this was lower than the countries closest to the liberal/minimal or sub-protective types of regime, it was higher than one of our employment-centred systems—The Netherlands. The higher proportions in poverty in Sweden were not due to higher poverty rates before social transfers, but rather to the lower efficacy of the transfer system in pulling people out of poverty. This may be related to the fact that the Swedish system operates a cut-off point after a year, in which the unemployed are obliged to accept training or employment-experience opportunities in order to retain eligibility for insurance. It may also reflect the fact that the take-up of voluntary insurance in Sweden was far from comprehensive in this period, possibly because of the success of governments in maintaining relatively low rates of unemployment through most of the 1980s. The higher rates of poverty in Sweden may reflect, then, the experience of those who fall out of the relatively generous safety net provided by the social insurance system.

After Denmark, the country that really stands out in reducing the financial hardship of unemployment was The Netherlands. Although the poverty rate was higher, at 25 per cent, and the experience of financial pressure somewhat sharper, deprivation with respect to household possessions was quite comparable with Denmark. The Netherlands might be termed a 'high-security' employment-centred system. While its welfare regime was primarily designed to favour those with employment experience, those eligible received both a high level of compensation and an unusually long period of support. This protection of living standards over a relatively long period was a feature shared with Denmark. In contrast, the unemployed in both France and Germany were under substantially higher levels of financial pressure. It is clear that there were substantial variations in outcome between the countries that were closest to an employment-centred regime, reflecting detailed differences in their institutional design. At their most generous, the average level of protection they provided was comparable with that of universalistic systems.

Turning to the countries where we expected the unemployed to experience severe financial difficulties, it was certainly the case that two of the three—Italy and the UK—had by far the worst outcomes. Italy came closest to the sub-protective type, although it was seen that major regional differences confound any simple classification. As was shown in Chapter 4, family solidarity helped to offset some of the disadvantages of a virtually non-existent system of public social support, at least for young adults. But income poverty remained very severe. It is likely that the availability of family financial support was limited by the relatively low incomes of those who were in work. Moreover, supporting the unemployed could well have contributed to the more general impoverishment of families already facing very difficult economic circumstances. The main benefit of the strength of family ties for the unemployed was that, by sharing family accommodation, they were less marginalized in their household living conditions. It is particularly Southern Italy that exemplifies the implications of low protection. While the overall level of poverty was very high among the unemployed in Italy—the highest after the UK—this was mainly because of the very high poverty rate in Southern Italy, which rose to 65 per cent of the long-term unemployed. This was accompanied by high levels of financial pressure and poor living conditions. There was no evidence that financial hardship in these countries led to greater resentment about people's financial situation; the wide prevalence of financial difficulty appears to have led to relatively restricted comparative reference groups. But the overall conclusion must be that family support was unable to prevent a very high level of financial hardship in systems with weakly developed systems of state welfare.

The highest level of poverty of all was to be found in the UK, the country closest to the liberal/minimal model. The unemployed in the UK emerge as the most severely marginalized in terms of their financial situation, accompanied by high levels of financial pressure and very poor living conditions. But again it was clear that there could be substantial variations within countries which could be seen as broadly similar in terms of their regime principles. In Ireland, the relative poverty rate was much lower and so was the distance between the unemployed and those in work in terms of financial pressure. While the unemployed experienced very high levels of financial difficulty, this partly reflected the fact that they were living in a poorer society.

The difference between the two 'liberal/minimal' countries appears to be strongly related to the level of social transfers. As was seen in Chapter 5, the poverty rate among the unemployed before social transfers was worse in Ireland than in the UK. However, the situation was quite different when social transfers were taken into account. The efficacy of the Irish transfer system in pulling people out of poverty, while falling well short of the Danish, was not that far behind the Dutch and French systems. But, while 46 per cent of the unemployed were lifted out of poverty by social transfers in Ireland, this was the case for only 19 per cent in the UK. The UK transfer system was by far the least effective in combating poverty among the unemployed of any of the countries that we were able to examine. The evidence about change over time also underlines the importance of specific policies rather than general regime constraints. While the situation of the unemployed deteriorated sharply in the UK between the 1980s and the 1990s, in Ireland there was a reduction of the proportion in poverty. This appears to have reflected different policies with respect to the level of benefits, with the Irish intentionally seeking to raise the living standards of the most vulnerable sectors of the population relative to the general population.

In sum, taking the overall level of financial deprivation, there is evidence that the universalistic and the employment-centred systems provided higher levels of financial protection for the unemployed than the liberal/minimal and sub-protective systems. But, there were substantial variations between countries which approximated the same regime model, emphasizing the crucial role played by specific social policy decisions in determining the financial experiences of the unemployed.

It might be argued that unemployment regimes would be distinctive less in terms of the average level of poverty than in terms of its distribution. In particular, those with more demanding rules of eligibility in terms of prior employment experience might be particularly disadvantageous for women. But the evidence on poverty rates and poverty experience among the unemployed did not indicate that this was the case. In general, men experienced higher poverty rates than women, the only exception being Denmark. If one takes, as a measure, the efficiency of the transfer system in lifting people out of poverty, while Denmark was the most egalitarian of the countries, it was women rather than men that benefited most in the two employment-centred systems for which information was available: Germany and France. The only example of a major sex inequality in favour of men was in the UK. However, this clearly reflected the specific workings of UK policies rather than any intrinsic characteristic of liberal/minimal type regimes, since Ireland was the country where the transfer system most strongly favoured women.

It is important however to bear in mind that this generally lower risk of poverty among unemployed women conceals important differences in the situation of women depending on their household situation. As is shown in Chapter 9, lone mothers experienced exceptionally high poverty rates in all countries. Similarly the more detailed analysis in Chapter 15 of Denmark, Italy, the UK, and France indicates that, with the exception of the UK, there was little difference in poverty risks among single men and women. The sex difference was, above all, due to the different poverty risks of married men and married women.

This suggests that, while women may not have been more vulnerable to poverty, this may have depended on their ability to rely on other incomes in the family. Thus protection may have been bought at the price of increased family dependence. The expectation from a comparison of the benefit structure was that universalistic systems would make it easier for people to escape poverty without depending on the income of other family members. It was clear from Chapter 3 that the extent of relative disadvantage of the unemployed differed considerably in most countries depending on whether there was another earner in the household. However, the employment status of others in the household had no significant impact on poverty risk in either Denmark or Sweden, consistent with the view that universalistic systems reduce family dependence. In contrast, the effects were very strong in all other regime types, although it should be noted that they were in most cases strong for both men and women.

In summary, universalistic systems achieved relatively good outcomes in terms of protecting the unemployed against poverty, and they did so in a way which permitted the unemployed person to be relatively independent of other household income. The employment-centred systems were very varied in terms of outcomes. At their most generous, the unemployed were overall as well-protected as in the universalistic systems, but the important difference was that their financial position was more heavily dependant on other household resources. The greatest financial deprivation was experienced by those in the liberal/minimal or sub-protective systems, where dependence on the household was also very high. However, the comparison of Ireland and the UK shows that systems governed by broadly similar principles could have very different levels of effectiveness depending on how these were implemented with respect to specific policies about the levels of benefits.

LABOUR MARKET MARGINALIZATION

The second dimension of exclusion upon which our analyses focused was that of marginalization from the labour market. We have looked at this from both an attitudinal and a behavioural viewpoint. It could be argued that such marginalization would be most complete where the unemployed lost their interest in having employed work and retreated into a sub-culture where work values had little salience. However, even if commitment remains strong, there is still the issue of how difficult it is for people to re-enter the labour market once they are unemployed, and how difficult it is for them to re-enter without a penalty of downward mobility into jobs that are likely to offer little long-term security.

There has been little consensus about the determinants of labour market marginalization. Some have argued that it is heavily conditioned by the nature of welfare provision for the unemployed. Where unemployment compensation is high or of long duration, it is suggested, it will lower the motivation to find work and encourage long spells of unemployment or even effective exit from the labour market. From this perspective, it is systems that are closest to a freely functioning market that will provide the lowest levels of marginalization. However, an alternative view is that there is no natural tendency for the market to clear and that active state employment policies are needed to give the unemployed a bridge back into work. Both views are premised on the assumption that institutional effects are important. However, it might be the case that these are relatively insignificant compared to the effects of changes in economic structure. The difficulty of matching the unemployed to jobs may depend primarily on the extent and rapidity of economic restructuring, which may reflect either international economic constraints or governmental macro-economic policies.

We take first the issue of how far the unemployed had come to develop attitudes to work that were likely to reinforce their marginalization in the labour market. The first point to note is that there was no evidence that any substantial proportion of the unemployed had lost their commitment to employment. Indeed, if the level of commitment among those in work is taken as the relevant yardstick, it is clear that the unemployed were more committed to employment than people who were currently in jobs. This was the case not only with respect to the average figures for the EU, but it was true in every single country. It was true just as much for women as for men. While employment commitment among the long-term unemployed tended to be a little lower than that among people who had been unemployed less than a year, it was still higher than among those in work.

Was there any evidence to support the view that high unemployment compensation was corrosive of work motivation? Was there a trade-off between maintaining people's living standards and keeping them attached to the labour market? If this were the case, one would expect employment commitment to be particularly low in countries closer to the universalistic type, which, as has been seen, were particularly successful at protecting people's living standards and reducing the risk of poverty. In contrast, employment commitment should be particularly high in the countries closest to the liberal/minimal and sub-protective systems, where financial support for the unemployed was very low.

The evidence in Chapter 6, however, showed that the unemployed in Denmark and Sweden—the countries that came closest to the universalistic type—were at least as strongly attached to having a job as those in either Britain or Italy—the countries that came closest to the liberal/minimal and sub-protective types. Commitment was also very high for The Netherlands, which was a particularly generous version of the employment-centred system. Similarly, there was no consistent evidence that the unemployed in these more generous welfare systems were less flexible in the way they went about looking for a job. It was the case that the Danes were generally less willing than the British or the Italians to make concessions in order to get a job. However, the Swedes were *more* flexible than the British and the Italians with respect both to their readiness to take a job with lower pay, and their willingness to move to a different part of the country to find work. The unemployed in the relatively high welfare system of The Netherlands also showed greater flexibility with respect to pay and geographical mobility than the British.

Overall then, a more generous welfare system did not erode commitment to employment or have any necessary consequences for job search flexibility. The only consistent evidence of a 'benefits effect' that we were able to detect was with respect to women in societies with more traditional gender cultures. Where a woman's role was still primarily defined in terms of her responsibilities as wife and mother, then there was a tendency for the receipt of benefit to be associated with lower commitment and flexibility. It was, then, the interaction between benefits and the particular type of cultural tradition with respect to the family that was crucial in this respect.

Processes of labour market marginalization are not then best understood as resulting from attitudinal change involving a decline of commitment to work among the unemployed, despite the fact that the issue of work incentives is given such prominence in policy discussions. Rather it is important to examine the constraints that arise on the one hand from changes in the structure of jobs and the distribution of skills and, on the other, from the institutional mechanisms of job allocation.

The level of long-term unemployment is strongly related to the overall level of unemployment, albeit often with a significant time lag. It is then affected both by the economic cycle and by specific economic crises. But there are also longer-term processes of economic change at work which are unlikely to be offset by any simple process of market adjustment. In all of the EU countries there has been a general tendency for lower-level skills to become redundant. It is this that accounts for the disproportionate share among the unemployed of people who were previously in manual work, whether skilled or non-skilled. As was seen in Chapter 8, even after a wide range of factors had been taken into account, a person's skill level remained a very powerful predictor of their unemployment risk in countries as diverse in their regime type as the UK, Sweden, Italy, and The Netherlands.

In addition, most countries have seen major shifts in their economic structure, with a relative decline of manufacturing industry and the growth of the service sector. The type of work involved in these sectors differs fundamentally: in the former it is primarily concerned with the production of objects, in the latter with the servicing, caring, or manipulation of people. There is little reason to expect that the skills learned in one sector will be readily transferable to the other. The high level of gender segregation in most

European societies, with men disproportionately concentrated in manufacturing and women in the services, both reflects and reinforces this skill divide. These general problems posed by the shift from manufacturing to services have been compounded in some countries by particularly acute problems flowing from the rapid reduction and restructuring of the agricultural sector.

The nature of the prevailing economic circumstances clearly has a particularly sharp effect on the problems that new entrants to the labour market experience in acquiring suitable jobs or indeed any job at all. When unemployment is high, young people are likely to be constrained to take temporary jobs, or jobs which require lower levels of skill than they would expect on the basis of their qualifications. In certain countries, our evidence suggests that the effects of the conditions that they experience at the beginning of their careers will carry over and effect their long-term career chances. As is shown in Chapter 7, this is particularly the case where the labour market is organized in a way that provides very strong protection for those already employed and emphasizes the divide between 'insiders' and 'outsiders'. The two countries that came closest to this form of labour market were Italy and France, and in both cases there was evidence of very long-term effects of the level of unemployment that people encountered when they were at the beginning of their work lives. In these societies, once people were forced into a disadvantageous labour market position, they became trapped into a situation in which they had markedly higher risks of later unemployment. The rigidity of the employment structure made it difficult to recoup lost position in the labour market. In contrast, in a country such as the UK, where there was greater in-career flexibility in both hiring and firing, such early labour market experiences did not have the same lasting consequences for people's later careers.

An important part of the process of labour market marginalization relates, then, to the changing skill structure of the workforce, given the specific conditions of economic restructuring. However, as well as the barrier of skill mismatch, there is also considerable evidence that the unemployed have to face the additional hurdle of the 'scarring effect' of unemployment. The fact of having been unemployed tends to leave a long-term shadow over a person's future career chances. Once a person has been unemployed once, they find it more difficult to get a job, and this increases with the duration of time that they have been out of work. Moreover, those who do get a job find themselves at increased risk of becoming unemployed again. People find themselves in a vicious cycle of unemployment, insecure work, and further unemployment.

An important factor underlying scarring effects is likely to be the constraints on job choice imposed by the need for a rapid escape from unemployment. People whose skills are no longer in demand may often be forced to trade down into less-skilled work, where the knowledge and experience necessary to carry out the job can be picked up rapidly. The analysis in Chapter 8, which compared the types of jobs that people obtained after being unemployed in the UK, Sweden, Italy, and The Netherlands suggests that in each of these countries there was an increased probability of moving into non-skilled manual work after a spell of unemployment. This was likely to have significant long-term costs in that such jobs tend to be in less secure sectors of industry, such as construction or distribution, where there is a high risk of further job loss and unemployment.

However, while there are processes of a rather general type that help account for labour market marginalization, our evidence suggests that the institutional system in a country may to some degree mediate such effects. In the first place, institutional provision may help mediate the transitions between jobs. The scarring effect of unemployment is likely to be particularly marked if people have to choose jobs rapidly as a result of financial pressure. It is notable that, of the four countries in which people's careers could be followed in detail over time, it is only in Sweden that we found that past unemployment does not increase the future risk of job loss. It seems plausible that this is in part an effect of the relatively high protection of living standards and the active labour market policies in that country. Systems that provide greater financial security will also permit longer periods of job search, increasing the chances of people finding work that suits them. Further, countries with active labour market policies are likely to ensure a better flow of information and thereby more effective matching of skills to types of work. It is also possible that the quality of lower-level jobs is higher in Sweden, as a result of a stronger emphasis on the quality of working conditions. As a result, even when people are downwardly mobile after unemployment, they may be less likely to find themselves in a precarious sector of the labour market.

Our evidence also confirms that institutional factors can play an important role with respect to women's employment chances, by reducing the problems of compatibility between domestic and work roles. These are likely to be particularly great where there are still young children in the household. The extreme case of this dilemma is where the mother is a lone parent. The importance of the nature of public childcare provision for the employment chances of lone mothers emerges strongly from the comparison of Denmark and the UK. The analyses in Chapter 9 suggest that the fact that 62 per cent of UK, but only 23 per cent of the Danish lone mothers were out of employment, was strongly related to the nature of childcare provisions in the two countries. In the UK, until recently, care for children has been seen as the responsibility of the parent, and the public provision of day-care has been very limited. Lone mothers are likely to have weaker informal support networks to assist with childcare. But the high costs of obtaining formal childcare tend to be a major barrier for people who are likely to have relatively low incomes when in work. In such cases, the boundaries between unemployment and non-activity become blurred, with women finding it difficult, for reasons that may well be beyond their control, to meet the availability for work criterion required for official classification as unemployed. In Denmark, childcare is predominantly provided through public services and it is heavily subsidized—indeed for families with low incomes it is free of charge. As a result the barriers to re-entry to employment faced by Danish mothers were very much lower than for their UK equivalents.

Finally, institutional factors may effect the nature of the groups that bear the brunt of the burden of long-term unemployment. This is particularly clear when Italy—which in this respect reflects well the experience of the other Southern countries—is compared with the central and northern European countries. The combination of the strong employment protection of the 'insiders', who already have jobs, and the sub-protective nature of Italian welfare provision for the unemployed generates a pattern whereby the costs of unemployment fall particularly heavily on the young. While parental support and the fact that young people can have a future perspective of integration in the labour market may help deflect some of the pressures, it is clear from the evidence both on poverty and life satisfaction that the costs of labour market marginalization remain very high.

SOCIAL INTEGRATION

The last dimension of the experience of unemployment that we have examined is social integration. We have focused in particular on three issues with respect to social integration. The first is the extent to which people participate in the normal forms of social life of their societies; the second is the distance between their subjective well-being and that of people in work; and third, we have looked at public attitudes to the unemployed, to see whether there is evidence of the type of disapproval and rejection that could lead to the social isolation of the unemployed through processes of stigmatization.

The issue of social integration in terms of social relationships, or its converse, social isolation, has in many ways been at the heart of the concern with social exclusion. It raises the issue of whether labour market marginalization is accompanied by the breakdown of everyday social networks, thereby reinforcing the rupture from the world of employment by cutting people off from information about jobs and undermining their self-esteem. In principle, such social isolation could come about for a variety of reasons. It might reflect the reactions of the unemployed individual, who withdraws from sociability either through financial pressure or loss of self-confidence. Or it might come about through the way in which those in work come to stigmatize the unemployed and thereby make social relationships more difficult.

In approaching these issues we have distinguished between different spheres of sociability: the primary sphere which involves immediate family and household relations, the secondary sphere with concerns interactions with neighbours, friends and relatives outside the household, and the tertiary sphere which relates to participation in organizational and associative life. The relative importance of these spheres for people's social life may vary between societies, and unemployment may have quite separate effects from one sphere to another.

The most important factor with respect to primary sociability is whether people are living on their own. It may not reflect a collapse of sociability, since people may have chosen to live in this way long before they were unemployed. But, once confronted with difficulties on the labour market, it implies that people are unable to call on household resources when they need either emotional or material support. It is clear that the type of household situation in which a person is likely to find themselves varies a great deal between societies, reflecting different family traditions. Young people, for instance, are much more likely to move out and form independent households in the northern than in the southern European societies, irrespective of whether they are unemployed.

As was shown in Chapter 12, there were wide country variations in the household situation of the unemployed. For instance, in Denmark 30 per cent of unemployed people were living in one-person households, while in Ireland the proportion was only 7 per cent and in Italy less than 3 per cent. The difference is even more striking with respect to young unemployed people. Of unemployed people aged 20 to 29, only 14 per cent were living with their parents in Denmark, whereas the proportion rose to 87 per cent in Italy. In general, people were most likely to be living on their own in the universalistic regimes, and least likely in the sub-protective regimes.

The impact of unemployment on the extent to which people lived on their own also varied substantially between countries. There was a tendency for unemployed people to be more likely than others to be on their own in Denmark, the UK, and The Netherlands, and for some groups of the unemployed in France, Germany, and Ireland, even when age and gender had been taken into account. However, in Italy Spain, and Portugal, the living patterns of the unemployed did not differ from those with stable jobs. Indeed, in Greece, unemployed people were less likely to be living on their own. This underlined the contrast between the southern European countries compared to all others. In the southern countries, family solidarities were stronger and alternative resources for living independently were far scarcer. The degree of social isolation in the primary sphere partly depended on the broader structure of household relationships in the society and partly on the differential impact of unemployment in societies with different family traditions and different levels of public support for the unemployed.

Household situation could also be a source of social isolation where unemployed people lived with partners who were themselves without work. As was seen earlier, the presence or absence of another earner in the household was a major determinant of the risk of poverty in most countries. But it was also likely to have an effect on the flow of information that came into the household and the knowledge that a person could have of the job opportunities that were available in the local labour market. As is shown in Chapter 13, a number of factors contribute to the concentration of unemployment in households. Partners are likely to share similar educational backgrounds and this will heighten the joint risk for those with low qualifications given the tendency for jobs to require higher levels of skill. Similarly, both partners in a couple may be vulnerable to unemployment where restructuring leads to the collapse of a dominant local industry and hence high regional unemployment rates. There were also variations between countries. Double unemployment appeared to be particularly strong in countries with high levels of female labour market participation and it could be accentuated by a social security system that placed a heavy penalty on other earned income in the household.

With respect to secondary sociability, our starting point was the finding of inter-war research that unemployment tended to lead to the disruption of social networks in the community. However, we are again confronted with the fact that there are major variations in typical patterns of sociability between countries, so the contexts in which the effects of unemployment emerge are quite different. The general level of sociability was far higher in the southern countries. For instance, while only 32 per cent of Danes and 19 per cent of the Dutch spoke to their neighbours on most days, the proportion rose to 47 per cent in Italy—a figure that was still relatively low compared to the other southern European countries. Similar differences emerge with respect to the frequency of meeting up with friends and relatives outside the household. The unemployed, then, were likely to experience very different levels of sociability depending on the country they belonged to. But, except in the case of France, we found no consistent evidence that unemployment was in itself an important factor reducing people's social networks. Indeed, in many countries, the unemployed tended to be more sociable than those in permanent jobs. This sharply contradicts theories of the effects of unemployment that were based on evidence about people's experiences in the inter-war period.

Finally, there were also important country differences in the extent to which people participated in associations and other organizations in their community. While social life in the southern countries revolved primarily around informal social networks, formal organizations played a much more important role in the northern countries. Thus while 59 per cent of people in Denmark and 50 per cent in The Netherlands participated in some type of club or organization, the proportion was only 18 per cent in Italy. The general level of associative participation clearly effected the likelihood that unemployed people would also have such community involvement. For instance, over 40 per cent of the unemployed in Denmark and The Netherlands participated in an organization, but in Italy this was the case for less than 13 per cent. But, although the experience of membership was primarily conditioned by the broader pattern prevalent in the society, it is notable that unemployment had a greater impact in reducing the level of participation in the northern and central European countries than in the southern.

Taking the overall pattern for the unemployed, the major difference is between Italy—which reflects well in this respect the broader distinctiveness of the southern countries—and the northern European countries. Primary and secondary forms of sociability were considerably stronger in Italy, while tertiary sociability was weaker. Denmark and The Netherlands represent the sharpest contrast with this pattern. They have a high proportion of people living on their own, relatively low levels of informal sociability and high levels of participation in formal associations. It is likely that different types of sociability are to some degree complementary. But the pattern of social life in the northern societies required a relatively high level of resources for the unemployed. While the welfare system in general permitted people to maintain the pattern of sociability characteristic of the wider society, it was somewhat more disruptive of the more expensive forms of sociability of people in the northern countries than of the largely informal sociability of the southern countries.

In general, then, the level of social isolation an unemployed person confronted was less the result of unemployment *per se* than of the wider patterns of household structure and sociability in the country in which they lived. Our results suggest that in most countries people's sociability outside the household proved fairly resilient in the face of unemployment, and this has been shown to be important for their personal well-being. But we found little evidence that the extensiveness of these social networks made it easier for a person to get a job. As was seen in Chapter 10, in none of the countries did the extensiveness of 'relational' resources make a significant difference to the chances that an unemployed person would get work. This is likely to be in part because of the qualitative nature of the social networks of the unemployed. While people continue to meet friends they are more likely to be involved in networks that consist predominantly of other unemployed people, who themselves lack useful job contacts.

Moreover, even the resources that people could draw upon, in terms of the occupational position and the educational background of other people in the household, were only important in helping people get a job in labour markets—such as those of the UK and Ireland—where there was relatively little regulation of hiring and firing procedures. In part this reflects the exceptionally closed character of some labour markets, which impose a stronger insider/outsider divide. As has been shown in Chapters 10 and 11, Italy presents a very clear case of this. There is effectively a form of collective exclusion of the outsiders—primarily young adults—which affects those from all social backgrounds. People's social resources are mainly important in more open 'market-based' labour markets, where educational qualifications are heavily reinforced by the information and contacts to which a person has access. Yet, even when there is a high level of flexibility in recruitment practices, the presence of effective active labour market policies, in a country such as Denmark, curbs the role of people's informal social resources and places the emphasis primarily on educational qualifications.

A second essential dimension of social integration is people's sense of well-being in their society. The measure of satisfaction that was available related to people's main daily activity, their financial situation, and their housing situation. The most notable feature of the results in Chapter 14 was the powerful effect of unemployment on such subjective satisfaction in all of the countries of the study, and indeed more widely in the countries of the EU. It is clear that neither the strong material support given by some of the northern countries, nor the high level of family solidarity in the southern countries could neutralize the destructive effect of unemployment on the subjective quality of people's lives.

There were however some significant country variations in the impact of unemployment on well-being. In terms of the general contrast between the unemployed and those in work, the two countries where unemployment had least effect on life satisfaction were Denmark and The Netherlands, suggesting a convergence in the outcomes of the universalistic and the more generous employment-centred regimes. When account had been taken of differences relating to age, sex, class, and financial deprivation, the pattern becomes more complex. Denmark still stands out as a country in which the impact of unemployment is relatively low, but this is also the case for Greece and Spain. Our evidence then strongly confirms the efficacy of the universalistic Danish system in securing subjective integration. But it is also suggests there are conditions in which the Southern countries, with their high level of informal social integration, can produce comparable outcomes in mediating the impact of unemployment.

In examining the factors that affected subjective integration, it is clear that it was linked to, but far from accountable by, the degree of financial deprivation and the extensiveness of 'secondary' sociability. In particular, the extent to which people were deprived in terms of their household living conditions had a marked effect on their subjective response to unemployment. Deprivation in living conditions accounted for approximately one-third of the overall impact of unemployment on people's well-being. In contrast, greater sociability with neighbours and friends tended to increase satisfaction. But any overall account of the effects of unemployment on subjective well-being would need to take account of more general influences that impact on people in widely different types of institutional system.

A long-standing issue has been whether women are better protected from the impact of unemployment than men, possibly because they can retain their sense of meaning and their links to the community through placing a greater emphasis on an alternative role as wife or mother. With respect to the wider measure of well-being, unemployment did appear to have a less severe impact on women than on men. But as is shown in Chapter 15, this did not imply that women felt any less deprived about not having a job. Comparing Denmark, Italy, Britain, and France, it was found that it was only in Italy that there were significant sex differences in terms of employment deprivation. Women's domestic role was only significant in reducing such deprivation for those with children under five years of age. However, a factor that was very influential for women's attitudes to being without a job was the extent to which they held traditional views about the division of gender roles. It was such broader values rather than domestic position that most clearly mediated the impact of unemployment.

Finally, was there any sign of public rejection of the unemployed that might have been an important source of increased social isolation? Chapter 16 shows that in general there was widespread sympathy for the unemployed across the seven countries for which comparable data were available. The proportions thinking that unemployment was an important problem ranged from 60 per cent in The Netherlands to 93 per cent in Ireland. There were significant country variations in the salience given to the issue. These could not be accounted for simply in terms of the level of unemployment or indeed of the level of long-term unemployment. It depended to some extent on whether people thought that the employment situation was improving or deteriorating. It also reflected the level of protection and assistance that already existed. It is notable that the two countries where unemployment was least likely to be regarded as a major problem—The Netherlands and Denmark—were both countries where social protection for the unemployed was, and was seen to be, particularly effective. Finally, there was some evidence that sympathy towards the unemployed was influenced by broader systems of social interpretation, reflected in people's political allegiances. It was an issue that had greater salience for those with left-wing than for those with right-wing political views. It seems likely that the former were more likely to regard it as a problem that resulted from the malfunctioning of society, whereas the latter viewed it in more individualistic terms.

Was there any evidence that generous welfare provision had the unintended consequence of creating a backlash against the unemployed and thereby enhancing their social isolation? This was examined by looking at the restrictiveness of the conditions that people thought should be imposed on the unemployed. It was a very widely held view that the unemployed should show some flexibility in their efforts to get back to work. For instance, in all countries most people agreed that they should accept retraining to get a job, and a majority felt that they should not be allowed to turn down a job if it was within reasonable distance from where they lived. But there is little evidence that such views were linked systematically to any particular type of welfare regime or even to the level of generosity of welfare benefits. While it was the case that the relatively generous system in The Netherlands was accompanied by the most restrictive attitudes to the unemployed, this was clearly not a direct effect of generosity. For, in Denmark, which gave the best protection of all to the unemployed, there was no evidence of a particularly high level of restrictiveness. Again the close link between people's broader political attitudes and their attitudes to the unemployed suggests that such views are far more influenced by political culture than by the characteristics of welfare regimes.

In short, the evidence suggests that, in the period of mass unemployment with which we are concerned, there was little public rejection of the unemployed in any of the societies under study. Nor was there any evidence that welfare regimes, either because of their implicit ethos about incentives or their generosity, played any role in increasing suspicion of, or hostility towards, the unemployed. Public perceptions of unemployment were most clearly linked to political beliefs, as mediated by party and ideological identification.

THE SOCIAL REGULATION OF UNEMPLOYMENT AND THE RISK OF SOCIAL EXCLUSION

While the nature of welfare provision was clearly of major importance for the quality of life of the unemployed, our evidence suggests that this can only be partially understood in terms of types of 'regime'. Differences at the level of detailed institutional design and of government policy meant that there could be substantial variations in outcome in countries whose welfare systems for the unemployed shared similar broad principles.

The domain in which welfare institutions clearly made the most substantial impact was that of financial deprivation. The 'universalistic' systems of

Denmark and Sweden provided a relatively high level of protection of living standards, and they did so in a way which did not make people dependent on other income in the household. But employment-centred systems were not necessarily associated with higher levels of poverty. The living standards of the unemployed in The Netherlands, a particularly generous version of the employment-centred system, were also well protected, although an importance difference was that this involved a greater dependence on other family resources. Our evidence confirmed that the countries closest to the liberal/minimal and sub-protective regime types provided the weakest protection of the living standards of the unemployed, although the comparison between the UK and Ireland revealed that the extent to which this was the case depended very much on specific government policies. Overall, then, the heterogeneity of the employment-centred systems blurred any simple relationship between regime type and poverty risk. It must be remembered moreover that the significance of regime type was primarily with respect to relative poverty. The absolute difficulties that the unemployed confronted in terms of the difficulty of meeting payments and the harshness of living conditions were strongly influenced by the general level of economic development of the society. The unemployed faced the most severe shortages in societies that were less advanced in the process of industrialization, although managing financially was also much harder in these societies for people in work.

The extent to which the unemployed were marginalized with respect to the labour market clearly depended to a very considerable extent on macro-economic conditions, particularly on the extensiveness and rapidity of economic restructuring. Long-term unemployment, which is the most significant indicator of such marginalization, is heavily dependent on the overall level of unemployment. This in turn is partly related to the business cycle and partly to the extent to which the particular location of a country in the international economy leads to pressures to transform the sectoral composition of the economy. The policies of governments may partly help to account for the abruptness of such transitions, which in turn may exacerbate the difficulty of labour market assimilation. But the long-term similarities in the sectoral trajectories of the European economies suggests that there are powerful underlying processes of a more general type. It is clear that the difficulties of assimilating the unemployed in the southern European countries and in Ireland were related to the fact that a sharp reduction in the size of the agricultural sector compounded the difficulties of restructuring the traditional manufacturing industries.

Nevertheless, there was evidence that the nature of welfare institutions could have an impact on the extent to which economic change led to individual entrapment. It was notable that Sweden, which had the most advanced policies for assisting the unemployed to find and retrain for jobs, was the only country which escaped the general pattern whereby an experience of unemployment 'scarred' a person in a way which made them more vulnerable to future unemployment. It was clear too that the strong childcare provision in Denmark helped prevent the marginalization from the labour market of women with young children, leading to high employment rates even among lone mothers. Both Sweden and Denmark had relatively low rates of long-term unemployment. It has to be taken into account that the economic shock resulting from sectoral change was less marked in Denmark than in other countries. But it seems likely that the relative success of these two countries in preventing long-term labour market marginalization was at least in part due to the policies of active intervention in the labour market characteristic of universalistic regimes.

The sphere in which there was least evidence for the direct impact of welfare regimes on the experience of unemployment was that of social isolation and social integration. It is possible that there is some long-term historical relationship between welfare systems and the typical forms of household structure in a society. More generous public welfare may make it easier for people to create and sustain independent households. Low levels of public welfare may reinforce inter-generational family and friendship solidarities, by providing them with a vital and highly visible function. Similarly, there may be more perceived pressure for the development of public welfare provision in societies where family structures are less stable. But whatever the extent of such reciprocal causation, there is no automatic mechanism whereby such solidarities offset lack of public provision. In several of our societies, it is clear that those who fell outside the provisions of public welfare had little that they could depend upon in terms of resources from family or friends. The patterns of household formation and sociability in societies have then their own distinctive dynamics, which have longer-term historical roots in very different paths of economic and cultural development.

The extent to which the unemployed were likely to experience social isolation was strongly influenced by these distinctive societal patterns of household organization and sociability. In the Southern countries, young unemployed adults were far more likely to be living at home with their parents. But this was not specifically because they were unemployed, but because young people in general in these societies were more likely to live in this way. They were also far more likely to meet regularly with neighbours, friends, and relatives. Again this mainly reflected the fact that the frequency of sociability was much higher in the society at large. In countries such as Denmark and The Netherlands, informal sociability was very much rarer for the unemployed and those in work alike. But instead there was more active participation in formal organizations. In Germany, again largely reflecting the more general pattern in the society, the unemployed had low levels of informal

TABLE 17.1. *Unemployed who are both in poverty and socially isolated, by country* (%)

	Poor and living alone	Poor and no daily contact with friends
Belgium	4.0	13.8
Denmark	3.7	2.8
France	4.4	27.7
Germany	9.9	21.0
Greece	1.3	10.4
Ireland	2.8	8.7
Italy	0.6	14.9
Netherlands	5.7	18.3
Portugal	0.0	14.9
Spain	0.7	7.4
United Kingdom	9.6	24.6

Notes: Poverty defined as <50% of the mean equivalized household income.
Source: European Community Household Panel (1994). Data were not available for Sweden.

sociability, but at the same time they also had relatively low participation in formal social life in the community.

The relationship between these different aspects of deprivation is of fundamental importance in any assessment of the risks of social exclusion for unemployed people. Social exclusion refers to a situation where people suffer from the cumulative disadvantages of labour market marginalization, poverty, and social isolation. The different aspects of deprivation become mutually reinforcing over time, leading to a downward spiral in which the individual comes to have neither the economic nor the social resources needed to participate in their society or to retain a sense of social worth.

Table 17.1 presents a picture of the empirical distribution of cumulative disadvantage involving both financial deprivation and social isolation. The data is given for both types of sociability which could be expected to have a significant affective dimension: primary sociability, involving the household, and secondary sociability, involving close informal links in the community. The results are drawn from the first wave of the European Community Household Panel in 1994; there are no data for Sweden as it was not included in the survey. The measure of poverty taken is that of people with equivalized household income less than half of the mean.

The evidence for Denmark confirms that only a very small proportion of the unemployed experienced the dual deprivation of poverty and social isolation. This is true whichever indicator is taken of social relationships. The southern European countries also showed a pattern of low cumulative disadvantage given the virtual absence of unemployed people who are both poor and living on their own. Ireland comes close to the southern pattern.

The Netherlands and Belgium have intermediate levels of cumulative dis-advantage with respect to both measures. The countries with the highest proportion of people with double deprivation were the UK, Germany, and France. Nearly 10 per cent of the unemployed in both the UK and Germany were both poor and living on their own, and more than 20 per cent were both poor and without daily contacts with friends. In France, there was an exceptionally high proportion, 28 per cent, that was both poor and had weak informal ties with others in the community.

The country differences show that there is no simple relationship between unemployment and social exclusion. Instead, we would suggest that the likelihood of cumulative deprivation depends on the predominant model of social regulation of unemployment that prevails in the society. Models of social regulation of unemployment can be seen as constituted by the inter-relationship between the responsibilities attributed to public welfare provision on the one hand and to family organization on the other. They are ideal types, designed to capture differences in the logic of different principles of social organization. While particular societies may be closer to one model than another, we should not expect any society to reflect the model in its pure form. We can distinguish three principal types of model: the public individualist model, the shared responsibility model, and the familialistic model.

The public individualist model is informed by the assumption that it is the society collectively that has responsibility for the problem of unemployment and hence for the well-being of the unemployed. Since individuals are not assumed to be responsible for their own unemployment, the objective of the welfare system is primarily that of protecting living standards. This requires a highly developed system of public welfare that will provide the resources for social participation irrespective of the particularities of the individual's market or family position. Given the level of public support, there is no strong normative obligation on the family to support its members when unemployed. But, since responsibility for unemployment is attributed to the society rather than to the individual, it is a model in which unemployment is not likely to undermine social relations between the individual and the local community.

The familialistic model, in contrast, rejects central collective social re-sponsibility for unemployment, but places a strong emphasis on the duties of the family, both in the sense of the immediate household and the wider kinship network, to look after its members. In so far as public policy has a role, it is to safeguard against threats to the integrity of the family, so that it is in a position to fulfil its supportive function. The implicit assumption is again that the individual is not personally to blame for being unemployed and therefore has a right to a share of family resources for the duration of their period out of work. Responsibilities for the unemployed are much akin to responsibilities for dependent children. Given everyday involvement in family life and its ongoing pattern of sociability, unemployment is also unlikely to threaten social relations with the community.

Finally, the shared-responsibility model divides the responsibility for providing for the unemployed between the public authorities and the family. It may define the frontiers of these responsibilities in different ways. Responsibilities may be synchronic, with public provision for minimum needs and family provision for a broader protection of living standards. Alternatively the relationship may be defined temporally, with public provision for the early phase of unemployment and family provision for longer spells of unemployment. The implicit assumption of such systems is that there is a possibility that the individual may be personally responsible for their unemployment. The limits set to public provision reflect a presumption that people may prefer unemployment to employment; hence attention must be paid to the potential disincentives of protecting their standard of living for any substantial duration of time. The residual role attributed to the family implies that it is not a responsibility that the family would normally expect to have to assume. Hence family support is likely to be accompanied by substantial pressures on the individual to re-enter the labour market. Family support becomes part of a system of social control of the unemployed. Given the restrictive conditions of public support and its implication of the potential responsibility of the individual, there is a higher probability that unemployment will undermine people's self-identity in a way that will encourage social withdrawal.

The different modes of social regulation are likely to lead to different outcomes in terms of social exclusion. The public individualist system will mitigate the effects of unemployment for social exclusion by providing relatively high protection of living standards. This will allow people to maintain their sense of self-worth as citizens by participating in associational life. However, its individualist emphasis will lead to a risk of social isolation in terms of more intimate relationships. In part this is because the material conditions are such that people will be in a position to continue to maintain independent households; in part it is because there is limited normative responsibility on kin to offer material or emotional support. The familialistic system will tend to provide only poor support for living standards. Essentially existing family resources are spread more thinly. To the extent that the unemployed are drawn from less-skilled, and poorer, backgrounds, then the responsibility for supporting the unemployed will lead to a greater risk of family impoverishment. However, the familialistic system protects against social exclusion by maintaining the sociability of the unemployed. This is in part a consequence of the fact that the unemployed are likely to live with their kin, so that they have regular social contact through their residence; in part it reflects the greater normative pressure on the wider kin network to take an interest in the welfare of a disadvantaged family member.

It is the shared-responsibility system that is most likely to pose the risk of social exclusion. To some degree this derives directly from its implicit definition of unemployment as potentially due to the failings of the individual, thereby increasing the risk that the unemployed will not be treated as equal citizens or indeed as equally deserving family members. These are inherently lower trust systems, which are subject to the defensiveness and interpersonal conflict such systems inspire. However, it also results from the fact that it is the system whose normative structure is least clearly defined and indeed where there is the possibility of significant normative conflict. There can be little in the way of rational criteria for deciding at what point public support should cease and family support begin; hence disagreement about what constitutes legitimate responsibilities may be chronic. The family is likely to be slow to step in to take up a burden which it feels should be shouldered by the state, and if it does so, this is likely to be in a grudging way that will increase the difficulties of relations within the family. There is then a much greater risk that the welfare of the unemployed individual will get lost in the interstices of the system, with the person neither receiving the resources for autonomy from the state nor being accepted as deserving of family sympathy and support.

The extent of the problems associated with the shared-responsibility model will clearly be conditional upon the specific nature both of the system of public welfare and of the ethos of the family. Where shared-responsibility is associated with a relatively high level of compensation for an extended period of time, it will be less corrosive of individual well-being than where it takes the form of very low level or short duration financial assistance from the state. Where, for reasons such as religion, family norms are particularly strong, then the family is more likely to offer support to offset the shortfall of state provision than in societies where the dissolution of traditional conceptions of the family has spread more widely in the society. For such institutional and cultural reasons, it can be expected that there will be significant country variations between countries that can be broadly classified as closest to the shared-responsibility model.

With respect to the societies that have been the focus of our analyses in this book, it is only Denmark and Sweden that provided the conditions for a high level of individual autonomy. As has been noted this may have been at the cost of some degree of social isolation with respect to their immediate household situation. But in general the evidence for Denmark confirms that such systems present a very low risk of social exclusion. At the other end of the spectrum, it was the southern European societies that came closest to a familialistic model of social regulation. The unemployed suffered from very high levels of financial hardship and had very little in the way of individual income, but socially they remained strongly integrated both in terms of relations in the household, where very frequently they lived with their parents and participated in the social life of the family, and in terms of maintaining high levels of sociability with neighbours and friends in the community.

The problems of the shared-responsibility dilemma could be expected to be most visible in the countries with liberal/minimal or employment-centred welfare institutions. But the strength of such effects will vary depending on the generosity of the welfare system and the strength of family values. In Ireland, not only was there a relatively generous system of social transfers compared with the UK, but the risk of social isolation was heavily reduced due to the strength of family ties—perhaps linked to the influence of Catholicism—and their impact on the protective role of the family. This led to levels of social integration closer to those of the southern countries. The Netherlands and Belgium were the most generous of the employment-centred systems in terms of their financial provision, and this is reflected in intermediate levels of double deprivation.

It is clear that the risk of the type of cumulative disadvantage that underlies the process of social exclusion was greatest in the countries where the respective normative responsibilities of the public authorities and of the family were least clearly delineated. Germany, France, and the UK were countries where the level of public financial support was at best intermediate and, in the case of the UK, very low. At the same time, these were countries in which the institutional responsibilities of the family were relatively weakly defined. It was in these societies, then, that there was the highest risk that unemployed people would simultaneously confront both poverty and social isolation, thereby creating the conditions for social exclusion.

APPENDIX A

The European Community Household Panel

The European Community Household Panel (ECHP) is under the responsibility of Eurostat, the Statistical Office of the European Communities. It is a large-scale comparative survey, involving interviews with the same households and individuals over a number of years. It is designed to contribute to the development of comparable social statistics on income and other social indicators relating to the living conditions of both households and individuals.

ECHP data are collected by 'National Data Collection Units' (NDUs). In the first wave (1994) a sample of some 60,500 nationally representative households, approximately 130,000 adults aged 16 years and over, were interviewed in twelve Member States: Germany, Denmark, The Netherlands, Belgium, Luxembourg, France, the United Kingdom, Ireland, Italy, Greece, Spain, and Portugal. In the second wave in 1995, when coverage was extended to thirteen Member States with the addition of Austria, some 60,000 households and 129,000 adults were interviewed. Sweden was not included in the original survey. Luxembourg has usually been excluded from the analyses in this study, given the small sample numbers for the unemployed (Eurostat 1998).

DATA-SET AVAILABILITY

Between 1996 and 1999, a number of different versions of the data set were released:

1. *The Production Data Base (PDB)*. The original Wave 1 data-set, released in 1996, was later revised and improved using a more complete and refined procedure for imputation of missing income data. These imputation measures were applied to both Waves 1 and 2 and, in 1998, a revised version of Wave 1 was released along with Wave 2. German data were not available outside that country in the 1996 release.

2. *The User Database (UDB)*. A non-confidential anonymized version of the first two waves, 1994 and 1995, was created in 1998 and released in 1999: the User Database (UDB). This has both advantages and disadvantages. Germany is included, but the data are restricted to a random subsample of 90 per cent of the original data records for households. All households with more than eight members have also been excluded for Germany. There are more derived variables, but there is a reduction in the number of original variables in the data set. The matching variables for linking Waves 1 and Waves 2 were not made available until 1999.

As a result of the date of release of the variables for matching Wave 1 and Wave 2, it was only possible in the time of the research programme to make use of Wave 1 in the analyses. As the research for the book took place over the whole period of the release of successive versions of the data sets, different chapters are based on different versions. Chapters 4, 9, 14 and most of the analyses in Chapter 15, were based on the original 1996 release of Wave 1. Chapters 3 and 12, as well as Tables 15.6, 15.9, and 15.10 used the anonymized 1998 version, which included the revised imputed income data. A major problem in the earlier version of the data was the absence of Germany from the common data set. Where work was based on the 1996 data-set, separate runs were prepared for Germany by the team for that country, but Germany could not be used in the analyses that required a pooled data set.

SAMPLING AND COVERAGE

For each country with the exception of The Netherlands and Belgium, a new random sample was selected for the first wave (1994) from the target population of private households. In general, a two-stage sampling procedure was adopted. At the first stage, sample areas were selected and, at the second, a small number of addresses or households was chosen within each area. Generally, larger countries received larger sample sizes but these were not in proportion to their size. In The Netherlands and Belgium, the panel was based on two modified pre-existing panels. In The Netherlands this was the Socio-Economic Panel survey (SEP) which had started in 1984. Belgium, Spain, and Portugal allowed substitution from pre-selected substitute samples, the remaining surveys did not allow substitutions. The result is considered to be a set of nationally representative random samples of private households, involving, overall, interviews with around 60,000 households and 130,000 adults in the European Union. A break down of the sample numbers by country is given in Table A1 (Verma and Clemenceau 1996).

At any subsequent wave, sample persons include all living initial Wave 1 residents who are still eligible, that is have not emigrated or entered an institution, children as they become 16, and household members aged 16+, who leave to form, or join, new households. Where original sample members joined new households, all adult members of the new household were added to the sample. As a result of these procedures, the sample is considered to reflect demographic changes and to remain representative of the population over time.

RESPONSE RATES

Table A1 gives response rates for the Wave 1 and Wave 2 samples distinguishing those where the ECHP began in 1994 from those where it was integrated into existing national panels (Verma and Clemenceau 1996). The average response rates of around 70 per cent are comparable to those generally found in comparable complex surveys on household budgets. The rates were much higher in the south, 90 per cent in Greece and Italy, than in the north, less than 50 per cent in Germany and Luxembourg. In the two pre-existing panels, Belgium and The Netherlands, the original (first wave) response rate was around 50 per cent. The Netherlands panel was able to interview 92 per cent of the households already in the sample but only

TABLE A1. *ECHP Response rates, waves 1 and 2*

	Wave 1				Wave 2				
	Households selected	Household interviews completed	Personal interviews completed	Household response rate %	Target for interview	Number interviewed	Response rate %	Interviewed in Waves 1 and 2	Attrition rate % W1 to W2 %
New panels									
Italy	7,841	7,115	17,730	90.7	7,844	7,128	90.9	6,697	5.1
Greece	6,131	5,523	12,492	90.1	5,897	5,219	88.5	5,060	7.7
Portugal	5,492	4,881	10,054	88.9	5,436	4,916	90.4	4,654	3.6
France	9,239	7,344	14,331	79.5	7,548	6,723	89.1	6,518	10.7
UK	8,104	5,779	10,517	71.3	5,398	4,549	84.3	4,405	23.3
Spain	7,108~	7,206	17,908	87.0	7,505	6,521	86.9	6,295	12.4
Denmark	5,580	3,482	5,903	62.4	3,847	3,228	83.9	3,014	11.5
Ireland	7,252	4,048	9,915	55.8	4,369	3,587	82.1	3,433	14.4
Germany	10,604	5,054	9,887	47.7	5,177	4,755	91.8	4,657	7.7
Luxembourg	2,485	1,011	2,046	40.7	1,027	962	93.7	945	6.2
Existing national panels*									
Netherlands	5,926	5,187	9,408	87.5	4,596	5,067			
Belgium	4,963	4,189	7,852	84.4		3,988	86.8	3,723	10.3
EU (12)	83,293	60,819	128,043	73.0					

Notes: ~ Spain, selected households, 7108 + 4822 substitutes.
* Response rates are for the national panel wave corresponding to ECHP Wave 1. Original first wave rates in both countries were around 50%.

36 per cent of new entrants. In Belgium, all ECHP Wave 1 sample cases came from the pre-existing panel, of which 80 per cent were interviewed (Eurostat 1996d).

Within-household Non-response

The problem of within-household non-response is generally not significant at the national level—around 3 per cent—but it can substantially affect the data for the particular households with missing personal interviews. It has not been considered necessary to undertake complete imputations of personal income for such non-respondents.

INTERVIEW PROCEDURE

Face-to-face personal interviews were carried out with a 'reference person' providing information on the household questionnaire and each individual in the household being asked to answer the personal questionnaire. Apparently, there were few proxy interviews and telephone interviewing was rare.

Structure of Schedules

The questionnaire was designed centrally at Eurostat, in close consultation with Member States, but allowed some flexibility for adaptation to national specificities and interests. This blue-print questionnaire was used in all countries except The Netherlands and Belgium where pre-existing survey questionnaires for on-going panel studies were modified slightly (Verma and Clemenceau 1996).

The interview schedule consisted of two types of questionnaire: a Household questionnaire and a Personal questionnaire. The *Household Questionnaire* asked for information on migration status of the household, tenure of accommodation, housing amenities, possession of durable goods, major sources of income, details of the household's income, and various indicators of financial situation.

Subsequently, every household member aged 16 years or older was asked to complete a detailed *Personal Questionnaire*. This was designed to include information on a number of different life domains. It covered economic activity and personal income in detail and also a range of topics including social relations, health, personal characteristics, education, and levels of satisfaction with various aspects of life and work. Economic activity was collected both for current status and retrospectively for the previous calendar year. For the previous year, people were asked to recall their main activity in each successive month, using a list of pre-coded options. Being in paid employment was defined as working 15 hours or more. Apart from some changes in Wave 2, changes to the questionnaire have been minimized over time to permit longitudinal analysis.

Household and Personal Income

In each wave, income data are available for two years. For the calendar year preceding that of interview, 1993 for Wave 1, the survey contains very detailed income information on annual income. There is also a relatively simple question, focusing on the time of interview, where respondents were asked to state their overall household income after taxes in the previous month. All amounts on income and income components are in national currency (NC).

While the principal income measure was designed to be the detailed 1993 income, a problem arises when studying unemployment. It is difficult to match current unemployment with current income. The detailed income measure is for annual income, whereas activity status may change over the year. This necessitates using the less detailed current monthly figure. Nevertheless, it can be shown that the national proportions below the 50 per cent mean poverty lines agree remarkably well whichever set of questions on income is used (Jacobs 1998).

For the detailed set of income questions, people other than those in self-employment were asked for both gross and net income from earnings. Most other income components were presumed reported net of tax and other deductions, with the exception of rental income and income from capital. With the exception of France, all gross amounts have been converted to net.

Where possible, imputations were performed for missing components of income and for inadequate detail such as income given only as a range. Imputations were also performed for components at a higher level of aggregation. This was considered to provide data that are substantively more meaningful and comparable across countries, better correlated to household and personal characteristics, and less prone to response variance. Imputed figures have been flagged in the data-set. In common with most other surveys on household income, the proportions imputed were particularly high for income from self-employed and capital income.

INTERNATIONAL DIFFERENCES

Apart from country differences in sampling mentioned earlier, there are some national variations in the data available, partly reflecting differential views on the requirements to ensure anonymity, and partly differences in the design of particular national schedules. Several variables were considered confidential for Germany and were not given in the anonymized data. These include date of interview and some income components. For The Netherlands, questions relating to the previous calendar year, to past unemployment experience, and financial situation were not asked. In France, because of the particularities of the tax system, all income components in the detailed income measure for the previous calendar year have been collected as gross and only total household income for the previous year has been converted to net. The French also used a different response set for the questions collecting information about the frequency of social contacts.

SAMPLE WEIGHTS

The data files contain weights to be applied in analysis of the data. There are three types of weights: cross-sectional and longitudinal weights for each individual and a household weight for each household. All residents in interviewed households in Wave 1 are 'sample persons' and received a non-zero base weight. In Wave 1 cross-sectional weights are identical to base weights. Wave 2 weights were computed on the basis of Wave 1 weights, modified to take into account non-response and the required adjustment of the achieved sample to external control distributions. These adjustments were applied to the weights of 'sample persons' to determine their longitudinal weights. The statistical procedure used for weighting ensured that all interviewed persons in the same household in Wave 1 received the same cross-sectional weight. The household weight is proportional to the uniform cross-sectional weight received by each of its members. The household and person weights given in the data files have been 'normalised', i.e. scaled to average 1.0 per unit within each country. Technical details of the weighting procedure developed at Eurostat are described in ECHP documentation (Verma 1995a, 1995b, 1997). The analyses in the book have used the Wave 1 individual cross-sectional weighting variable supplied with the particular version of the data-set.

DEFINITIONS OF EMPLOYMENT AND UNEMPLOYMENT

The main subsamples used in our analyses were those of people in employment and the unemployed. For current labour market status *Employment* refers to those who, during the reference week, had been in, or were temporarily absent from, paid or self-employment for at least 15 hours per week. *Unemployment*, adopting the International Labour Office (ILO) definition, refers to those who, during the reference week, were without work, and were either actively searching for work and available to start within two seeks, or had already found a job but had not yet started. The sample numbers for these categories is given in Table A2. Duration of unemployment was calculated using the first and second wave calendar recall data. In this case unemployment is self-defined.

TABLE A2. *Sample numbers: unemployed and total workforce*

	WG	DK	NL	BE	FR	UK	IRE	IT	GR	SP	PT
Total Unemployed	241	331	352	359	934	592	848	1426	937	2109	458
Total Workforce	2975	3559	5176	2762	9936	3610	5171	8969	6552	9130	6451

Source: European Community Household Panel, 1994, anonymized data.

APPENDIX B
Replacement Rates in Europe

The commonly used notion of the 'replacement rate' refers to the proportion of the income that would have been obtained in work that is replaced by unemployment benefit and its associated allowances. This has been an important focus of attention in part because of its political implications. Some economists argue that the generosity of benefits is itself one of the causes of unemployment. Similarly government policies aiming at applying more rigorous criteria for benefit eligibility are often based on the assumption that high replacement rates lead the unemployed to become satisfied with their situation and to reduce their job search efforts. Empirical evaluation of these claims depends crucially on the ability to develop a valid measure of the replacement rate. However, this is by no means unproblematic. We present below the methods and results developed by the OECD, as well as some evidence from our own analyses of the European Community Household Panel.

THE APPROACH OF THE OECD

The method developed by the OECD is based on the analysis of the situation of specific 'types' of unemployed person. It involves calculating the overall amount of benefits and allowances that an unemployed person would receive under specific conditions. For instance, as can be seen in Table B1, taking the situation of an unemployed person aged forty with a dependant wife, there are wide differences between countries.

The gross replacement rate in the first year of unemployment is higher than 70 per cent in The Netherlands, Sweden, and Denmark. It is particularly low in the United Kingdom, at 29 per cent. In several countries, the rate diminishes from the second year. This is particularly the case in Sweden, Italy, Spain, and Greece. The net replacement rate after tax and including housing allowances is higher than the gross in all countries except Italy. It should be noted that the effect of moving from the gross to the net rate calculations is particularly strong in Sweden for the second year of unemployment, and for the United Kingdom.

Estimates of the replacement rate depend heavily on the characteristics of the unemployed person's situation that are taken as the point of departure. For instance, the results can be very different depending on whether the estimates are for an unmarried person or for a married person with a working partner. Given the arbitrariness of choosing any one specific type of situation, the OECD has developed a synthetic indicator. This is the arithmetic mean of eighteen replacement rates derived for combinations of the following characteristics of an unemployed person aged 40:

TABLE B1. *Gross[a] and net[b] replacement rates for an unemployed person aged 40 with a dependent partner, for different durations of unemployment*

	Year 1		Years 2 and 3		Years 4 and 5	
	gross	net	gross	net	gross	net
Belgium	51	70	51	64	51	64
Denmark	73	83	73	83	73	83
France	58	80	40	62	25	60
Germany	38	74	34	72	34	72
Greece	53	—	19	—	0	—
Ireland	42	58	43	58	43	58
Italy	45	43	15	13	0	0
Netherlands	70	90	58	88	48	85
Portugal	65	—	43	—	0	—
Spain	65	70	30	55	0	39
Sweden	76	81	6	100	0	101
UK	29	75	30	74	30	74

[a] Benefits rights before tax as a percentage of pre-tax earnings.
[b] Post-tax benefit rates together with housing allowance, as a percentage of post-tax earnings. Rent is assumed to correspond to 20% of the earnings of an average industrial worker in the country concerned.
Source: OECD data base on unemployment benefits and replacement rates, see Martin (1976).

(1) Duration of unemployment: less than a year, between one year and less than three years, between three years and less than five years;
(2) Family situation: unmarried, married with a dependant spouse, married with a spouse who works;
(3) Level of previous earnings: average earnings and two-thirds of average earnings.

Defined in this way, the synthetic indicator gives the picture of the relative generosity of the benefits system of different countries that can be seen in Table B2.

Taking 1995, the country that emerges as the most generous is Denmark with an index of 70.3, while the least generous was the United Kingdom (18.1), followed by Italy (19.7) and Greece (22.1). France, Belgium, and The Netherlands were in an intermediary situation. It should be noted that the synthetic indicator varies across time. This reflects the fact that countries may choose to adopt more restrictive, or more generous policies with respect to financial assistance to the unemployed. The index increased between 1991 and 1995 in Denmark and also in Italy. However, it decreased in The Netherlands, even though this country retained its position as one of the most generous in Europe.

The approach adopted by the OECD has the merit of taking account of diverse reference situations. It has however some disadvantages. Reasoning in terms of typical cases necessitates choices that are to some degree arbitrary. Given that the economic and social realities are so diverse within Europe, certain typical cases are much more important in some countries than in others. When 40 per cent of the unemployed are under 25 years of age in Italy, for instance, how satisfactory is it to take as the reference point an unemployed person of 40 years of age? Can

TABLE B2. *Synthetic indicator of generosity of benefit systems*[1]

	1991	1995
Belgium	42.3	41.6
Denmark	51.9	70.3
France	37.2	37.5
Germany	28.1	26.4
Greece	17.1	22.1
Ireland	—	26.0
Italy	2.5	19.7
Netherlands	51.3	45.9
Spain	33.5	31.7
Sweden	29.4	27.3
UK	17.5	18.1

[1] Benefit rates before tax as a percentage of previous pre-tax earnings for an unemployed person aged 40.
Source: OECD database on unemployment benefits and replacement rates.

one place sufficient reliance on a simple average between a number of selected situations without considering the statistical representativeness of given situations and the way this varies between countries? Is it sensible to give equal weight to estimates that reflect the situation of the majority of the unemployed and those that reflect the situation of a minority?

It should also be noted that the procedure adopted by the OECD does not take account of social assistance provided at regional or local level. This could give a very misleading picture in countries with more decentralized structures. This is likely to be the case for Germany, for instance, which gives the local authorities considerable autonomy to provide complementary assistance to meet the needs of people judged to be in severe financial difficulty. The relatively low replacement levels and overall generosity indicator given for this country might then be an artefact of the procedures used.

Finally, the approach of the OECD assumes that the unemployed take up their rights. Given the complexity of the legislation and the numerous administrative steps that need to be taken by the unemployed to get access to benefits, it is likely that a proportion of the unemployed do not get to take full advantage of their entitlements. Several studies have pointed to the gap between formal provision and actual take-up. Atkinson and Micklewright (1991), for instance, have underlined that take-up remains very incomplete in certain OECD countries, particularly when social assistance is subject to means-testing.

EVIDENCE FROM THE EUROPEAN COMMUNITY HOUSEHOLD PANEL

Another approach to assessing the replacement rate is to take as the point of departure not a selected set of 'typical cases' but rather the actual benefit income of the unemployed. This can be estimated from survey data and we have carried out an exploratory analysis using data from the first wave of the European Community Household Panel, carried out in 1994[1]. This contains relatively full income data for the previous calendar year, which can be related to labour market history experience over that year.

The procedure was to compare the average net annual income from benefits of people who had been unemployed throughout 1993 with the average net annual income from earnings of two categories of people: all full-time workers employed throughout the year, and manual full-time workers employed throughout the year. The decision to focus on the long-term unemployed was guided by the need to ensure that none of the income could be attributed to a period in the year in which people had been in work. The analysis has been confined to those who were in receipt of benefit to avoid confounding the issue of coverage with that of the generosity of benefits for those who were covered. To provide greater comparability, the results were standardized using a multiple classification analysis to take account of age, level of education, and the presence of young children. Replacement rates were calculated taking account of different sets of benefits: 1) unemployed insurance and assistance, 2) unemployment insurance, unemployment assistance and housing benefit and 3) all benefits.

Taking first the replacement ratios calculated with respect to all full-time employees, it can be seen from Table B3 that Denmark still emerges as the country in which the unemployed receive the best financial compensation. The replacement rate is 0.68 taking account of unemployment benefit and social assistance; it rises to 0.70 when housing benefit is included and to 1.28 if all types of benefit are taken into account. The country where the unemployed in receipt of benefits were least well supported was Greece with 0.23 for unemployment benefit/assistance and 0.47 for all types of benefits. The situation in the United Kingdom was close to that in Greece with 0.34 for unemployment insurance benefit and social assistance. Although it rose to 0.69 when all types of benefit were included, it remained the second lowest of the countries. France, Germany, Italy, and Spain are in an intermediate position. For the last two of these countries, it is particularly important to remember that this applies only to those in receipt of benefit, since a very small proportion of the unemployed were covered. This was also the case for Portugal, where the few who received benefit were in a particularly favourable position. It is also interesting to note that Ireland comes out as more generous than the UK, despite the broad similarities in the principles underlying welfare provision.

The ordering of countries remains very much the same when the comparison is restricted to manual full-time workers, who are in the most similar labour market segment to the unemployed. There is some increase in the replacement ratios for most countries, although they are very far from suggesting that benefits replace earnings potential. Greece and the United Kingdom remain the least generous and Denmark the most generous.

This analysis clearly also has its disadvantages in providing an overall picture. It only concerns the longer-term unemployed, which makes it difficult to assess

[1] These analyses were devised by Sten-Ake Stenberg and Charlotte Samuelsson of the Swedish Institute for Social Research, Stockholm and were implemented with the assistance of Sheila Jacobs, Nuffield College, Oxford.

TABLE B3. *Annual mean income of long-term unemployed 1993, who receive unemployment benefits, relative to income of full year FT employed*

(a) Compared with all full-time workers

	UB + Soc Ass	UB + SA + Hs Ben	All Benefits
Belgium	0.40	0.40	0.77
Denmark	0.68	0.70	1.28
France	0.41	0.43	0.78
Germany	0.37	0.38	0.74
Greece	0.23	0.23	0.47
Ireland	0.46	0.47	0.84
Italy	0.39	0.39	0.75
Portugal	0.54	0.55	1.03
Spain	0.38	0.38	0.74
UK	0.34	0.40	0.69

(b) Compared with working class full-time workers

	UB + Soc Ass	UB + SA + Hs Ben	All Benefits
Belgium	0.38	0.38	0.79
Denmark	0.73	0.75	1.41
France	0.46	0.49	0.91
Germany	0.42	0.44	0.85
Greece	0.25	0.25	0.50
Ireland	0.48	0.48	0.92
Italy	0.43	0.43	0.83
Portugal	0.63	0.64	1.23
Spain	0.43	0.43	0.85
UK	0.34	0.42	0.77

Note: Standardized for age, education and presence of minor children. These are modified versions of tables originally constructed for the EPUSE project by Sten-Ake Stenberg and Charlotte Samuelsson of the Swedish Institute for Social Research.
Source: ECHP (1994) anonymized data.

the decline of benefit with unemployment duration. It probably underestimates the benefits in systems like the French and Spanish, which make stronger efforts to support the living standards of the unemployed in the first year. This is likely to diminish the differences between these countries and those such as the UK and Ireland where benefits start low but are sustained at broadly similar levels for relatively long periods of time. The estimates also depend on personal declarations of income, which may be affected by problems of recall accuracy and are necessarily approximate.

Nonetheless, while a good deal of further work needs to be done to provide a well-validated picture of relative replacement rates, there is a reasonable level of convergence between different sources in terms of the relative position of countries, which provides general support for the classification used in the volume.

REFERENCES

ABOWD, J., CORBEL, P., and KRAMARZ, F. (1995) *The entry and exit of workers and the growth of employment: an analysis of French establishments*, Working paper No. 9542, CREST, INSEE, Paris.

—— KRAMARZ, F., and MARGOLIS, D. N. (1994) *High wage workers and high wage firms*, Working paper No. 9454, CREST, INSEE, Paris.

ALLMENDINGER, J. (1989) Educational system and labour markets outcome. *European Sociological Review* 3: 231–50.

ALOGOSKOUFIS, G., BEAN, C., BERTOLA, G., COHEN, D., DOLADO, J., and SAINT-PAUL, G. (1995) *Unemployment: Choices for Europe*, London: Centre for Economic Policy Research.

ALTHAUSER, R. P. (1989) Internal Labor Markets. *Annual Review of Sociology*, 15.

ANDERTON, B., and MAYHEW, K. (1994) *A Comparative Analysis of the UK Labour Market*, Cambridge: Cambridge University Press.

ANDRESS, J. H., and STRENGMANN, W. K. (1994) Income packages in low-income households. An analysis with data from Socio-Economic Panel and the Bielefeld Social Assistance Data Bank. In R. V. BURKHAUSER, and G. G. WAGNER (eds.) *Proceedings of the 1993 International Conference of German Socio-Economic Panel Study Users*, Verteljahreshefte zur Wirtschaftsforschung, 36–41.

ASHTON, D. N. (1984) *Unemployment Under Capitalism: The Sociology of British and American Labour Markets*, Brighton: Wheatsheaf Books Ltd.

ATKINSON, A. (1983) *The Economics of Inequality*, 2nd edn. Oxford: Clarendon Press.

—— and MICKLEWRIGHT, J. (1991) Unemployment compensation and labour market transitions: a critical review. *Journal of Economic Literature* 29/4: 1679–727.

—— and MOGENSEN, G. V. (1993) *Welfare and Work Incentives*, Oxford: Clarendon Press.

—— RAINWATER, L., and SMEEDING, T. M. (1995a) *Income Distribution in European Countries*, Luxembourg Income Study Working Paper No. 121.

—— —— —— (1995b) *Income Distribution in OECD Countries*, Social Policy Studies No. 18. Paris: Organisation for Economic Cooperation and Development.

ATKINSON, J. (1984) Manpower Strategies for Flexible Organisations. *Personnel Management* 15: 28–31.

—— and MEAGER, N. (1986) Is 'Flexibility' Just a Flash in the Pan? *Personnel Management* 17: 26–9.

AVERITT, R. (1968) *The Dual Economy*, New York, NY: Norton.

BAKKE, E. W. (1940a) *The Unemployed Worker: A Study of the Task of Making a Living without a Job*, New Haven, CT: Yale University Press.

—— (1940b) *Citizens without Work*, New Haven, CT: Yale University Press.

BARBAGLI, M. (1974) *Disoccupazione intellettuale e sistema scolastico in Italia*, Bologna: Il Mulino.

BARBIERI, P. (1997a) IL tesoro nascosto. La mappa del capitale sociale in un'area metropolitana. *Rassegna Italiana di Sociologia* 3: 343–70.

—— (1997b) Non c'è rete senza nodi. Il ruolo del capitale sociale nel processo di incontro fra domanda e offerta di lavoro. *Stato e Mercato* 1: 67–110.

388 *References*

BARON, J. N., and BIELBY, W. T. (1984) The Organization of Work in a Segmented Economy. *American Sociological Review* 49: 454–73.

BAUDELOT, C., and GLAUDE, M. (1989) Les diplômes se dévaluent-ils en se multipliant? *Economie et Statistique* 225: 3–16.

—— and GOLLAC, M. (1997) Le salarié du trentenaire: question d'âge ou de génération? *Economie et Statistique* 304–305: 17–35.

BECKERMAN, W. (1979a) The Impact of Income Maintenance Payments on Poverty in Britain. *Economic Journal* 89: 261–79.

—— (1979b) *Poverty and the Impact of Income Maintenance Programmes*, Geneva: ILO.

BEGGS, J., and HURLBERT, J. S. (1997) The Social Context of Men's and Women's Job Search Ties: Membership in Voluntary Organization, Social resources, and Job Search Outcomes. *Sociological Perspectives* 40: 601–22.

BENOIT-GUILBOT, O., and GALLIE, D. (1994) *Long-Term Unemployment*, London: Pinter Publishers.

BERNARDI, F. (1999) Does the husband matter? Married women's careers in Italy. *European Sociological Review* 15/3: 285–300.

BERNASCO, W. (1994) *Coupled Careers: the effects of Spouse's Resources on Success at Work*. Amsterdam: Thesis Publishers.

—— DE GRAAF, P. M., and ULTEE, W. C. (1998) Couples Careers: effects of spouse's resources on occupational attainment in The Netherlands. *European Sociological Review* 14: 49–68.

BERTOLA, G. (1990) Job security, employment and wages. *European Economic Review* 4: 851–86.

BETTIO, F., and VILLA, P. (1996) *A Mediterranean perspective on the break-down of the relationship between participation and fertility*, Discussion paper, Department of Economics, University of Trento.

BIANCO, M. L. (1996) *Class e reti sociali. Risorse e strategie degli attori nella riproduzione delle diseguglianze*, Bologna: Il Mulino.

BISON, I., PISATI, M., and SCHIZZEROTTO, A. (1996) Diseguaglianze di generre e storie lavorative. In S. PICCONE STELLA, and C. SARACENO (eds.) *Genere. La costruzione sociale del maschile e del femminile*, Bologna: Il Mulino, 253–79.

BJORKLUND, A., and HOLMLUND, B. (1989) *Effects of Extended Unemployment Compensation in Sweden*, Reprint Series No. 243. Swedish Institute for Social Research.

BLANCHARD, O., and SUMMERS, L. (1986) Hysteresis and the European Unemployment Problem. In S. FISHER (ed.) *NBER Macroeconomics Annual I*, Cambridge: National Bureau of Economic Research.

BLANK, R. (1994) *Social Protection versus Economic Flexibility*, Chicago IL: University of Chicago Press.

BLOSSFELD, H. (1992) Is the German Dual System a Model for a Modern Vocational Training System? *International Journal of Comparative Sociology* 3–4: 168–81.

—— and ROHWER, G. (1995) *Techniques of Event History Modelling: New Approaches to Causal Analysis*, New York NY: Erlbaum.

BLUNDELL, R., and BOND, S. (1995) *Initial Conditions and moment restrictions in dynamic panel data models*, IFS Working Paper Series No. W95/17, London: Institute for Fiscal Studies.

BONNAL, L., FOUGÈRE, D., and SÉRANDON, A. (1994) L'impact des dispositifs d'emploi sur le devenir des jeunes chômeurs: une évaluation économétrique sur données longitudinales. *Economie et Prévision* 115: 1–28.

BORCHORST, A. and SIIM, B. (1987) Women and the advanced welfare state—a new kind of patriarchal power? In A. SHOWSTACK SASSOON (ed.) *Women and the State*, London: Hutchinson.

BOTT, E. (1971) *Family and Social Network*, London: Tavistock.

BOURDIEU, P. (1979) *La Distinction*, Paris: Les Éditions de Minuit.

—— (1980) Le capital social. *Acte de la recherche en sciences sociales* 31: 2–3.

—— (1994) *Raisons pratiques: sur la théorie de l'action*, Paris: Editions du Seuil.

—— DARBEL, A., RIVET, J., and SEIBEL, C. (1963) *Travail et Travailleurs en Algérie*, Paris: Mouton.

BOXMAN, E., DE GRAAF, P. M., and FLAP, H. D. (1991) The impact of social and human capital on the income attainment of Dutch managers. *Social Networks* 13: 55–73.

BRADLEY, H. (1996) *Fragmented Identities, Changing Patterns of Inequality*, Cambridge: Polity Press.

BRADSHAW, J., KENNEDY, S., KILKEY, M., HUTTON, S., CORDEN, A., EARDLEY, T., HOLMES, H., and NEALE, J. (1996) *The employment of lone parents: a comparison of policy in 20 countries*, London: Family Policy Studies Centre.

BREEN, R. (1998) The Persistence of Class Origin Inequalities Among School Leavers in the Republic of Ireland 1984–1993. *British Journal of Sociology* 49: 275–98.

—— and GOLDTHORPE, J. (1997) Explaining Educational Differentials: Towards a Formal Rational Action Theory. *Rationality and Society* 9: 275–305.

BREUER, W. (1999) La pauvreté en Allemagne: un problème résolu? In S. PAUGAM (ed.) *L'Europe face à la pauvreté. Les expériences nationales de revenu minimum*, Paris: La Documentation Francaise.

BRIDGES, W. P., and VILLEMEZ, W. J. (1986) Informal hiring and income in the labor market. *American Sociological Review* 51: 574–82.

BROWNING, M. (1992) Children and household economic behavior. *Journal of Economic Literature* 30: 1434–75.

BRYSON, A., FORD, R., and WHITE, M. (1997) *Making work pay: Lone mothers, employment and well-being*, York: Joseph Rowntree Foundation.

BYNNER, J., and ROBERTS, K. (1997) *Youth and Work: Transition to Employment in England and Germany*, London: Anglo German Foundation.

CAHUC, P., and ZYLBERBERG, A. (1996) *Economie du travail*, Brussels: De Boeck Universite.

CALENDER, C., and METCALF, H. (1991) *Recruitment Procedures and Job Search Behaviour, 169*, Brighton: Institute of Manpower.

CALLAN, T., and SUTHERLAND, H. (1997) Income Supports in Ireland and the UK. In T. CALLAN (ed.) *Income Support and Work Incentives: Ireland and the UK*, Policy Series Paper No. 30, Dublin: Economic and Social Research Institute.

——, NOLAN, B., and WHELAN, C. T. (1993) Resources, Deprivation and the Measurement of Poverty. *Journal of Social Policy*, 22/2: 141–22.

CALMORS, L., and DRIFFILL, J. (1988) Centralisation of Wage Bargaining and Macroeconomic Performance. *Economic Policy* 6: 13–61.

CAMPBELL, K. E., MARSDEN, P. V., and HURLBERT, J. S. (1986) Social resources and socioeconomic status. *Social Networks* 8: 97–117.

CARROLL, E. (1997) *Development of Social Rights for the Unemployed: Assessing Competing Theories of Welfare State Extension with Techniques of Pooled Time Series Analysis*, Mimeo. Swedish Insitute for Social Research.

CASTLES, F. (1993) *Social Security in Southern Europe*, Paper presented at a conference organized by the Sub-committee on Southern Europe of the American Social Science Research Council, Bielefeld, July.

CAVALLI, A. (1993) La prolongation de la jeunesse en Italie: ne pas brûler les étapes. In A. CAVALLI and O. GALLAND (eds.) *L'allongement de la jeunesse*, Arles: Actes Sud.

—— and GALLAND, O. (1995) *Youth in Europe*, London: Pinter.

CEPR (1995) *Unemployment: Choices in Europe*, London: Centre for Economic Policy Research.

CHENU, A. (1997) *Le devenir professional des ouvriers et des employés: promotion, mise à son compte, risque de chômage 1968–1990*, Paper presented at the seminar of the Laboratoire de sociologie quantitative, CREST, INSEE, Paris.

CLARK, A. (1998) *The Positive Externalities of Higher Unemployment: Evidence from Household Data*, Unpublished paper.

—— and OSWALD, A. (1994) Unhappiness and Unemployment. *Economic Journal* 104: 648–59.

—— —— (1998) *Unhappiness and Unemployment in Panel Data*, Unpublished paper, University of Orléans.

COBALTI, A., and SCHIZZEROTTO, A. (1994) *La mobilità sociale in Italia*, Bologna: Il Mulino.

COHEN, D. (1994) *Les infortunés de la prospérité*, Paris: Julliard.

COLEMAN, J. (1988) Social capital in the creation of human capital. *American Journal of Sociology* 94: 95–120.

—— (1990) *Foundations of Social Theory*, Cambridge, MA: Harvard University Press.

—— (1991) Matching Processes in the Labor Market. *Acta Sociologica* 34: 3–12.

COMMISSION OF THE EUROPEAN COMMUNITY (1995) *Employment in Europe*, Luxembourg: Office for Official Publications of the European Union.

COMMISSION DI INDAGINE SULLA POVERTA E SULL' EMARGINAZIONE (1996) Rome: Poulo.

CRAGG, A., and DAWSON, T. (1984) *Unemployed Women: A Study of Attitudes and Experiences*. London: Dept. of Employment, Research Paper No. 47.

DALY, M. (1996) *Social Security, Gender and Equality in the European Union*, Brussels: European Commission.

—— (1997) Welfare States under Pressure: Cash Benefits in European Welfare States over the last ten years. *Journal of European Social Policy* 7: 129–46.

DANISH MINISTRY OF LABOUR (1996) *The Unemployment Insurance Scheme*, Copenhagen: Arbejdsministeriet.

DE GRAAF, N. D., and FLAP, H. D. (1988) 'With a little help from my friends': social resources as an explanation of occupational status and income in West Germany, The Netherlands and the United States. *Social Forces* 67: 452–72.

DE GRAAF, P. M. and ULTEE, W. C. (1991) Labour market transitions of husbands and wives in the Netherlands between 1980 and 1986. A contribution to the debate on the new underclass. *The Netherlands' Journal of Social Sciences* 27: 43–59.

DE TOCQUEVILLE, A. (1994) *Democracy in America*, London: Allen and Unwin.

DE VREYER, P., PAUGAM, S., PRÉLIS, J., and ZOYEM, J. P. (1996) *From Precariousness to Social Exclusion: A perspective on European Research*, EPUSE working paper No. 2. Nuffield College, Oxford.

DELEECK, H., VAN DEN BOSCH, K., and DE LATHOUWER, L. (1992) *Poverty and the Adequacy of Social Security in the EC*, Aldershot: Avebury.

DELL'ARINGA, C., and SAMEK LODOVICI, M. (1996) Policies for the Unemployed and Social Shock Absorbers: The Italian Experience. *South European Society and Politics* 3: 172–97.

—— —— (1997) *Policies for the Unemployed and Social Shock Absorbers: The Italian Experience*, London: Frank Cass.

DEVINE, T. J., and KIEFER, N. M. (1991) *Empirical Labor Economics. The Search Approach*, Oxford: Oxford University Press.

DEX, S., GUSTAFSSON, S., SMITH, N., and CALLAN, T. (1995) Cross-national comparisons of the labour force participation of women married to unemployed men. *Oxford Economic Papers* 47: 611–35.

DITCH, J., BARNES, J., BRADSHAW, J., COMMAILLE, J., and EARDLEY, T. (1996) *A Synthesis of National Family Policies 1994*, York: Social Policy Research Unit, University of York.

DRÈZE, J., and MALINVAUD, E. (1994) Growth and Employment: The Scope of a European Initiative. *European Economic Review* 38/3–4: 489–504.

DUNCAN, A., GILES, C., and WEBB, S. (1995) *The Impact of Subsidising Childcare*, Manchester: Equal Opportunities Commission.

EARDLEY, T., BRADSHAW, J., DITCH, J., GOUGH, I., and WHITEFORD, P. (1996) *Social Assistance in OECD Countries: Country Reports*, Research Report No. 47. Paris: OECD.

EDWARDS, R. C. (1975) The Social Relations of Production in the Firm and Labour Market Structure, *Politics and Society*, 5/1: 83–109.

—— (1979) *Contested Terrain*, New York: Basic Books.

ELIAS, N., and SCOTTSON, J. L. (1965) *The Established and the Outsiders*, London: Frank Cass and Co.

ELIAS, P. (1996) *Who forgot they were unemployed?* Working papers of the ESRC Research Centre on Micro-social Change, Paper 97-19, Colchester, University of Essex.

ELMESKOV, J., and PICHELMANN, K. (1993) Interpreting unemployment: the role of labour force participation. *OECD Economic Studies* 21: 139–60.

EMERSON, M. (1988) Regulation or Deregulation of the Labour Market: Policy Regimes for the Recruitment and Dismissal of Employees in the Industrialised Countries. *European Economic Review* 32: 775–817.

ERIKSON, R., and GOLDTHORPE, J. (1992) *The Constant Flux*, Oxford: Clarendon Press.

ESPING-ANDERSEN, G. (1987) The comparison of policy regimes: an introduction. In M. REIN, G. ESPING-ANDERSEN, and L. RAINWATER (eds.) *Stagnation and renewal in social policy. The rise and fall of policy regimes*, New York, NY: M. E. Sharpe Inc.

—— (1990) *The Three Worlds of Welfare Capitalism*, Oxford: Polity Press.

—— (1994) Welfare states and the economy. In N. J. SMELSER, and R. SWEDBERG (eds.) *The handbook of economic sociology*, Princeton, NJ: Princeton University Press.

ESPING-ANDERSEN, G. (1996) *Welfare States in Transition: National Adaptation in Global Economies*, London: Sage Publications.

—— (1997) *Welfare States at the End of the Century. The impact of Labor Markets, Family and Demographic Change*, Paris: OECD Publications.

—— (1998) *Labor market regulation and unemployment. A review of the evidence from comparative research*, Unpublished paper, Department of Sociology and Social Research, University of Trento.

—— (1999) *Social Foundations of Postindustrial Economies*, Oxford: Oxford University Press.

—— ROHWER, G., and SORENSEN, S. L. (1994) Institutions and Occupational class mobility: scaling the skill barrier in the Danish labour market. *European Sociological Review* 10: 110–34.

EUROPÄISCHE KOMMISSION (1997) *Europäische Wirtschaft No. 64*, Brussels/Luxembourg: Office for Official Publications of the European Community.

EUROPEAN COMMISSION (1993) *Social Protection in Europe*, Luxembourg: Office for Official Publications of the European Union.

—— (1995) *Social Protection in Europe*, Luxembourg: Office for Official Publications of the European Union.

—— (1996a) *Social Protection in Europe*, Luxembourg: Office for Official Publications of the European Community.

—— (1996b) *Social protection in the member states of the European Union*, Luxembourg: Office for Official Publications of the European Communities.

—— (1996c) *Employment in Europe, 1995*, Luxembourg: Office for Official Publications of the European Union.

EUROPEAN COMMISSION NETWORK ON CHILDCARE (1996) *A Review of Services for Young Children in the European Union*, Brussels: European Commission Directorate General V.

EUROSTAT (1995) *Statistics in Focus Regions: Unemployment in the Regions of the European Union in 1994*, Luxembourg: Office for Official Publications of the European Union.

—— (1996a) *Social Protection Expenditure and Receipts 1980–1994*, Luxembourg: Office for Official Publications of the European Union.

—— (1996b) *Social Portrait of Europe*, Luxembourg: Office for Official Publications of the European Union.

—— (1996c) *Employment and Unemployment. Aggregates 1980–1994*, Luxembourg: Office for Official Publications of the European Union.

—— (1996d) *ECHP Wave 2 Evaluation: Longitudinal Response Rates-Empirical Results* Doc. PAN 72/96. Luxembourg: Eurostat.

—— (1997) *Statistics in Focus Income Distribution and Poverty in the European Union, 1993*, Brussels: Eurostat.

—— (1998) *ECHP Longitudinal Users Database Waves 1 and 2 Manual*. Luxembourg: Eurostat.

EVANS, M., PAUGAM, S., and PRÉLIS, J. A. (1995) *Chunnel Vision: Poverty, social exclusion and the debate on social welfare in France and Britain*, London School of Economics, STICERD, Welfare State Programme. Working Paper No. 115.

FAHEY, T., and LYONS, M. (1995) *Marital Breakdown and Family Law in Ireland*, Dublin: Oak Tree Press.

FAINI, R., GALLI, G., and ROSSI, F. (1996) *Mobilita e disoccupazione in Italia: un'analisi dell'offerta di lavaro*, Rome: Società Italiana di Publicazioni Industriali.

FERRERA, M. (1993) *EC Citizens and Social Protection. Main results from a Eurobarometer survey.* Brussels: European Commission Directorate General V.

—— (1996) The 'Southern Model' of Welfare in Social Europe. *Journal of European Social Policy* 6: 17–37.

FLEURBAEY, M., HERPIN, N., MARTINEZ, M., and VERGER, D. (1997) Mesurer la pauvreté? *Economie et Statistique* 308–309–310: 23–33.

FLORENS, J-P., and FOUGÈRE, D. (1993) *Chômage et transitions sur le marché du travail.* Rapport à la MIRE. Toulouse: MIRE.

FORSÉ, M. (1997) Capital Social et Emploi, *L'Anneé Sociologique*, 47/1: 143–81.

FOUGÈRE, D., and KAMIONKA, T. (1992) Un modèle markovien du marché du travail. *Annales d'Economie et Statistique* 27: 149–88.

FREEMAN, R. B. (ed.) (1994) Working Under Different Rules, New York, NY: Russell Sage.

FRIDBERG, T. (1988) *Lone-parents in Denmark*, mimeo. Copenhagen: Danish National Institute for Social Research.

FRYER, D. (1986) Employment Deprivation and Person Agency During Unemployment. *Social Behaviour* 1: 3–23.

—— (1990) The Mental Costs of Unemployment: Towards a Social Psychological Concept of Poverty. *British Journal of Clinical and Social Psychiatry* 7: 164–75.

FURNISS, N., and TILTON, T. (1977) *The Case for the Welfare State*, Bloomington, Indiana: University of Indiana Press.

FURSTENBERG, F., and HUGHES, M. (1995) Social capital and successful development among at-risk youth. *Journal of Marriage and the Family* 57: 580–92.

GALBRAITH, J. (1969) *The New Industrialised State*, Boston: Houghton.

GALLIE, D. (1998) *Unemployment, the Household and Social Networks in Europe*, Paper for European Science Foundation Conference on Inequality and Social Exclusion in Europe: The Role of the Family and Social Networks. Castelvecchio Pascoli, Italy, April 1998.

—— (1999) Unemployment and Social Exclusion in the European Union. *European Societies*, 1/2: 139–67.

—— and RUSSELL, H. (1998) Unemployment and Life Satisfaction: A Cross-cultural comparison. *European Journal of Sociology* 2: 248–80.

—— and VOGLER, C. (1994) Unemployment and Attitudes to Work. In D. GALLIE, C. MARSH, and C. VOGLER (eds.) *Social Change and the Experience of Unemployment*, Oxford: Oxford University Press, 115–53.

—— GERSHUNY, J., and VOGLER, C. (1994) Unemployment, the Household and Social Networks. In D. GALLIE, C. MARSH, and C. VOGLER (eds.) *Social Change and the Experience of Unemployment*, Oxford University Press, 231–63.

—— MARSH, C., and VOGLER, C. (eds.) (1994) *Social Change and the Experience of Unemployment*, Oxford: Oxford University Press.

—— WHITE, M., CHENG, Y., and TOMLINSON, M. (1998) *Restructuring the Employment Relationship*, Oxford: Oxford University Press.

GANZEBOOM, H. B., and TREIMAN, D. J. (1996) Internationally Comparable Measures of Occupational Status for the 1988 International Standard Classification of Occupations. *Social Science Research* 25: 201–39.

GERSHUNY, J., and HANNAN, C. (1997) *Unemployment: Blame the Victim?* Working papers of the ESRC Research Centre on Micro-social change, Paper 97-23, Colchester, University of Essex.

—— and MARSH, C. (1994) Unemployment in Work Histories. In D. GALLIE, C. MARSH, and C. VOGLER (eds.) *Social Change and the Experience of Unemployment*, Oxford: Oxford University Press.

GOLDTHORPE, J. (forthcoming) *Social Class and the Differentiation of Employment Contracts*. In J. GOLDTHORPE, *Numbers and Narratives: Essays for a Future Sociology*. Oxford: Clarendon Press.

GORNICK, J., MEYERS, M., and ROSS, K. (1997) Supporting the Employment of Mothers: Policy Variation across Fourteen Welfare States. *Journal of European Social Policy* 7: 45–70.

GRANOVETTER, M. (1973) The strength of weak ties. *American Sociological Review* 78: 1360–80.

—— (1974) *Getting a job. A study of contacts and careers*, Cambridge, MA: Harvard University Press.

—— (1982) The Strength of Weak Ties. A Network Theory Revisited. In P. V. MARSDEN, and N. LIN (eds.) *Social Structure and Network Analysis*, London: Sage.

GREENE, W. H. (1993) *Econometric Analysis* (2nd Ed.), Englewood Cliffs: Prentice Hall.

GRIECO, M. (1987) *Keeping it in the family: social networks and employment chance*, London: Tavistock.

GROTE, J. R. (1997) *Interorganizational Networks and Social Capital Formation in the South of the South*, European University Institute, R. SCHUMAN Centre Paper No. 38.

GRUBB, D. (1994) *Direct and Indirect Effects of Active Labour Market Policies in OECD Countries*, Cambridge: Cambridge University Press.

—— and WELLS, W. (1993) Employment regulation and patterns of work in EC countries. *OECD Economic Studies* 21: 7–58.

GUSTAFSSON, S. (1996) *Tax Regimes and Labour Market Performance*, Cheltenham: Edward Elgar.

HAKIM, C. (1982) The Social Consequences of High Unemployment. *Journal of Social Policy* 11/4: 433–67.

—— (1996) *Key Issues in Women's Work: Female Heterogeneity and the Polarisation of Women's Employment*, London: Athlone Press.

—— (1998) *Models of the family, labour force participation and welfare systems: a new perspective from Preference Theory*, Paper presented at the European Science Foundation Conference, Castelvecchio, Pascoli, April 1998.

HALSEY, A. H., LAUDER, H., BROWN, P., and WELLS, A. S. (1997) *Education, Culture, Economy and Society*, Oxford: Oxford University Press.

HANNAN, C. (1998) *Social Cohesion and Unemployment Exit Rates*, Paper presented at European Science Foundation Conference, Castelvecchio, Pascoli, April 1998.

HANSEN, H., HEINSEN, N., SALOMAKI, A., VIITAMAKI, H., AMIRA, S., KNOLICH, B., SEMRAU, P., CAPELLEN, A., BALL, J., EINERHAND, M., METZ, H., VAN GALEN, J., ERIKSSON, I., and LINDHOLM, L. (1995) *Unemployment Benefits and Social Assistance in seven European Countries*, The Hague: Ministerie van Sociale Zaken en Werkgelegenheid.

HAUSER, R., and NOLAN, B. (1998) *Changes in Income Poverty and Deprivation Over Time: A Comparison of Eight European Countries from the Mid-1980s to the Mid-1990s with Special Attention to the Stituation of the Unemployed*, EPUSE Project Working Paper 3, Nuffield College, Oxford.

HEATH, A., and CHEUNG, S. Y. (1998) *Education and Occupation in Britain*, Oxford: Oxford University Press.

HECKMAN, J. J. (1974) Effects of Child-Care Programs on Women's Work Effort, *Journal of Political Economy*, 82/2: 5136–63.

HOLLINGER, F., and HALLER, M. (1990) Kinship and social networks in modern societies: a cross-cultural comparison among seven nations. *European Sociological Review*, 2: 103–24.

HOLMLUND, B. (1998) Unemployment Insurance in Theory and Practice. *Scandinavian Journal of Economics* 100: 113–41.

HSIAO, C. (1986) *Analysis of Panel Data*, Cambridge: Cambridge University Press.

HUSTER, E. (1996) *Armut in Europa*, Oplanden: Leske + Budrich.

ICHINO, A., and BERTOLA, G. (1995) Crossing the river. *Economic Policy*, 21: 361–420.

—— and ICHINO, P. (1994) A chi serve il diritto del lavoro, *Rivista Italiana di Diritto del Lavoro*, 4: 459–505.

JACKMAN, R., LAYARD, R., and NICKELL, S. (1996) *Combatting Unemployment: Is Flexibility Enough?* Centre for Economic Performance/LSE discussion paper No. 293.

JACOBS, S. (1998) Poverty and Unemployment in the European Union, Paper given to the Sociology Seminar, Nuffield College, Oxford.

JAHODA, M. (1992) *Employment and Unemployment: A Socio-Psychological Analysis*, Cambridge: Cambridge University Press.

—— (1998) Economic Recession and Mental Health: Some Conceptual Issues. *Journal of Social Issues* 44: 13–23.

JONES, G. (1992) *Short-term reciprocity in parent-child economic exchanges*, London: MacMillan.

JURADO GUERRERO, T., and NALDINI, M. (1997) Is the South so Different? Italian and Spanish Families in Comparative Perspective. In M. RHODES (ed.) *Southern European Welfare States. Between Crisis and Reform*, London: Frank Cass & Co Ltd.

KASL, S., and COBB, S. (1979) Some Mental Health Consequences of Plant Closings and Job Losses. In W. A. FERMAN and J. P. GORDUS (eds.) *Mental Health and the Economy*. Kalamazoo, MI: The Upjohn Institute.

KAZAMAKI, E. (1991) *Firm Search, Sectoral Shifts and Unemployment*, Stockholm: Almqvist & Wiksell International.

KELVIN, P., and JARRETT, C. (1985) *Unemployment: its Social Psychological Effects*, Cambridge: Cambridge University Press.

KEMPERMAN, M., and VISSERS, A. (1999) De l'assistance passive à l'assistance active aux Pays-Bas. In S. PAUGAM (ed.) *L'Europe face à la pauvreté. Les experiences nationales de revenu minimum*, Paris: La Documentation Francaise.

KESSLER, R., BLAKE, S., TURNER, J., and HOUSE, J. S. (1989) Unemployment, Reemployment and Emotional Functioning in a Community Sample. *American Sociological Review* 54: 321–53.

Korpi, T. (1995) Effects of Manpower Policies on Duration Dependance in Re-employment Rates: the Example of Sweden. *Economica* 62: 353–71.

König, W., Lüttinger, P., and Müller, W. (1988) *A Comparative Analysis of the Development and Structure of Educational Systems: Methodological Foundations and the Construction of a Comparative Educational Scale*, CASMIN Working Paper No. 12, University of Mannheim.

Kramarz, F., Lollivier, S., and Pele, L. P. (1995) *Wage inequalities and firm-specific compensation policies in France*, Working paper No. 9518, CREST, INSEE, Paris.

Krief, P. (1998) *La construction sociale du chômage. Une étude sur le cas-limite des demandeurs d'emploi de très longue durée*, PhD thesis in Sociology. Paris: Ecole des Hautes Etudes en Sciences Sociales.

Lampard, R. (1994) An examination of the relationship between marital dissolution and unemployment. In D. Gallie, C. Marsh, and C. Volger (eds.) *Social Change and the Experience of Unemployment*, Oxford: Oxford University Press.

Lane, R. (1991) *The Market Experience*, Cambridge: Cambridge University Press.

Layard, L., Nickell, S., and Jackman, R. (1984) *On Vacancies*, Discussion paper 165, London: LSE Center for Labour Economics.

——— ——— ——— (1991) *Unemployment. Macroeconomic Performance and the Labour Market*, Oxford: Oxford University Press.

——— ——— ——— (1994) *The Unemployment Crisis*, Oxford: Oxford University Press.

Lazarsfeld, P., Jahoda, M., and Zeisel, H. (1933) *Marienthal: The Sociology of an Unemployed Community*, London: Tavistock.

Lescure, R., and L'Horty, Y. (1994) Le chômage d'inadéquation en France: une évaluation, *Economie et Prévision* 113–14: 139–54.

Lewis, J. (1992) Gender and the Development of Welfare Regimes. *Journal of European Social Policy* 2: 159–73.

——— ed. (1997) *Lone Mothers in European Welfare Regimes*, London and Philadelphia: Jessica Kingsley Publisher.

Liebfried, S. (1992) Towards a European Welfare State. In Z. Ferge, and J. E. Kolberg (eds.) *Social Policy in a Changing Europe*, Boulder, CO: Westview Press, 245–79.

Liem, R. (1987) The Psychological Consequences of Unemployment: A Comparison of Findings and Definitions. *Social Research* 54: 321–53.

Lin, N. (1982) Social Resources and Instrumental Action. In P. V. Marsden and N. Lin (eds.) *Social Structure and Network Analysis*, London: Sage.

——— (1999) Social Networks and Status Attainment. *Annual Review of Sociology* 25: 467–87.

——— and Dumin, M. (1986) Access to occupations through social ties. *Social Networks* 8: 365–85.

——— Dean, A., and Ensel, W. M. (1996) *Social Support, Life Events and Depression*, New York, NY: Academic Press Inc.

——— Ensel, W. M., and Vaughn, J. C. (1981a) Social resources and strength of ties: structural factors in occupational status attainment. *American Sociological Review* 46: 393–405.

——— Vaughn, J. C. and Ensel, W. M. (1981b) Social resources and occupational status attainment. *Social Forces* 59: 1163–81.

LINDBECK, A. (1993) *Unemployment and Macroeconomics*, Cambridge, Mass: MIT Press.

—— and SNOWER, D. J. (1988) *The Insider-Outsider Theory of Employment and Unemployment*, Cambridge, Mass: MIT Press.

LOLLIVIER, S., and VERGER, D. (1997) Pauvreté d'existence, monétaire où subjective sont distinctes. *Economie et Statistique* 308–309–310: 113–42.

MABBETT, D. (1996) *The Organisation of the Danish Cash Benefit System. Analysis and Issues*, CWR Working Paper 4, Copenhagen: Centre for Welfare State Research.

MADDALA, G. S. (1983) *Limited Dependent and Qualitative Variables in Econometrics*, Cambridge: Cambridge University Press.

MAGUIRE, M. (1992) *The Role of Employers in the Labour Market*, London: Routledge.

MARSDEN, P. V., and CAMPBELL, K. (1984) Measuring tie strength. *Social Forces* 63: 482–501.

—— and HURLBERT, J. S. (1988) Social resources and mobility outcomes: a replication and extension. *Social Forces* 66: 1038–59.

—— and LIN, N. (1982) *Social Structure and Network Analysis*, London: Sage.

MARSH, C., and ALVARO, J. (1990) A Cross-cultural Perspective on the Social and Psychological Distress Caused by Unemployment: A Comparison of Spain and the United Kingdom. *European Sociological Review* 6: 327–55.

MARSHALL, G. (1997) *Repositioning Class. Social Inequality in Industrial Societies*, London: Sage.

MARSHALL, T. H. (1950) *Citizenship and Social Class*, Cambridge: Cambridge University Press.

MARTIN, J. P. (1976) Indicateurs de taux de remplacement aux fins de comparaisons internationales, *Revue Économigue de L'OCOE*, 26: 115–32.

MASSEY, D. S., and ESPINOSA, K. E. (1997) What's Driving Mexico-U.S. Migration? *American Journal of Sociology* 4: 939–99.

McFATE, K. (1995) Western states in the new world order. In K. McFATE, R. LAWSON, and W. J. WILSON (eds.) *Poverty, Inequality and the future of social policy. Western states in the new world order*, New York, NY: Russell Sage Foundation.

MÉNY, Y., and RHODES, M. (1998) *The Future of European Welfare. A New Social Contract?* London: Macmillan.

MICHIE, J., and GRIEVE SMITH, J. (1996) *Creating Industrial Capacity. Towards Full Employment*, Oxford: Oxford University Press.

MIDDLEMANS, J., and PASERMAN, R. (1996) Vivre sous le même toit. Modèles familiaux dans l'Union Europénne. *Insee Première*, 43: 1–4.

MINGIONE, E. (1991) *Fragmented Societies: a Sociology of Economic Life Beyond the Market Paradigm*, Oxford: Basil Blackwell.

MITCHELL, D. (1991) *Income Transfers in Ten Welfare States*, Aldershot: Avebury.

MORTENSEN, D. T. (1977) Unemployment and job search decisions. *Industrial and Labor Relations Review* 30: 505–17.

MOSS, L., and GOLDSTEIN, H. (1979) *The Recall Method in Social Surveys*, London: University of London.

MÜLLER, W., and SHAVIT, Y. (1998) *The Institutional Embeddedness of the Stratification Process: A Comparative Study of Qualifications and Occupations in Thirteen Countries*, Oxford: Oxford University Press.

MURRAY, C. (1992) *The Emerging British Underclass*, London: Institute of Economic Affairs.

MYRDAL, G. (1960) *Beyond the welfare state*, London: Duckworth.

NEGRI, N. (1998) Les failles d'un système localisé en Italie. In S. PAUGAM (ed.) *L'Europe face à la pauvreté. Les expériences nationales de revenu minimum*, Paris: La Documentation Francaise.

—— and SARACENO, S. (1996) *Le politiche contro la povertà in Italia*, Bologna: Il Mulino.

NICKELL, S. (1997) Unemployment and Labour Market Rigidities: Europe versus North America. *Journal of Economic Perspectives* 3: 55–74.

NOLAN, B. and WHELAN, C. (1996) *Resources, Deprivation and the Measurement of Poverty*, Oxford: Clarendon Press.

NORTH, D. C. (1990) *Institutions, institutional change and economic performance*, Cambridge: Cambridge University Press.

O'CONNOR, J. (1973) *The Fiscal Crisis of the State*, New York, NY: St Martin's Press.

—— (1996) From Women in the Welfare State to Gendering Welfare State Regimes. *Current Sociology* 44: 1–124.

OECD (Organization for Economic Co-operation and Development) (1989) *OECD Country Survey: The Netherlands*, Paris: Organization for Economic Co-operation and Development.

—— (1990a) *Employment Outlook*, Paris: Organization for Economic Co-operation and Development.

—— (1990b) *Labour market policies for the 1990s*, Paris: Organization for Economic Co-operation and Development.

—— (1991a) *Employment Outlook 1991*, Paris: Organization for Economic Co-operation and Development.

—— (1991b) *Economic Outlook*, Paris: Organization for Economic Co-operation and Development.

—— (1993a) *Breadwinner or Child Rearers: The dilemma for lone mothers*, Paris: Organization for Economic Co-operation and Development, Labour Market and Social Policy Occasional Papers.

—— (1993b) *Employment Outlook*, Paris: Organization for Economic Co-operation and Development.

—— (1994a) *Employment Outlook*, Paris: Organization for Economic Co-operation and Development.

—— (1994b) *The OECD Jobs Study. Evidence and Explanations. Part II*, Paris: Organization for Economic Co-operation and Development.

—— (1994c) *The OECD jobs study*, Paris: Organization for Economic Co-operation and Development.

—— (1994d) *The OECD Jobs study. Facts, Analysis, Strategies*, Paris: Organization for Economic Co-operation and Development.

—— (1995a) *Income Distribution in OECD Countries*, Paris: Organization for Economic Co-operation and Development.

—— (1995b) *Job Gains and Job Losses: Recent Literature and Trends*, The OECD Jobs Study Working Papers No 1. Paris: Organization for Economic Co-operation and Development.

—— (1996) *Employment Outlook*.

—— (1997a) *Historical Statistics 1960–1995*, Paris: Organization for Economic Co-operation and Development.

—— (1997b) *Employment Outlook*, Paris: Organization for Economic Co-operation and Development.

—— (1997c) *The Tax/Benefit Position of Production Workers*, Paris: Organization for Economic Co-operation and Development.

—— (1997d) *Family, Market and Community. Equity and efficiency in social policy*, Paris: Organization for Economic Co-operation and Development.

—— (1998a) *Benefit Systems and Work Incentives*, Paris: Organization for Economic Co-operation and Development.

—— (1998b) *Employment Outlook*, Paris: Organization for Economic Co-operation and Development.

OECD-CERI (1997) *Education at a glance*, Paris: Organization for Economic Co-operation and Development.

OFFICE FOR NATIONAL STATISTICS (1996) *Labour Market Trends*, London: Office for National Statistics.

ORLOFF, A. S. (1993) Gender and the Social Rights of Citizenship: the Comparative Analysis of Gender Relations and Welfare States. *American Sociological Review* 58: 303–28.

ORME, C. (1996) *The initial conditions problem and two-step estimation in discrete panel data models*, Manchester: University of Manchester Discussion Paper, No. 96–33.

PAUGAM, S. (1991) *La disqualification sociale. Essai sur la nouvelle pauvreté*, Paris: Presses Universitaires de France.

—— (1993) *La Societe Francaise et ses Pauvres. L'Experience du Revenu Minimum d'Insertion*, Paris: Presses Universitaires de France.

—— (1996) Poverty and Social Disqualification: A Comparative Analysis of Cumulative Social Disadvantage in Europe. *Journal of European Social Policy* 6: 287–303.

—— (1997) *La disqualification sociale. Essai sur la nouvelle pauvreté*, Paris: Presses Universitaires de France, coll. 'Sociologies' 4ème édition.

—— (1998a) Poverty and Exclusion: A Sociological View. In Y. MÉNY, and M. RHODES (eds.). *The Future of European Welfare. A New Social Contract?* London: Macmillan.

—— (1998b) *To Give, to Receive and to Give Back. The Social Logic of Family Support*, Paper for European Science Foundation Conference on Inequality and Social Exclusion in Europe: The Role of the Family and Social Networks. Castelvecchio Pascoli, Italy, April 1998.

—— and ZOYEM, J. (1996) Pauvreté et Transferts Sociaux: Une Dépendance Accrue des Ménages à Bas Revenus. *Solidarité Santé* 1:

—— —— and CHARBONNEL, J. (1993) *Précarité et risque d'exclusion en France*, Paris: La Documentation Francaise. Documents du centre d'étude des revenus et des côuts.

—— (ed.) (1999) *L'Europe face à la pauvreté: Les expériences nationales de revenu minimum*. Paris: La Documentation Francaise.

PAYNE, J. (1987) Does unemployment run in families? Some findings from the general household survey. *Sociology* 21: 199–214.

PAYNE, J., and PAYNE, C. (1992) Recession, Restructuring, and the Fate of the Unemployed: Evidence in the Underclass Debate. *Sociology* 28: 1–19.

PEARLIN, L. (1989) The Sociological Study of Stress. *Journal of Health and Social Behaviour* 30: 241–56.

—— MENEGHAN, E., LIEBERMAN, M., and MULLAN, J. T. (1981) The Stress Process. *Journal of Health and Social Behaviour* 19: 2–21.

PEDERSEN, P. J., and SMITH, N. (1995) *The Welfare State and the Labour Market*, Centre for Labour Market and Social Research, Denmark, Working Paper 95–17.

PFAU-EFFINGER, B. (1998) Culture or Structure as Explanations for Differences in Part-time Work in Germany, Finland and the Netherlands. In J. O'REILLY, and C. FAGAN (eds.) *Part-Time Prospects*, London: Routledge.

POLLERT, A. (1988) The 'Flexible Firm': Fixation or Fact? *Work, Employment and Society* 2: 281–316.

PORTES, A. (1998) Social Capital: Its Origins and Applications in Modern Sociology. *Annual Review of Sociology* 24: 1–24.

—— and LANDOLT, P. (1996) The Downside of Social Capital. *The American Prospect* 26: 18–21.

PUGLIESE, E. (1993) *Sociologia della disoccupazione*, Bologna: Il Mulino.

PUTNAM, R. (1993) *Making democracy work*, Princeton, NJ: Princeton University Press.

—— (1996) The Strange Disappearance of Civic America. *The American Prospect* 24: 34–48.

RAINWATER, L., REIN, M., and SCHWARTZ, M. (1986) *Income packaging in the Welfare State*, New York, NY: M.E. Sharpe.

REICH, M., GORDON, D. M., and EDWARDS, R. C. (1973) A Theory of Labour Market Segmentation. *American Economic Review* 63: 359–65.

REIN, M., ESPING-ANDERSEN, G., and RAINWATER, L. (1987) *Stagnation and renewal in social policy. The rise and fall of policy regimes*, New York, NY: M.E. Sharpe.

REYNERI, E. (1994) A long wait in the shelter of the family and safeguards from the State. In O. BENOIT-GUILBOT, and D. GALLIE (eds.) *Long-Term Unemployment*, London: Pinter.

—— (1996) *Sociologia del Mercato del Lavoro*, Bologne: IL Mulino.

RINGEN, S. (1997) *Family Change and Family Policies: Great Britain*, Oxford: Oxford University Press.

ROTTMAN, D. (1994) *Income Distribution within Irish Households: Allocating Resources within Irish Families*, Combat Poverty Agency, Research Report Series No. 18, Dublin.

ROUSSEL, L. (1989) *La famille incertaine*, Paris: Odile Jacob.

ROWNTREE, S. (1901) *Poverty: A Study of Town Life*, London: Longman.

RUBERY, J., and WILKINSON, F. (eds.) (1994) *Employer Strategy and the Labour Market*, Oxford: Oxford University Press.

—— FAGAN, M., and GRIMSHAW, D. (1998) *Women and European Employment*, London: Routledge.

RUSSELL, H. (1996) Women's Experience of Unemployment: A Study of British Women in the 1980s, Unpublished D.Phil. thesis, University of Oxford.

—— (1997) *Seeking Work: Gender Differences in Job Search Behaviour and Outcomes among the Unemployed*, Paper presented at the Third European Conference of Sociology, University of Essex, August 1997.

—— (1999) Friends in Low Places: Gender, Unemployment and Sociability. *Work, Employment and Society* 13: 205–24.

SALAIS, R., BAVEREZ, N., and REYNAUD, B. (1986) *L'invention du chômage. Historie et transformation d'une catégorie en France des années 1890 au années 1980*, Paris: Presses Universitaires de France.

SAMEK LODOVICI, M. (1997) *Labour Market Regulation and Unemployment in Italy*, Milan: Instituto per la Ricerca Sociale.

SARACENO, C. (1988) *Sociologia della famiglia*, Bologna: Il Mulino.

—— (1992) *National Policies to Combat Social Exclusion in Italy*, Brussels: EC.

—— (1994) The Ambivalent Familism of the Italian Welfare State. *Social Politics* 1: 60–82.

—— (1997) *Family Change, Family Policies and the Restructuring of Welfare*, Paris: OECD.

SCARPETTA, S. (1996) Assessing the role of labour market policies and institutional settings on unemployment: a cross-country study. *OECD Economic Studies* 26: 44–97.

SCHADEE, H. M. A., and SCHIZZEROTTO, A. (1990) Processi di mobilità maschili e femminili dell'Italia contemporanea. *Polis* 4: 97–139.

SCHIZZEROTTO, A., and BISON, I. (1996) Mobilità occupazionale tra generazioni e mobilità di carriera: un confronto intergenerazionale. In G. GALLI (ed.) *La mobilita dell società Italiana S.I.P.I.—Centro Studi Confindustra*, Rome: SIPI.

—— and COBALTI, A. (1998) *Occupational Returns to Education in Comtemporary Italy*, Oxford: Oxford University Press.

SCHNAPPER, D. (1981) *L'épreuve du chômage*, Paris: Gallimard.

SEXTON, J. J. (1988) *Long-term unemployment. Its wider labour market effects in the countries of the European Community*, Luxembourg: Office for Official Publications of the European Communities.

SHACKLETON, J. R. (1996) *Training for Employment in Western Europe and the United States*, Aldershot: Edward Elgar.

SHAVIT, Y., and BLOSSFELD, H. P. (1993) *Persistent Inequality*, Boulder, CO: Westview Press.

—— and MÜLLER, W. (1998) *From School to Work. A Comparative Study of Qualification and Occupation in Thirteen Countries*, Oxford: Oxford University Press.

SIAROFF, A. (1994) *Work, Welfare and Gender Equality: A New Typology*, London: Sage.

SIEBERT, H. (1997) Labor market rigidities: at the root of unemployment in Europe. *Journal of Economic Perspectives* 3: 37–54.

SIIM, B. (1993) *The Gendered Scandinavian Welfare States: The Interplay between Women's Roles as Mothers, Workers and Citizens in Denmark*, Aldershot: Edward Elgar.

SIMMEL, G. (1997) *Les Pauvres*, Paris: Presses Universitaires de France.

SIMONAZZI, A., and VILLA, P. (1997) *Flexibility and growth*, Working Paper, University of Trento.

SMELSER, N. J., and SWEDBERG, R. (1994) *The handbook of economic sociology*, Princeton, NJ: Princeton University Press.

SMITH, N., WALKER, I., and WESTERGÅRD-NIELSEN, N. (1993) *The Labour Market Behaviour of Danish Lone Mothers*, Amsterdam: North Holland.

SNEESENS, H., and SHADMAN-MEHTA, F. (1995) Real Wages, Skill Mismatch and Unemployment Persistence (France 1962–1989), *Annales d'Economie et de Statistique* 37–38: 255–92.

SOCIAL SECURITY ADMINISTRATION (1995) *Social Security Programs Throughout the World—1995*, Research Report No. 64.

SOSKICE, D. (1990) Wage Determination: the Changing Role of Institutions in Advanced Industrialised Countries. *Oxford Review of Economic Policy* 6: 36–61.

STATISTICS CANADA (1986) *Labour and Household Surveys. Family characteristics and labour force activity: annual averages 1977–1984*, Ottawa: Ministry of Supply and Services.

STENBERG, S. (1998) Unemployment and Economic Hardship. A Combined Macro- and Micro-level Analysis of Relationship between Unemployment and Means-Tested Social Assistance in Sweden. *European Sociological Review* 14: 1–13.

SVALLFORS, S. (1996) *Välfärdsstatens moraliska ekonomi—Välfärdsopinionen i 90-tallets Sverige*, Umeå, Sweden: Boréa Bokförlag.

SYSDEM EMPLOYMENT OBSERVATORY (1995) *Trends 22 (Annual Report)* Brussels: SYSDEM.

TAJFEL, H. (1978) *Differentation between social groups. Studies in the social psychology of intergroup relations*, London: Academic Press.

TAYLOR-GOOBY, P. (1995) Who wants the welfare state? Support for the state welfare in European countries. In S. SVALLFORS (ed.) *In the eye of the beholder— Opinions on welfare and justice in comparative perspective*, Umeå, Sweden: Impello Säljsupport.

TEACHMAN, J. D., PAASCH, K., and CARVER, K. (1997) Social Capital and the Generation of Human Capital. *Social Forces* 75: 1343–59.

TITMUSS, R. (1958) *Essays on the Welfare State*, London: Allen and Unwin.

TOFT, C. (1996) Constitutional choice, multi-level government and social security systems in Great Britain, Germany and Denmark. *Policy and Politics* 24: 247–61.

TOPALOV, C. (1994) *Naissance du chômeur, 1880–1910*, Paris: Albin Michel.

TRIGILIA, C. (1992) *Sviluppo senza autonomia: effeti perversi delle politiche del Mezzogiorno*, Bologna: Il Mulino.

ULTEE, W. C., and LUIJKX, R. (1990) Educational heterogamy and father-to-son occupational mobility in 23 industrialised nations: General societal openness or compensatory strategies of reproduction? *European Sociological Review* 6: 125–49.

—— DESSENS, J., and JANSEN, W. (1988) Why does unemployment come in couples? An analysis of (un)employment and (non)employment homogamy tables for Canada, the Netherlands and the United States in the 1980s. *European Sociological Review* 4: 111–22.

US DEPARTMENT OF LABOR (1986) *Employment and earnings, May*, Washington, DC: Bureau of Labor Statistics.

VÄISÄNEN, I. (1992) Conflict and Consensus in Social Policy Development. A Comparative Study of Social Insurance in 18 OECD-countries. *European Journal of Political Research* 22: 307–27.

VERMA, V. (1995a) *European Community Household Panel (ECHP): Weighting for Wave 1* Doc. PAN 36/95. Luxembourg: Eurostat.

—— (1995b) *European Community Household Panel (ECHP): Longitudinal Weighting* Doc. PAN 51/95. Luxembourg: Eurostat.

—— (1997) *European Community Household Panel (ECHP): Longitudinal Weighting for Wave 2 (Technical Specifications)* Doc. PAN 87/97. Luxembourg: Eurostat.

—— and CLEMENCEAU, A. (1996) Methodology of the European Community Household Panel. *Statistics in Transition* 2/7: 1023–62.

VOGLER, C. (1989) *Labour Market Change and Patterns of Allocation within Households*, ESRC Social Change and Economic Life Initiative Working Paper No. 12, Oxford: Nuffield College.

—— and PAHL, J. (1993) Social and Economic Change and the Organisation of Money within Marriage. *Work Employment and Society* 7: 71–95.

VRANKEN, J. (1999) Le Minimex en mutation en Belgique. In S. PAUGAM (ed.) *L'Europe face à la pauvreté. Les expériences nationales de revenu minimum*, Paris: La Documentation Francaise.

WARR, P. (1987) *Work, Unemployment and Mental Health*, Oxford: Oxford University Press.

WEGENER, B. (1991) Job mobility and social ties: social resources, prior job and status attainment. *American Sociological Review* 56: 60–71.

WEINBERG, D. (1987) Poverty Spending and the Poverty Gap. *Journal of Policy Analysis and Management*, 6/2: 230–41.

WHELAN, C. T. (1992) The role of Income, Life-Style Deprivation and Financial Strain in Mediating the Impact of Unemployment on Psychological Distress: Evidence from the Republic of Ireland. *Journal of Occupational Psychology* 65: 331–44.

—— (1993) The Role of Social Support in Mediating the Psychological Consequences of Economic Stress. *Sociology of Health and Illness* 15: 86–101.

—— (1994) Social Class, Unemployment and Psychological Distress. *European Sociological Review* 10: 49–62.

—— HANNAN, D., and CREIGHTON, S. (1991) *Unemployment, Poverty and Psychological Distress*, Dublin: The Economic and Social Research Institute.

WILLETTS, D. (1992) *Theories and Explanations of the Underclass*, London: Policy Studies Institute.

WILLIAMSON, O. E. (1985) *The Economic Institutions of Capitalism*, New York, NY: Free Press.

—— (1994) *The Economics and Sociology of Organisations*, New York, NY: Aldine de Gruyter.

WINKELMAN, L., and WINKELMAN, R. (1998) Why are the Unemployed so Unhappy? Evidence from Panel Data. *Economica* 65: 1–15.

WOLBERS, M., and DE GRAAF, P. (1996) Langetermijnontwikkelingen in de opbrengsten van diploma's op de Nederlandse arbeidsmarkt (Long term developments in the returns to education credentials on the Dutch labour market). *Tijdschrift voor Arbeidsvraagstukken* 12: 296–309.

WONG, S., and SALAFF, J. (1998) Network capital: emigration from Hong Kong. *British Journal of Sociology* 49: 358–74.

AUTHOR INDEX

SUBJECT INDEX